to Abe,

from Ima

July 2002

The Gaon of Vilna

THE S. MARK TAPER FOUNDATION

IMPRINT IN JEWISH STUDIES

BY THIS ENDOWMENT

THE S. MARK TAPER FOUNDATION SUPPORTS

THE APPRECIATION AND UNDERSTANDING

OF THE RICHNESS AND DIVERSITY OF

JEWISH LIFE AND CULTURE

The Gaon of Vilna

THE MAN AND HIS IMAGE

IMMANUEL ETKES

TRANSLATED BY JEFFREY M. GREEN

UNIVERSITY OF CALIFORNIA PRESS
Berkeley Los Angeles London

The Publisher gratefully acknowledges the generous contributions to this book provided by the Lucius N. Littauer Foundation

University of California Press
Berkeley and Los Angeles, California

University of California Press, Ltd.
London, England

Library of Congress Cataloging-in-Publication Data

Etkes, I.
[Yaòhid be-doro. English]
The Gaon of Vilna : the man and his image / Immanuel Etkes ; translated from the Hebrew by Jeffrey M. Green.
p. cm.
Includes bibliographical references and index.
ISBN 0-520-22394-2
1. Elijah ben Solomon, 1720–1797. 2. Rabbis—Lithuania—Vilnius—Biography 3. Hasidism—History—18th century. 4. Elijah ben Solomon, 1720–1797—Influence. 5. Vilnius (Lithuania)—Biography. I. Title.

BM755.E6 E8513 2002
296.8'32'092—dc21 2001008254

Manufactured in the United States of America

10 09 08 07 06 05 04 03 02
10 9 8 7 6 5 4 3 2 1

The paper used in this publication is both acid-free and totally chlorine-free (TCF). It meets the minimum requirements of ANSI/NISO Z39.48–1992 (R 1997) (*Permanence of Paper*).

Contents

Acknowledgments

The initiative for publishing the Hebrew edition of this book originated in the various events that took place to commemorate the bicentennial of the Gaon of Vilna's death. One significant experience was a week's tour of Vilna and other Jewish sites in Lithuania in which I took part, along with dozens of colleagues who study the Jews of eastern Europe and their culture. The book was published in Hebrew in Jerusalem in 1998 by Merkaz Zalman Shazar.

I am deeply grateful to my teacher, the late Yakov Katz, and to my friends and colleagues David Assaf, Yisrael Bartal, Ada Rapoport-Albert, Elhanan Reiner, and Yisrael Yuval for reading the chapters of this manuscript and making useful comments. I would also like to mention Nehama Feintuch and Ido Werker, my students at the Hebrew University in Jerusalem who served as my research assistants and helped me greatly with their diligence and intelligence.

I would like to thank Stanley Holwitz and David Gill of the University of California Press for leading the production of this book. I am especially grateful to Jeffrey M. Green, the translator, and to Bonita Hurd, the copyeditor, for their dedicated and professional work.

The English translation of this book was made possible by grants allocated by various funds of the Faculty of Humanities of the Hebrew University of Jerusalem and by the Litauer Foundation. I thank them all.

Introduction

Rabbi Eliyahu, the son of Shlomo Zalman, known as the Gaon of Vilna—or by the acronym Ha-GRA, for "ha-Gaon Rabbi Eliyahu"—enjoyed exceptional authority during his lifetime. Even among his rivals the Hasidic leaders, whom he persecuted, were those who acknowledged his status as the greatest scholar of his generation and who applied to him the epithet "unique in his generation." In the eyes of his disciples and admirers, the Vilna Gaon was not only unique in his generation but also unparalleled in many generations. Some disciples and admirers accorded him the same status as the Sages of the Talmud, while others made the lesser comparison to the Geonim of Babylonia. They all viewed him as a kind of angel from heaven, sent by divine providence to guide his generation in the proper way of studying Torah.

It is not out of place to wonder how and why the Vilna Gaon attained this status. Unlike other great rabbis in his generation, the Gaon never held an official post. He never served as a rabbi, nor was he the head of a yeshiva. The disciples who studied Torah with him were few in number, and they were not disciples in the common sense of the word—students who acquired most of their knowledge from him. In fact, they were mature scholars who visited him from time to time or stayed with him for a brief period. Moreover, the Vilna Gaon's writings were published only posthumously. Hence, the fame he enjoyed during his lifetime cannot be attributed to them. How, then, and why, did this man become such an admired and influential figure?

The first chapter of this study is an effort to answer this question, if only partially. That chapter focuses on descriptions of the Gaon written by his sons and several of his disciples. These are evaluations, impressions, and testimony included in the introductions that these men added to editions of his writings. True, they were written after his death and evidently display the familiar tendency of authors to emphasize and exaggerate their admiration for a great person who has recently departed from life. Nevertheless these accounts are the most immediate and reliable testimony regarding the Vilna Gaon as he was perceived and interpreted by his disciples and associates. These descriptions are important not only because they were written by men who had spent time in his presence but also because these men were among the small number of "those who saw his face." Hence it may be presumed that these men played a considerable role in forming the public image of the Vilna Gaon during his lifetime as well.

In the first chapter I also describe the unusual distinction of the Gaon's achievements as a Torah scholar, a distinction that made him a symbol and model of greatness in Torah scholarship in the eyes of his disciples and, through them, in the eyes of many others. However, his exceptional scholarly achievements represent only one aspect of his image. The second aspect is embodied in his pious and ascetic way of life. Because of his conduct, the Gaon was called *he-Ḥasid* by his admirers. Of course they meant *ḥasid* in the sense of that term before the growth of the Hasidic movement founded by Rabbi Israel Ba'al Shem Tov. In my opinion, the key to understanding the distinguished status of the Vilna Gaon, in the view of his contemporaries as well as in that of following generations, is his embodiment of these two aspects, a combination expressed in the pair of epithets commonly applied to him: ha-Gaon he-Hasid.

One of the main expressions of the Gaon as a Hasid was his affinity for Kabbalah. This refers not only to the decisive impact of Kabbalistic ideas on his worldview, nor only to the commentaries he wrote about Kabbalistic works, but also to mystical experiences that he underwent. The principal source of our knowledge on this subject is the unique testimony written by Rabbi Ḥayyim of Volozhin. This testimony indicates that the Gaon rejected repeated offers of *maggidim* who wished to reveal the secrets of the Torah to him. Similarly, he did not attribute great importance to the knowledge he gained by means of ascent of the soul. He viewed the knowledge of the Torah that he acquired by force of hard intellectual work as the most exalted expression of divine revelation, for in his opinion intellectual work was inspired by divine grace. Thus we have before us an exceptional and original view of the encounter between human intelligence and divine revelation.

The force and authority embodied by the Gaon were expressed in the myth that developed around him after his death. One of the manifestations of this myth is that of the Gaon as a maskil. This myth is known in several versions, some of them contradictory, and all of which are related to the tense and complex encounter between traditional Jewish life in eastern Europe and the secularizing tendencies of the Haskalah movement. The early stages of the development of Haskalah in eastern Europe were characterized by a pronounced effort to prove its religious legitimacy. Underlying this effort was the conviction that, far from uprooting traditional Jewish life, Haskalah was consistent with it. Thus it is not surprising that proponents of Haskalah fostered an image of the Gaon as a maskil and used it to mobilize support. The source of this image lies in the position taken by the Gaon on the matter of involvement with "external wisdom," or areas of knowledge that transcend the boundaries of rabbinical culture. He believed that not only was it permitted to deal with this "wisdom," it was even vital, because this knowledge was a necessary tool for studying Torah. He himself studied several fields of science and even left manuscripts of works in these areas. This is the factual basis on which the myth of the Vilna Gaon as a maskil was constructed.

The Gaon's position regarding the study of non-Jewish wisdoms was not unique among the traditional scholarly elite. Similarly, it is doubtful whether, when expressing this position, he was at all aware of its possible consequences regarding the Haskalah movement. Nevertheless, the closeness in time of the Vilna Gaon to the origins of Haskalah in eastern Europe, along with, of course, his enormous authority, fostered the image of the Gaon as a maskil and led to the exploitation of this image as an instrument of propaganda by proponents of Haskalah. However, opponents of Haskalah of various types also promoted the image of the Gaon as a maskil and clung to it for their purposes. His expertise in non-Jewish wisdom and science proved, in their opinion, that the way of the maskilim offered nothing, for although the Gaon was not inferior to the greatest of their scholars, he did not deny the values of the tradition. On the contrary, he was a model of devotion to those values. Most ironically, the opponents of Haskalah had an interest in exaggerating his mastery in fields of general knowledge, for the greater he was in wisdom and science, the more his figure served as a powerful weapon to strike at the maskilim.

The second chapter in this book deals with the myth of the Vilna Gaon as a maskil among both proponents and opponents of Haskalah. The chapter also follows later traces of this myth as reflected in the historiography of the Haskalah movement. This discussion shows that the matter of the Gaon and Haskalah is an instructive example of the continuity between Haskalah literature of the nineteenth century and Jewish historiography of the end of that century and the first half of the next. Following the survey of historical writing, the chapter offers a critical examination of the image of the Gaon as a maskil. This examination compares the image with various sources and tries to determine the real place of the Gaon with regard to the beginnings of the Haskalah movement in eastern Europe.

Chapters 3 through 5 deal with various aspects of the controversy between the Hasidim and the Mitnagdim. At the center of chapter 3 stands my effort to reconstruct the first moves in the development of the controversy. This reconstruction is meant to examine the role played by the Vilna Gaon in the struggle against Hasidism. According to both Hasidic and Mitnagdic sources, which confirm and complement each other, the Gaon initiated and led the struggle against Hasidism. This finding contradicts the view that the struggle against Hasidism began as an initiative of the oligarchy, and that the Gaon merely served as a figurehead that the establishment was pleased to use. Not only did the Gaon initiate the attack, he also prevented reconciliation between the warring camps during his lifetime. These findings are, of course, important for understanding the motives for the struggle against Hasidism. Naturally, the more prolonged and complex a controversy of this kind is, the more it is bound up with various and sundry motives. However, my findings regarding the role played by the Gaon at the beginning of the controversy clearly prove that the basic motives underlying the struggle against Hasidism were spiritual and religious, and not political and social.

How did the persecuted Hasidim regard their persecutor? How did the Hasidic leaders explain to themselves and to their flocks the fact that their chief opponent was the greatest scholar of their generation? I discuss this question in chapter 4. I have based my examination primarily on a number of letters written by Rabbi Shneur Zalman of Lyady. This prominent leader of the Hasidim of White Russia was involved in the controversy with the Mitnagdim from its beginning in the early 1770s until its final, harsh manifestations near the end of the eighteenth century. Moreover, Rabbi Shneur Zalman of Lyady was himself a victim of informers and twice was arrested by the Russian authorities. Hence his responses to the Mitnagdim in general and to the Vilna Gaon in particular are of great interest.

Rabbi Shneur Zalman's response to the role played by the Vilna Gaon in the struggle against Hasidism was dual: on the one hand, he acknowledged the Gaon's eminence as the greatest scholar of his day, and, on the other, he absolutely challenged his authority to determine that Hasidism was a heresy. Rabbi Shneur Zalman bridged the distance between these two positions by explaining that the Gaon was acting in innocence but was deceived by perjurers. He also offered a dialectical interpretation, according to which the struggle against Hasidism ultimately proved beneficial to Hasidism. Rabbi Shneur Zalman went so far in this direction as to present outbursts against Hasidism as products of divine providence seeking to abet Hasidism.

The two lines of argument found in Rabbi Shneur Zalman's writings influenced the approach taken by Habad historiography to the phenomenon of opposition to Hasidism. Indeed, the question of the meaning of the struggle against Hasidism, and the fact that the Gaon led that struggle, continued to concern and disturb Hasidim during the generations that followed. Hasidic historiography—mainly that connected with Habad—sought to present a picture that would heal the wounds of the past and serve the needs of the present. In chapter 4 of this book I survey and examine three prominent examples of this kind of historical writing, as well as examples of the discussion of the struggle against Hasidism in the works of various orthodox writers, including some who had a pronounced affinity with the Mitnagdic heritage. One may point to three main types among these writers: those that apologize, those that harmonize, and those that deny. Writers of the first type admit that the Hasidim were persecuted, but they justify the Gaon and his supporters with the claim that these persecutions rescued Hasidism from severe and dangerous degeneration. Those who take the harmonistic line bring out the advantages that both sides gained from the struggle between them. Allegedly, both the Hasidim and their opponents learned from each other and were positively influenced. As a result, the gap between the two viewpoints was narrowed and everyone benefited. The writers of the third type ignore the persecution of the Hasidim. These writers share a common orthodox outlook, viewing both the Hasidim and the Mitnagdim as "true Jewish believers" who were supposed to have cooperated to defend the values of the tradition against external threats.

Chapter 5, too, discusses the controversy between Mitnagdim and Hasidim and is devoted to Rabbi Ḥayyim of Volozhin's response to Hasidism. It is somewhat ironic that this rabbi, who was regarded as the greatest of the Vilna Gaon's disciples, waged the struggle against Hasidism in a style entirely different from that initiated and led by his teacher and master. In contrast to the unrelenting war waged by the Gaon, which was intended to eliminate the deviant sect, Rabbi Ḥayyim chose to struggle against Hasidism on the plane of ideas and education. Behind that response lay his realization that the Hasidim were not heretics and their motives were pure. At the same time, Rabbi Ḥayyim had no doubt that the Hasidic way of worshiping God was mistaken. Most of all, he was apprehensive about the blow Hasidism dealt to the status of Torah study and its practitioners.

Rabbi Ḥayyim's polemics against Hasidism were characterized by a restrained and seemingly impartial tone. As one who knew the doctrine of Hasidism firsthand, Rabbi Ḥayyim could expose what appeared to him to be its principal weak points. However, his response to Hasidism was not restricted to polemics. In his book *Nefesh Ha-ḥayyim,* Rabbi Ḥayyim set out systematic theological doctrine, which can be seen as a response to Hasidism. Central to this doctrine is the effort to restore the status of Torah study to its former place at the head of the hierarchy of Jewish values. One of the conspicuous innovations in this thought can be called the mystification of Torah study, or the effort to endow Torah study with mystical significance.

In chapter 5, I also discuss Rabbi Ḥayyim's establishment of the Volozhin yeshiva, the innovations in organization and content that characterized it, and the role it played in the confrontation with Hasidism. In a certain sense, Rabbi Ḥayyim's thought and the yeshiva he both established and led were two faces of the same coin, for by means of the yeshiva he sought to translate the religious ideals he had developed into educational activity that formed a pattern of life. It is also possible to say that, with his intellectual and educational project, Rabbi Ḥayyim sought to make the heritage of the Gaon widely available.

The relations between Torah scholarship and the institution of the rabbinate in nineteenth-century Lithuania are central to chapter 6. What at first appear to be two complementary phenomena prove on deeper inspection to be an intricate and complex web of relationships. One expression of these relationships is the apparent contradiction between the ideal of *Torah lishma* (Torah study for its own sake) and the rabbinate. Among the explanations of this contradiction one may point to the roles played by the heritage of the Vilna Gaon and that of Rabbi Ḥayyim in shaping the ideal of Torah study. Of course, other contemporary factors were present. In any event, inspired by the ideal of Torah study, scholars tended to relate to the rabbinate as a livelihood that would permit them to continue studying Torah. In these two respects the rabbinate occasioned them bitter disappointment.

The seventh and last chapter of this book closes the circle by returning to the Vilna Gaon himself. In it I discuss his outlook and practice regarding the relationship between the value of Torah study and that of *yira*. The ancient rabbis were extravagant in their praise of Torah study, but they were severely critical of great scholarship not accompanied by *yira*. These attitudes of the Sages made the question of the relationship between Torah and *yira* an immanent issue in Jewish culture. Over the generations, questions arose repeatedly regarding the nature of the required *yira* and the correct equilibrium between it and Torah study. Examination of the Gaon's outlook and way of life regarding these questions fills in the picture of the ha-Gaon he-Hasid with which this study began.

Naturally it is very difficult to estimate the influence of a person such as the Vilna Gaon on his contemporaries and on Jewish culture in the generations that followed him. Nevertheless, it is possible to point to two areas in which his influence is especially notable: the struggle against Hasidism, and the flourishing of the world of Torah in Lithuania.

The struggle against Hasidism that the Gaon initiated and led is a fascinating example of an individual's ability to influence the course of history. Considering the decisive role played by the Gaon in this controversy, it is doubtful that the struggle would have assumed such a fierce character and been so protracted without him. Recall that the authority of the Gaon was not anchored in any official post. Instead, his power was the personal authority of a man viewed as Gaon and Hasid, and with it he guided the leaders of the Vilna community—and, after them, those of other communities—in unrelenting warfare against Hasidism. The Gaon's success in mobilizing the community leadership shows both the exceptional force of his personality and the devotion of the Jewish society in Lithuania to the values that he symbolized.

Although the confrontation between Hasidism and its opponents took on an entirely different guise after the Gaon's death, it would be no exaggeration to say that the consolidation of two principal camps in eastern European Jewry, existing side by side and competing with each other, drew on the formative experience of the Gaon's struggle against Hasidism. Certain manifestations of tension between Hasidim and Mitnagdim persist to this day, and one of them is the political division of the Haredi community in the state of Israel. Moreover, the confrontation that took place several years ago between the Lubavicher rebbe and Rabbi Schach, the centenarian leader of the Lithuanian yeshivot in Israel, can be seen as a late and distant echo of the conflict between the Vilna Gaon and Rabbi Shneur Zalman of Lyady in the eighteenth century.

The influence of the Gaon on the flourishing of the world of Torah in Lithuania was not as direct and transparent as was his involvement in the struggle against Hasidism, for his writing, his method of study, and his Halakhic decisions were not widely disseminated. However, this cannot diminish the vitality and power radiated by the Gaon as a symbol and source of inspiration. The secret of his influence can be attributed to the fact that he appeared to the members of his own generation and those following him as the perfect embodiment of the values of Torah and *yira.* Thus the significance of a historical personage need not depend on his or her success in shaping new concepts and ways of life but may have extensive and prolonged influence because he or she is viewed as epitomizing the values and ideals to which the society is committed.

1 Ha-Gaon He-Hasid

IN HIS OWN TIME AND FOR SUCCEEDING GENERATIONS

During his lifetime the Gaon of Vilna wielded comprehensive and exceptionally powerful authority. Striking testimony to this effect is found in the words of the Hasidic leader Rabbi Shneur Zalman of Lyady to his followers in Vilna in 1797: "According to all accounts, no one in the districts of Lithuania will raise his heart so high as not to yield his own opinion before that of ha-Gaon he-Hasid and to say wholeheartedly that the truth is not in his mouth, perish the thought."[1] Rabbi Shneur Zalman's remarks imply that, even were it possible to persuade rabbinical authorities that the path of Hasidism was correct, they would not dare disagree with the Vilna Gaon. The organized campaign against Hasidism in 1772 offers a forceful demonstration of the Gaon's public status, for he led that struggle from the start, and he imbued it with his authority.[2]

How can we explain the extraordinary authority of this man? This question becomes more acute when one recalls that he had very little public exposure. He never held official office. Moreover, he sought to cut himself off from the people around him and studied Torah intensely in the seclusion of his home. The number of his students, those counted among "the ones who saw his face," was severely limited.[3] Moreover, his writings were not published until after his death. What, then, was the secret of the Gaon's enormous influence during his lifetime? Most probably the few people who frequented him—his students and the members of his family—served as agents of a kind, spreading his reputation far and wide. The few people in direct contact with him were deeply impressed by his personality; they interpreted it, and they shared their impressions and interpretations with others. Thus was fashioned the figure of the Vilna Gaon as pictured by the public. Naturally, the myth around him that arose after his death was nourished by these impressions and interpretations.

In this chapter I shall try to reconstruct the figure of the Gaon as it was conceived and interpreted by those few who "saw his face." For this reconstruction I have relied on the introductions written by the Gaon's two sons and a few of his students to his posthumously published works. These introductions are the earliest extant written testimony about the character of the Gaon. This testimony also provided the basis for biographical works about him, the first of which was published more than fifty years after his death.[4]

THE GAON

As a point of departure for examining the figure of the Vilna Gaon, as it was understood and interpreted by those close to him, let us consider the two epithets that were commonly applied to him: ha-Gaon he-Hasid. The term *gaon* indicates the Gaon's extraordinary achievements in the study of Torah, while the adjective *ḥasid* relates to his way of life and character. I shall begin the discussion with those features of the Gaon's personality for which he was called *gaon*. One of the outstanding traits, one mentioned repeatedly in accounts by his students and sons, was the astounding breadth of his knowledge of Torah. Here are the words of Rabbi Ḥayyim of Volozhin, who was regarded as his chief disciple: "And he could quote by heart the entire Babylonian and Jerusalem Talmuds, and the *Mekhilta* and *Sifri,* and the *Tosefta,* and all of the Midrashim, and the Zohar, and the *Ra'aya Mehemna,* and the *Zohar Ḥadash,* and the *Tiqunim* and *Sefer Yeẓira* and *Pirqei de Rabbi Eliezer,* and in general all the teachings of the Tannaim and Amoraim in our possession, both the exoteric and the esoteric teachings."[5] Thus the Gaon's knowledge of Torah was exceptional in the extreme. He was not content with study of the Babylonian Talmud, which had been the custom of most Torah scholars for generations, but he also mastered the Jerusalem Talmud. Other strata of Halakhic literature that he included in his studies, though it was unusual to take them up, were the *Tosefta* and Halakhic Midrash. Furthermore, unlike other Jewish scholars of his generation, who concentrated on the Halakhic component of rabbinic literature, the Gaon studied Midrash and Aggadah as well. And, as if that were not enough, he also included the various strata of Kabbalistic literature in his studies. Another expression of the exceptional breadth that characterized his knowledge of Torah is the list of works that he wrote, as presented by his sons: "For he considered, investigated, and prepared treatises in this order: on the Bible, the Mishnah, the Babylonian and Jerusalem Gemara, the *Tosefta, Mekhilta, Sifra, Sifri, Seder Olam, Pirqei de Rabbi Eliezer,* Zohar, several volumes of the *Tiqunei Zohar, Sefer Yeẓira, Heikhalot, Ra'aya Mehemna, Sifra Deẓeni'uta,* on the Four *Turim* of the *Shulḥan 'Arukh,* on several tractates, on the *Avot de Rabbi Nathan* . . . more than a hundred new principles and also some old ones, on astronomy, and algebra, and triangles."[6] Thus the Gaon composed commentaries on the Bible, on the various levels of rabbinic literature, and also on some of the major works of Kabbalah. Moreover, he wrote treatises on several areas of science, which he viewed as an essential resource for understanding the Torah.[7]

This describes the areas of the Gaon's knowledge and its breadth. But what about the quality of that knowledge? In other words, to what degree did he master that enormous literary domain? A typical answer to this question is found in the story recounted by Rabbi Israel of Shklov, in the name of a "great rabbi" who frequented the Gaon's home. According to Rabbi Israel, the Gaon instructed his students to learn at least one tractate of the Talmud by heart, so that when they were walking on the way somewhere they could review that tractate and not succumb to the transgression of ceasing Torah study. One of the students responded to the Gaon's instruction and learned the tractate *Succah* by heart. When he came before him and reported this, his teacher asked him to list the number of differences of opinion mentioned in that tractate between certain Tannaim and Amoraim. This was a particularly difficult test of memory, and it is no wonder that the student found it difficult to pass. In contrast, the Gaon displayed astounding mastery:

> Then our master opened his holy mouth and listed, as one who counts pearls, cutting the components of the tractate into tiny pieces: how many times it mentioned controversies between Tannaim and Amoraim, and how many times the Halakhah followed one or another of them, and how many *sugiyot* and methods of Halakhic interpretation there are, and how many laws from the *Toseftot* and the Jerusalem Talmud, and *succoth* that were unfit . . . And he listed the types of acceptable *succoth* mentioned in this tractate . . . and such was his mastery of the entire Babylonian Talmud, the Jerusalem Talmud, and the entire Torah.[8]

This story shows that the Gaon was endowed with an astounding memory, as though photographs of all the pages of the tractate were collected in his mind, so that he was capable of analyzing their components one by one. As noted, the story quoted here is merely an example. In general it may be stated that both the disciples of the Gaon and his sons had the impression that the extensive and voluminous rabbinical literature that he had studied was all stored in his memory and available for immediate use.

How did the Gaon attain such marvelous mastery of the vastness of Torah? At this stage I offer two answers to this question, which emerge from the testimony of his sons and disciples. First, the man was gifted with extremely rapid comprehension, so that his accomplishments in Torah study were exceptional. Thus, for example, his disciple Israel of Shklov testifies that he would "review the entire Babylonian Talmud every month all his life."[9] The Gaon's rapid comprehension was evident even in his childhood. His sons reveal that "when he was nine years old, his hands were full of the Bible, Mishnah, and Gemara," and that he learned all the writings of Lurianic Kabbalah within half a year.[10]

Second, the Gaon reviewed his studies countless times. Thus his exceptional achievements in Torah studies were the product of a combination of outstanding intellectual ability and a mighty mental effort. The importance that he attributed to review of Torah studies emerges from a story that Rabbi Ḥayyim of Volozhin told his students:

> Our rabbi said, When he came before the Vilna Gaon of blessed memory he was then about nineteen years old, in the full power of his acuity and the freshness of his intellect and the greatness of his diligence at that time, and great was his memory as you know, and he said to the Vilna Gaon of blessed memory, I have reviewed the Order *Mo'ed* fourteen times and it is still not sharp and clear in my mouth. His master the Vilna Gaon of blessed memory answered him in surprise, From fourteen times you wish it to be clear for you? And he [Rabbi Ḥayyim] said to him, Should it be a hundred and one times? He [the Vilna Gaon] smiled to him and said: There is no limit at all to the matter, and all the days of your life you should stand and review.[11]

Thus the Gaon regarded review and repetition as an endless process. Rabbi Ḥayyim complained that the tractate of the Talmud he had studied was still not "sharp and clear" for him, though he had reviewed it fourteen times. Hence the goal of repetition was not only to engrave the studied material on one's memory but also to attain penetrating and exhaustive understanding of it. In Rabbi Ḥayyim's opinion, the main test of exhaustive understanding of the Torah was the ability to overcome all the difficulties and doubts that arise during the study of a text. He attributed that marvelous degree of exhaustive and penetrating understanding to his teacher, the Vilna Gaon: "For the Gaon, may he rest in peace, possessed complete mastery of the entire Torah, without any doubt, having learned the Bible, the Mishnah, the Babylonian and Jerusalem Talmuds, the *Mekhilta, Sifra* and *Sifri* and *Tosefta,* the Midrashim and the Zohar, and all the extant teachings of the Tannaim and Amoraim. He knew them all perfectly and settled the doubts that are born from their words."[12] Thus not only was the literature that the Gaon studied astounding in its extent, but the quality of his mastery of the material was also extraordinary.

What characterized his method of study? What was innovative in his method of interpreting texts? In light of his disciples' and sons' testimony we may pinpoint four principal traits that typified the Gaon's method of Torah study:

1. Commitment to the Truth of the Torah

The Gaon opposed methods of study that made intellectual acuity a goal in itself. He required his students to study with commitment to the truth and to refrain from posing artificial questions and seeking solutions to problems that were not vital to clarifying the passage under discussion. His sons describe the instructions he issued on this matter:

> Then he admonished [us] about the way to study in the sea of the Talmud: to read Rashi's commentaries carefully, because the wise reader will find them very apt, and also the innovations of the authors of the *Tosafot* of blessed memory. He stipulates that the study must be directed toward truth; he [the scholar] must hate raising artificial difficulties; he acknowledges the truth, even if stated by young pupils, and all of [the scholar's] desire for intellectual display is of no value compared to the truth. Thus he will succeed and gain knowledge in his studies. And he ordered [us] to avoid clever reasoning.[13]

Sharpness of wit and the raising of many difficulties are presented here as contrary to the search for truth, or at least deleterious to it. Evidently this does not refer to intellectual acuity that serves the search for truth, but rather to cleverness that is a goal in itself. Thus commitment to the truth and striving to attain it involve willingness to forgo the mental satisfaction and, of course, the social prestige that can be derived from keen and casuistic learning.

How successful was the Gaon in his effort to influence his contemporaries' method of study? Rabbi Abraham Simḥah of Amcislaw, the nephew of Rabbi Ḥayyim, writes, "And it was famed in all of our country that he of blessed memory was the light of Torah for our path; from him and henceforth was practiced the way of studying Torah among the vast majority of the Sages of the generation and the scholars: only the straight path to the truth of the Torah."[14] These remarks reflect the prevalent opinion, that the Gaon did indeed succeed in reforming the methods of study. However, we are unable to determine the degree of that success. In any event, it is known that the Gaon's disciples sought to follow their master's path in this matter. An important expression of this is Rabbi Ḥayyim's effort, in the yeshiva that he established, to base Torah study on uncompromising commitment to the truth.[15]

2. *Textual Editing of Rabbinical Literature and Kabbalistic Works*

The medieval commentators on the Talmud, chiefly Rashi and the authors of the Tosafot, frequently refer to the question of the correct reading of the talmudic text they sought to interpret. The fact that there are different readings of certain passages of the Talmud required the commentators to determine which one was correct. Unlike the commentators on the Talmud known as the Rishonim (the first, or former), who were active until the fifteenth century, the Aharonim (last, or latter) commentators did not refer to the issue of textual criticism and relied on what had been decided by the Rishonim.[16]

However, unlike his contemporaries and immediate predecessors, the Vilna Gaon did refer to the problem of textual criticism. In this sense he acted as though he were one of the Rishonim. Moreover, he was not content with deciding among various readings extant in manuscripts of the Talmud, but he audaciously proposed emending the Talmud when an existing reading appeared faulty to him. He also revised many passages of the *Tosefta*.[17] These revisions were based on extremely extensive mastery of talmudic literature. By virtue of this mastery, the Gaon could support his emendations by citing parallels in rabbinical writing. Indeed, his disciple Rabbi Israel of Shklov states that the Gaon did not permit himself to revise an existing reading except

> after much searching and groping and weighing in his mind as broad as the sea, and seeking after seeking in the two Talmuds and in all the words of the Tannaim and the Amoraim, which were arrayed before his eyes, whether his method or reading went according to them in a well-trodden way, . . . because [regarding] any method or reading that he innovated openly, he did not determine it unless that reading or method

> did not solve at least fifteen or twenty difficult *sugiyot* in all the words of the Tannaim and Amoraim that are in our possession.[18]

Thus the Gaon's enormous expertise in all the strata of Halakhic literature served him not only as a resource for his textual criticism but also as a check and balance. The test of every revision was not limited to the solution of a local difficulty; instead every emendation was supposed to accord with many passages in the Talmud. The Gaon initiated yet another daring innovation: he made emendations in Kabbalah as well. Here, too, he did not dare to emend the existing reading unless the revision was based on many good arguments.[19]

3. *Connection between the Late Strata of Torah and Its Ancient Sources*

The sons and disciples of the Gaon noted his method of revealing the ancient sources of later strata in the development of Halakhic literature. A well-known example is found in his commentary on the *Shulḥan 'Arukh,* where he revealed the talmudic sources on which the rulings of Rabbi Joseph Karo are based. What is the meaning of this procedure? The Gaon believed that the source of Halakhic authority was the words of the Sages found in the Babylonian and Jerusalem Talmuds. Therefore, revealing that the teachings of the Sages were the source of the rulings in the *Shulḥan 'Arukh* implied acceptance of the authority of those rulings. However, this implies that in any instance of lack of agreement between a passage in the Talmud and a ruling in the *Shulḥan 'Arukh,* the ruling must be changed in accordance with the words of the Sages. And in fact, the Gaon was not reluctant to disagree with the author of the *Shulḥan 'Arukh* or with other Halakhic authorities of earlier generations whenever he concluded that a ruling did not derive from a passage in the Talmud or its precise interpretation.[20]

The Gaon's efforts to reveal the connection among various strata of Halakhic literature was not limited to clarification of the *Shulḥan 'Arukh.* Another example of a similar procedure can be found in his commentary on the Mishnah, where he points out the roots of later discussion in the Babylonian and Jerusalem Talmuds and allusions to the *Tosefta* and *Barai-*

tot.[21] The foundation of the Gaon's commentaries was thus an assumption of the unity and perfect completeness of Torah, encompassing all of Jewish religious literature in all its strata. The task confronting a commentator on Torah is to reveal that unity by laying bare the ancient roots of the later layers of Halakhah. This outlook regarding the character of the Torah and the purpose of its commentators applied not only to Halakhic literature, the manifest aspect of the Torah, but also to Kabbalistic literature, its esoteric aspect. In reference to this attitude, Rabbi Ḥayyim of Volozhin describes the Gaon's commentary on *Sifra Deẓeni'uta:* "He also did wonders, and we have shown his great and awesome fire in his commentary on *Sifra Deẓeni'uta,* which [encompasses] all the orders of the Secrets of Creation and the Secrets of the Chariot, which are arranged in the Holy Zohar and *Adrot* and the *Tiqunim* and the writings of the ARI [Rabbi Isaac Luria] of blessed memory . . . included and arranged in their order and correctly in the source of sources in this exalted and holy book *Sifra Deẓeni'uta.*"[22] Thus in the Gaon's view, the status of *Sifra Deẓeni'uta* was parallel to that of the Mishnah, and the status of the Zohar, the *Adrot,* and the *Tiqunim* is parallel to that of the Gemara. Consequently, just as it is proper to reveal the sources of the Sages of the Gemara in the Mishnah, thus it is also proper to reveal the roots of the Zohar, the *Adrot,* and the *Tiqunim* in *Sifra Deẓeni'uta.*

4. *Revealing the Connection between the Manifest and the Hidden in the Torah*

The assumption that there is a close connection between the manifest and hidden aspects of the Torah is fundamental to Kabbalistic thought. Hence it is necessary to presume that there can be no contradiction between Halakhah and Kabbalah. However, that presumption appears to be refuted by the disparity between certain Halakhic rulings and statements in the Zohar on those matters.[23] In the face of this difficulty, the Gaon stands out as a scholar who was able to reconcile the manifest with the hidden. Rabbi Ḥayyim describes the Gaon's accomplishment in this area:

> As for what people are accustomed to saying, that in certain laws the esoteric Sages disagree with the exoteric Sages, this is because they did not

> understand how to interpret the words of the Holy Zohar in truth. For how is it possible that the esoteric way in our holy Torah should contract with the exoteric? We must praise and thank the Lord with great gratitude for sending us a holy light from heaven . . . our great and holy rabbi ha-Gaon he-Hasid, our teacher rabbi Eliyahu of Vilna, may he rest in peace, in whose mouth and on whose tongue both hidden and manifest [teachings] were fluent and preserved in his heart and arranged in every respect to concord with each other.[24]

Thus Rabbi Ḥayyim attributes extensive knowledge to the Gaon of both the exoteric aspect of the Torah and its esoteric aspect, as well as their full reconciliation. Impressive testimony on this matter is found in the words of the Gaon's student Rabbi Menahem Mendel of Shklov: "And I shall tell correctly what I heard from the holy mouth explicitly, that he never interpreted a difficult verse unless he knew its secret meaning, and he garbed it in the simple meaning of the verse."[25] This is stated in relation to the Gaon's commentary on Proverbs, a commentary he dictated to Rabbi Menahem Mendel. Another of his students, Rabbi Israel of Shklov, states that in some instances the Gaon based an emendation of talmudic text on esoteric doctrine.[26]

Hitherto we have considered the extent of the Gaon's knowledge of Torah, the quality of his mastery of it, and the character of his interpretations and innovations. In the eyes of his disciples and sons, the Gaon appeared to be someone brimming with new interpretations of the Torah of an extent and at a pace that are difficult to grasp. These characteristics are related to a turning point in his life that occurred when he reached the age of forty. Reports of this are varied and complement each other.

Let us begin with the words of his son Abraham: "For until the age of forty he studied for himself, and after the age of forty his whole purpose was to teach others."[27] Rabbi Abraham Simḥah of Amcislaw presents a far-reaching statement on this matter in the name of his uncle Rabbi Ḥayyim of Volozhin: "For I have heard from my late uncle that the whole quantity of his teaching and writings, which our late rabbi wrote on exoteric and esoteric matters, he wrote them all before he reached forty, the age of understanding, for since then his understanding was greatly increased, and [he had so] many insights that time was not sufficient to write them."[28] The Gaon's disciple Rabbi Israel of Shklov recounts:

> Regarding all his writings, he composed them all until he was forty years old, and afterward he did not write and did not compose except by his disciples, because he was a running stream, so that it was impossible for anyone to write them. I have heard from his son, the great rabbi of blessed memory, that he heard from his [father's] mouth that he had one hundred and fifty interpretations of one verse of the Song of Songs, and no person was found who could write as fast as his mind and he did not want to misuse his holy time for that.[29]

Despite differences in tone among the various reports, they corroborate each other and indicate that, when the Gaon reached the age of forty, a highly significant turning point took place in his self-awareness and manner of studying. The most conspicuous expression of this turning point was his decision no longer to write his new insights himself but to assign this task to his disciples. He apparently reached this decision because he realized that the rate of flow of his ideas and new insights was impeded or blocked by the need to formulate them in writing. He opted for the abundant flow of ideas and delegated the task of writing them down to his disciples, as best they could.

In his disciples' view, the Gaon was now an abundant source of new insights into the Torah that could not be contained. Rabbi Ḥayyim offers an apt expression of this feeling: "And like the value of a drop against the great sea thus was the value of his compositions against his enormous wisdom. And if a man lived a thousand years, he would not manage to write down all of his wisdom that was revealed to him truly like a flowing stream."[30] The comparison of all the Gaon's writings to a drop of the sea, in contrast to the inexhaustible plenitude of his wisdom, is repeated in the writings of his students and sons, and it probably reflects their exciting experience of learning Torah from him.

How can that abundance be explained? Is a person of flesh and blood, talented and diligent though he or she may be, capable of containing so much learning? Questions and perplexities of this kind evidently preoccupied the Gaon's disciples, and they underlie the following remarks of Rabbi Ḥayyim: "Therefore all the wonders of his deeds and great discoveries did not amaze me. For his reward came: this is the Torah and this is its reward. He merited it from heaven as his portion for all of his labor."[31]

Thus the Gaon's exceptional achievements in his studies were not only the fruit of his talents and perseverance, but they also had an element of divine grace. Rabbi Ḥayyim goes on to explain why and for what purpose the Gaon merited that supreme gift: "For we possess a tradition from the Tanna Rabbi Meir that he merits many things." This refers to the words of Rabbi Meir: "Whoever deals in Torah for its own sake merits many things, . . . and the secrets of the Torah are revealed to him, and he becomes like an abundant spring and like a river that does not cease" (*Avot* 6:1). Rabbi Ḥayyim viewed the Gaon as the miraculous embodiment of the study of Torah for its own sake and thus saw it as no surprise that he received what he merited.

My discussion of the image of the Gaon as a scholar would not be complete unless I referred to a ceremony he held when he completed his commentary on the Song of Songs. A description of the ceremony has come down to us as formulated by Rabbi Israel of Shklov, who heard about it from Rabbi Menahem Mendel of Shklov. The event took place in the community of Serahai, where the Gaon lived for some time in the home of his son's father-in-law, who served as the local rabbi. His disciple Menahem Mendel stayed with him there, and it was he who wrote down the interpretation of the Song of Songs. When he had nearly finished the commentary, the Gaon invited his son's father-in-law and his son Judah Leib to join him. The Gaon asked to have the windows closed and that many candles be lit, although it was still full daylight:

> And when he completed his interpretation he raised his eyes on high with mighty devotion, blessings, and thanks to His great Name, may it be blessed, Who enabled him to conceive the light of all the Torah from within and from without. Thus he said, All the wisdoms are needed for our holy Torah and are included in it, and he mastered them all perfectly. And he recalled them: the wisdom of algebra and triangles and geometry and the wisdom of music; . . . and of the wisdom of philosophy, [the Gaon] said he knew it perfectly. And he brought only two good things out of it . . . and the rest must be thrown out. Then he said, thank God the entire Torah which was given at Sinai, he knew it thoroughly, and all the Prophets and Writings and *mishnayot* and the oral law, how they are hidden in it, and no doubt was left to him about any Halakhah or *sugiya* in the whole Torah in his old age, and he knew the entire oral

> Torah and all the Halakhic authorities up to the recent ones on the *Shulḥan 'Arukh,* and he clarified them and shined lights on the darkness of flawed readings; . . . and in hidden things all that was in our possession, the Zohars and the *Tiqunei Zohar* and *Sefer Yeẓira* and the writings of the ARI of sacred memory and the PARDES, he had studied them and knew them. . . . And he revised them with evidence as clear as the sun; only two grave things in the mysteries of the Torah of the Zohar were questionable for him. . . . And those, if he knew who knew them, he would go on foot to him and then wait with him for our righteous messiah, and with this he finished.[32]

This is the essence of what Rabbi Israel heard from his colleague Rabbi Menahem Mendel about the ceremony that the Gaon held when he finished his interpretation of the Song of Songs. I use the word *ceremony* because from the testimony presented here it appears that the Gaon did indeed initiate an event of exceptional character. The invitation of his son's father-in-law and his son to join him and his disciple, and the instruction he gave to close the windows and light candles in full daylight, and of course the words he said to those present—all of this indicates his intention to make the conclusion of his commentary on the Song of Songs into an event of ceremonial character. This should not seem trivial to us, for we are dealing with a man who led a life of severe asceticism. In light of the words he spoke on that ceremonial occasion it appears that the Gaon wished to mark not only the completion of his commentary on the Song of Songs but also all his accomplishments in the study of Torah. His words express a deep sense of joy and gratitude that he had managed to study the entire Torah. The great joy and feelings of gratitude that swelled in his soul explain the need he felt to share this event with his son and his son's father-in-law.

These remarks of the Gaon sum up his life, a life whose principal content and goal was the study of Torah. He lists the areas of his studies one after the other, from the elementary to the difficult. He was required to study science because he viewed it as an essential auxiliary for studying Torah. He examined philosophy and found it worthless.[33] From here he passes on to the main point: the written and oral law, Halakhic literature in all its strata, and all the major works of Kabbalah. The quantitative aspect of mastery of the Torah is complemented by the qualitative aspect:

the Gaon's success in revealing the connections among the various strata of the Torah, and in emending faulty readings that he found in rabbinical and Kabbalistic literature. In general, he regarded himself as having successfully included the entire Torah in his studies. A graphic expression of this awareness is found in his admission that he found only two passages in the Zohar difficult to understand, and that if he knew someone who could explain them, he would go to him by foot and then await the advent of the messiah.

HE-HASID

The second epithet applied to the Gaon by his disciples and admirers was, as noted, *he-Ḥasid*. This epithet relates to his way of life, to his virtues, and to his mental world. Use of this epithet might appear surprising, since the Gaon led the opposition to Hasidism. However, the term *ḥasid* in this context does not imply any connection with the Hasidic movement founded by Rabbi Israel Ba'al Shem Tov (the BESHT). By calling their revered rabbi *he-Ḥasid*, the Gaon's disciples intended to associate with him the attributes that had been bound up with that title in the generations prior to the emergence of Hasidism.

The concepts *ḥasid* (a pious or saintly person) and *ḥasidut* (piety or saintliness) were used for many generations to indicate a certain type of religious life. A *ḥasid* is an individual who stands above others in the quality and intensity of his worship of God. *Ḥasidut* is the concept that characterizes the *ḥasid's* way of life and his degree of spiritual elevation. The *ḥasid's* character and the contents of *ḥasidut* underwent changes over the generations.[34] Particularly important for this discussion is the type of *ḥasid* that developed under the inspiration of the moral and religious ethos of the Kabbalists of Safed during the sixteenth century.[35] The main traits of this form of *ḥasidut* were (1) intense occupation with esoteric doctrine, in addition to Halakhic literature; (2) a severely ascetic way of life, in the spirit of the instructions of Kabbalistic ethical literature; and (3) forms of worship that differentiated between *ḥasidim* and the rest of the community, such as the use of the ARI's version of the prayers and frequent ritual immersion. Individual *ḥasidim* and fellowships of *ḥasidim* were a familiar phenomenon in various areas of eastern Europe during the seventeenth and eighteenth centuries.[36] They usually were honored and respected by the community at large. At the same time, they tended to separate themselves from the public and refrained from accepting the burden of leadership.

In the eyes of his disciples and admirers, the Gaon was the spectacular embodiment of a *ḥasid.* This assessment found many expressions in the introductions to his works written by his sons and disciples. Among the traits attributed to the Gaon, his asceticism is outstanding. He withdrew from society and from any secular activity, and his main goal in this withdrawal was to direct most of his time and resources to Torah study. In chapter 7, I shall again discuss this manifestation of the Gaon's piety, as well as others. Here, I shall concentrate on another aspect of his *ḥasidut:* his Kabbalism and mysticism.

I have indicated the breadth of the Gaon's grasp of Kabbalistic literature and noted his manner of interpreting it. Naturally, the image of the Gaon as someone who penetrated to the greatest degree the depths of esoteric doctrine is one of the most important revelations of his piety *(ḥasidut).* Therefore it is not surprising that Rabbi Ḥayyim of Volozhin responded sharply to rumors that challenged the status of the Gaon as a Kabbalist. I shall present some of Rabbi Ḥayyim's replies to such rumors and then try to make clear their intention and meaning:

> Regarding that which my ear caught of the slander of many ignorant and empty people in distant regions, who never saw the light of his Torah and sanctity in their lifetimes, people without a yoke on their mouth and a tongue speaking haughtily to attribute a defect to the holy men of heaven. . . . They say of the holy rabbi, who was content with the holy divine spirit, that the ARI of blessed memory was not significant to him, perish the thought. This and even more, some of them go deeper to speak ill, saying that even the Holy Zohar was not fit in his eyes, perish the thought, to designate as material for study in his lifetime. May the lips of those who speak impudently of that saint, the foundation of the earth, be silenced.[37]

Who are those who slandered the Gaon by saying that he did not highly regard the ARI and showed no interest in the Zohar? Scholars who have addressed this issue assumed they were Hasidim.[38] Indeed, we do possess a Hasidic source that reveals a controversy between Hasidim and the Gaon regarding the status of Lurianic Kabbalah. In a letter from Rabbi Shneur Zalman of Lyady to his followers in Vilna, written in 5557 (1797), we find:

> And it is known to us with utmost clarity that ha-Gaon he-Hasid, may his candle burn brightly, does not believe that the Kabbalah of the ARI of blessed memory in general is all from the mouth of Elijah of blessed memory, [but that] only a very little bit is from the mouth of Elijah and the rest is of [the ARI's] great wisdom, and there is no obligation to believe in it, . . . and [that] a man who has such [wisdom] has the judgment, the option of choosing for himself the good and the blameless from all the sanctified holy writings of the ARI of blessed memory, which is not what we believe.[39]

Thus the controversy between the Hasidim and the Gaon is focused on the question of whether the writings of the ARI possess binding authority. The Hasidim claimed that the ARI wrote all his works on the basis of a revelation from Elijah the Prophet, and therefore no one is permitted to disagree with him or deviate from his teaching. The Gaon, in contrast, believed that the ARI usually based his teachings on his own wisdom and not on a revelation from Elijah, and therefore it is not necessary to adopt his method in interpreting the Zohar. Nevertheless, there is a certain disparity between the words of Rabbi Shneur Zalman and the words attributed by Rabbi Ḥayyim to those who slandered the Gaon. Rabbi Shneur does not claim that the Gaon did not honor the ARI, but rather that he did not view him as a binding authority. Thus, Rabbi Ḥayyim might not have been responding specifically to the letter of Rabbi Shneur Zalman but rather to attitudes and opinions regarding the Gaon prevalent in Hasidic circles. In any event, the rumors that arrived from "distant regions"—that is to say, the areas into which Hasidism had spread—about the Gaon's alleged contempt for Lurianic Kabbalah and the Zohar definitely aroused Rabbi Ḥayyim's ire. This is evident in the blunt style he uses against the slanderers, a style unmatched in its sharpness in all his writings.

In his effort to refute the calumny, Rabbi Ḥayyim refers to the Gaon's enormous expertise in the literature of the Zohar. Moreover, the Gaon's studies of this literature were accompanied by "a flame of love and awe of the Exalted and sanctity and purity and marvelous devotion." On the Gaon's attitude toward the ARI, Rabbi Ḥayyim writes, "My eyes saw the precious holy splendor of the ARI of blessed memory in the eyes of our great rabbi, may he rest in peace. For whenever I spoke to him about [the ARI], his entire body would recoil, and he would say, What can one say or speak about the divine glory of a holy and dreadful man of God like him?"[40]

Is there any basis to Rabbi Shneur Zalman's claim that the Gaon did not view the ARI as a binding authority? An answer to this question can be found in the recent work of Y. Avivi on the Gaon's Kabbalism.[41] Avivi shows that in a number of matters the Gaon did not follow in the footsteps of the ARI and interpreted the Zohar in his own way. Avivi also offers a convincing explanation of the assumption that probably guided the Gaon in this area. The latter viewed Zohar literature as part of ancient rabbinical literature and, therefore, acknowledged its obligatory authority. He saw the ARI, in contrast, as a late commentator on the Zohar. Therefore, despite the great esteem in which he held the ARI, he did not believe that his commentaries obliged everyone who followed after him. This is a consideration similar to that which guided the Gaon in his studies of Halakhic literature. As noted, he disagreed with *posqim* who preceded him, whenever he thought they had misunderstood the relevant *sugiya.*

Was Rabbi Ḥayyim aware of this fact? If we examine his words carefully, we shall find that they do not necessarily contradict either Rabbi Shneur Zalman's argument or Avivi's findings. On the one hand, Rabbi Ḥayyim never argues that the Gaon acknowledged the binding authority of Lurianic Kabbalism. Nor, on the other hand, does he admit that the Gaon deviated from the ARI's interpretations. It is not possible to determine exactly how Rabbi Ḥayyim grasped the relationship between the Gaon's Kabbalah and that of the ARI. However, beyond any doubt he is deeply wounded by the rumors coming from Hasidic sources regarding the Gaon's allegedly contemptuous attitude toward the teachings of the ARI and the Zohar. Rabbi Ḥayyim's sharp response to those rumors shows not only the sensitivity, veneration, and loyalty that he felt toward his master but also, it is reasonable to assume, the significance attributed to Kabbalah in general, and to Lurianic Kabbalah in particular, among the Jews of eastern Europe at the end of the eighteenth century. That society viewed the study of Kabbalah as a necessary and important characteristic of saintliness, and it regarded the ARI as a preeminent authority in Kabbalah. These assumptions were common to both Hasidim and their opponents.

However, Rabbi Ḥayyim is not content with merely emphasizing the Gaon's expertise in Kabbalah and his deep spiritual relationship to it. Further on in his response to the slander against his master, he presents a revelatory and fascinating description of the mystical revelations attributed to the Gaon. This particular testimony is often mentioned in articles and books about the Gaon and has been the subject of research;[42] nevertheless, I cannot refrain from citing it here in this discussion. Here is the essence of Rabbi Ḥayyim's testimony:

> For I heard from his holy mouth that many times several *maggidim* from heaven visited him, asking and requesting whether he would allow them to transmit secrets of the Torah to him without any labor. And he did not lend an ear to them at all. And one of the *maggidim* implored him very greatly. Nevertheless he did not look on his great aspect and answered, saying to him: I do not wish my understanding of His Torah, may His Name be blessed, to be through any intermediary at all. My eyes are raised solely to Him, may His Name be praised, what He wishes to reveal to me, and to give my part in the Torah, may its name be praised, with my labor at which I have labored all my life, and may He, may His Name be praised, give me wisdom from His mouth and knowledge and understanding, that He may give me an understanding heart, and may my kidneys act like two wells. And let me know that I have found favor in His eyes. And I want only what is in His mouth. And achievements by angels and *maggidim* and ministers of the Torah for which I have not labored and not [attained with] my wisdom, I have no desire for them.[43]

In the light of this testimony, the Gaon appears to be a mystic who received revelations from higher powers. This fact in itself is not surprising, for the Gaon was very deeply involved in the world of Kabbalah. However, it is surprising that the Gaon rejected the offer of the *maggidim* to reveal the secrets of the Torah to him. The phenomenon of the *maggid* was regarded for generations as the supreme desire of mystics. Two famous examples of the appearance of a *maggid* stood before the Gaon's eyes and those of his generation and were likely to exert an influence on their expectations. These were connected to the names of Rabbi Joseph Karo and Rabbi Moses Ḥayyim Luzzatto.[44] Rabbi Joseph Karo documented the appearance of the *maggid* in a work that became famous and widely circulated, and a *maggid's* appearance to Rabbi Moses Ḥayyim Luzzatto was also widely known because of the controversy that broke out surrounding the messianic pretensions that Luzzatto developed, inspired by the *maggid*.[45]

The Gaon explained his decision to reject the seductive proposal of the *maggidim* by stating that he was not interested in having any intervening factor mediate between him and the divinity. He was not contemptuous of revelations. On the contrary, he believed that the insights and innovations he attained while laboring at the study of Torah came to him directly from the "mouth" of God. The process of Torah study appears here to be an event endowed with pronounced mystical significance. Understanding Torah is a gift of divine grace, for God grants the student wisdom and understanding, by virtue of which he has the merit of producing new Torah teachings. From this point of view the revelations offered by the *maggidim* are of lesser value than one's own studies. Another explanation of the Gaon's reserved attitude toward *maggidim* can be found in a story related by Rabbi Ḥayyim near the same place:

> And it happened to me that our rabbi sent me to my young brother, . . . our teacher Rabbi Shlomo Zalman of eternal memory, saying to him on order in his name that he should receive no *maggid* who might come to him. Because in a short time a *maggid* would come to him. And he said, Although our rabbi *Beit Yosef* had a *maggid*, that was two hundred years ago,[46] and the generations were as they should be, and he was on holy soil. Not so is it now: so many violate the norms, especially outside the land [of Israel], that it is fully impossible for it to be all holy of holies without any admixture at all.[47]

In light of the instruction sent by the Gaon to his student Shlomo Zalman, the revelations of *maggidim* appear to be not only of secondary importance but also dangerous.[48] Rabbi Joseph Karo could adopt without apprehension the guidance of the *maggid* who appeared to him, for he was living in the land of Israel[49] at a time when the generation was fit. The situation abroad was different, mainly since it was a period when "so many break out." In such circumstances there were grounds to fear that the words of the *maggid* would not be purely holy. In other words, it was conceivable that *maggidim* might not be acting as agents of divine powers but rather serving the powers of the *sitra ahra* (the forces of evil).

Who were those who "broke out"? In using this expression, the Gaon was most probably referring to the Frankists, a sect of secret Sabbateans, the disciples of Jacob Frank, who were concentrated in Podolia. Revelation of the antinomian character of this sect in the 1750s developed into a stormy and painful episode and left a harsh impression on the Jews of Poland and Lithuania.[50] It is easy to imagine that, from the Gaon's point of view, the Frankists were acting on inspiration by the forces of the *sitra ahra*. It is also not impossible that, in referring to those who "break out," the Gaon included the Hasidim. According to a tradition that has come down to us, the Gaon claimed that, since the Hasidim "shout in their prayer, 'Bo, Bo,' . . . he knows that this is a great *qelipa*."[51] Thus it appears that various manifestations of the action of the *sitra ahra* so close together in time and place aroused the Gaon's misgivings about responding to the proposals of *maggidim*.

The Gaon's apprehension regarding any contact with the forces of the *sitra ahra* also was evident when he recoiled from the opportunity that came his way to exorcise a dybbuk. This event is central to a "marvelous story" told by Rabbi Abraham Simḥah of Amcislaw in the name of Rabbi Ḥayyim of Volozhin:

> Once an evil spirit entered a man in Vilna in the courtyard of the synagogue, and a great noise was made there from the multitude that gathered to see the marvel. Our rabbi opened the window of his house of study, which was then in the courtyard of the synagogue, and looked out to see why there was noise. As soon as the man possessed by the spirit saw the face of our rabbi he began to shout, Rabbi, you are the one about whom they proclaim on high: Beware of Elijah and of his Torah. If you sentence me, even if only with your own mouth (he meant to say with-

> out holy names), that I must leave this man, I must leave. Our rabbi of blessed memory answered, In my whole life I never wanted to have any business with you, and now, too, I do not want to talk to you at all.[52]

Thus we find that the Gaon took a consistent line regarding contact with the powers of the *sitra ahra.* The circumstances of the two cases are, indeed, different: in one case the Gaon directed his disciple not to respond to the overtures of a *maggid,* lest he might be impure; in the second case he refrained from offering assistance to a man possessed by an evil spirit. However, both episodes have in common his absolute rejection of any contact with the forces of pollution. This attitude can be seen as another expression of the Gaon's piety. Fear of the *sitra ahra* and the struggle against it played an important role in the world of old-style *ḥasidim.* From this point of view, the Gaon walked in a path trodden by those who molded the *ḥasidic* ethos of former generations.

The pronounced contrast between the Gaon's position in this matter and that attributed to the BESHT is noteworthy. Not only did the latter not recoil from contact with the powers of the *sitra ahra,* he actually sought to confront them face-to-face on his own initiative. Among other things, he struggled against spirits, he negotiated with Samael, and he tried to redeem the soul of Shabbetai Ẓevi.[53] These confrontations, the BESHT believed, were an important component of his mission as a leader. In contrast, the Gaon did not think that his mission as a leader obliged him to struggle directly against the powers of the *sitra ahra.*

I have mentioned the reasons why the Gaon rejected the offers of *maggidim.* Rabbi Ḥayyim, citing the Gaon, also presents surprising remarks regarding another form of revelation—the ascent of the soul. This refers to a mystical experience expressed by the departure of the soul from the body and its ascent to upper realms.[54] One of the famous men favored with an ascent of the soul was the ARI. During an ascent of the soul, the ARI studied in the Yeshiva on High, where marvelous secrets were revealed to him. He, in turn, revealed some of those secrets to his disciples.[55] The BESHT also was graced with ascents of the soul, but for him these were essentially an opportunity to try to exert influence in the upper realms on the fate of the Jewish people.[56] However, according to Rabbi Ḥayyim, the Gaon did not attribute great importance to secrets of the Torah revealed to a person in his sleep by means of the ascent of the soul. This attitude is surprising, for among Kabbalists the ascent of the soul was regarded as a supreme desire. Why did the Gaon deviate from the prevalent position in that matter? Rabbi Ḥayyim explains, "The essence of what a person achieves in this world is by labor and effort when he chooses the good and directs himself to words of Torah; . . . and this is the essence of a man in dealing with His Torah, may His Name be blessed. But what the soul attains in sleep, which is without effort and without choice and will, is only the receiving of a reward that the Holy One, blessed be He, provides him in this world as a semblance of the world to come."[57] Thus a person's purpose in our world is the study of Torah based on choice, on will, and on effort. The secrets revealed to a person without exertion are mere reward and do not partake of the essence of a person's purpose in this world. In other words, with all the importance that the Gaon attributed to the understanding of the Torah that a person may attain, no less important in his eyes was the way by which one attained that understanding. The process of learning was the essence of human life.

In light of the Gaon's statement that he did not greatly value understanding achieved by the ascent of the soul, Rabbi Ḥayyim concludes that the Gaon did indeed experience ascent of the soul: "And the meaning of his holy words was that he had experienced an ascent of the soul every night from the day when he came into holy self-awareness. For one of his disciples told me that he had heard as much uttered explicitly from his holy mouth."[58] Perhaps there is a degree of irony here, in that what was not so important in the eyes of the Gaon is used by his disciple as a most important means of acclaiming his name. In any event, Rabbi Ḥayyim presents further testimony regarding manifestations of the elevated powers with which the Gaon was favored. Among other things, he states that he found in the writings of the Gaon "supreme, holy secrets, what was revealed to him by Jacob the Patriarch, may he rest in peace, and Elijah of blessed memory."[59] Furthermore, unusually, the Gaon had no recourse at all to specific *kavanot* and *yihudim* in order to attain revelations. They came to him naturally, without any striving on his part. This astounding phenomenon appeared self-evident to Rabbi Ḥayyim in relation to the Gaon: "Since all the words of his mouth and the meditations of his heart and his thoughts day and night constantly . . . were only concerned with the words of the Torah, with revealed things, with the Secrets of Creation, and with *ma'ase merkavah,* . . . and everything was pure and with marvelous sanctity, is it not so that one is only shown the thoughts of one's heart, and what need is there for *kavanot* and *yihudim?*"[60]

One way that the Gaon's disciples expressed their impression of his exceptional preeminence was the statement that no Sage had reached his high level for many generations. In this spirit Rabbi Ḥayyim characterizes the innovations of the Gaon in his interpretation of the Order *Zera'im* as such that "none of the Sages of the generations before us equaled them since the time that the Talmud was completed."[61] The Gaon's son Rabbi Abraham stated in that vein: "Who saw such a thing and who heard the like of them from the days of our rabbis the Savoraim and the heads of the yeshivot and the Geonim."[62] From the estimation that a Sage on the level of the Vilna Gaon had not appeared in our world for generations, it is but a small step to state that his appearance in that generation was a matter of divine grace. The view that the Gaon was the emissary of God appears in the words of Rabbi Ḥayyim within a more comprehensive conception: God promised that the Torah would not be lost from the Jews. This promise was especially important during the period of exile, for the tribulations of exile made it harder to study Torah. If that is true in the field of exoteric knowledge, it is even more applicable in the esoteric domain.

Against the background of these difficulties, the Gaon's mission becomes clearer, according to Rabbi Ḥayyim: "With God's compassion for us, to establish His good word, that it will not be forgotten, etc., He sent us a holy guardian angel from heaven. A man in whom the spirit of God dwells. . . . And he illuminated our eyes by his holy writings on revealed and hidden things. He brought to light mysteries of wisdom, which he revealed to us from their hiding places."[63] Thus, had the Gaon not appeared, the generation would have been forsaken in darkness.

Another of his disciples, Rabbi Menashe of Ilia, describes the Gaon's mission as being messianic in character:

> As it appears, the length of our exile shows that we must be near to the footsteps of our messiah, and we must clear the way before him, the way

> of truth; . . . and as it appears that the Lord sent us a holy guardian angel from heaven, the famous Gaon our teacher Rabbi Eliyahu of blessed memory of Vilna, who began somewhat to restore the glory of Torah to its former status, according to the way of truth and simplicity, and we must follow him and add to him here and there, until matters attain the fullness of correction, until we shall be worthy of having the divine light and abundance affect us by the hands of the messiah.[64]

Whereas Rabbi Ḥayyim emphasized the Gaon's contribution in revealing the secrets of the Torah, Rabbi Menashe, a rationalistic scholar influenced by Haskalah, describes the Gaon as someone who had paved the way for the advent of the messiah by rehabilitating the path of plain meaning and truth in the study of Torah. Nevertheless, both men perceived the appearance of the Gaon in their generation as a sign of divine grace: the Gaon was sent to our world to guide the members of his generation along the paths of Torah study. This perception was shared by all his disciples.

IN HIS GENERATION AND FOR GENERATIONS

In summing up this discussion of the image of the Gaon as it was perceived and described by his disciples and sons, the first concept that comes to mind is perfection. The Gaon appears in the testimony of these men as the perfect embodiment of a Jewish scholar, a *Talmid Haham,* and of a *ḥasid.* His studies encompassed the entire Torah, both written and oral, revealed and hidden. His mastery of Torah literature was enormous in its proportions and was complete without any qualification. Moreover, in his commentaries and innovations the Gaon managed to connect early and late and revealed and hidden, to clear the text of scribal errors and resolve all doubts. Not only did he study and know the entire Torah, but he also demonstrated clearly that Torah, including all its strata and aspects, is a unified entity.

The Gaon also entirely embodied the highest level of piety. He withdrew from all the delights of the world and immersed himself in Torah and the commandments. His study was for its own sake, and for that reason he was graced with revelations of the secrets of the Torah. However, in this matter he adopted an original approach: he rejected the proposals of *maggidim* to reveal the mysteries of the Torah to him, and he did not value highly the secrets of Torah that were revealed to him by the ascent of the soul. More than anything, the Vilna Gaon sought to gain revelations directly from the "mouth" of God—that is to say, the insights and innovations that he gained through his intellectual labor in studying Torah. We find that to some degree the Gaon blurred the distinction between the revealed and the hidden: on the one hand, he preferred to attain the secrets of the Torah by intellectual effort; on the other hand, he also regarded the new insights he gained in the area of Halakhah as the fruit of divine revelation. Thus it may be said that the Gaon regarded all Torah study, both exoteric and esoteric, as an event of mystical significance.

In various ways the Gaon's disciples and sons expressed their conviction that before them was a person of superhuman dimensions: the sum of his writings represented merely a drop of the sea of his wisdom, his Torah was like a flowing stream impossible to contain, and a man on his high level had not appeared in our world for many generations. To be precise: the essence of the Gaon's greatness was not expressed in supernatural attributes or deeds but in the total actualization of human attributes. However, the appearance of a man who embodies such human perfection can only be interpreted as a marvelous event: the Gaon was sent from on high by divine grace in order to enlighten his generation with Torah.

When we consider that conception of the Gaon, a number of questions arise: Do we have a realistic portrait of the Gaon here, or could this be merely a legendary portrait? To what degree is it possible to regard the descriptions and impressions of his sons and disciples as reliable testimony? Another question to be asked in this context is: What was the secret of his influence on those around him and on his contemporaries? Why were his disciples drawn to him, and why did he receive such extensive recognition and authority among his contemporaries? Furthermore, what is the meaning of his sons' and disciples' efforts to erect a monument to him in the introductions they wrote to his works? Finally, how is it that, of all the great Torah scholars who lived and were active during the eighteenth century, such a powerful myth should have grown up around the Vilna Gaon? The latter question is especially important because this man neither served as rabbi of an important community nor left a body of Halakhic rulings. Moreover, his writings did not become extensively circulated study material in yeshivot and houses of study, and most of the components of his system of study failed to become widely accepted. Why then did the collective memory of eastern European Jewry seize upon this figure in particular?

These and similar questions are, of course, open to estimation, and various and sundry answers may be proposed for them. I shall suggest answers that appear reasonable to me, both in consideration of the sources in our possession and the circumstances and spirit of the period. The various descriptions of the Gaon were written by his sons and disciples after his death. Apparently his demise left a great void in their souls, and they felt a powerful need to present him as they knew him. In such circumstances writers tend to glorify and intensify the figure dear to them. However, even if we assume that in the portrait before us there is some degree of exaggeration and idealization, we cannot avoid the conclusion that it expresses an encounter with a personality endowed with extraordinary intellectual abilities and psychic powers. It appears to me that what underlay the various descriptions of the Gaon was first of all the direct experience of being in his presence and studying under his direction. That experience left in the hearts of his disciples the impression that he had monumental dimensions, and it aroused in them the feeling of self-abnegation and submission to him. An apt expression of this feeling is found in the words chosen by Rabbi Ḥayyim to conclude his introduction to the Gaon's commentary on the Zohar: "These are my words, I being so tiny and minuscule, for I was able to taste of the sweetness of the words of our great and holy rabbi only as a dog licks. And all of my body trembles in awe before the heights of his holy Torah in revealed and hidden things to no limit. His good memory is the joy of my soul."[65]

What was so enchanting about the Gaon for those privileged to be among those who "saw his face"? What is the source of the veneration they felt for him? Why did they display such self-effacement before him? No doubt, since they themselves were scholars, the encounter with a man who possessed such outstanding capabilities and achievements aroused astonishment and admiration in their hearts. However, most likely it was not only his abilities and achievements that riveted them but also his personality. Here, it is fitting to point out several of the Gaon's traits, which have been discussed at length by H. H. Ben-Sasson: the Gaon was aware of his merit and radiated authority and leadership. He was also endowed with a powerful will, which was expressed in his way of life and his daily schedule.[66] It appears that his mental abilities and powers—rare in their intensity—combined with his reclusive way of life, increased the power of his attraction both for those who had the privilege of being in his company and for those who were nourished by rumors and stories about him.

In addition to all this, the Gaon was a source of inspiration for his disciples and admirers. In his personality, his scholarly achievements, and his way of life, he exemplified a living model of religious values and ideals such as scholarship and piety. From the mid–eighteenth century on, those values had begun to erode. The new movement of Hasidism, on the one hand, and the harbingers of Haskalah, on the other, challenged the scholarly ethos and the ethical ideals of the old style of *ḥasidut.* For circles of Jewish scholars who wished to maintain those values, the Gaon served as a moral support and source of authority. Hence it is no surprise that his disciples and sons joined together in an effort to document his greatness in the introductions they composed to his writings. However, during succeeding generations, authors recast the figure of the Vilna Gaon in relation to the needs of their time and in the light of their propensities. In this respect the Gaon exemplifies a kind of prestige and an authority that retained their force long after the time and place in which they were developed. In the coming chapters we shall take note of some of the features added to the picture of the Gaon over the generations.

2 The Vilna Gaon and Haskalah

THE VILNA GAON VIEWED AS A MASKIL BY THE MASKILIM

The cornerstone of the image of the Vilna Gaon as one of the forefathers of Haskalah in eastern Europe was laid by Rabbi Barukh of Shklov (1744–1808), also known as Barukh Schick, one of the pioneers of Haskalah in eastern Europe. In the introduction to his Hebrew translation of Euclid's *Elements,* Rabbi Barukh claims that, when he visited the revered sage in the winter of 1777–78, the latter advocated secular studies: "I heard from the holy one that, to the extent that a person is lacking in knowledge of secular subjects, he will lack one hundredfold in the wisdom of the Torah. For the Torah and secular knowledge are bound together. . . . He commanded me to translate whatever possible of the secular subjects into our holy tongue in order to recover what they [the

Gentiles] had devoured, . . . so that knowledge should proliferate among our people of Israel."[1]

Rabbi Barukh's self-assumed mission was to promote secular studies among the Jews of eastern Europe,[2] to which end he wrote, translated, and published books on secular subjects. As his efforts in this vein met with hostile reactions, it is reasonable to assume his claim that the Gaon approved his activities was motivated by a desire to benefit from the Gaon's enormous prestige. Rabbi Barukh's testimony regarding this "approval" was widely quoted by Haskalah writers and historians of later generations, probably because it was the first evidence of its kind, it could be attributed to the primary source, and it seemed particularly trustworthy in that it had appeared in print during the Gaon's lifetime.

This portrayal of the Gaon as a supporter of Haskalah was to develop still further. The next stage can be illustrated by *Te'udah BeYisrael* (Admonition in Israel) by Isaac Baer Levinsohn (1788–1860). In this book, the first programmatic work of the Haskalah movement in Russia, Levinsohn took pains to prove that the aims of Haskalah were consistent with Jewish tradition, and that its very roots could be traced back to that tradition. Arguing this point, Levinsohn cited a long list of Jewish leaders of the past who had not been averse to secular studies, notwithstanding their prowess as men of Torah. In this list Levinsohn included the Gaon of Vilna, relying on the above-cited testimony of Rabbi Barukh of Shklov.

However, his account seems to add some new elements. The Gaon, says Levinsohn, had not merely acknowledged the importance of secular studies and instructed Rabbi Barukh to translate scientific literature into Hebrew; he himself had been "learned in many of the sciences and he would earnestly encourage the study of sciences." Moreover, Levinsohn stated that the Gaon's position in this regard had influenced his disciples, among whom was Rabbi Solomon Zalman of Volozhin, a close disciple of the Gaon, whom Levinsohn described as "learned in grammar and geometry and the other secular subjects necessary for understanding the Talmud." Levinsohn then generalized, adding that "thus were all the holy society of the disciples of Our Master Eliyahu of Blessed Memory."[3]

Elsewhere, in discussing Levinsohn's efforts to prove the correctness of Haskalah within the tradition, I wrote:

> The customary image of the Haskalah movement in eastern Europe tends to focus on elements of transformation and innovation that threatened to undermine the patterns of traditional society and to question the validity and authority of its values. This picture is certainly justifiable, even with respect to the movement's more moderate manifestations, such as that represented by Levinsohn, and it is all the more valid if one considers its later, more radical developments. However, in viewing Haskalah as advocated by Levinsohn and his contemporaries through the prism of its future evolution, one runs the risk of overlooking one of its most basic characteristics: Levinsohn and many other contemporary maskilim were largely rooted in the traditional world, both as regards their personal behavior, education, and cultural background and as regards their ideologies. The claim that Haskalah was compatible with tradition—the central thesis of Levinsohn's book—was not just a propaganda slogan intended for external consumption; it was first and foremost an expression of Levinsohn's innermost feelings, and indeed of the views of those maskilim he represented.[4]

Consequently, it is easy to see why invoking the Gaon's authority was of vital significance for Levinsohn and his colleagues. Considering the enormous amount of prestige and respect the Jews of Lithuania accorded the Gaon, his image as a supporter of Haskalah was not only important as evidence that could be presented to opponents outside the movement, but it also helped shore up the maskilim's self-image.

A definitive overview of the Gaon's reputation among Russian maskilim may be found in a book called *Safah Laneemanim,* by Samuel Joseph Fin.[5] Fin, one of the leading Lithuanian maskilim from the 1840s on, discusses the Gaon's attitude to Haskalah in a historical survey of the movement's origins in Russia, and he describes it as marking a turning point. Prior to the Gaon's arrival on the scene, Jewish culture in Poland had been at a low ebb, exemplified by the prevalent method of casuistry *(pilpul)* in the study of the Torah and by the complete neglect of secular studies and sciences. It was the Gaon of Vilna, writes Fin, who

> destroyed and smashed all the castles in the air of casuistry . . . and laid the way for plain and literal interpretation. . . . He also realized the usefulness of the sciences in expanding Torah knowledge, and the merit of the scientific method in religious education. And, in addition to teaching

> himself the whole theory of grammar and language, and all the theoretical sciences, he urged wise men versed in languages to translate into the holy tongue books of secular knowledge by Gentile scholars.

As further proof of the Gaon's favorable attitude to the goals of Haskalah, Fin cites the testimony of the great rabbi's sons regarding their father's ideal curriculum:

> First of all he cautioned . . . to be expert in all twenty-four books [of the Bible,] with their vocalization and cantilation. And above their army [should be] the banner of grammar, . . . and after that he commanded that the six Orders of the Mishnah should be familiar in his [the student's] mouth, with generalizations and explanations. . . . Then he admonished [us] about the way to study in the sea of the Talmud, . . . stipulating that the study must be directed toward truth; it must hate raising artificial difficulties; it acknowledges the truth, . . . and his [a scholar's] desire to demonstrate intellectual skills should not be equal in value to his commitment to the truth.

Though Fin added no comments or interpretation, it may be inferred from the context in which he placed the quotation that the Gaon was an advocate of educational reform compatible, at least in part, with the aims of the maskilim.

Fin not only depicts the Gaon as a pioneer of Haskalah but also holds that he exerted considerable influence on his contemporaries. Though a saint and a recluse, he "nevertheless . . . offered the Jews of Lithuania and Poland a new light, to illuminate their path to knowledge of the Torah via the route of the plain interpretation, and proceed from there to religious and scientific education." Indeed, when Fin discusses contemporaries of the Gaon who had taken up secular studies, he attributes their inclination to do so to the Gaon's inspiration.

Fin admits that the road leading from this reappraisal of secular learning—due primarily to the Gaon—to the rise of the Haskalah movement in Russia during the first half of the nineteenth century was by no means smooth or continuous. In the late eighteenth century, the Mitnagdim were diverted from pursuing secular studies by the increasing spread and vigor of the Hasidic movement, which led them to apply themselves rigorously to study of Torah. Moreover, rumors were now reaching eastern Europe that many of the German maskilim had rejected religious observance, and such rumors could not but create a negative attitude to Haskalah in Russia. However, Fin reports that "it was not long before a steadfast spirit was renewed among the wise men of Israel . . . to arouse the people to secular studies, . . . to teach the Children of Israel knowledge of the duties of the Israelite toward himself, his religion, his king and the country of his birth." Fin thus maintains that the reservations regarding Haskalah, common even among Mitnagdim, reflected a deviation from the Gaon's views and cannot be cited as evidence that he had not launched the movement in Russia.

THE IMAGE OF THE VILNA GAON AS A MASKIL AS A WEAPON IN THE HANDS OF ORTHODOX JUDAISM

The maskilim were not the only ones to cultivate the image of the Gaon as well versed in secular knowledge. Spokesmen for Jewish orthodoxy, too, embraced the idea, out of a desire to do battle with their opponents on the latter's own ground. For an instructive example, we turn to a letter written by Rabbi Eliyahu Rogoler, then rabbi of Kalisz and one of the most prominent figures of the rabbinic world in nineteenth-century Lithuania.[6] Rabbi Eliyahu's letter, written at the behest of an orthodox leader, Rabbi Zvi Lehren of Amsterdam, was intended to express the response of Russian and Polish rabbis to the first synod of German Reform rabbis, held at Braunschweig in 1844.

One of Rabbi Eliyahu's arguments against the Reform rabbis was that their attempt to introduce religious innovations was closely bound up with their university education. "Apostate philosophy" and the secular sciences—which Rabbi Eliyahu regarded as a single entity—were inspiring the Reform leaders to undermine the foundations of Halakhah and providing them with the doctrinal basis for that attempt. To combat the academic authority of the Reform rabbis, Rabbi Eliyahu drew support from

> our holy master, the divine teacher . . . Rabbi Eliyahu of Vilna, about whom the entire world would bear witness that the greatest scholars

> and professors were not worth a straw in comparison to him, being utterly incompetent before him in all the seven sciences. . . . Nevertheless, behold and see what the late Gaon wrote . . . denouncing philosophy, and he took Maimonides to task for having been attracted in some respects to the accursed philosophy. . . . He would always declare that one should study no science but the Talmud, save the science of grammar alone, and he would never study the other sciences except in a place where it was forbidden to meditate on the Torah [i.e., in the toilet].[7]

Whereas the Haskalah depiction of the Gaon as learned in secular knowledge was meant to serve as a model worthy of emulation, the picture drawn in Rabbi Eliyahu's letter had a completely different purpose. First and foremost, here was a person of astounding achievement in secular studies who could therefore serve as an authoritative witness as to the nature of "philosophy." Second, the Gaon was an eloquent illustration of the marginal significance that should be attributed to secular subjects in comparison with the essential study—that of the Torah.

The image of the Gaon as an enlightened scholar assumed yet another aspect in a book titled *Aliyot Eliyahu*, by Rabbi Yehoshu'a Heschel Levine. This book, published in 1856, was the first biography of the Gaon of Vilna. In it Levine combined bona fide biographical elements with highly fanciful descriptions of the Gaon's virtues, producing what could be called a "Mitnagdic" equivalent of a literary genre that was popular in Hasidic circles: namely, fanciful biographies of Hasidic leaders—especially of Rabbi Israel Ba'al Shem Tov, the founder of Hasidism. One of the Gaon's virtues, according to Levine, was his familiarity with secular knowledge: "When he was twelve years old, there was no science too difficult for him. . . . All natural and theoretical sciences were ruled by his strong hand." To corroborate these and other, equally florid, descriptions, the author cites passages in the Gaon's writings in which his secular knowledge is apparent.[8]

Further confirmation of the Gaon's amazing proficiency in the secular sciences could be derived—so claimed Levine—from the "enemy camp" itself. *Aliyot Eliyahu* includes two episodes concerned with scientists' impressions of the Gaon. The first episode relates that when the Gaon paid a visit to Berlin, he was approached by a German professor, head of three celebrated universities, who presented the Gaon with a complicated problem that he and his colleagues had been unable to solve. To the German scholar's astonishment, the Gaon easily solved the problem.[9] Though Levine leaves the German professor anonymous, his other witness to the greatness of the Gaon is none other than the celebrated philosopher Solomon Maimon (1753–1800). A letter purporting to be from Maimon's hand relates that, having heard of the Gaon's stature as a secular scholar, the writer decided to discover the truth for himself. Following a detailed description of his visit to the Gaon and the conversation that ensued, Maimon sums up his impressions with the statement that "in all the scholars of the Gentiles, etc., there is none like him."[10]

Unlike Eliyahu Rogoler, who used the Gaon's alleged proficiency in secular knowledge as an argument against such knowledge, Yehoshu'a Heschel Levine claims that the Gaon was in favor of disseminating secular knowledge among the Jews. Essentially, Levine's goal was to portray the Gaon as an ideal of the balanced and correct inclusion of secular learning within the tradition. The Gaon's sanction of secular learning depended on its total subordination to the Torah: "All the sciences appeal to him: Take us to be your perfumers and cooks [1 Samuel 8:13]. . . . And he waved his hand to them and raised his voice: Come, ye blessed ones, to the gates of Torah and piety. For I have seen the breaches in the ranks of our people, among whom [the sciences] have caused many, many casualties. However, the light of the Torah will reform them."[11] In other words, the Gaon was allegedly aware of the great danger involved in secular studies; nevertheless he was willing to permit them—provided they remained within suitable bounds. In fact, Levine presents the Gaon as having achieved a golden mean between the extreme nonreligious Haskalah, on the one hand, and uncompromising orthodoxy that entirely rejected any dealings with the secular sciences, on the other.[12]

It is clear that Yehoshu'a Heschel Levine is projecting the confrontation between Haskalah and orthodoxy in the 1850s back to the time of the Gaon, more than fifty years earlier.[13] This anachronistic approach, as well as the description of the Gaon as having advocated the adoption of a moderate brand of Haskalah within the limits of tradition, constitute, of course, a reflection of the views of the author and his circle. Both Levine and Rabbi David Luria of Bykhow (1798–1855), the Lithuanian scholar who helped him prepare the book, belonged to a rather small group of Lithuanian scholars who combined Torah knowledge with some measure of secular science.[14] Levine's portrayal of the Gaon could be invoked as a justification of such a moderate approach in the face of possible criticism from orthodox circles. Simultaneously, the picture of the enlightened Gaon-as-maskil was a weapon to be wielded against the godless Haskalah movement.

Indeed, there is no doubt that this was exactly Levine's intention. At the beginning of *Aliyot Eliyahu,* he cites an exchange of letters with several persons who had assisted him; one of these was Rabbi Jacob Zvi Meklenburg (1785–1865; renowned rabbi, author of the Torah commentary *Haketav Vehakabbalah*). In his letter to Levine, Rabbi Jacob Zvi Meklenburg explicitly states that the immediate motive for publishing the book was to aid the struggle against the radical Haskalah:

> To enlighten the rash. How foolish are these ignoramuses of our generation, and how they have sinned. Upon merely smelling the odor of science, they regard it as the most supreme poetry [literally: "as Heman and Darda," cf. 2 Kings 5:11]. And it affects them as a plague. And lo, the Gaon will serve them for eyes, to see a holy man of God, for whom the secrets of all the secular sciences were as an open book, and he adhered to them. However, he adhered even more to the love of God and His Torah with greater vigor, in sanctity and purity, all his life.[15]

Thus, the Gaon was living proof that familiarity with secular knowledge was no justification for a relaxation of religious observance. Having served as rabbi of Koenigsberg (1830–65), Rabbi Jacob Zvi Meklenburg had witnessed the gradual deterioration of traditional values.[16] It is not surprising, therefore, that he was inclined to draw the publication of *Aliyot Eliyahu* into the struggle against radical Haskalah.

The author of that volume and the Lithuanian scholars who helped him viewed their work in the immediate context of the ongoing conflict with Haskalah, as is evident from the end of the manifesto "Aharit Vetikvah Tovah" (The End and Good Hope), which apparently was written by Levine himself and included in the book as an appendix. This manifesto provides clear evidence of the new energy within the Haskalah movement and of the turmoil within orthodoxy following the accession to the throne of the new czar, Alexander II. In this changing context Levine's book assumed a polemical significance, not lacking in apologetic overtones. The figure of Eliyahu of Vilna as a *maskil* was held up as refutation of the accusation that the orthodox establishment was opposed to the policies of the "enlightened" czar. At the same time, the very figure who combined secular knowledge with Torah and piety was a weapon to be brandished against "those for whom knowledge and piety have become mutual enemies . . . and whose faith has been lost and rooted out of their mouths."

For a Hasidic version of the Gaon's role in the early Haskalah movement, we turn to the writings of Rabbi Joseph Isaac Schneersohn,[17] the leader of Habad (Lubavich) Hasidism from 1920 to 1950 (he was the father-in-law of the last rebbe). In his *Divrei Hayamim Hahem,* he describes the Gaon of Vilna as one who "diligently pursued his studies with unprecedented perseverance—twenty-four hours a day; Torah piety and integrity were his craft." Rabbi Joseph Isaac also reports the Gaon's alleged interest in secular studies and his desire "to increase secular knowledge within Israel in addition to knowledge of the Torah." However, claims the author, despite the Gaon's sterling qualities and virtues, he failed to discern the danger involved in such studies. This shortsightedness was responsible—albeit unintentionally—for the contamination of Lithuanian Jewry with the Berlin brand of Haskalah. In Rabbi Joseph Isaac's words:

> For many years the Gaon had told his disciples, his respected brother Rabbi Issachar, and his respected son Rabbi Abraham, of his deep regret that the five books of Moses had not been translated into the Jewish vernacular—Yiddish—with an easily understood commentary, properly arranged and accessible to all.
>
> The Gaon's brother and son, besides being incomparable scholars of the Torah, also possessed a wide knowledge of various sciences and spoke Polish, German, and French. And when it was heard that a great and meticulously observant scholar in Berlin [Moses Mendelssohn] had translated the Pentateuch into lucid German, they chose five of the best students . . . and sent them to Berlin to investigate the character of the learned translator of the Pentateuch and to copy the translation.

> The students who had been sent remained in Berlin for more than a year and copied many pages of the translation of the Pentateuch, and brought them to the aforementioned scholars. The latter liked the translation and praised it to the Gaon himself; and his permission was secured for the students to make several dozen copies of the translation, to distribute them among literate persons and set times for public instruction.
>
> The distribution of Mendelssohn's translation among students of Torah and literate persons not only detracted from the brilliance of the Torah's sanctity but served as a bridge over which dozens of pious and highly talented young men from the study houses of Vilna, Shklov, Slutzk, Brisk and Minsk made their way to Berlin to learn the German language and the sciences of medicine, astronomy and geometry, among them Rabbi Barukh Schick, Rabbi Benjamin Zeev Rivelish of Shklov, Rabbi Menasseh of Ilya, Rabbi Pinchas Eliyahu of Vilna (the author of *Sefer Haberit*), and the well-known grammarian Rabbi Solomon Dubnow.

In other words, it was this deplorable error on the part of the Gaon and his disciples that had paved the way for the Berlin Haskalah to infiltrate Lithuania. The Hasidic leaders, however, had taken great care to avoid such unfortunate intrusions because of an admonition handed down to them in the name of the Ba'al Shem Tov, according to which Mendelssohn was a tool of the devil and his desire was "to entice Israel with false opinions . . . to produce those who would deny the Lord and His Torah." It is highly ironic that Rabbi Joseph Isaac adopts the Haskalah position here, which is that the Gaon truly did play a decisive role in the spread of Haskalah in Lithuania. However, what the *maskilim* held to the Gaon's credit was held against him by the Hasidic leader.

The story of the role played by the Gaon and his disciples in introducing Haskalah to Lithuania is a strange mixture of truth and imagination, typical of the historical writing of Rabbi Joseph Isaac. It is true that the men mentioned at the end of the quotation did study science, and some of them were close, to one degree or another, to the tendencies of the Haskalah movement. However, the story of the dissemination of Mendelssohn's translation of the Torah in Lithuania by permission of the Gaon and by his disciples is groundless. Nevertheless, the story does express faithfully the view that was common in Hasidic circles during the nineteenth century: namely, that the Mitnagdim were influenced by the heretical Haskalah movement, whereas the Hasidim courageously defended the bastions of tradition.

THE HISTORICAL VIEW OF THE VILNA GAON AND HASKALAH

Before seeing how historiography treats the issue of the Gaon and Haskalah, we must make an important distinction between historians whose chronological and ideological proximity to nineteenth-century Haskalah or orthodoxy led them to adopt either group's creed without further question, and later authors who tended to take a more critical stance. Jacob Raisin belongs to the first category.[18] At the beginning of his book he waxes eloquent over the amazing emergence of Russian Jewry from the Dark Ages to the life and light of the West. Raisin's emotional kinship with the Haskalah movement, in which he sees the principal manifestation of Russian Jewry's renascence, is also evident in, inter alia, the dedication of the book to his father, whom he describes as one of the maskilim. Small wonder, then, that when such strong views and emotions joined forces with rather blunt tools of criticism and analysis, the result was once again a picture of the Gaon of Vilna as a veritable maskil, with certain additions made by Raisin himself.[19]

In fact, Raisin pictures the Gaon as a nineteenth-century liberal revolutionary. He fought against *pilpul,* declared that talmudic literature alone was the supreme and exclusive source for Halakhic decisions, and tried to free Jewish life of the centuries-old accumulation of customs *(minhagim)* that encumbered religious practice, in particular those customs rooted in the *Shulḥan 'Arukh.* However, in Raisin's view, the Gaon's main influence was not in the area of Torah study and ritual customs but rather in the dissemination of secular studies. As corroboration for his assertion that the Gaon was actually the founder of the Haskalah movement in Russia, Raisin points to the Gaon's contribution to the reform of Jewish education. He even cites an opinion that the educational reform advocated by the Gaon was more revolutionary than that formulated by

Naftali Hertz Wessely in his *Divrei Shalom Veemet* (Words of Peace and Truth).[20] Furthermore, the Gaon is alleged to have urged his disciples to engage in secular studies; indeed, the example set by the Gaon himself in this respect encouraged the maskilim to take up the banner of general education.

While Raisin's uncritical praise of the Gaon-as-maskil stemmed from his sympathy with the Haskalah movement, the historian Zeev Yavetz expressed a similar evaluation from quite different motives. In his lifestyle and outlook, Yavetz embodied an eastern European version of the modern orthodox ideal of *Torah 'im derekh eretz.* The person and activities of the Gaon provided Yavetz with the ideal founder and source of authority for his own ideology.[21] In a sense, he was following the lead of Yehoshu'a Heschel Levine. However, whereas the latter's barbs had been aimed at the radical Haskalah of the 1850s, the target of Yavetz's criticism was the *Wissenschaft des Judentums* in Germany, and in particular its greatest historian—Heinrich Graetz. Yavetz accuses Graetz of having ignored the contribution of Polish scholars to Jewish scholarship and claims that the Gaon introduced the critical method into rabbinical literature. His example inspired a new generation of Polish scholars fully familiar with the critical approach who, while also engaging in Torah study, were not averse to studying and delving into secular subjects. In stark contrast to the Gaon, "the father of faithful criticism," the learning of Mendelssohn's disciples soon proved to be false, in that they threw off the yoke of religious observance.

Yavetz's emphasis of the maskil element in the world of the Gaon and his disciples was so far-reaching that, according to his account, during the lifetimes of Mendelssohn and the Gaon, relations between the "capital of the Torah" and the metropolis of Haskalah were perfectly harmonious. To this idyllic picture, Yavetz adds:

> And who knows the benefit that would have accrued to Israel [by virtue of the good relations between Vilna and Berlin], were it not for the evil winds that emanated on the one hand from *Wissenschaft,* which began to ring false after Mendelssohn's death, and on the other hand from the winds of falsehood [Hasidism,] . . . which considers itself above all criticism, whereas in the eyes of the wise beholder it is beneath all criticism,

> a system promising wonders that are comprehensible neither to itself nor to its audience.

In Yavetz's view, then, the confrontation between Torah and secular knowledge derived from both the deterioration of Mendelssohn's disciples and the rise of Hasidism; in contrast, the great luminaries—the Gaon and Mendelssohn—had urged a balanced combination of the two.

Among the historians who have critically discussed the attitude of the Gaon of Vilna to Haskalah are Ben-Ẓion Katz, Joseph Klausner, Israel Zinberg, Louis Greenberg, and Raphael Mahler.[22] These authors, though differing in various details, display remarkable similarities in their conceptions of the Gaon's position and role in relation to the beginnings of Haskalah in eastern Europe. In contrast to the one-dimensional image of the Gaon-as-maskil—some versions of which we have been considering—the picture painted by the critical historians is complex and even rather ambivalent. On the one hand, they point to the gaping abyss between the Gaon's spiritual world and the goals of the Haskalah movement, as exemplified by the Gaon's hostility toward philosophy and his deep regard for Kabbalah, his tendency to stringent decisions in Halakhic matters, and his adoption of an ascetic lifestyle. Needless to say, the aforementioned historians reject the exaggerated descriptions of both Haskalah and orthodox spokesmen regarding the Gaon's familiarity with secular knowledge. Katz even takes pains to present detailed arguments contradicting the fabulous episodes in *Aliyot Eliyahu*.[23] Nevertheless, though these historians place the Gaon's roots and worldview squarely in the old world, they claim that his views and activities reveal the seeds of certain new elements. Moreover, they are inclined to see him as exerting some influence on the development of the Haskalah movement.

The Gaon's positive attitude to what would ultimately characterize the Haskalah movement, according to the aforementioned authors, is exemplified first and foremost in his favorable approach to secular studies. For example, Katz holds that, although the Gaon rejected philosophy, he loved and greatly admired the natural sciences. In Klausner's view, the fact that the Gaon permitted the study of secular subjects, studied them himself, and urged the translation into Hebrew of books that some of his colleagues viewed as abominations was "a step forward . . . toward the Haskalah." Zinberg ventures the opinion that the Gaon's views in this regard were almost heretical. Both Klausner and Zinberg are of the opinion, therefore, that the Gaon's attitude to secular knowledge was a break with traditional norms and a move in the direction of Haskalah.

The reader of Zinberg and Mahler is left with the impression that the Gaon encouraged secular studies among the Jewish public as well. It is in this spirit that one should understand Mahler's statement that the Gaon "also urged his disciples and associates to translate books of science into Hebrew from foreign languages." Zinberg asserts that the Gaon not only "urged" but "instructed" his disciples to do so. Both authors appeal to Rabbi Barukh of Shklov as their witness for these assertions (see above). Most of these historians mention the scientific books written by the Gaon himself; they, too, provide some evidence for his alleged activities in propagating secular studies.

The critical historians Klausner and Mahler also imply that the Gaon "preached" or "demanded" the reform of traditional education, in the form of a more systematic and rational approach to the teaching of Torah subjects. Zinberg implies that the Gaon actually demanded the incorporation of secular subjects into the traditional curriculum, while Greenberg states categorically that the Gaon shared the dissatisfaction of the maskilim with the traditional education system, as is evident in his attempts to modify it and introduce improvements. To summarize, most of the historians mentioned above believe that the Gaon encouraged—or even actively furthered—reforms in traditional education that were similar in spirit to those demanded by the maskilim. Needless to say, most of these historians stress the Gaon's opposition to *pilpul* and his efforts to base the study of Halakhah on the plain interpretation of the text; in this connection, some of them regard him as one of the pioneers of the critical school in Talmud research.

Not only do these historians find harbingers of the new tendencies in the Gaon's opinions and actions, but they also attribute real influence to him in the development of the Haskalah movement in eastern Europe. Katz, for example, holds that the Gaon's immense prestige inspired people to emulate him even in regard to secular studies.[24] Similarly, Zinberg states, "The Gaon, whose authority was tremendous, became a fortress and a support for all devotees of secular science. Those whose stormy spirit could not find satisfaction in the secrets of practical Kabbalah or in fruitless *pilpul* saw the Gaon as a central figure, shield and protection, and all lovers of knowledge flocked to him."[25] Klausner, for his part, asserts confidently that, if the Haskalah movement penetrated the masses in Lithuania more easily than in other parts of eastern Europe, this was due to "the Vilna Gaon's system of education and his attitude to study of the Bible, grammar and the secular subjects."[26] Mahler even introduces a dialectical component: "The elements of the new system that the Vilna Gaon introduced into the study of the old Torah played a historical role contrary to his own intentions; for, instead of reinforcing the traditional spiritual world, they undermined its foundations and accelerated its decline."[27] As a rule, therefore, the historians whose views we have surveyed agree in regarding the Gaon of Vilna as one of the harbingers, or heralds, of the Haskalah movement in eastern Europe.[28] In comparison with the earlier, more rhapsodic version of the Gaon-as-maskil, the views of these historians seem more sober and balanced. Nonetheless, I contend that their descriptions of the Gaon's affinity with the goals of Haskalah and his influence on the development of the movement are exaggerated. Before embarking on a reevaluation of the sources, however, I believe it is necessary to review certain methodological aspects of the term *harbinger.*[29]

It seems to me that the term *harbinger,* as it should be used in the present context, is based on the historian's assumption that any new cultural phenomenon, before actually appearing full-fledged on the historical stage, takes shape gradually over a long time. Hence an examination of the continuum of events leading from the old reality to the new should reveal a number of intermediate phenomena that, though not identical with the new reality, nevertheless tend toward it and are its harbingers, for they betray certain deviations from the outlines of the old in the direction of the new. According to this definition, one can distinguish between different levels or degrees of harbinger. Determination of the level of a harbinger may be based on a quantitative estimate of the elements characteristic of the new phenomenon to which it is connected, on an evaluation of the relative weight of these new elements in its world, and on the degree of intensity of its connection with them. In general terms, one might distinguish between a definite harbinger—that is, one whose affinity with the new phenomenon is very close—and a remote harbinger, whose world is still largely anchored in the old environment.

The historian engaged in an attempt to discover and describe the harbingers of a new phenomenon must, however, beware of a pitfall: any discussion of "harbingers" must necessarily be after the fact. Not until a new phenomenon has become integrated into our historical consciousness can we take up the quest for its harbingers. Accordingly, the historian risks the temptation to interpret the motives and intentions of a so-called harbinger in light of future developments, rather than in terms of the immanent rhythm of its own environment. Moreover, even if this risk is avoided, the meaning of the term *harbinger* should still be treated with some reserve. After all, the harbinger himself would not have viewed himself as such within the historical continuum; he could not very well have evaluated himself in relation to a phenomenon as yet unborn![30] The origin of the concept is rooted, therefore, in our historical consciousness, which seeks to impose certain categories of understanding and significance on reality.

Our definition of harbingers disregards the question of their direct influence on the historical process that ultimately produces the new phenomenon. It is quite possible, for example, for an "immediate harbinger" to exert minimal influence on the historical development of the phenomenon, while the influence of a "remote harbinger" will be considerable. Consequently, we have seen fit to separate discussion of whether the Gaon of Vilna was indeed a harbinger of Haskalah from the question of the degree to which he may have influenced the development of the movement.

WAS THE VILNA GAON A HARBINGER OF HASKALAH?

Before reconsidering the description of the Gaon as a harbinger of Haskalah, we must attempt an accurate reconstruction of the facts: that is, of those elements in the Gaon's biography that seem to express his affinity with the goals of Haskalah. Along with these facts, the Gaon's motives and intentions should also be considered. To understand these, we shall have to examine his inner world, its values, concepts, and criteria. We shall then apply the following criteria: (1) to what degree do the elements that allegedly express the Gaon's affinity with Haskalah indeed constitute a deviation from the characteristic norms and patterns of traditional society, and (2) how far do these elements approach the goals of Haskalah in its most mature manifestations?

Secular Study

First, let us consider the Gaon's attitude to secular studies. Did he really "instruct" his disciples and associates, or "urge" them, to translate secular books into Hebrew? As we have seen, the sole evidence cited by Klausner, Zinberg, Mahler, and others for this assertion is the testimony of Rabbi Barukh of Shklov in the introduction to his translation of Euclid's *Elements.* Now, while we have no reason to doubt Rabbi Barukh's word, neither do we have any reason or justification to generalize and to infer that the Gaon enjoined his disciples to translate secular texts. Furthermore, it should be noted that Rabbi Barukh's activities in spreading secular knowledge began before his meeting with the Gaon and in fact were not connected with that meeting; nearly one year before, in 1777, he had published a medieval Hebrew work on astronomy and a book of his own on astronomy and human anatomy. Consequently, Rabbi Barukh probably came to the Gaon to request support for his project. The Gaon, who perceived the benefit to be derived from the translation of scientific texts into Hebrew, gave Rabbi Barukh his blessing after the fact.[31]

We do have some further evidence as to the Gaon's interest in the translation of scientific texts. Rabbi Abraham Simḥah of Amcislaw reports, on the evidence of his uncle, Rabbi Ḥayyim of Volozhin, that the Gaon told his son Abraham of his desire "to have the sciences translated from other tongues into the holy tongue, and to have the Book of Josippon to the Romans translated, so that we should be able to understand the intention of our Sages in the Talmud and the Midrashim."[32] This testimony supports that of Rabbi Barukh of Shklov—but also restricts its validity, insofar as it delineates the permissible limits of what should be translated and specifies the purpose. To summarize, then, we can state that the Gaon took a favorable view of translating secular texts that could contribute to an understanding of rabbinical literature. At least in one case, when approached by an individual who had devoted himself to such an undertaking, the Gaon encouraged him. However, it by no means follows that the Gaon "instructed" his disciples to undertake the translation of secular books, with all that this statement implies.

The reader will recall the frequent mention of books on secular subjects written by the Gaon. These works are supposed to demonstrate the great sage's interest in the promotion of secular studies among the masses. As listed by most authors, the Gaon's works in this area include *Sefer Dikduk Eliyahu,* a brief account of the rules of grammar, published in Vilna in 1833; and *Sefer Ayil Meshullash,* devoted to geometry and published in Vilna in 1834. Mention is also made of a text in geography, *Sefer Tsurat Haarets,* and a work on astronomy; the latter was never published, but its existence is inferred from late traditions concerning a manuscript, seen by someone, in which the Gaon had noted his innovations in astronomy.[33] The so-called geography textbook, published in Shklov in 1802, is a commentary on Joshua, chapters 15–19—which deal with the division of the land of Israel among the tribes—and on the chapters in Kings and Ezekiel that deal with the building of the temple. Naturally, the Gaon's commentary on the chapters from Joshua includes geographical details, but it can in no way be considered a systematic work on geography! Indeed, the Gaon's interest in this case was no different from that of many previous commentators on these chapters, including Rashi.

It still seems incontrovertible that the Gaon wrote books on grammar and geometry. However, the authors who cite them as evidence for the Gaon's image as a maskil ignore—intentionally or otherwise—the essential difference between these books and those published by the real harbingers and pioneers of Haskalah. The latter's intention—explicit and avowed—was to spread secular knowledge among the Jewish masses, as is evident from the nature and style of their books. The Gaon, on the other hand, had no intention of distributing his books widely. In fact, a cursory inspection shows that they were simply notes and summaries that the Gaon had jotted down for his own use, a common practice among scholars of the day.[34] The publication of these privately written notes as "books" or "works" had nothing to do with the Gaon's own initiative or even wishes; it essentially reflects the immense reverence of some of his followers for anything written by the Gaon's "holy hand." The many traditions transmitted by the Gaon's contemporaries and disciples contain no hint of his taking any initiative to spread secular studies among Jews.[35]

What, then, was the nature of the Gaon's interest in secular subjects, as reflected in his notes? What weight did he attach to them, and what was their significance in the context of his overall spiritual activity? Evidence from two sources combine to throw light on these questions. The first, cited earlier in this article, is Rabbi Barukh of Shklov's quotation of the Gaon's own words, to the effect that "to the extent that a person is lacking in knowledge of secular subjects, he will lack one hundredfold in the wisdom of the Torah. For the Torah and secular knowledge are bound together." The second source is a statement in the Gaon's name by Rabbi Israel of Shklov (d. 1839; a disciple of the Gaon who later headed the community of the Gaon's disciples in Eretz Israel): "All the sciences are necessary for our Torah and included therein, and he [the Gaon] knew them all perfectly and mentioned them: algebra and triangles and geometry and the theory of music. And he praised the latter greatly, saying that most of the cantilation of the Torah, and the secrets of the Levites' songs and the secrets of *Tiqunei Hazohar* cannot be known without its aid."[36] In both cases, the emphasis is on the necessity of familiarity with the sciences in order to increase knowledge of the Torah. The secular sciences are valueless in themselves: they are merely indispensable tools for study of Torah, in the nature of "perfumers and cooks."[37] This "instrumentalist" view is in keeping with the Gaon's overall conception of Torah study as central and exclusive. Indeed, the ideal of total devotion to Torah study implies that any independent interest in secular studies is without value.

It is true that, farther on in the introduction to his translation of Euclid, Rabbi Barukh of Shklov attributes to the Gaon yet another explanation for the importance of secular studies: "He commanded me to translate whatever possible of the secular subjects into our holy tongue in order to recover what they [the Gentiles] had devoured, so that they will spread through the land and knowledge should proliferate among our people of Israel; in order to eliminate the tyrants' pride and haughtiness, the impudence of peoples and the tongue of nations that rush like the rushing of waters, saying to us, where is your wisdom—and the name of Heaven is profaned." However, there are good grounds to suspect that this is more an expression of Rabbi Barukh's own point of view than a faithful representation of what he had heard from the Gaon. Whereas Rabbi Barukh's desire to restore respect for the Jews among the Gentiles was the principal motive for his program of general education, no such justification for the adoption of secular studies can be found in the above-cited testimony of Rabbi Israel of Shklov, nor is it attributed elsewhere to the Gaon.

Nevertheless, the Gaon might have been in agreement with the underlying assumptions of the argument, namely, that in the distant past Jewish scholars were well versed in the secular sciences; it was they who had taught the sciences to the Gentiles. Only the tribulations of the Diaspora caused the Jews to forget their knowledge; and in fact, the Bible was alluding to the sciences when it said, "For this is your wisdom and your understanding in the sight of the peoples" (Deuteronomy 4:6). Such ideas were common among many Sephardic Jewish scholars during the Middle Ages, and were not unknown among some Ashkenazic scholars in later generations. It is quite possible, therefore, that the Gaon held such opinions. Significantly, however, unlike Rabbi Barukh, the Gaon did not carry such ideas one step farther and actively preach the study of secular subjects.

At this point in our discussion, the pertinent question is: Was the Gaon's interest in secular subjects, as just described, at variance with the accepted norms of Ashkenazic Jewry at the end of the Middle Ages? As we have seen, those who describe the Gaon as a pioneer or harbinger of the Haskalah movement tend to assess his favorable attitude to secular studies as a departure from and breach of traditional patterns. This assessment presupposes the commonly held historiographic view that medieval Ashkenazic Jewry lived strictly within the narrow confines of Halakhah, with the secular sciences excluded as forbidden territory. However, recent research has shown that not a few leading scholars of Ashkenazic Jewry in the fourteenth and fifteenth centuries were favorably inclined to the study of philosophical literature, and even to its dissemination.[38]

A similar reservation is in order regarding the sixteenth to eighteenth centuries. Although the study of secular subjects and sciences was not a central element of traditional life in the late Middle Ages, we can cite a considerable number of prominent people in central and eastern Europe who engaged to some extent in such study. Among those known to have engaged in secular studies are Rabbi Moses Isserles (the "Rema," 1525–72), Rabbi Judah Loew of Prague (the "Maharal," c. 1512–1609), Rabbi Yom Tov Lipmann Heller (1579–1654), Rabbi Yair Bachrach (1638–1701), Rabbi Yehonatan Eybeschuetz (1690–1764), and Rabbi Shlomo Ḥelma (1715–81).[39] Needless to say, there were differences in these scholars' fields of interest within the secular sciences and in the way they and others like them explained—or justified—their excursions into secular knowledge.[40] Some of them delved into both philosophy and the sciences, while others eschewed the study of philosophy altogether. Some explained their secular studies as motivated by a thirst for knowledge, pure and simple, whereas others justified their activities in traditional terms. A common justification was the argument, mentioned above, that the sciences originated among the people of Israel; they had been forgotten because of the adversities of exile, and it was necessary to relearn them in order to restore respect for the Jewish people among the Gentile nations. Of course, the sciences could also be employed as "perfumers and cooks" to the Torah, insofar as they were useful in clarifying various Halakhic problems. Whatever the motive, such constant recourse to secular knowledge among the rabbinic elite furnishes us, I believe, with sufficient grounds to assert that the Gaon's behavior in this respect was no breakthrough or deviation from his social context. This conclusion is not at variance with those of Gershom Scholem and Ḥayyim Hillel Ben-Sasson regarding the penetration of Kabbalah and the rejection of the influence of rationalistic thought in Poland during the late Middle

Ages.[41] For in the Gaon himself a deep affinity with Kabbalah and reservations about philosophy are combined with the acquisition of secular knowledge.[42]

It should not be assumed that the positive attitude to secular studies on the part of specific scholars met with universal approval. Far from it: at times they faced fierce criticism.[43] One might mention in this context the public dispute that arose between Rabbi Aaron of Prague, then head of the Poznan yeshiva, and the young Rabbi Abraham Horowitz. In a public sermon, Rabbi Aaron fiercely attacked those engaging in philosophy and other secular studies. Rabbi Abraham responded in a pamphlet with an enthusiastic defense of Maimonides, his school, and his followers.[44] However, this polemic did not reach the level of vituperation that was later to be characteristic of the strife between the Haskalah movement and its opponents in the modern era.

The dispute may have remained relatively moderate because whatever interest then existed in secular studies was evinced largely by members of the scholarly elite who had no intention of advocating the dissemination of such studies among the Jewish masses. Even more significant, however, at the end of the Middle Ages the dispute remained within traditional society, both parties sharing a common ideological and normative basis. In the modern era, study of the secular sciences was tantamount to a new ideological orientation seeking to supplant traditional values. It follows, therefore, that those historians who describe the Gaon's position as a breakthrough, one bordering on heresy, are guilty of anachronism. Their conception of the Gaon's approach is derived from a later and entirely different historical context—that of the fierce struggle between Haskalah and orthodoxy in nineteenth-century Russia. As we have shown, the Gaon's opinions regarding secular study were firmly rooted in medieval tradition, which attributed no heretical significance to an interest in secular knowledge.[45]

Educational Reform

We now take up another aspect of the Gaon's alleged affinity with Haskalah goals—his advocacy of educational reform, seen by some authors as heralding the later proposals of the maskilim. In fact, as mentioned above, some have even gone so far as to identify the Gaon's proposed "reforms" with those outlined by Wessely in his *Divrei Shalom Veemet.*[46] Can this claim be substantiated?

The most detailed available evidence of the Gaon's position regarding the methodology of learning, on which the above-mentioned authors rely, is the statement of his sons:

> Over and above his wisdom, he taught the people knowledge and encouraged them to study in a proper order. . . . First he admonished them . . . to be familiar . . . with the twenty-four books [of the Bible], including the vocalization and cantilation accents. And together with these—the science of grammar. . . . He then commanded that one should be fluent in the Six Orders of the Mishnah, with all the commentaries thereon. . . . He then admonished us as to methods of studying the "sea" of the Talmud; and the thorough perusal of Rashi's commentary . . . and the *novellae* of the Tosafot; . . . and it is a precondition that one should study with integrity, detesting the proliferation of difficulties; . . . and he commanded that one should eschew witty interpretations.[47]

These admonitions could hardly be considered a detailed proposal for educational reform. Moreover, their wording does not seem to imply that they were aimed directly at the formal system of education. Nevertheless, they do convey, albeit indirectly, criticism of the traditional system of study,[48] insofar as the Gaon's positive prescriptions indicate what he considered the weak points of that system. These seem to be the weak points: (1) the Bible as a whole was not taught systematically; (2) there was no systematic instruction in Hebrew grammar as applied to Bible studies; (3) the Mishnah was not studied independently of the Gemara (it is not clear whether this criticism was didactically motivated—that is, a recommendation to teach the Mishnah as an intermediate stage, permitting gradual progression from the Bible to the Talmud—or whether it was a methodological comment intended to convey to students of the Torah the importance of studying the Mishnah independently); and (4) the "witty" interpretations that the Gaon condemns clearly refer to *pilpul,* which was then widespread.

It might be claimed that there is a direct line from the Gaon's indirect criticism of the traditional system of study to the explicit criticism voiced by Haskalah spokesmen.[49] The latter, too, repeatedly stressed the importance of teaching the entire Bible and Hebrew grammar systematically; they urged the gradual progression from the Bible to the more difficult Talmud, with the Mishnah serving as an intermediate stage; and, of course, they were firmly opposed to *pilpul,* favoring a literal approach to the text. However, before we consider whether there was indeed a direct connection between the Gaon's criticism and that of the maskilim, we must point out that the former was by no means the first representative of the rabbinic elite to venture such opinions. He was preceded in this respect by such scholars as the Maharal of Prague, Rabbi Ephraim Luntshits, Rabbi Isaiah Horowitz, and others.[50] In fact, the writings of these and other scholars contain criticism more explicit and strongly worded than that attributed to the Gaon. Are these sufficient grounds to present them, too, as harbingers of Haskalah? Is there really a direct, continuous line from this traditional criticism to the strictures of Haskalah spokesmen?

The criticism of the traditional world of learning leveled by the Gaon and his predecessors was essentially a demand for a more systematic and rational approach to study and teaching. There was no intention to breach the value framework of traditional education. However, since this demand was in harmony with the goals of Haskalah, it is not surprising that representatives of that movement took it up, at times even citing the traditional criticism as their authority. Their purpose was, of course, to demonstrate that their new criticism was not really new but a continuation of the old. Nonetheless, it will be readily seen that this continuity was of a rather limited scope. In fact, the question of a more rational approach to the methodological and didactic aspects of Torah study was merely one element in the comprehensive educational reform advocated by the Haskalah movement; the central element in that reform was inclusion of secular subjects in the curriculum.

Furthermore, the educational program of Haskalah embodied a basic value transformation, succinctly expressed in Wessely's assertion that "the Torah of man" was an end in itself, an educational goal to be nurtured no less than "the Torah of God." For the Haskalah movement, educational reform was a tool for reshaping and reorienting Jewish society, and in this the maskilim were inspired by the humanism and rationalism typical of the European Enlightenment.[51] Needless to say, this concept was entirely at variance with the traditional concept of education, which embraced study of the Torah to the exclusion of any other subject and saw the production of Torah scholars as the supreme goal of Jewish education.

Evidently, then, rather than the Gaon and his predecessors heralding the future aims of Haskalah, it was the maskilim who appropriated those elements of traditional criticism that accorded with their own views. Moreover, once these elements had been incorporated into the general fabric of the Haskalah educational program, they took on new and different meanings and intentions. For example, the Gaon's recommendation to teach the whole of the Bible was most probably rooted in his comprehensive and all-embracing understanding of the concept of "Torah."[52] For the Gaon, all levels and offshoots of the Torah were one organic unity, with the oral Torah implicit in the written Torah. The Gaon's concept may also have had a methodological motive: familiarity with the Bible provides an important basis for productive study of talmudic literature. However, Haskalah's demand for systematic Bible studies was part and parcel of an entirely new trend seeking to shift the center of attention from the Talmud to the Bible; the latter, after all, was more appropriate to the universalist orientation of Haskalah, whereas the Talmud was an expression of the particularism so abhorred by the maskilim.

A similar reservation applies to the Gaon's advocacy of the plain interpretation *(peshat)* of the text as against *pilpul.* The traditional objections to *pilpul,* including those of the Gaon, were aimed at the method of *pilpul* and *ḥiluqim* that began to spread among Torah scholars in the fifteenth century.[53] The gist of these objections was that the elaborate logical constructions devised by the adherents of *pilpul* represented a major deviation from the truth as expressed by the text in its literal meaning. However, regarding study of the Bible, the Gaon never considered the plain interpretation *(peshat)* as superior in any way to homiletic *(derash)* or esoteric *(sod)* interpretations. Although we do find the call for an increased awareness of the differences between *peshat* and *derash,* which can be traced to the influence of the Gaon, this by no means implied a degradation of *derash* or *sod.*[54] The Gaon himself was a master of homiletic interpretation and regarded the hidden, esoteric content of the Torah to be of supreme significance. On the other hand, the maskilim, in their emphasis on *peshat,* were referring primarily to plain interpretation of the Bible; moreover, they considered the *peshat* as eminently superior to *derash* and *sod,* which they wished to banish from the study houses.[55]

Although one cannot speak of an unbroken line leading from rabbinic criticism of traditional education to the objections of the maskilim, one cannot ignore certain unique elements implicit in the Gaon's methodological approach that seem to presage future developments. I am not referring to his rejection of *pilpul,* which was not new or unique, but to his innovative approach to the study of Halakhic literature.[56] It is well known that the Gaon frequently emended the standard texts of the Mishnah, Tosefta, Babylonian Talmud, and Jerusalem Talmud, where they had been corrupted—in his opinion—by erring copyists.[57] Medieval commentators on the Talmud were concerned with determining correct readings, but later scholars were not; hence the Gaon was a conspicuous exception in his time. He was also unusual in the extent and breadth of his emendations, in the significance he attributed to them, and in the extraordinary range of Halakhic literature on which he based them. The Gaon's work in this area has inspired numerous authors, including eminent representatives of critical research, to call him "the father of modern Talmud criticism."[58] It should nevertheless be emphasized that the Gaon differs from modern exponents of philological research in that he based his emendations on logical deduction and on mastery of the literature rather than on ancient manuscripts.[59]

The Gaon's critical approach is also evident in his tendency, at times, to interpret the Mishnah in a manner other than what follows from the Gemara.[60] This was his practice when it appeared to him that the Gemara's interpretation was at variance with the *peshat*—the plain meaning of the Mishnah. It is evident that in doing so the Gaon was deviating from the accepted norms of traditional interpretation. Moreover, in his commentary on the *Shulḥan 'Arukh,* where he aspired to base the accepted Halakhic ruling on primary sources, he did not hesitate to take issue with the greatest commentators and Halakhic authorities of previous generations, including the author of that code, whenever he believed that they had misunderstood the talmudic argument.[61] Even more, whenever he deemed the accepted practice to be in error, he ruled it invalid and replaced it with what he believed to be in accordance with the talmudic sources.[62]

Taken together, the various manifestations of the critical approach that characterized the Gaon's approach to scholarship show a certain resemblance to the spirit of rational criticism that characterized the European Enlightenment of the eighteenth century and which was to become an important component in the Jewish Enlightenment movement of eastern Europe. From that point of view it may be said that something of what is called "the spirit of the age" affected the Gaon. On the other hand, it must again be emphasized that the Gaon's critical spirit was restricted to the area of methods of scholarship, whereas the critical spirit of Haskalah was directed at many elements within the traditional way of life and even challenged its fundamental values.

Was the Vilna Gaon a Harbinger of Haskalah?

Were historians correct in describing the Gaon as a harbinger of Haskalah? Here are the main conclusions I have drawn so far:

1. Nowhere in the available sources have we found evidence that the Gaon actually advocated the dissemination of secular studies and sciences among his contemporaries.
2. The Gaon's interest in secular studies was not different in nature or motivation from that found among certain representatives of the scholarly elite in previous generations. He viewed the sciences as an auxiliary tool for the clarification of certain Halakhic problems, whereas Haskalah valued them as ends in themselves. For the maskilim, a positive attitude to the cultural and scientific heritage of European society was a prerequisite for the Jews' social and political integration into that society, and this was the motive behind the maskilim's struggle to introduce secular studies into the curriculum of Jewish education. No trace of either these views or these aspirations can be found in the Gaon's outlook.

3. The Gaon did not initiate or plan any reform in Jewish education. His critical comments on educational matters did not deviate from those of some of his predecessors. The maskilim were able to identify with certain elements in this traditional critique, and they incorporated them in their own program; however, this is not sufficient to justify presenting the Gaon and the critics who preceded him as harbingers of Haskalah. The Haskalah movement envisaged a far-reaching transformation of traditional values; hence, even the traditional elements that they appropriated assumed new significance through their inclusion in the Haskalah program.

It follows, then, that evaluations of the Gaon as a precursor of the modern Haskalah movement cannot stand the test of careful examination. Such evaluations err doubly: by inaccurate presentation of the facts and by misinterpreting them in anachronistic fashion. I have nevertheless shown that the critical approach displayed by the Gaon in methodological matters may be seen to some extent as a harbinger of the critical attitude that was to characterize Haskalah. One might therefore call the Gaon a "distant" harbinger of Haskalah, that is, a figure firmly rooted in the traditional realm, with the innovative nature of his message limited at best.

My thesis, that the Gaon cannot be reckoned among the "immediate" harbingers of eastern European Haskalah, can presumably be reinforced and clarified by comparing him with his contemporaries who indisputably fall into that category.[63] In this context I shall confine my discussion to one of those figures—Rabbi Barukh of Shklov, whom I have already had occasion to mention.[64]

For many years, Rabbi Barukh worked devotedly and energetically to further the study of secular subjects in the Jewish community. In 1777 he journeyed to Berlin, where he published *Yesod Olam*, a medieval Hebrew work on astronomy based on a manuscript by Rabbi Isaac ben Joseph Hayisraeli. That same year he published his own book *Ammudei Hashamayim Vetiferet Adam* (The Pillars of Heaven and the Glory of Man), part of which was concerned with astronomy, and the remainder with the structure of the human body. Some two years later, in 1779, Rabbi Barukh published in The Hague another work, called *Derekh Yesharah* (Straight Path), consisting of guidelines in health and hygiene. In the introduction to this work he wrote, inter alia, that he was preparing a book about medications (it was never published). In 1780, in The Hague, Rabbi Barukh published his translation of Euclid's *Elements.* After a long interval, in 1793, he published a book entitled *Kne Hamiddah* (The Measuring Rod), essentially a reworked Hebrew version of an English textbook on trigonometry.

Rabbi Barukh's literary activity, which involved considerable effort and expense, was accompanied by a public relations campaign aimed at rendering the study of secular subjects socially acceptable. This objective is discernible in the introductions to his books, in which he crosses swords with the opponents of secular studies and presents an array of proofs and arguments for the significance and importance of secular knowledge.

Although Rabbi Barukh's motives and general philosophy undoubtedly differed from those of the Haskalah movement in its mature form, they definitely point toward goals that ultimately were to characterize Haskalah. For example, his book on health and hygiene reveals a utilitarian approach characteristic of Haskalah; books intended for the edification of the public were a prominent genre in Haskalah literature.

One of Rabbi Barukh's most frequent arguments in favor of secular education, which evidently represents his primary motivation, was the need to restore the Gentiles' respect for Israel. This argument rests on a theory that I have already outlined: the sciences were originally developed by the Jews, who passed them on to the other nations but forgot them, owing to their sufferings in the Diaspora. This lack was responsible for the contempt in which the Gentiles held the Jews. I have also mentioned that many Jewish scholars of medieval Spain, and even Ashkenazic scholars of the late Middle Ages, held similar views. Rabbi Barukh's innovation was the practical conclusion that he drew from the theory: the need to promote the dissemination of secular studies among his contemporaries. No such conclusion was drawn by most members of the scholarly elite who had dabbled in the secular sciences. An instructive example of the attitude of such rabbis is that of Rabbi Yehonatan Eybeschuetz.[65] Familiar with secular knowledge—and even proud of it—he, too, believed that the Jews had forgotten their knowledge in exile, but held that this would be remedied only after the arrival of the messiah.

The view that it was necessary to spread secular knowledge among the Jews in order to enhance their prestige among the nations also hints at a way of thinking that was to characterize Haskalah. Rabbi Barukh never departed from the particularistic self-image typical of traditional society. However, in the following respects he anticipated Haskalah and served as its harbinger: his sensitivity to Jewish honor in the eyes of other nations, the idea that certain faults in Jewish society should be rectified in order to increase the Jews' prestige among their neighbors, and his willingness to criticize Jewish society in light of an external criterion not immanent in the tradition. One does not find such features in the ideas and attitudes of the Gaon.

DID THE VILNA GAON INFLUENCE THE GROWTH OF THE HASKALAH MOVEMENT IN LITHUANIA?

It remains now to ascertain whether the Gaon, albeit unintentionally and unwillingly, influenced the development of the Haskalah movement in eastern Europe. Recall that some of the historians whose views I have surveyed answer this question in the affirmative. For example, Katz and Zinberg imply that the Gaon played a highly important role in the beginnings of Haskalah in eastern Europe; Klausner goes even farther, claiming that the Gaon and his activities were responsible for the exceptional diffusion of Haskalah among Lithuanian Jewry. However, a careful examination of the available sources shows that such assertions have no basis in fact.

Among the closest disciples and associates of the Gaon—those who had direct access to him and publicized his teachings—we find only two persons who could justifiably be considered harbingers of Haskalah: Rabbi Barukh of Shklov and Rabbi Menasseh of Ilya.[66] Of these, only the latter was a genuine disciple of the Gaon, for Rabbi Barukh's contact with the great sage was apparently episodic.[67] On the other hand, numerous individuals active at that time in eastern Europe who can readily be defined as harbingers—or even pioneers—of the Haskalah movement had no contact whatsoever with the Gaon of Vilna. Moreover, a perusal of the autobiographical writings of the early maskilim in Lithuania yields no indication that the Gaon or his literary output played any part in their spiritual development.[68]

It seems, therefore, that the mistaken evaluation of Katz, Zinberg, and Klausner was the direct result of an erroneous analogy. They incorrectly attributed to the Gaon actions and views that could be interpreted as betraying leanings toward Haskalah goals; and since they were aware of the authority wielded by the Gaon, they succumbed to the temptation of seeing him as having influenced the development of Haskalah in eastern Europe as well. The source of the fallacy most probably lies in the image of the Gaon-as-maskil—created and cultivated, as we have seen, by Haskalah authors of the nineteenth century. Although these historians did express reservations about that image, they did not sufficiently free themselves of it.

Indeed, if one may speak of the role played by the Gaon in relation to the origins of Haskalah in Russia, it is mainly a role played by the image of the Gaon-as-maskil, of which we have seen several versions above. This image was constructed by arbitrarily choosing certain traits from the historical figure of the Gaon, by offering an inexact presentation of the facts, and above all, by taking them out of their authentic context and viewing them anachronistically. Thus it cannot show anything about the Gaon's true relationship to Haskalah. Rather, it shows the deep need of the maskilim to base their approach on his authority. In other words, the Gaon had no initial influence on the growth and development of the Haskalah movement. However, once that movement emerged as a result of other factors, the maskilim fostered an image of the Gaon as a fellow maskil and made use of it.

One may well ask why the maskilim chose the Gaon rather than someone else. The answer appears to lie in the unique combination of his tremendous prestige and authority in his contemporaries' eyes and certain traits that could be interpreted as giving him an affinity with Haskalah. Obviously, were it not for those characteristics, the figure of Gaon-as-maskil could never have been created. However, it is no less obvious that the maskilim chose the Gaon to put the stamp of approval on their movement not because they believed he exemplified adherence to their values and aspirations but because of that prestige, which was a direct consequence of his learning and piety.

The Gaon's attraction might also have been due to his role in the controversy with Hasidism, an implacable foe of the Haskalah movement.[69] Finally, the Gaon's active life coincided with the early stages of Haskalah in eastern Europe. In fact, it was only because some of the real harbingers and pioneers of Haskalah were active during the Gaon's lifetime that both the Haskalah authors of the nineteenth century and some twentieth-century historians influenced by those authors were able to postulate a continuous link and cause-and-effect relationship between the Gaon and the beginnings of Haskalah. Of course, there is no need to stress that chronological proximity alone is no proof of influence.

As members of a small minority swimming against the stream, the Russian maskilim seized on the image of the Gaon-as-maskil to give legitimacy to their ideals. The Gaon's apparent leanings toward the goals of their movement bolstered the self-image of the maskilim, who believed that Haskalah did not contradict tradition. In fact, this image continued to play a legitimizing role among the Russian maskilim, especially in Lithuania, until Haskalah took a new turn in the 1860s and 1870s.[70] Perhaps the best evidence for the vitality of that image in Haskalah consciousness is the fact that its echoes continued to appear in Haskalah literature throughout the early twentieth century[71] and in subsequent historiography.

THE COMBINATION OF TORAH AND SECULAR LEARNING AMONG TRADITIONAL SCHOLARS

Even if one accepts my conclusion that the Gaon did not actually influence the development of the Haskalah movement in Russia, one may well ask if, and to what extent, his critical approach to the study of Halakhic literature, and his positive attitude to secular subjects as "perfumers and cooks" to the Torah, had any influence within the circles of his disciples and admirers in the traditional camp.

The widespread belief that the Gaon successfully eradicated *pilpul* seems more than a little exaggerated.[72] The extent and depth of his influence in this respect still await thorough investigation. Nevertheless, it seems certain that the attempts by the Gaon's disciples to propagate their master's attitudes did leave their mark on the scholarly world in Lithuania.[73] Similarly, some of the Gaon's disciples show a tendency to emphasize the value of Bible studies, favoring the study of grammar in this connection. However, only a few scholars actually went so far as to emend talmudic texts, as the Gaon had done: among these few were such figures as Rabbi Samuel Strashun of Vilna and Rabbi David Luria of Bykhow.[74] Finally, the literary activity of the Gaon's son Rabbi Abraham in the field of Midrash also shows a critical investigative approach.[75]

We need not be surprised that most of the Gaon's disciples refrained from making textual emendations after the manner of their master. Indeed, for anyone steeped in traditional attitudes that tend by their very nature to sanctify and canonize ancient texts, such a course of action required considerable daring. In addition, precisely because of their adulation of the Gaon and their respect for his charismatic authority, they concluded that practices permissible and suitable for him were not so for themselves. Consequently, though the disciples devoted considerable efforts to studying their master's emendations and commentaries, most of them avoided adding emendations of their own. Their attitude to the Gaon's modification of religious customs was similar: they described his religious practices, strove to emulate them, and sometimes also tried to trace their sources in traditional texts.[76] One might say that the Gaon did not really bequeath his critical methods to his followers; rather, the latter adopted his conclusions, institutionalizing them and establishing them as new norms.

It remains to determine the influence exerted on the traditional camp by the Gaon's position regarding secular studies. An answer to this question may be found in the valuable work of David Fishman on the Jews of Shklov. In the late eighteenth century the city of Shklov in White Russia was an important economic center. Among the Jews of that city arose a new economic elite that fostered ties with the regime. As a result, the members of that elite began to adopt the cultural patterns prevalent among officials. In other words, in the late eighteenth century one could discern signs of cultural adaptation in the community of Shklov. Against this background, the Gaon's attitude toward secular wisdom is significant. Fishman emphasizes that it is not a coincidence that, among the disciples of the Gaon, those who lived in Shklov brought out the positive attitude of the Gaon toward secular study. These men, who belonged to the learned elite of the community, found it important to promote the possibility of coexistence between Torah and secular learning. One of the most prominent of the Gaon's disciples, Rabbi Benjamin Rivlin, embodied this combination, though with the reservation that secular study was intended to serve as an aide to Torah study and nothing more.[77]

The trend to combine Torah study with secular study among the Gaon's students in Shklov was a relatively brief episode and did not persist beyond the end of the eighteenth century. However, certain Jews in Lithuania continued this trend during the first half of the nineteenth century. I refer to a rather thin stratum of men, generally belonging to the scholarly elite, who combined their study of Torah with some measure of secular studies. Among these were Rabbi Abraham, son of the Gaon, who published a book dealing with, inter alia, geography;[78] Rabbi Samuel ben Joseph, rabbi of Lucenec, who published the Gaon's book on geometry and added a commentary of his own; Rabbi Samuel Strashun and Rabbi David Luria, already mentioned above; Rabbi Ya'aqov Barit of Vilna, a prodigious scholar and the teacher of young scholars who were preparing themselves for the rabbinate; and several others.[79]

An attempt at a programmatic outline of the place and value of secular studies may be found in the writings of the Gaon's grandson Rabbi Ya'aqov Moshe ben Abraham. We may reasonably assume that his views largely represent those of the aforementioned circle. Rabbi Ya'aqov addressed himself to the problem in his introduction to *Ayil Meshullash,* his grandfather's work on geometry.[80] He expressed a generally favorable attitude to secular studies, but with the following provisos: (1) one should not enter the gateway of secular knowledge until one is full of Torah and *mitzvot;* (2) the study of the sciences should not be regarded as an end in itself but rather as an ancillary means to the study of Torah; and (3) one should limit the time spent on secular studies and engage in the study of Torah.

In other words, Rabbi Ya'aqov regarded secular studies as mere "perfumers and cooks" to the Torah; nevertheless, despite this seeming accord with his grandfather's views, his position has a significance of its own. In the case of one living and writing in the mid-1830s, a favorable attitude to the sciences as "perfumers and cooks" cannot be considered a direct and simple continuation of the Gaon's views. This is because, unlike his grandfather, the grandson was faced with the Haskalah movement, which was then effecting a spiritual transformation among the Jews and posing a threat to tradition. Hence, the new element implicit in Rabbi Ya'aqov's position was his personal view of the stand to be taken with respect to the spiritual environment in which he lived. The Gaon's grandson presents his approach as midway between Haskalah, which in his view overvalues secular knowledge, and extreme orthodoxy, which utterly negates any contact with such knowledge.

Indeed, one might point to the decision to sanction limited secular study confined within the bounds of Torah study and subordinated to it, in spite of the threat Haskalah posed to tradition, as an important characteristic of this particular group of scholars. However, the typical attitude of this circle regarding secular studies follows the lines laid down by the Gaon. Moreover, we may safely assume that in adopting this stance the Gaon's son, his grandson, and their associates were emulating what they believed to be his example.

This interesting cultural trend among the Lithuanian Mitnagdim of the nineteenth century deserves thorough research into its nature and salient features, as well as the extent and depth of its influence. For the moment, a few remarks will suffice. First, not all the Gaon's disciples and associates held such views. For example, in his writings Rabbi Phinehas ben Judah, a member of the Gaon's inner circle, engages in violent polemics against the secularizing influence of Haskalah and, in the process, totally rejects secular studies.[81] We may assume that other disciples and admirers of the Gaon reacted similarly to the Haskalah movement. At the same time, a prominent member of the Gaon's inner circle, Rabbi Abraham Abeli, referred to his positive attitude toward the sciences and to his critical methodology in arguing for a positive response to the more moderate brand of Haskalah. Rabbi Abraham, a respected rabbi and teacher in Vilna in the early decades of the nineteenth century, wrote a *haskamah* (note of approval, generally appended to new religious texts) to Isaac Baer Levinsohn's book *Te'udah BeYisrael.*[82] We see, therefore, that the Gaon's "testimonial" concerning the proper response to the Haskalah phenomenon was by no means unequivocal but lent itself to varying interpretations.

In conclusion, it is reasonable to suppose that the borderline between the Haskalah movement and the circle described here was not as clear-cut as I have made out: most probably there were several gradations of opinion. It would be wrong, however, to think of this group as a transitional stage in the development of Haskalah, for it persisted alongside that movement while fighting against it.

3 The Vilna Gaon and the Beginning of the Struggle against Hasidism

THE QUESTION OF MOTIVATION FOR THE STRUGGLE AGAINST HASIDISM

During the intermediate days of Passover in 5532 (1772), the organized struggle against Hasidism was launched. The community of Vilna, the largest and most important of the Jewish communities of Poland and Lithuania, initiated the struggle and called on other communities to follow in its footsteps. This was not a struggle over ideas between two currents or what may be called a Kulturkampf. The community of Vilna and the communities associated with it started a total war against what they viewed as a deviant sect. The aim of this war was to remove Hasidism and the Hasidim from the world. For that purpose the community organizations used a variety of means at their disposal: testimony was gathered about the "crimes" of the Hasidim, Hasidic writings were seized and burned, Hasidic leaders were arrested and punished, and above all, it was forbidden, under pain of excommunication, to maintain Hasidic minyanim (prayer quorums).

The central questions in the present chapter are: Why did the struggle against Hasidism break out? and What role did the Vilna Gaon play in that struggle? However, before taking them up, one must consider several other questions that historical investigation of the opposition to Hasidism must address: Why was the organized struggle against Hasidism not launched before 5532, more than thirty years after the "revelation" of the Ba'al Shem Tov and his first activity in the public arena? Why did that struggle begin in Lithuania, where Hasidism began to penetrate only in the late 1760s, and not in the Ukraine, the cradle of Hasidism? And of course, who initiated and led the struggle against Hasidism, and what were his motives?

Shimeon Dubnow describes the struggle's outbreak according to his general conception of the essence of Hasidism, on the one hand, and of the "rabbinate," on the other. He defines the rabbinate as "the system of the religion of the book, a religion consisting principally of study; expertise in literature thousands of years old, in laws, and in infinitely minute concatenations of law upon law; and scrupulous obedience to the commandments in all their precise details."[1] In Dubnow's opinion, the rabbinate, in this sense, laid the normative foundations of the community organization and established its values.

Dubnow regarded the struggle against Hasidism as a natural response, even a necessary one, of the rabbinate and the community leadership against a movement that rebelled against them and challenged them. As he says, the aim of Hasidism was essentially to challenge the scholarly foundation of the religion and to replace it with the element of hidden faith, to emphasize emotion and devotion in the observance of the commandments rather than piling up heaps of regulations on them.[2]

As for why the response of the rabbinate and the community organization was so late in coming, and why it appeared in Lithuania and not in the Ukraine, Dubnow responds that, after the abolition of the Council of the Four Lands in 1764, the power of the community organization was considerably diminished. In the Ukraine, groups of Hasidim exploited the collapse of communities' power to create forums for themselves. However, when Hasidism began to expand into White Russia and Lithuania in the late 1760s, it encountered a different situation. According to Dubnow, although the central authority had been destroyed, each community still had a rabbinical leadership, the teachers and guides of the people. Since Hasidism aspired to overthrow the pillars of the rabbinate and create its own teachers and leaders, the rabbis in Lithuania were aroused to go to war against the "ruiners and destroyers." At the head of the warriors stood the Gaon Rabbi Eliyahu of Vilna.[3]

Dubnow did not ask who drew whom into the war against Hasidism. Was it the community leadership who began the struggle and then claimed the authority of the Gaon, or did the Gaon take up the struggle and then mobilize the community leadership to assist him? Since the Gaon and the community leadership were partners in identifying with the system of the rabbinate, it was only reasonable that they should act in concert to eradicate Hasidism. Dubnow explains the Gaon's position as the chief warrior by characterizing him as the embodiment of the rabbinate. However, that determination is hardly ever expressed in his account of the course of events, aside from the notation that the Gaon imprinted his fanaticism and severity on the struggle.

To supplement this explanation of the outbreak of the struggle against Hasidism, Dubnow notes that at that time the Frankists had not yet died out, and in faraway Lithuania they might well have thought that in the Ukraine, the birthplace of Frankism, a new conspiracy against Judaism was emerging.[4]

In his *Tradition and Crisis,* Jacob Katz proposes a different conception, both with respect to the innovation embodied by Hasidism and regarding the motivation of its opponents.[5] At the same time, Katz agrees with Dubnow's estimation that the arousal of opposition to Hasidism was inevitable. Katz interprets Hasidism as a "two-fold revolution, religious and social." Religiously, the revolution was expressed in "the shift in emphasis from the actual performance of the precept to the attainment of ecstasy through that performance." And socially, the revolution was expressed in the consolidation of new patterns of leadership and social cohesion: the Zaddik—a leader whose authority derived from personal charisma as opposed to the institutional authority of the rabbi; and the Hasidic band, which gathered around the Zaddik spontaneously and voluntarily. According to Katz, this double revolution "could not take place without a clash with the exponents of the traditional society."[6] As to why the struggle against Hasidism began in the early 1760s in Lithuania and not earlier in the Ukraine, Katz's explanation is similar to Dubnow's:

> The weakening of *kehila* community leadership and the geographical dispersal of Jewish settlements in the provinces of Podolia and Volhynia apparently helped Hasidism to gain its first foothold in those regions. The abolition of the Council of the Four Lands, which took place around the time of the BESHT's death (1765), removed the primary organizational instrument that might have checked the movement's spread. The struggle against Hasidism would now fall to communal officials—rabbis and *parnasim* [lay leaders]—individuals such as R. Elijah, the "Gaon" of Vilna, who considered themselves responsible for the fate and leadership of Judaism.[7]

Since, by the nature of his discussion, Katz does not deal with events in detail, he does not address the question of the role played by the Gaon versus that played by the community leaders. However, regarding the motivations for opposition to Hasidism, it appears from Katz's account that the Gaon and the community leaders acted from identical motives: the defense of the tradition against those who deviated from it and threatened its integrity.

While Dubnow and Katz believed that the Gaon and the community leaders acted from identical motives, Ḥayyim Hillel Ben-Sasson contends that "there were two circles of warriors here, each of which had its own emphasis and preference regarding the purposes of the war and its means."[8] On the basis of a comparative analysis of the polemical writings—those that were, in his opinion, written with the direct inspiration of the Gaon versus those composed by the community leaders—Ben-Sasson reached the conclusion that the Gaon and his circle combated Hasidism because of "matters of faith and ways of worshiping the Creator," whereas the community leaders opposed Hasidim because of their damage to "communal and religious order." Even when the leaders of the

Vilna community raised claims identical to those raised by the Gaon, they phrased them "from the point of view of the regime and in formal terms."[9] Like his predecessors, Ben-Sasson ignores the question of who drew whom into the struggle against Hasidism—whether the Gaon aroused the community leadership or vice versa. His account implies that the Gaon and the community leadership worked in parallel, though with different motives.

Ben-Ẓion Katz took up the question of the role played by the leaders of the Vilna community versus that played by the Gaon.[10] He commences his account of the beginning of the struggle against Hasidism by presenting a series of difficulties, the purpose of which is to prove that it is impossible to understand the events as described in the sources in the literal sense. Later Ben-Ẓion Katz suggests a general explanation that resolves all those difficulties. He argues that the question that primarily concerned the Jews of Lithuania on the eve of the struggle against Hasidism was, Who represented the correct way of worshiping God, the Ba'al Shem Tov or the Vilna Gaon? He maintains that the struggle against Hasidism was initiated and managed by the heads of the community of Vilna in order to negate the Hasidic option and fortify the authority of the Gaon. Thus the Gaon was the *casus belli* and the symbol around which the warriors rallied, but he was not the driving force. The initiators and directors of the struggle were, in his view, "the heads of the community of Vilna."

The following discussion will reexamine some of the conclusions reached by the historians briefly surveyed above. At the same time I shall identify more precisely the role played by the Vilna Gaon in the beginning of the struggle against Hasidism. The central questions in the discussion are: Is it true that the battle against Hasidism was the inevitable reaction of the traditional establishment against those who defied it? Was the position of the Gaon at "the head of the warriors" expressed only in that he endowed with his authority and prestige the struggle waged by the traditional establishment, or did he exert a direct influence on the course of events? As for the motivations behind the struggle against Hasidism, was Ben-Sasson right in distinguishing between the motives of the Gaon and those of the community leaders?

In order to answer, let us trace the course of events at the beginning of the struggle against Hasidism, keeping in mind these questions: who made the decision that the struggle against Hasidism must begin, how was that decision made, and why? The full meaning of these questions will be clear if we note the two stages in the development of opposition to Hasidism: before the spring of 5532 and after it.

During the first stage, scattered signs of criticism appeared in response to the phenomenon of a new kind of Hasidism. Gershom Scholem, who has analyzed certain literary expressions of this criticism, views them as the earliest testimony to the activities of the Ba'al Shem Tov and his band.[11] According to Scholem's interpretation, some of these literary sources express the criticism by adherents to the old style of Kabbalistic *ḥasidut* against the new type of Hasidism, with its enthusiastic and popular character. Several scholars have expressed doubts and reservations regarding Scholem's view that certain passages of the criticism of the new Hasidism relate to the Ba'al Shem Tov and his followers.[12] However, even those who agree with those reservations and believe that the documents Scholem discovered do not relate specifically to the Ba'al Shem Tov can infer from them how adherents to the old style of Kabbalistic *ḥasidut* responded to the Ba'al Shem Tov and his circle. Confirmation of this supposition can be found in the book *Shivḥei HaBESHT,* which records several manifestations of opposition toward those close to the Ba'al Shem Tov. Thus, for example, it is stated that Rabbi Nahman of Kosov led the prayers in a house of study where he happened to be. When it became clear to the congregation that Rabbi Nahman had dared to stray from the standard form of the prayers, Nusah Ashkenaz, preferring the version of the ARI, "all the men of the House of Study opened [their mouths] and said to him: How did you have the audacity to lead the prayers without permission and to change the formula in a way that our fathers and our fathers' fathers, who were great Torah scholars, did not pray[?]"[13] From another story in *Shivḥei HaBESHT,* we learn that a group of Hasidim who were active in Kotov were held in contempt by certain individuals in the community."[14]

Typically, opposition to Hasidism before the spring of 5532 was scattered, incidental, and unorganized, and it was also relatively moderate.

In general it was expressed as criticism or mockery. In contrast, the second stage of opposition to Hasidism, that which began in Vilna in the spring of 5532, was not only organized and systematic but was also animated by a severe purpose: total war against Hasidism until it was extirpated, at least from Lithuania. Thus the question arises again: how, why, and by whom was the decision made to undertake total war against Hasidism?

THE COURSE OF EVENTS BEFORE THE SPRING OF 5532

I shall use both Mitnagdic and Hasidic sources in my effort to reconstruct the course of events during the first stages of the struggle against Hasidism. My primary source is article six in the anthology *Zemir 'Aritsim Veḥarvot Tsurim* (The Pruning Hook of Tyrants and Swords of Flint), published in 5532 in Aleksnitz, which is near Brody.[15] This anthology contains polemics against the Hasidim written in the spring of 5532, mostly in Vilna. Unlike the other items in the anthology, article six stands out because it presents a systematic and rather detailed survey of the course of events. While the identity of its author is unknown, he evidently followed the course of events closely and apparently had access to sources of information within the community leadership of Vilna.[16] Article six appears to be a reliable account: its style is restrained, and the author avoids polemical claims; there is also an inner logic to the course of events as he describes them. However, beyond these considerations, we may assume that article six is reliable because it is consistent with Hasidic sources. I refer to two letters from Rabbi Shneur Zalman of Lyady: one dated 5557 (1797) and addressed to his followers in Vilna, and the second dated 5565 (1805), to Rabbi Abraham of Kalisk.[17]

While article six was written soon after the events it describes, the letters of Rabbi Shneur Zalman were written many years afterward. Thus one may wonder how accurate his account may be. However, the testimony of Rabbi Shneur Zalman must be taken seriously for two reasons: first, he was personally involved in some of the events he describes; second, these events were crucial for Hasidism, and it is unlikely that they would have been easily forgotten. Moreover, just as the account of Rabbi Shneur Zalman corroborates that contained in article six, so, too, article six confirms the letters of Rabbi Shneur Zalman. Let us now trace the events in question, basing our reconstruction on a combination of these two sources.

The descriptions of the beginning of the struggle against Hasidism generally focus on events that took place in Vilna in the spring of 5532. However, existing documents contain echoes of two earlier events with which we must begin this discussion. The first was the effort made by Rabbi Menahem Mendel of Vitebsk and Rabbi Shneur Zalman of Lyady to gain an audience with the Vilna Gaon in the winter of 5532. The second event is the "debate" that took place in Shklov during that winter. Here is the description of these two events as presented by article six:

> And when our rabbi and teacher Mendel of Minsk was here last winter with the true Gaon, the man of God, our master and rabbi, Rabbi Eliyahu the Hasid, may his candle be bright, he did not see the face of the Gaon all that winter long.[18] He [the Gaon] said that he had a commentary on a passage in the Zohar composed by their sect, in which there was heresy. . . . And when the writings arrived from Shklov here in the holy congregation of Vilna, then the Gaon said: The holy congregation of Shklov is right, and as for the aforementioned sect, they are heretics and must be brought low.[19]

Additional information that supplements and clarifies the picture is found in a passage from the letter of Rabbi Shneur Zalman of Lyady:

> We went to the Gaon he-Hasid, may his candle burn brightly, to his house to debate with him and to remove his complaints from us, while I was there with the Hasid rabbi our late teacher Rabbi Mendel Horosener of blessed memory, and the Gaon closed his door before us twice. And when the great people of the city spoke to him, [saying]: Rabbi, the famous rabbi of theirs has come to debate with his venerable, holy Torah, and when he is defeated, certainly thereafter there will be peace upon Israel, he put them off with delays. And when they began to implore him greatly, he left and went away and traveled from the city, remaining there until our departure from the city. . . .

> Afterward in our country we traveled to the holy congregation of Shklov also to debate, and we did not succeed. And they did something to us that was not right, they broke their word and the promise they had given us at first not to do anything to us. Only when they saw that they had nothing to respond to our words did they come with a strong arm and suspend themselves from a high tree, ha-Gaon he-Hasid.[20]

From these two accounts, we may infer the following probable sequence of events: during the winter of 5532 rumors reached the Gaon regarding the new type of Hasidim and their strange customs. The source of the rumors was apparently in the community of Shklov, in White Russia, where several rabbinical scholars lived who were closely associated with the Gaon. When the Hasidic leaders in White Russia learned that the Gaon was hostile to Hasidism because of what he had heard about it, they decided to set out for Vilna to mollify him and prove to him that the accusations against them were groundless. The initiative of Rabbi Menahem Mendel of Vitebsk and Rabbi Shneur Zalman of Lyady was probably based on a sober estimate of the enormous authority of the Gaon and of the potential danger to Hasidism, should he decide to act against them.

An interesting detail in the account of Rabbi Shneur Zalman is the claim that differences of opinion broke out between the Gaon and "the great people of the city," apparently the *parnasim* of Vilna. The latter entreated the Gaon to receive the Hasidic delegation, but the Gaon rejected that entreaty categorically. Things reached such a pass that the Gaon left the city to avoid the pressure of the local notables. The *parnasim* of Vilna were probably aware that the Gaon's qualms about Hasidism might develop into an open conflict. Those who pressured the Gaon to receive the Hasidic delegation probably supposed and hoped it would be possible to smooth over the differences in direct negotiations, in the course of which the Gaon would impose his authority on the new-style Hasidism. However, the Gaon's stubborn refusal to receive the Hasidim shows that at that stage he had already formed a rather definite opinion regarding the essence of the new sect.

What rumors had reached the Gaon regarding the Hasidim? Why was he so resolute in his decision not to meet the two Hasidic leaders who came to knock on his door? From evidence presented below, we find that the Gaon had heard from his followers in White Russia that the Hasidim were contemptuous of rabbinical scholars. Furthermore, a strange custom was common among the Hasidim: some of them performed a kind of headstand or handstand before praying. Later I shall discuss the reliability of these two accusations. For the moment let us consider a third accusation, to which Rabbi Shneur Zalman explicitly referred in his letter: a Hasidic interpretation of a certain passage of the Zohar, which the Gaon viewed as a sign of heresy. We do not know what passage of the Zohar Rabbi Shneur Zalman refers to, nor how the Hasidim interpreted it.[21] In any event, it is worthwhile to take note of further information that Rabbi Shneur Zalman included in his letter in which he sought to vindicate the Gaon and the way he acted toward the delegates of Hasidism:

> And in truth we exonerated him, since the matter had already been decided by him absolutely without any doubt in the world, and the trial was over for him based on the gathering of testimony from many people who appeared trustworthy. Accordingly, when he heard about some Torah matter from a well-known intermediary, . . . he did not look favorably and change it to positive, [thinking] that perhaps the intermediary had changed the words slightly, for it is known that with a slight change of the words the [meaning of] a matter can truly change completely from one extreme to the other, and certainly it did not cross his mind that perhaps [the Hasidim] have the words of the Lord according to *gilui eliyahu,* separating and stripping off the corporeality that is in the Holy Zohar in a manner hidden and beyond him, only that it requires reception from mouth to mouth and not through the aforementioned intermediary, because great and mighty sanctity is necessary for such a high level, and truly the opposite of what was confirmed to him according to witnesses reliable in his honor's eyes; . . . and for this reason he did not want to receive any claim or answer or excuse in the world about a Torah matter that he had heard, nor anything in the world from us.[22]

Most probably the Gaon's suspicions and reservations regarding the Hasidic interpretation of the Zohar were increased because of their pretentious claim that the new interpretation had reached them by means of a revelation from Elijah. That would be a high-level revelation, which only select individuals could merit. He totally rejected the possibility that the Hasidim had indeed received a revelation from Elijah, on the strength of the rumors that had reached him earlier regarding the deviant behavior of the Hasidim.[23] Moreover, the "intermediary" who had reported to the Gaon about the Hasidic interpretation of the Zohar had given him a distorted version of it. For this reason, Rabbi Shneur Zalman explains, the Gaon was unwilling to hear the version of the Hasidim regarding their interpretation of the Zohar. Apparently, rumors that seemed authentic and reliable to him about the deviant behavior of the Hasidim, combined with the report about the falsification of an idea appearing in the most important work of Kabbalah, shaped the Gaon's attitude toward the Hasidim at that stage.

Although the Gaon's opinion of the Hasidim was so definite that he refused adamantly to receive their representatives, he nevertheless initiated no action against them at that time. His decision to wage a public campaign against the Hasidism was made only after he received "writings" from Shklov, including the report about the results of the "debate" that had been held there. That debate, which was held in the winter of 5532, was the second of the two events that preceded the outbreak of the struggle against Hasidism that had been launched in the spring of that year. What was the nature of this so-called debate? From the various sources that relate to the event, it appears that the term *debate* is to be understood here as it was used in reference to controversies between religions during the Middle Ages. Thus it refers to a verbal confrontation in which one side maligns and accuses the other side, which defends and justifies itself. Following this pattern, the initiators of the debate in Shklov raised a series of accusations against the Hasidism, who were supposed to respond to and refute them.

Another letter of Rabbi Shneur Zalman's, concerning the controversy that broke out between him and Rabbi Abraham of Kalisk in the 1790s, presents some of the arguments against the Hasidim and explains the connection between the debate at Shklov and the launching of the struggle against Hasidism.[24] In the letter sent to Rabbi Abraham in 5565 (1805) Rabbi Shneur Zalman surveys the development of the relations between them and, while doing so, he recalls earlier offenses: in the summer of 5532 the leaders of Hasidism held an emergency assembly in the home of Rabbi Dov Ber, the *maggid* of Mezhirech, who was then living in the town of Rovna. Rabbi Abraham of Kalisk and Rabbi Shneur Zalman made their way to that city together. Upon their arrival in Rovna, Rabbi Abraham feared the *maggid's* wrath and refrained from entering the town. He asked Rabbi Shneur Zalman to ask Rabbi Menahem Mendel of Vitebsk to "speak favorably for him with our holy rabbi, may his soul rest in peace, and to give him permission to come to him." Why was the *maggid* so angry at Rabbi Abraham that the latter was afraid to come to his house? The answer emerges in the continuation of Rabbi Shneur Zalman's letter:

> I went with him to the room of our great rabbi, whose soul is in heaven, and my eyes saw and my ears heard that he spoke severely to him about the evil of his leadership of our fellow believers in the state of Russia, . . . whose conversation all day long was debauchery and levity, and also to mock all the scholars and to have contempt for them with all sorts of derision and throwing off of the yoke and great frivolity. And they also constantly turned themselves over with their head down and their feet up (which is called *kuleyen zikh*) in the markets and the streets, and the name of Heaven is profaned in the eyes of the uncircumcised, and also of other kinds of mirth and joking in the streets of Kalisk. And in the winter of 5532, after the debate that was held in Shklov, he could make no answer to that accusation or the likes of it. And the sages of the holy community of Shklov wrote to report to the late Gaon of Vilna, until they made it enter his heart to judge them as detractors, perish the thought, like a judgment against an *apikoros* who scorns Torah scholars, and about the turning of the feet upward he said that it is from Pe'or etc.;[25] and so they wrote from Vilna to Brod and there they printed the tract *Zemir 'Aritsim* in the aforementioned summer. This caused great grief to all the Hasidic leaders of Volhyn, and they could not sit in their houses, and they gathered all of them together in the holy community of Rovna at that time with our great rabbi, whose soul is in heaven, to take counsel.[26]

We find that the *maggid's* wrath was directed at the path of Rabbi Abraham of Kalisk as the leader of the Hasidim in White Russia. It appears that Rabbi Abraham and his company were inspired by a radical spirit, expressed by, among other things, mockery of Torah scholars and by headstands. These gymnastics served the members of the company as a means of attaining the virtues of modesty and humility, for in their cultural and social context, headstands were regarded as contemptible and frivolous pranks.[27] Indeed, the opponents of Hasidism regarded headstands as an ugly and contemptible practice, and the Gaon even associated it with a certain form of idol worship. As for the mockery of Torah scholars, it may be assumed that the members of the company confronted the traditional elites, criticized them harshly, and were disrespectful of them. They did so in the name of the truth of the new Hasidism, which did not attribute value to erudition that was not accompanied by moral and spiritual qualities. One way or another, the behavior of Rabbi Abraham and the members of his company aroused the wrath of the men of Shklov, and it was the focus of the debate that they initiated against the Hasidim. Since the answer given them by the Hasidic leaders did not satisfy them, they wrote to the Gaon that the Hasidim were tantamount to heretics. The Gaon adopted their position, as we read in article six: "And when the writings arrived from Shklov here in the holy congregation of Vilna, then the Gaon said: The holy congregation of Shklov is right, and as for the aforementioned sect, they are heretics and must be brought low."[28]

Most probably the initiators of the Shklov debate raised further claims against the Hasidim, but Rabbi Shneur Zalman decided to emphasize the arguments that were directed against Rabbi Abraham of Kalisk and the members of his company. For our purposes, it is highly significant that Rabbi Shneur Zalman states that these accusations, to which Rabbi Abraham of Kalisk "found no answer," were what motivated the Gaon to proclaim that the Hasidim were heretics. Thus Rabbi Shneur Zalman confirms the version of the author of article six, according to whom the Gaon's decision to declare total war against the Hasidim was made after he received the "writings" from Shklov.[29]

Who are these "sages of the holy community of Shklov" who waged the controversy against the Hasidim? Were they the rabbi and *dayyanim* (religious judges) of the community, or were they scholars who held no public office? On the basis of the sources in our possession, it is difficult to respond to that question with certainty.[30] Nevertheless, it is rather clear that the action taken against the Hasidim in Shklov was coordinated with the Vilna Gaon. This is indicated by the remarks of Rabbi Shneur Zalman quoted above: "Only when they saw that they had nothing to respond to our words did they come with a strong arm, and suspend themselves from a high tree, ha-Gaon he-Hasid." This indicates that the rabbis of Shklov acted with the authority of the Gaon. But in turn the Gaon depended on the rabbis of Shklov. Though he had already passed judgment on the Hasidim when he rejected their leaders' request to meet with him, he did not see fit to launch a public campaign against them before the scholars of Shklov wrote to him and reported the outcome of the debate.

How the Shklov debate influenced the Gaon's decision to launch the struggle can be clarified in two ways: first, although the Gaon had formed a negative opinion of Hasidism even before the debate, he was still in doubt as to how to treat it. The report that arrived from Shklov about the disrespect for Torah scholars tripped the balance.[31] Second, while it is possible that the Gaon had resolved to wage war against Hasidism even before the Shklov debate, in order for that war to gain wide support a public event was needed, at which the guilt of the Hasidim could be exposed to all eyes. The *parnasim* of Vilna tried, as noted, to soften the Gaon's categorical position regarding Hasidism. Now the Gaon could find support in the opinion of the scholars of Shklov when he came to impose his position on the leaders of Vilna.

THE COURSE OF EVENTS IN THE SPRING OF 5532

Let us now follow the chain of events in Vilna after the Gaon decreed that it was necessary to pursue the Hasidim and combat them. The author of article six describes the confrontation between the Hasidim and their opponents in Vilna as follows:

> And within the aforementioned sect the first head was *morenu* Issur [meaning "prohibition"; his real name was Issar], as he should be called, and the second was the rabbi *morenu* Ḥayyim, the preacher here. And important and eminent men, the sect of those who saw the face of the true Hasid, our teacher the rabbi Eliyahu, said to the aforementioned,

> our teacher Ḥayyim: how long will you keep hopping on two boughs [1 Kings 18:21], for there is nothing to add to the words of the Gaon, etc. And our teacher Ḥayyim answered about the aforementioned Gaon, that he was a lie and his Torah was a lie and his faith was a lie.[32]

Thus we find that, at this stage, the community establishment of Vilna was not yet involved in the struggle against the Hasidim at all. The entire initiative was concentrated in the hands of the Gaon's associates. They addressed Rabbi Ḥayyim, a leader of the Hasidim in Vilna, and commanded him to withdraw from the customs of Hasidism. Whether the Gaon ordered his associates to take this step or whether they acted on their own initiative, there is no doubt that the Gaon's determination regarding the essence of Hasidism underlay their action. The reply that the author of article six places in the mouth of Rabbi Ḥayyim is extremely insolent, and his account might well be exaggerated. In any event, it is certain that Rabbi Ḥayyim's rejection of the demand that he abandon the customs of Hasidism entailed a challenge to the Gaon's authority.

In the view of the Gaon's associates, this rejection was a severe injury to their master's honor. This is evident in the following stage of the struggle:

> The event took place during the intermediate days of Passover. The leaders and two groups of *dayyanim* had convened on the matter on the Passover holiday. There was a sentence to drive out and disperse the minyan of Karliner, and to drive the minyan out immediately. And that the aforementioned *morenu* Ḥayyim should beg forgiveness . . . for the honor of the Place [i.e., God] and for the honor of the Torah and for the honor of the Hasid [the Gaon], and also that he would receive a reprimand and a ban as a Torah judgment, and also that he would go with ten men and ask forgiveness of the Hasid. And when he came to the Hasid, the Hasid responded in these words: My [dis]honor is forgiven to you, and the [dis]honor of the Place and the [dis]honor of the Torah, this transgression will not be forgiven to you until you die. And *morenu* Ḥayyim said: Give us expiation. And the Gaon our teacher the Hasid Rabbi Eliyahu replied to him: There is no forgiveness for heresy. And *morenu* Rabbi Ḥayyim also withdrew from preaching. And our teacher Ḥayyim accepted a reprimand and a ban on himself.[33]

The direct involvement of the community leadership in the struggle against the Hasidim began only after informal efforts by the Gaon's associates failed. However, the connection between the action of the leadership and the Gaon's authority and his position regarding the Hasidim is absolutely clear. Not only did the leadership seek to vindicate the Gaon's honor, but the decision to disperse the Hasidic minyan was also an institutional expression of the verdict issued earlier by the Gaon against the Hasidim. The community leaders' dependence on the Gaon also emerges clearly from the following steps:

> And the leaders and the court sent people out to search for their books and writings, and they found strange writings there, that it is impossible to write openly and the space is too small. And a ban was proclaimed after testimony was given about their actions. And a legal hearing was held about their unseemly actions, also their foolishness of the upper parts below and the lower parts above. And one of them was polluted with lying with a man, and he confessed to this before the court . . . and also other ignoble things, and they interrupted their prayers with words in Yiddish. And the leaders visited the Gaon he-Hasid to ask his opinion, and he said that it was a duty to repel them and pursue them and reduce them and drive them from the land.[34]

We find that after the community leadership took up the task of directing the struggle against the sect of Hasidism, the leadership could no longer continue acting without depending on testimony brought before it by means of formal procedures. Perhaps its decision to gather testimony before a court was also intended to prepare the ground for taking severe punitive measures against Hasidim. In any case, it is instructive that, after hearing testimony, the leadership had to determine the meaning of that testimony and the conclusion to be drawn from it, and for that purpose the leaders turned to the Gaon and asked for his guidance. His verdict, that "it was a duty to repel them and pursue them," underlay the following steps taken by the community leadership:

> Then the leaders sat and also two groups of the judges, and the Rabbi was the chief justice. And there was a verdict to burn their writings at the *kune* [pillory] before the welcoming of the sabbath. And *morenu* Issar the head of the sect should go up to the topmost step on the sabbath before the prayer, "He dwells eternal," and in all the synagogues and the houses of study there should be no minyan here, but only in the syna-

> gogue and the great house of study, and he should confess there in the formula that would issue from the court. And then the warden should excommunicate them and all those associated with them and should write letters of peace to all the major communities, to the holy community of Shklov and to the holy community of Minsk.[35]

The means for suppressing Hasidism decided on by the Vilna leadership—public confession of the leader of the sect and proclamation of a ban against the Hasidim—were not sufficient for the Gaon, as we find in the continuation of the account by the author of article six:

> And when the verdict against *morenu* Issar was issued, the Hasid was not present here [in Vilna], but in Antikolya, and on Friday, before the holy sabbath, he assembled the leaders and was angry with them: Why have you been lenient in your judgment? If it depended on me, I would have done to them as Elijah the Prophet did to the Prophets of Ba'al. And the Hasid wished to place *morenu* Issar in the pillory, only the leaders did not desire that. And they struck him with a rubber whip in the *kahal* room before the welcoming of the sabbath. And then they burned their writings before the pillory. And before "He who dwells eternal," he went up to the upper step, and the Hasidim, his comrades, stood at his right, . . . and afterward they banned him. And all that week he sat in prison in the jail of the citadel that they call "Schloss." And on the sabbath night he was held in the *kahal* room.[36]

The main gap dividing the Gaon and the community leaders concerned their attitude toward Rabbi Issar, a leader of the Hasidim in Vilna. The Gaon's demand to pillory him was probably intended to give public and extremely forthright expression to the condemnation of Hasidism. The Gaon's reprimand of the Vilna community leaders for having been "lenient" in their verdict regarding Rabbi Issar is consistent with the conclusion that emerges from the course of events as clarified so far. That is to say, the Gaon played a decisive role at the start of the struggle against Hasidism. The community organization did not start the struggle and then seek support in the Gaon's authority. Rather, the Gaon initiated the struggle and made the community organization a tool in directing and promoting it.

A possible objection to this conclusion might be based on the argument that the author of article six attributed great prominence to the part played by the Gaon at the start of the struggle against Hasidism, either because he was one of his associates or for other reasons. Nevertheless, against such an objection stands the testimony of Rabbi Shneur Zalman, which also attributes decisive significance to the Gaon in leading the struggle against Hasidism. It is unlikely that Rabbi Shneur Zalman would be interested in emphasizing the role of the Gaon, since, despite the controversy, he acknowledged the Gaon's greatness and related to him with veneration. On the contrary, from his point of view it would have been preferable to attribute the struggle against Hasidism to the leaders of the Vilna community. However, not only does he describe the Gaon as the initiator and leader of the struggle at the start, but he also argues that the Gaon's uncompromising stand prevented reconciliation between the Hasidim and their opponents. Moreover, he wrote his account twenty-five years after the struggle between them had begun.

In his letter of 5557 (1797) to his Hasidim in Vilna, Rabbi Shneur Zalman responded to the suggestion that he should arrange a debate with the leaders of the Mitnagdim in order to bring the controversy to a close. Those who proposed that idea most likely assumed that in the course of such a debate Rabbi Shneur Zalman would manage to refute the accusations against the Hasidim, and thus achieve reconciliation. Rabbi Shneur Zalman rejected the initiative as hopeless. In support of this pessimistic prognosis, he described the events that took place in the spring of 5532, emphasizing the role played by the Gaon. Following that description, on which the above discussion relies, Rabbi Shneur Zalman went on to argue:

> And what is different today? For even now, at this time, nothing is heard from him,[37] no retraction or regret for the past, to say that now some doubt has been born to him that perhaps they made an error. . . . For it is known to them that, in certainty, I have refuted all the objections, for all the objections are known and published in our country; but they did not accept the explanations, as we saw with our own eyes in the community of Shklov. And if so why should I toil in vain? . . . Even the more so with regard to us after a great and mighty event, many and grave evil deeds

> have been done to our people in our countries of Lithuania and Reissen by the proclamation of the Gaon he-Hasid.[38]

Farther on in the letter, Rabbi Shneur Zalman discusses another component in the initiative of the Hasidim of Vilna. They proposed that the outcome of the confrontation between them and their opponents be decided by two arbiters acceptable to both parties. Rabbi Shneur Zalman responded, "It was not wise of them to ask for that, for certainly their importance was insignificant before him to decide against the opinion of the Gaon he-Hasid; . . . for it is heard that no one in the states of Lithuania would raise his heart so high as not to abnegate his own opinion before that of the Gaon he-Hasid and say with confidence that what he says is incorrect, perish the thought."[39]

Another expression of Rabbi Shneur Zalman's view that the Gaon was the one who prevented reconciliation between the Hasidim and the Mitnagdim is found in a later letter of his, from 5575 (1815):

> Many years after the death of the Gaon he-Hasid of blessed memory, the merit of his Torah sustained him and all those who gathered in his shadow no longer to spill blood in vain, when it became evident in the eyes of all and the truth was known and seen clearly, that we have no hint of heresy, perish the thought, nor even a hint of a hint. For that reason the tribes were permitted to intermingle and they always intermarry with us, and likewise the other rejections and decrees, stringent and severe, of 5532 were annulled.[40]

With these words Rabbi Shneur Zalman, though he does so subtly and by allusion, connects the cessation of the struggle against Hasidism with the demise of the Gaon. In other words, as long as the Gaon was among the living, it was impossible to arrange a reconciliation between the Hasidim and their opponents in Lithuania, because the Gaon clung to his position and no one dared disagree with him.

SUMMARY AND CONCLUSIONS

Following this reconstruction of the course of events in the first stages of the struggle against Hasidism, I propose a number of conclusions:

1. The Vilna Gaon's determination that the Hasidim were heretics who should be persecuted motivated the beginning of the organized struggle against Hasidism, and it was fundamental to it.
2. Not only did the Gaon's associates act in his name and with his authority, but the community establishment also depended on his instructions, as he led the battle against Hasidism.
3. As long as the Gaon was alive, it was impossible to effect a reconciliation between the Mitnagdim and the Hasidim.

In light of these conclusions we must reject the opinion that opposition to Hasidism was an inevitable response of the traditional establishment. On the contrary, it is more likely that, were it not for the position and initiative of the Gaon, the establishment would not have waged total war against Hasidism, and the signs of opposition, had there been any, would have taken a decidedly different form.[41] This conjecture is supported if we examine the character of the opposition to Hasidism before the Gaon's intervention and after his death. Although those two periods are different from one another, with respect to both the scale of the opposition and the way in which it was expressed, they nevertheless have a common feature: during them the struggle against Hasidism was essentially limited to the realm of ideas and propaganda and was not accompanied by punitive and repressive measures like those the community organization instituted under the initiative and inspiration of the Gaon.[42]

What is the meaning of the fact that the Gaon motivated and directed the organized struggle against Hasidism? The growth of the form of Hasidism established by the Ba'al Shem Tov and his disciples placed the spiritual and religious leadership of eastern European Jewry in a dilemma. On the one hand, the new form of Hasidism was like a continuation of the old type, which had been considered for generations to be the embodiment of worship of God on the most exalted level and, for that reason, enjoyed great prestige. Like the old form of Hasidism, that of the Ba'al Shem Tov was anchored in Kabbalah. Furthermore, the new form of Hasidism adopted forms of worship that derived from Kabbalistic circles. On the other hand, the Hasidism of the Ba'al Shem Tov was certainly not a simple continuation of the old form of Hasidism, for it was distinguished from what preceded it in its manner of worshiping God, in its thought, and in its social functioning. The traits that distinguished the new Hasidism were greatly emphasized in the polemical literature of the Mitnagdim, which presented it as a deviation from the correct path: ecstatic prayer accompanied by strange and even wild manifestations of body movement and raising of the voice; disdain for the element of erudition in the service of God, evidenced by transfer of the center of gravity from study to prayer; a forgiving, even permissive, attitude toward lapses, for the purpose of avoiding sadness; and the like.[43] Furthermore, they were critical of the effort to disseminate the ways of Hasidism by ignoring the traditional view that exemplary piety was expected of only a chosen few.[44]

In response to the complexity of the Hasidism founded by the Ba'al Shem Tov, in that it was both a continuation of the old Hasidism and a departure from it, the spiritual and religious leadership of eastern Europe had to decide: Was the new Hasidism a legitimate and respectable phenomenon? Or were the disciples of the Ba'al Shem Tov and their followers unworthy of being called Hasidim? As noted, the Gaon determined that the new Hasidism was nothing but a sect of heretics who should be persecuted. However, that decision was not inevitable, for not only were some rabbis and Torah scholars attracted to Hasidism, but others regarded it sympathetically, though they did not actually join it.[45] Similarly, some of them had only moderate objections to it and did not combat it.[46]

Why did the Gaon decide as he did, and what is the meaning of that decision regarding the essence of opposition to Hasidism? On the basis of the sources examined above, it may be stated that the Gaon acted from spiritual and religious motives rather than for social or political reasons. The Gaon judged Hasidism in the light of its manifestations, which he regarded as incontrovertible signs of heresy. The flawed interpretation of the passage from the Zohar, the phenomenon of scorn for Torah scholars, and the Hasidim's strange custom of standing on their heads were regarded by the Gaon as keys to evaluating the movement in general. Since to him these traits appeared to be manifestations of heresy, he drew a similar conclusion regarding other "deviations" that characterized Hasidic worship of God. Moreover, Dubnow is probably correct in pointing to the revelation of the Frankist heresy, which occurred about twenty years before the outbreak of the struggle against Hasidism, as a factor that influenced the Gaon's determination. Traditionally, it is maintained that the Gaon connected Hasidism with the evil forces of the *sitra ahra*. This is stated in the margins of article six: "I also heard from speakers of truth of the aforementioned holy community of Vilna, that they shout 'Baa! Baa!' during their prayers. And it was said in the name of the true Hasid, our master Eliyahu, that he knows that this is a great *qelipa*."[47]

It appears to be no coincidence that a personality such as the Gaon was needed to initiate the struggle against Hasidism and mobilize the community organization for that purpose. If the Hasidim had challenged the authority of the Halakhah and shown it disrespect, any local rabbi could have declared them heretics. However, the Hasidim did not challenge the obligatory authority of the Halakhah, and aside from the claim that they were not scrupulous about the proper times for their prayers, no accusations were leveled against them for failure to observe the commandments. Therefore, only someone who combined both Hasidism of the old kind—mastery of the hidden recesses of Kabbalah, erudition extraordinary in its scope and quality, intense zeal, and exceptional personal authority—such as the Gaon, would have been capable of ruling that the new Hasidism was a heresy, and only he could have motivated the community organization to carry out the actions required by that decision. In a certain sense Jacob Katz was right in describing the battle against Hasidism as an effort to defend the tradition against those who deviated from it.[48] But the estimation that Hasidism was a severe deviation from the tradition was not self-evident, and it was accepted as true and mandatory only following the Gaon's decision. Moreover, the Gaon did not act as a mere representative of the tradition but rather as an outstanding exemplar of the old style of Kabbalistic Hasidism. In other words, it is possible to interpret the Gaon's struggle against Hasidism as, among other things, rejection and condemnation of the new form of Hasidism by the old form.[49]

My conclusion regarding the motives underlying the Gaon's struggle against Hasidism are largely consistent with the view of the matter proposed by Ben-Sasson.[50] However, it is difficult to agree with his claim that the communal leaders, unlike the Gaon, acted against Hasidism for formal, institutional reasons. If my conclusion is correct, that the Gaon was the one who decreed that the Hasidim were heretics and had to be combated, then the community leaders acted out of identification with his motives or, at least, out of recognition of his authority. Naturally, as the quarrel between the Hasidim and their opponents continued it became more complex and additional motives became involved.[51] Hence it is not surprising that, over time, motives of an economic and political character were added. However, that development should not obscure the fact that, at the first and decisive stage, the struggle against Hasidism was decidedly spiritual and religious in character. Indeed, a letter by Rabbi Menahem Mendel of Vitebsk shows that the Hasidim themselves viewed the struggle in that manner at that time. In 5538 (1778), a few months after moving to the land of Israel at the head of a band of Hasidim, Rabbi Menahem wrote to the leaders of Vilna, calling for reconciliation between the camps: "Behold I stand today on holy ground, and may the Lord God be my witness, by Whom I swear and Whose Name I bear, that if there are among us those whose opinion and faith, perish the thought, have any hint of deviance or, perish the thought, of denial of our holy Torah, written and oral, even any reservation or limitation of a commandment, against the Lord and against His messiah, may that day not save us."[52]

In conclusion, the total warfare against Hasidism declared in Vilna in the spring of 5532 was not a response of the community establishment against those who rebelled against it but was primarily the struggle of those who regarded themselves as faithful to the tradition, against those who appeared to deviate from it. One might say that it was a struggle concerning the essence of the way of Hasidism in worshiping God. The greatest scholar of the generation, who was both a Hasid and a Kabbalist of the old kind and a Torah scholar of exceptional achievements, was the one who determined that the new Hasidism was a heresy, and it was he who brought the community establishment to fight against it.

4 The Vilna Gaon and the Mitnagdim as Seen by the Hasidim

The organized struggle against Hasidism, which began in Vilna in 5532 (1772), continued for about thirty years. During that time the Hasidim were the objects of persecution and oppression. Community leaders who took part in the campaign against Hasidism passed ordinances that led to the social ostracism of the Hasidim, interfered with their sources of livelihood, prohibited people from eating meat that they had slaughtered, and prevented them from holding prayers in the manner they wished. It is easy to imagine the suffering and humiliation of the Hasidim in the areas where they were persecuted.[1] How did they respond?

In discussing the response of the Hasidim, I do not refer specifically to the actions they took, but primarily to their response on the cognitive level. How did they explain to themselves the fact that the leaders of important communities, including rabbis and *dayyanim,* viewed them as heretics who must be expelled from the Jewish people? How did they reconcile themselves to the fact that among those who signed the writ of excommunication issued in Brod were the scholars of the *kloiz* (house of study), renowned as Torah scholars, expert in Halakhah and Kabbalah, and pious in their conduct? Moreover, how did they explain the fact that the man who led the struggle against them was none other than Rabbi Eliyahu, ha-Gaon he-Hasid of Vilna, who was regarded as the greatest sage of his generation?

RABBI MENAHEM MENDEL OF VITEBSK: A CALL FOR PEACE

In the month of Shevat 5538 (winter 1778), several months after reaching the land of Israel at the head of a "caravan" of Hasidim, and about six years after the outbreak of the struggle against Hasidism, Rabbi Menahem Mendel of Vitebsk sent an epistle from Safed to "the Ministers, Sages, and Judges of the States of Volhynia and Lithuania, and Russia." This epistle, as far as we know, was the first public call by a Hasidic leader for reconciliation between the warring camps.[2] These are its main points:

1. The Hasidim rejected all accusations leveled by the Mitnagdim against them and declared loyalty to the values of the tradition.[3]
2. They were willing to forgive the Mitnagdim for the wrongs they had done to the Hasidim during the persecutions, and they called for a new chapter in relations between the two camps.[4]
3. They recognized the authority of the community leaders to whom the letter was addressed, that is to say, the traditional establishment, and called for these leaders to recognize the righteousness of the Hasidim and to live in peace with them.[5]

Rabbi Menahem Mendel might have been satisfied with these declarations. However, he includes an important statement in the letter, alluding to the role played by the Vilna Gaon in the outbreak of the struggle:

> This has been my way from the start, before arriving in the Land of Israel I also yearned and desired for unity and unanimity. But what can I do? For between us was an orator who "testified lies" [Proverbs 14:5] and spoke falsehoods against us and "plotted evil plots" [Psalms 141:4] . . . and "were they wise, they would think on this" [Deuteronomy 31:32], that they had borne false witness against us. . . . For what can they do? Since one may judge only what one's eyes see and what one's ears hear, and the onus is on the witnesses.[6]

With these apparently obscure words Rabbi Menahem Mendel refers to a certain event well known to the recipients of his epistle: the journey to Vilna he made with Rabbi Shneur Zalman of Lyady in the winter of 5532, a few months before the organized struggle against Hasidism began. As noted in chapter 3, the two leaders of Hasidism in White Russia had wished to meet with the Gaon to dispel various rumors that had reached his ears. However, the Gaon was resolved not to receive these Hasidim, and they were forced to return home empty-handed.[7]

Mention of this event amounts to a rather severe accusation against the camp of Mitnagdim, and especially against their leader. For their part the Hasidim had endeavored to prevent the outbreak of the dispute, but their overture had been rejected. Along with that accusation, Rabbi Menahem Mendel also offers an explanation of the Gaon's behavior: false witnesses had leveled severe accusations against the Hasidim, and the Gaon trusted them. This explanation does not completely absolve the Gaon, "and 'were they wise, they would think on this,' that they had borne false witness against us." Nevertheless, "one may judge only what one's eyes see and what one's ears hear, and the onus is on the witnesses."

During the same year that Rabbi Menahem Mendel addressed the leaders of the Polish communities, he wrote an additional epistle addressed to the community leaders of Vilna.[8] In this epistle, he again claims that the Hasidim are meticulous in the observance of Jewish law, with all its strictures and minutiae. Thus all the accusations that the Mitnagdim leveled against them were groundless. Rabbi Menahem Mendel does admit that there were some Hasidim whose behavior was wild,[9] but these were the youthful actions of a minority and there was no reason to draw general conclusions from their behavior.

In the second epistle Rabbi Menahem Mendel again refers to the failed visit he had made to Vilna together with Rabbi Shneur Zalman of Lyady. He hints that had the Vilna Gaon been willing to lend an attentive ear, the controversy might have been avoided. But the Gaon was not to be held responsible, at least not solely. Again Rabbi Menahem Mendel repeats the argument that the Gaon had been deceived by false witnesses, "'according to whom every lawsuit and case of assault is judged' [Deuteronomy 21:5] and by them 'was poured the soul blood of the innocent poor'" (Jeremiah 2:34).[10]

One must look into the repeated claim that the Gaon and the community leaders who joined the battle against Hasidism had been misled by false witnesses. By advancing this claim, Rabbi Menahem Mendel apparently wished to bridge the gap between the argument that the Hasidim had been persecuted though they had done nothing wrong, and acknowledgement of the authority of the leaders of the Mitnagdim, acknowledgement implied in the very act of addressing them. At first glance, willingness to absolve the leaders of the Mitnagdim from the accusation of unjustified persecution seems to be a tactical measure required by reality. When all is said and done, those who wish to put an end to persecution must acknowledge the authority of those who instigate it, in accordance with the Halakhic axiom that "the mouth that forbade is the mouth that must permit."

However, Rabbi Menahem Mendel's claim appears to have a deeper motivation: if the Hasidim were declared heretics, they would have to be expelled from the Jewish community. Apprehension regarding such an eventuality certainly worried the Hasidic leaders greatly. The Sabbatean trauma—and especially its Frankist manifestation, which was close in time and place—influenced not only the Mitnagdim but also the Hasidim. While the former suspected that Hasidism was a Sabbatean-style sect, the latter feared they might meet a fate like the Sabbateans. The effort made by the Hasidic leaders to gain recognition as an integral part of the Jewish people is understandable against the background of this fear. This effort necessarily entailed recognition of the authority of the community leaders who contested them and, above all, the authority of the Vilna Gaon.

Placing most of the blame on false witnesses probably also played an important role in the inner world of the Hasidim. Certainly they were disturbed by the question of how they, whose entire lives were colored by the aspiration and effort to draw close to God, could have been seen by their opponents as deviants and heretics. How could it be explained that an exalted person such as the Gaon had made such a grave error about them? In other words, what was the explanation for the dreadful gap between their self-image and their image in the eyes of their opponents? The necessary conclusion was that the Gaon had acted innocently, and that false witnesses had led him astray. If he had known the facts as they were, he certainly would not have decreed that the Hasidim were heretics, nor would he have led the community of Vilna in the struggle against them.

RABBI SHNEUR ZALMAN OF LYADY: DEFENSE OF THE VILNA GAON

Rabbi Shneur Zalman of Lyady was the Hasidic leader who stood at the front during the struggle with the Mitnagdim. As noted, he accompanied his mentor and friend, Rabbi Menahem Mendel of Vitebsk, in the abortive voyage of reconciliation to Vilna in the winter of 5532. After Rabbi Menahem Mendel emigrated to the land of Israel in 5537, Rabbi Shneur Zalman took his place as leader of the Hasidim in White Russia.[11] Since that region was one of the main arenas of the struggle against Hasidism, Rabbi Shneur Zalman remained involved in the controversy with the Mitnagdim. He was also involved because the Hasidim living in Lithuania, including Vilna, were his followers.[12] Indeed Rabbi Shneur Zalman himself was the object of persecution by the Mitnagdim. He was arrested and interrogated twice because his enemies informed against him to the authorities.[13]

In light of all this, there is reason to ask once again: How did Rabbi Shneur Zalman understand the struggle waged by the Mitnagdim against the Hasidim? How did he explain to himself and his followers the fact that the man regarded as the greatest scholar of the generation had ruled that the Hasidim were heretics? How did he seek to clear Hasidism of the grave accusations leveled against it by the Mitnagdim? I shall draw answers to these questions from the letters of Rabbi Shneur Zalman. Some of these letters were sent to the leaders of the Mitnagdim, while others were sent to his followers, and they reflect various stages in the development of the conflict.

In the month of Kislev 5547 (1787) a proclamation was issued in Vilna calling for the renewal of the struggle against the Hasidim. Among other things the proclamation called for a great convention in Shklov on the New Moon of Tevet in order to develop a strategy for the war against the Hasidim. The convention was indeed held, and in its wake regulations were published calling for the breakup of Hasidic minyanim and for the isolation and ostracism of the Hasidim. Following the publication of these regulations, Rabbi Shneur Zalman wrote an epistle to the leaders of the community of Mohilev, asking them not to implement those regulations in the area under their authority.[14]

Rabbi Shneur Zalman's arguments were intended to invalidate the regulations. To accomplish this he employed the Halakhic principle that a court may not condemn anyone in absentia or without giving the accused an opportunity to defend himself. He maintains that this principle was universally acknowledged and accepted in monetary suits, hence all the more reason it should apply "in our case, which is truly a capital case." Furthermore, the authors of the regulations relied on false witnesses and ignored a multitude of reliable witnesses, neighbors of Hasidim prepared to testify that they were free of any transgression.[15]

After denying the validity of the procedures used by the authors of the regulations, Rabbi Shneur Zalman addresses the question of the authority on which they depended:

> For they do not build on their opinion unless it depends on that of others, and they are named the elders of the generation. And the elders, it is heard, hang from a great tree, ha-Gaon he-Hasid, our teacher Rabbi Eliyahu of Vilna, for it is widely known that he is unique in his generation. And truly he is a sole authority. . . . But a single person does not outweigh the majority who are with us, comrades and disciples of the holy rabbi, the *maggid meisharim,* our teacher Rabbi Duber, may he rest in peace, of Mezhirech. For who is greater for us than the great Rabbi Eliezer, that if all the Sages of Israel were in one pan [of a balance], he

would outweigh them all [*Avot* 2:8]. But nevertheless they voted against him and carried the vote.[16]

Rabbi Shneur Zalman was forced to deal with the issue of the Gaon's authority because the leaders of the Mitnagdim continually appealed to that authority, whenever objections were raised to their claims. In that matter as well, Rabbi Shneur Zalman advanced a Halakhic argument. He did not deny the view of the Mitnagdim that the Gaon was unique in his generation. However, against the opinion that one must obey the greatest authority of the generation without reservation, he advanced the principle of majority rule. True, the Gaon was unique in his generation, but he was still a single man, whereas the *maggid* of Mezhirech and the other Hasidic leaders were the majority. Altogether, the position that Rabbi Shneur Zalman took regarding the Gaon was ambivalent: he recognized his extraordinary personal merit, but he also denied his authority as a sole Halakhic arbiter. It would not be too much to say that there is a good deal of irony in the fact that the leaders of the Mitnagdim constantly had recourse to the Gaon's charisma, whereas the Hasidic leader based his argument on Halakhic principles.

As noted, the role played by the Gaon at the start of the campaign against Hasidism and the motivations that guided him occupied a considerable part of the letter sent by Rabbi Shneur Zalman to his Hasidim in Vilna in 5557 (1797). In the month of Tishrei of that year, the Gaon's call to do battle against the Hasidim was published once again.[17] Rabbi Shneur Zalman's Hasidim in Vilna were apprehensive and implored their rabbi to come to Vilna and bring the conflict to an end, either by holding a debate with the leaders of the Mitnagdim or by referring the case to arbitrators agreed on by both sides. In his letter of response, Rabbi Shneur Zalman explained that in the existing circumstances there was no possibility of resolving the controversy.[18]

To support this claim, he tells them about his first failed effort at reconciliation: the visit to Vilna in the company of his teacher and comrade, Rabbi Menahem Mendel of Vitebsk, in the winter of 5532. As noted, Rabbi Menahem Mendel also alluded to that event in his letters. It was apparently no coincidence that both men repeatedly told about that failed effort at reconciliation with the Gaon. Recounting the story implies that the rigid position taken by the Gaon at that time determined the entire course of subsequent events. Had the Gaon not refused stubbornly to receive the emissaries of Hasidism, perhaps things would have turned out differently.

Later in his epistle, Rabbi Shneur Zalman tells his Hasidim that, after the failed visit to Vilna, the Hasidic leaders traveled to Shklov to take part in the controversy initiated by the Mitnagdim there. When the Mitnagdim realized that they could not refute the arguments of the Hasidim, "they came with a strong arm and hung themselves from the great tree of ha-Gaon he-Hasid, may his light burn brightly." Thus the failure to appease the Mitnagdim in Shklov was also connected to the Gaon's authority. Rabbi Shneur Zalman further explains to his Hasidim that, not only had the Gaon prevented dialogue and reconciliation in the past, but until he changed his mind there was no hope for reconciliation and accommodation. Even if the arbitrators ruled that the Hasidim were right, their decision would have no weight, for "as you have heard, no one in the state of Lithuania would have the audacity not to subordinate his own opinion to that of ha-Gaon he-Hasid."[19]

The constant repetition of the statement that the Gaon was the one who had prevented and continued to prevent any possibility of reconciliation between the Hasidim and their opponents reflects recognition of the exceptional force of his authority. At the same time it constitutes a severe accusation. However, that is just one side of the coin. On the other side, quite surprisingly, is the effort to defend the Gaon and explain why he refused to receive the Hasidic leaders who sought an audience with him in the winter of 5532.[20]

As described in chapter 3, it all began with rumors that had reached the Gaon regarding the deviant conduct of the Hasidim. Among other things, they were accused of contempt for Torah scholars and wild behavior during prayers that culminated in the practice of doing headstands. The Gaon regarded the people from whom he received information as reliable witnesses whose word was not to be doubted. At that stage further information came to him: the "well-known intermediary," whose identity is unknown to us, told him of a Hasidic interpretation of a passage in the Zohar. The Gaon regarded that interpretation as "heresy and Epicureanism." Hence, when Rabbi Menahem Mendel and Rabbi

Shneur Zalman wanted to meet with him, he refused to receive them. In sum, the Gaon was to be exonerated. He acted as he did not arbitrarily but on the basis of testimony that appeared reliable to him.

Rabbi Shneur Zalman's response to the Gaon is marked by the ambivalence we found in the attitude of Rabbi Menahem Mendel of Vitebsk. On the one hand, he regards him as bearing general responsibility for the persecution of the Hasidim, since everyone took their authority from him. On the other hand, he exonerates him and explains that he acted innocently. How can one understand Rabbi Shneur Zalman's effort to explain the inner logic of the Gaon's position to his Hasidim? Why did he make such an effort to defend the man who was most responsible for their suffering?

The explanation lies in a combination of pragmatic considerations and deep spiritual motivations. As an astute public leader, Rabbi Shneur Zalman understood that a blow to the prestige and authority of the Gaon would not only fail to reconcile the Mitnagdim with Hasidism but also was liable to deepen the rift. Recognizing the Gaon's authority and exonerating him were intended to prevent exacerbation of the conflict. On a deeper, spiritual level, Rabbi Shneur Zalman probably felt a need to defend the Gaon for another reason: he aspired to clear Hasidism of the taint of heresy that had been cast on it by the greatest scholar of the generation. How could he accept the fact that an exalted personage such as the Gaon had erred so deeply regarding the nature of the Hasidim and Hasidism? The only escape from this severe difficulty was the explanation that the Gaon had been misled by people he trusted and who had given him false information.

THE *MAGGID* OF MEZHIRECH: THE STRATEGY OF RESTRAINT

Another letter sent by Rabbi Shneur Zalman to his followers in Vilna, also written in 5557 (1797), is of great interest.[21] This letter, too, responds to the distress of the Hasidim of Vilna following the renewal of the persecutions. It shows an effort to apply the path taken by the *maggid* of

Mezhirech when the conflict broke out in 5532 to the renewal of the persecutions. This letter therefore provides important information about the response of the Hasidic leaders when the conflict first broke out. Rabbi Shneur Zalman tells his Hasidim that, following publication of the Mitnagdic book *Zemir 'Aritsim Veharvot Tsurim* and its circulation in many communities, a wave of persecutions broke out, causing great suffering to the Hasidic leaders: "Truly it could not be believed if it were told: the greatness of the humiliations and torments done then to the famous Zaddikim of Volhynia, until they could not sit in their homes, and all of them came to take refuge beneath the wing of our great and lamented rabbi in the community of Rovna, may his memory be blessed, to consult and make a plan about what was to be done."[22]

It was known from another letter of Rabbi Shneur Zalman's that the Hasidic leaders gathered for an emergency meeting in the home of the *maggid* Dov Ber.[23] However, in the present letter, which was published only recently, Rabbi Shneur Zalman chose to describe the response of the *maggid* to the first persecutions against the Hasidim: "There were then many ways to do something and contradict and overturn their thought, and to write doubly and triply bitter things against them, . . . and to print them and send them among Jacob [i.e., among the Jews] and in many other ways. But our great rabbi of holy and blessed memory did not choose to do any act against them, just all the power of Israel was in their mouth, to cry out to the Lord who frustrates the plans of the cunning, that their hands might not be resourceful."[24]

Thus we find that various responses were considered during the conference held by the Hasidic leaders. Among other things they raised the possibility of publishing and circulating polemical writings against the Mitnagdim. They also considered other ways of struggling, which are not stated explicitly, though they were apparently belligerent. They might even have considered issuing proclamations of excommunication against the persecutors of Hasidism.[25] However, the *maggid* of Mezhirech, who was then regarded as the chief leader of Hasidism, decided by virtue of his authority that the path of restraint should be taken. Most likely the *maggid* believed that an aggressive response might deepen the rift between the Hasidim and their opponents and cause them to drive the Hasidim out of the Jewish people. One way or another, it may be stated that the strategy of restraint, exemplified by both Rabbi Menahem Mendel and Rabbi Shneur Zalman, originated in the course laid out by the *maggid* of Mezhirech at the outbreak of the controversy.

Later in this epistle, when he wishes to apply the instructions given by the *maggid* of Mezhirech in 5532 to the situation in 5557 (1797), Rabbi Shneur Zalman mentions the reward the Hasidim gained by virtue of their restraint:

> [What is described in] the verses "because of your tribulations to benefit you in the end" [Deuteronomy 8:16], "and your beginnings will be in grief and your end will greatly flourish" [Job 8:15], [is exactly what happened to us,] as our eyes, and not those of a stranger, have seen, for afterward they multiplied to thousands and scores of thousands of our comrades in every country, and seeing the exaggerated lies that were told against us, in fortifying themselves and arousing the world against us in a great noise and trumpet blast, and in this they awaken those slumbering in the vanities of the age to rouse from their slumber and see that the light is good, and to distinguish between truth and lying, . . . which would not have been the case had they not been suffering then and accepted torments with love; and had they provoked strife and controversy certainly thousands and scores of thousands would have been prevented, perish the thought, from seeing the truth; . . . and God did justice for us so that in that day to sustain a great multitude in true life.[26]

In retrospect, from a distance of twenty-five years, Rabbi Shneur Zalman finds a causal connection between the strategy adopted by the Hasidic leaders at the outbreak of the controversy and the vast expansion of Hasidism during the intervening years. The sharp disparity between the vociferous aggression that characterized the struggle of the Mitnagdim and the restrained response of the Hasidim is what aroused "thousands and scores of thousands" to understand the truth of Hasidism and join its ranks. Since this is the proper interpretation of previous events, the lesson to be drawn from it regarding the challenge before the Hasidim at that time is, according to Rabbi Shneur Zalman, as clear as day: "Behold now also the duty is incumbent on us to be silent and suffer and accept torments with love, because they are truly like birth pangs, and I am assured that the Lord has decreed for us that when the pangs and labor pains soon cease, God willing, thousands and scores of thousands will be born and be led to the Lord to serve Him[,] . . . and that will be your consolation."[27]

This was the consolation of the persecuted, that many joined them and thus confirmed the correctness of their path. Moreover, comparison of the persecutions to birth pangs, and the statement that "God did justice for us," shed new light on the phenomenon of opposition. Had it not been for the vociferous and mendacious attacks of the Mitnagdim on the Hasidim, perhaps the multitude "slumbering in the vanities of the age" would have remained immersed in sleep. Thus the phenomenon of opposition, with all its horrors and injuries, is "justice" done for them, for it hastened the strengthening and expansion of Hasidism. This appears to be the first attempt to propose a dialectical interpretation of the phenomenon of opposition and to view it in a positive light. Naturally, such a view was possible only from the standpoint of the late 1790s, when Hasidism had proven its resilience and vitality despite persecution since the early 1770s.

AFTER THE VILNA GAON'S DEATH: "NOT TO SPEAK ILL AFTER THE BIER OF A TORAH SCHOLAR"

The Vilna Gaon died during the intermediate days of Succot in 5558 (1797). A rumor spread among the Mitnagdim that the Hasidim were happy and rejoicing at the death of their venerated leader. Consequently the heads of the Vilna community initiated a new wave of persecutions against the Hasidim, fiercer than its predecessors. Things went so far that the persecuted Hasidim in Vilna addressed the Gentile authorities and involved them in the controversy.[28] Even then, the Mitnagdim showed no restraint. In May 1798 a letter defaming the Hasidim and their leader Rabbi Shneur Zalman was sent to the authorities. They arrested Rabbi Shneur Zalman in the following September, interrogated him, and released him in November, the Hebrew month of Kislev 5559.[29] Upon his release from prison, Rabbi Shneur Zalman wrote to his followers:

> Here is the announcement of a grave matter of controversy and unjustified hatred. Therefore it is worthy for the whole community whose heart has been touched with awe of God, and who fears for His word, to be very careful of being a cause or a cause of a cause of damage, . . . for therein also last year, after the passing of his honor the Gaon of blessed memory of Vilna, I wrote a dreadful warning to all of our faction not to speak ill after the bier of a Torah scholar, not a hint of reproach or the hint of a hint, without any permission in the world. But this time now, in the hard times we are undergoing, perhaps it might be suspected that the reins were loosed, perish the thought, because many people lean on the great tree, none other than his honor ha-Gaon he-Hasid of blessed memory. Therefore I have come again with a double and redoubled warning to our entire faction, near and far, in every place of their dwelling, without anyone giving permission to himself, to open mouth or tongue against the honor of the Torah, the honor of ha-Gaon he-Hasid of blessed memory. For it is clearly known to us that he was not responsible, perish the thought, for acting greatly against us, and all the days of his life the obstacle and error did not proceed from the ruler, perish the thought.[30]

Thus it turns out that, soon after the death of the Gaon, Rabbi Shneur Zalman warned his Hasidim not to dishonor his memory. Now, after his release from prison, he hastened to warn them again about the same thing. He knew that his Hasidim felt strong resentment against the Gaon. He probably was apprehensive lest those feelings might grow stronger and harsher because of his imprisonment. With his request to restrain such feelings, Rabbi Shneur Zalman argues that it was not the Gaon who had called for addressing the authorities. He repeats that statement in more general terms: "All the days of his life the obstacle and error did not proceed from the ruler, perish the thought." It is somewhat ironic that the degeneration of the struggle against the Hasidim to the level of informing against them to the authorities made it possible for Rabbi Shneur Zalman to say something to the credit of the Gaon. True, the Gaon had initiated and led the struggle against the Hasidim; however, he had never supported an appeal to the authorities.

Nevertheless, Rabbi Shneur Zalman's attitude toward the Gaon was far more complex than it appears. The very year that he wrote to his followers in favor of the Gaon, he wrote in a rather different spirit to Rabbi Phinehas Horowitz, the rabbi of Frankfurt am Main: "Please pardon me for burdening you with words relating to you all the tribulations I underwent from our adversaries in Vilna, who follow the opinion of their famous rabbi, who permitted the shedding of our blood like water in 5532."[31] It is easy to explain the disparity between the two letters. The first was sent to his followers to warn them not to dishonor the memory of the Gaon. The second was a personal appeal to a rabbi known for his affinity with Hasidism. Thus Rabbi Shneur Zalman did not hesitate to express his anger against the Gaon directly and explicitly for having permitted the persecution of the Hasidim.

Conciliatory tones toward the Mitnagdim, with the Gaon chief among them, are audible in a letter that Rabbi Shneur Zalman wrote to the scholars of the Vilna community several years later. These scholars had addressed Rabbi Shneur Zalman and warned him regarding the use of polished knives by Hasidic slaughterers in the Vilna area. Wishing to mollify the rabbis of Vilna, Rabbi Shneur Zalman refers to the words of Rabbi Ḥayyim of Volozhin, uttered at the time of his visit to White Russia in 5563 (1803): "For he said in the name of his revered teacher ha-Gaon he-Hasid of blessed memory, that there was no prohibition at all against slaughter with polished knives according to the law as studied in the Gemara and the *posqim.*" Rabbi Shneur Zalman goes on to explain that the prohibition against polished knives issued by the Mitnagdim in 5532 was motivated by "removal," that is to say, a social sanction, "like the other removals and decrees that were issued by error by the ruler in 5532 as though against an actual heretic: . . . everything according to the rumor, from men regarded as fit and dependable by His Honorable Torah."[32] The argument is repeated, that the Gaon acted innocently and was misled by witnesses whom he trusted. However, at that point Rabbi Shneur Zalman is able to go much further in clearing the Gaon of guilt:

> In the fullness of years, after the passing of ha-Gaon he-Hasid of blessed memory, the merit of his Torah stood by him and by all those who gathered in his shadow, to shed no more blood in vain [and] with the revelation to all eyes the truth was known clearly, that there is no hint of heresy among us, not a hint of a hint. Therefore, the tribes were permitted to mingle, and they have always intermarried with us. Likewise the remaining ostracisms and decrees were rescinded, both the lenient and severe ones of 5532, which were an error and misinformation in the eyes

> of the community. And of this it has been said, who can understand errors and clear me of hidden sins? [Ps. 19:13] And a person does not understand the words of Torah unless he has failed in them. And greater than that we have found an erroneous instruction even in the Great *Sanhedrin* in the Chamber of Hewn Stone . . . as it is written, "and the whole community of the Children of Israel shall be forgiven, for the whole nation is in error."[33]

The picture painted here is one of reconciliation between the warring camps. After it was clear to everyone that the suspicion of heresy that the Mitnagdim had cast on the Hasidim was groundless, the war against them came to an end. Not only were the "ostracisms and decrees" rescinded, but relations of brotherhood and cooperation began to be knit between the camps. This new structure of arrangements developed "in the fullness of years, after the passing of ha-Gaon he-Hasid." Most likely the Gaon's death was among the principal factors in stopping the war against the Hasidim. However, quite surprisingly, Rabbi Shneur Zalman attributes the improvement in relations to the positive influence of the Gaon: through the merit of his Torah, as it were, his disciples would "shed no more blood in vain." Yet it had been the Vilna Gaon who had "permitted the shedding of our blood like water" and led the campaign against the Hasidim. He was the one who had locked his door before the emissaries of Hasidism who sought to propitiate him in 5532, and he had thwarted any possibility of reconciliation in the succeeding decades.

What is the meaning of the statement that, by virtue of the Gaon's Torah, those following in his footsteps had ceased to persecute the Hasidim? This apparently means that heaven favored the Gaon by having his disciples cease from persecuting the Hasidim, by virtue of his Torah. In reading these words, one wonders whether they are a sincere expression of Rabbi Shneur Zalman's feelings, or whether they are courteous phrases intended to placate the leaders of Vilna. It is difficult to provide an unequivocal answer to these questions. Most likely, as the reconciled situation blurred memories of the persecution, making them a picture of a rapidly receding past, Rabbi Shneur Zalman was able to develop a more positive view of the Gaon. However, it is doubtful that even with the passage of years he was capable of changing his ambivalent attitude toward the Gaon into an entirely positive one. Even if he was truly convinced that by virtue of the Gaon's Torah his admirers had ceased from persecuting the Hasidim in vain after his death, he could not have forgotten that by virtue of that Torah the Gaon was able to lead the struggle against Hasidism as long as he remained alive.

In the letter cited here, Rabbi Shneur Zalman repeats the familiar claim that the Gaon and the leaders of Vilna acted in error. However, whereas in earlier statements he had been satisfied with stating that they acted innocently, in this epistle he adds Bible quotations and authoritative sources intended to show that that error is a common and legitimate phenomenon. Thus the opposition to Hasidism was also a legitimate phenomenon, though erroneous. With these words Rabbi Shneur Zalman plots the course for a train of thought that was to be prominent in Habad historiography in following generations.

MAẒREF HA'AVODAH: OPPOSITION TO HASIDISM AS A LEGITIMATE ERROR GUIDED BY THE HANDS OF HEAVEN

Another link in the chain of the reactions of Habad Hasidism to the phenomenon of opposition is found in the book *Maẓref Ha'avodah* (Purifier of Worship), first published in Koenigsberg in 5618 (1858). This work claims to describe "a debate that took place seventy-two years earlier between the two great rabbis of the generation, one from the sect of Hasidim and the other from the sect of Mitnagdim." The author, who hid behind a fictitious identity, was Ya'aqov Qidner, a Habad Hasid who lived in the first half of the nineteenth century.[34]

This work is an effort to present a systematic and well-argued answer to the criticism of Hasidism prevalent among Mitnagdim during the first decades of the nineteenth century. The author appears to have been particularly interested in influencing Torah scholars, as can be seen from the detailed, erudite discussion justifying the Hasidic custom of using the version of the prayer book attributed to the ARI (Rabbi Isaac Luria).[35] Another expression of this concern is found in his effort to respond to the criticism leveled against Hasidism by Rabbi Ḥayyim of Volozhin in his book *Nefesh Ha-ḥayyim* (The Soul of Life).[36]

During the "debate" the Mitnaged raises various questions and doubts about the path of the Hasidim. In so doing he also raises the issue of the position taken by the Gaon against Hasidism:

> For it is known and renowned among all the Jews from our rabbi, the great and true Gaon, the rabbi of all the people of the diaspora, his honor of holy name, our teacher Rabbi Eliyahu of Vilna, whose grasp of the revealed and the esoteric was as one of our great ancient Sages, and the greatness of his asceticism and his piety is known and famous to all . . . and from his holy mouth we have heard explicitly about your sect: that they are like the sect of Shabbetai Ẓevi may his name be blotted out; and also he explicitly forbade us to marry them and forbade us to consult their books, like the books of heretics, perish the thought. . . . And also their wine and bread is totally forbidden and especially their ritual slaughter is that of a heretic. And ha-Gaon he-Hasid also did not want to look in the face of any one of the sect; . . . and once one of their rabbis came to Vilna to argue with him, and he did not want to admit him into his presence.[37]

The description of the attitude of the Gaon was not meant to remind the reader of forgotten things. Following those words, the Mitnaged challenges the Hasid: how did he have the temerity to thrust his head in among the tall mountains, that is to say, the Gaon, on the one hand, and the Hasidic leaders, on the other, and to decide in favor of the latter against the stand of the Gaon? Underlying this challenge was the Gaon's authority. That authority, whose power permitted the persecution of the Hasidim, is here presented as a reason for rejecting their way.

The author of *Maẓref Ha'avodah,* who was well acquainted with Mitnagdim, apparently believed that the Gaon's stand toward Hasidism continued to influence the Mitnagdim during the first decades of the nineteenth century. Indeed, it is easy to imagine that the Gaon's struggle against Hasidism occupied a significant place in the collective memory of both Mitnagdim and Hasidim. As for his authority, it had not declined with the passage of time but had grown stronger. Thus it is no surprise that the author is not sparing with the words he places in the mouth of the Mitnaged in veneration of the Gaon's authority.

The Hasid responds to the Mitnaged's challenge:

> My friend, take the beam from between your eyes and straighten yourself out, because who permitted you to marry our daughters? For it is known and renowned to everyone that all the magnates of the sect of Mitnagdim marry with our daughters. And even the family of the Gaon of blessed memory. Please tell me, my friend, who permitted you to eat of our slaughter, for the whole sect of Mitnagdim eats of our slaughter. . . . Thus after these true words whoever has a brain in his head will understand the thing correctly, . . . that in this matter you are not at all wary of the words of the Gaon.[38]

Farther on, the Hasid explains that by ignoring the prohibitions and restrictions against contact with the Hasidim, the Mitnagdim acknowledge that the Gaon erred in what he said about the nature and character of the Hasidim. To make it easier for the Mitnaged to swallow such a coarse statement, the Hasid refers to the controversy between Rabbi Yakov Emden and Rabbi Yehonatan Eybeschuetz. It was known that, in Emden's opinion, Eybeschuetz was a Sabbatean and it was forbidden to read his books. Nevertheless, the Hasid states, no one heeded that prohibition anymore because it was clear to everyone that Emden was mistaken. Similarly, no one heeded the prohibitions imposed by the Gaon on contact with Hasidim, because everyone knew that his position was erroneous. Moreover, the entire controversy between Emden and Eybeschuetz occurred as a cautionary example to be recalled in the future, permitting the opponents of Hasidism to recognize the Gaon's error.[39]

The example of Rabbi Ḥayyim of Volozhin is an important component of the evidence presented by the author of *Maẓref Ha'avodah.* Rabbi Ḥayyim was regarded as the Gaon's greatest disciple and the heir to his position as leader of the Mitnagdim in Lithuania. Thus Rabbi Ḥayyim's authority counterbalances, at least to a degree, the position taken by the Gaon. Here the Hasid describes Rabbi Ḥayyim's attitude toward the Hasidim:

> I used to sit and study in the [yeshiva of] Volozhin with the true Gaon Rabbi Ḥayyim, and it is known to all that he was the chosen disciple of the Gaon of blessed memory, and I was among his associates and I saw the greatness of his fear and awe in remembering the holy name of his

> rabbi the Vilna Gaon; . . . and nevertheless regarding the warnings of the aforementioned Gaon about our sect, I realized that he gave no place at all to his words, . . . and I saw that several Hasidim were sitting in his yeshiva. And he also brought them close with all sorts of attractions, . . . and I also saw several travelers from the sect of Hasidim [who were passing] through Volozhin, and his highness Rabbi Ḥayyim the aforementioned Gaon kept them until the sabbath. And they celebrated the sabbath with him in great honor. And once the Hasid Rabbi Yisrael Yafe, the printer from the community of Kapost came, and he detained him until the sabbath and he celebrated the sabbath with him with great honor like one of the great rabbis; and during the meal he implored him to say some of those elevated words to him, that he had heard from his holy rabbi of Lyady, and he preached before him and it was viewed very well by him. And once again I saw more than the rest that his only son who was dear to him, our master Rabbi Isaac, he has in hand all the books of our rabbis . . . and he studies them and reads them with depth of mind.[40]

Rabbi Ḥayyim's friendly attitude toward the Hasidim who studied in his yeshiva and were guests in his home, the interest he showed in the teachings of their rabbis, and that fact that his son owned Hasidic books and studied them—all of these clearly prove that the Mitnagdim had some authority for ignoring the prohibitions imposed by the Gaon on contact with Hasidim.[41]

The argument that the Gaon's position regarding Hasidism was based on error is not new. As noted, this was the opinion of both Rabbi Menahem Mendel of Vitebsk and of Rabbi Shneur Zalman of Lyady. Both of them absolved the Gaon of malicious intention because he had been misled by false witnesses. Rabbi Shneur Zalman took a further step and presented evidence that even the Sages of the *Sanhedrin* were liable to err. Hence the error of a communal leader was a legitimate occurrence. However, the author of *Maẓref Ha'avodah* is not content with these explanations and seeks to endow the Gaon's error with a theological dimension:

> And if it may seem wonderful why God did this to us by placing in the heart of ha-Gaon he-Hasid of blessed memory invalid opinions to condemn wholehearted believers as heretics, perish the thought, I shall explain to you that there is no reason to raise that question at all. For we have found that when the ARI of blessed memory was revealed, there

> stood against him the holy Gaon Rabbi Solomon Luria of blessed memory, and he wanted to ban the ARI of blessed memory; . . . and this was also the case at the time of the revelation of the pure and bright holy light of the Ba'al Shem Tov and the holy rabbi our teacher Dov Ber of Mezhirech, there was prepared against them the aforementioned rabbi, the Gaon, to conceal their path and their way in sanctity. And one should not wonder why God did that. For it is known and famous in books that every pure and bright light cannot be revealed in this crude and murky world except by slight hiding and concealing. . . . And when God shined his bright light to create worlds He had to hide it so that the recipients could receive.[42]

We find that the Gaon's opposition to Hasidism was not simply a human error, but the product of the precise planning of divine providence. The Kabbalistic principle that every manifestation of divine light must be accompanied by an obscuration and concealment also applies to the revelation of the Ba'al Shem Tov. Hence the Gaon's opposition was a concealment necessitated by the abundance of light. This surprising explanation of the Gaon's struggle against Hasidism is a kind of "sweetening of judgments," for the severe persecution of the Hasidim was "sweetened" and its sting removed. The bans, the humiliations, and the bodily and economic injury to the Hasidim took place only to conceal the strength of the divine light that broke through with the revelation of the Ba'al Shem Tov and the *maggid* of Mezhirech. Thus it was possible to maintain both the honor and authority of the Gaon, and the righteousness and honor of Hasidism. This harmonious explanation, which can also be described as the mystification of the struggle between the Hasidim and the Mitnagdim, leaves no doubt as to which of the two warring camps received the divine light and which of them served as a veil meant to conceal it.

The effort of the author of *Maẓref Ha'avodah* to make sense of the opposition to Hasidism led by the Gaon expresses a viewpoint typical in the first decades of the nineteenth century. In the beginning of the century the organized struggle against Hasidism came to an end. The cessation of the persecution can be attributed to a number of factors: the Gaon's death, recognition by the Russian authorities of the right of the Hasidim to hold separate minyanim, and increasing recognition that the Hasidim were not heretics.[43] In the early nineteenth century a new system of relations between the two camps began to take shape. These relations were complex and were expressed in coexistence and a certain degree of cooperation on the social and interpersonal level and, at the same time, in competition and confrontation on the spiritual and religious level. In other words, the Mitnagdim stopped accusing the Hasidim of heresy and acknowledged their right to exist within the Jewish people. Nevertheless they retained the opinion that the Hasidic manner of worshiping God was erroneous.

Maẓref Ha'avodah was thus intended to present a convincing reply to the allegations and objections leveled against Hasidim and Hasidism. The author sought to lead his readers to the conclusion that Hasidism is not merely a phenomenon that must be tolerated retrospectively, but that it was, from the start, the preferable way of worshiping God. In his effort to instill this recognition in his readers, the author saw fit to refer to the Gaon's war against Hasidism. Being familiar with the state of mind of the Mitnagdim, especially in learned circles, Ya'aqov Qidner understood that even at this stage it was not possible to ignore the monumental figure on whom the Mitnagdim had leaned since the beginning of the struggle. The Gaon's enormous authority and the living memory of his campaign against Hasidism were obstacles in the path of anyone who wanted to change the Mitnagdim's attitude toward Hasidism. Therefore it was imperative to find a proper and convincing explanation of the Gaon's attitude toward Hasidism—an explanation that would not impair, perish the thought, his honor and authority—in order to change the tolerant, lukewarm, yet somewhat tense attitude of the Mitnagdim into acknowledgement of the virtue and correctness of Hasidism.

BEIT RABI—A CONTROVERSY FOR THE SAKE OF HEAVEN

So far we have dealt with the response of the Hasidim to the phenomenon of opposition in two periods: at the very time of the organized struggle against Hasidism, which is to say, the last three decades of the eighteenth century; and when persecution gave way to coexistence combined with a spiritual and cultural confrontation, or the first decades of the nineteenth century. However, the question of the character and meaning of opposition to Hasidism continued to preoccupy the Hasidim in the second half of the nineteenth century and on into the twentieth century. As a matter of course, because of the distance in time from the dramatic events of the late eighteenth century, the response to opposition became a matter of perception and interpretation of the past. The two principal channels of expression through which the Hasidim formed their picture of past opposition are hagiographic literature and historical writing. Below I shall concentrate on three examples of Habad historiography.

Ḥayyim Meir Heilmann's book *Beit Rabi* was published in Berditchev in 5562 (1902). The book is devoted to the history of the rebbes of Habad, from Rabbi Shneur Zalman of Lyady to those of the late nineteenth century. In the introduction to his book, Heilmann claims that he is making available to his readers a faithful and documented history of Habad Hasidism. In his opinion his version is preferable both to irresponsible hagiographic literature and the distorted historiography of the Haskalah school. To support this claim, Heilmann points to the multitude of reliable sources presented in his book and the lack of contradiction among the facts mentioned in it.

Heilmann claims that, along with these virtues, his book has another important feature: "All the letters presented here are not propaganda with insults and abuse; they do not revile those opposed to them, rather they find virtue in them; . . . and we copied hardly any malicious letters from major Mitnagdim."[44] The first part of this citation refers to the epistles of Rabbi Shneur Zalman of Lyady. By virtue of the moderate and restrained tone that characterizes them, these letters are worthy to be cited in a balanced and responsible historical study. The writings of the opponents of Hasidism, by contrast, are flooded with "insults and abuse," and therefore they are not worthy of inclusion. This statement is one of many indications of the author's personal affinity with Hasidism. In his presentation of the confrontation between the Hasidim and the Mitnagdim his leanings are evident.

Heilmann was a Habad Hasid who had been exposed to the influence of modern historiography and had even adopted some of its features.

Nevertheless, he cannot be viewed as a critical historian. Along with his aspiration to reveal the historical truth, Heilmann also displays deep commitment to the values and needs of two social circles to which he was attached: Habad Hasidism in particular and Haredi society in general.[45] This dual commitment influenced both the description of opposition to Hasidism and its interpretation. The connection to Habad Hasidism is expressed in acceptance of the version of events that Rabbi Shneur Zalman presents in his epistles. The attachment to the values and needs of Haredi society is expressed in an apologetic interpretation that presents the dispute as "a controversy for the sake of heaven."

Heilmann begins by warning the reader, "Do not be hasty in your opinion to judge harshly the rabbis who disagreed with our rabbi and spoke erroneously against them. Know well that the dissenting rabbis were great and very profound in Torah and *yira,* and all their actions were not ill-intentioned, perish the thought, to oppose the truth. Only from God did a cause come to turn them back."[46] To strengthen his claim that the leaders of the Mitnagdim acted in innocence, Heilmann suggests two explanations for the persecution of the Hasidim. First, at the time of the growth of Hasidism there were still secret Sabbateans in the Polish hinterland. Since the Sabbateans pretended to be pious Kabbalists, the Mitnagdim mistakenly thought that the new Hasidim were also Sabbateans. Second, the leaders of the Mitnagdim were misled by false witnesses who appeared to be fit witnesses.

The latter explanation is familiar from the epistles of Rabbi Menahem Mendel and of Rabbi Shneur Zalman. By contrast, the statement that the Frankist episode and the shock it left among the Jews lay in the background of the struggle against Hasidism sounds like an entirely historical explanation. However, Heilmann does not seek merely to propose a reasonable explanation of past events. His views have the no-less-significant function of attempting to shape the reader's attitude toward those events. Therefore he distinguishes between false witnesses who acted with malice and who deserved condemnation and the leaders of the Mitnagdim, who, even if they erred, had the sake of heaven in their intentions. In the light of this distinction he again warns, "But the righteous rabbis, at one with God and His Torah like the Vilna Gaon and [the author of] *Hanod'a Beyehuda* of blessed memory and those like them, heaven forfend that ill might be thought of them and that they might be spoken badly of."[47]

The repeated claim that the Gaon and the leaders of the Mitnagdim acted in innocence justified the demand not to offend their honor. However, this is an argument of legalistic and restricted character, leaving in its wake questions and doubts. In the end, why were the innocent Hasidim persecuted? Was it possible to dismiss the long and cruel campaign waged against them as a regrettable error and nothing more? Was it perhaps possible to reveal a hidden and deep reason that would give meaning to the persecution of the Hasidim?

Indeed, Heilmann goes on to suggest an interpretation of the struggle of the Mitnagdim against Hasidism: "But in truth they were all righteous and holy and pure, and the holy spirit appeared in their house of study, and their controversy was for the sake of heaven and not a simple controversy, but rather [one that dealt] with high and exalted things that stand at the height of the world; and also at the time of the controversy their hatred was not complete."[48] In defining the war against the Hasidim as a "controversy . . . for the sake of heaven," Heilmann seeks to give it a decent and respectable character.[49] And if this is not sufficient, he veils the meaning of the controversy in clouds of mystery: these were "high and exalted things that stand at the height of the world." Unquestionably, those great men who disagreed with one another had hidden reasons beyond our understanding. Heilmann also argues that the controversy between the Mitnagdim and the Hasidim was not at all an abnormal phenomenon. As noted, this argument exists in *Maẓref Ha'avodah.* However, Heilmann expands its scope and mentions a series of great men who were persecuted for no good reason and whom everyone, after a while, acknowledged were righteous. Among them were Rabbi Yehonatan Eybeschuetz, the ARI, and Maimonides. Controversies of that kind also took place at the time of the Sages of the Talmud, and such was the controversy between Saul and King David. Thus, controversy is a familiar and legitimate phenomenon from time immemorial. However, in his generation, Heilmann adds, the controversy received particular significance: "Now in the footsteps of the messiah . . . Satan knows and sees that his end is near, etc., and therefore when a new light shines in the world he is fearful lest perhaps because of this his day will come sooner.

And therefore he confuses the world and increases controversy among the Jews so as to prolong by that the time of exile, perish the thought. And this, too, is caused by God so as not to do away with choice so that it will be free, etc."[50]

Here we have an effort to reveal the metaphysical meaning of the struggle against Hasidism. In the background stands the Lurianic conception of the messianic redemption. According to this conception, redemption depends on completion of the process of *tiqun* (repair), which means increasing the powers of sanctity over those of the *sitra ahra* (the forces of evil).[51] The appearance of Hasidism, as Heilmann interprets it, is a "new light" that advances the messianic process. By contrast, the controversy against Hasidism is the product of the ruses of the forces of impurity, which endeavor to delay redemption. Clearly, to present those who disagree with Hasidism as tools of Satan is no great compliment. However, Heilmann softens the barb somewhat by explaining that even the initiative of Satan is governed by divine providence. The latter allows Satan to arouse controversy in order to permit "free choice." What is the nature of this free choice? Heilmann must be referring to a choice between the worthy path of the Hasidim and the erroneous way of the Mitnagdim.

This position reflects Heilmann's ambivalent attitude toward the leaders of the Mitnagdim. He spares no words in emphasizing their innocence and integrity; however, the explanation he offers regarding the meaning of the controversy leaves no doubt about the superiority of the Hasidim over their persecutors. This ambivalent position also appears in the principle that Heilmann states at the conclusion of his discussion of this matter: "In all the controversies that were among great [rabbis], when one was right in his judgment, nevertheless the worth of the opponent is not diminished, and his honor remains in its place. But this, too, you will find, tried and true, that in every controversy among the great [rabbis], the persecuted one was on a special level, and his persecutors did not attain the height of his eminence."[52] Thus the honor of the Gaon and the other rabbis of the Mitnagdim was unimpaired, but the persecuted Hasidim were on a higher level.

As noted, Heilmann's position was shaped by his relationship to two circles of identity and commitment: the Habad circle and the Haredi circle. Heilmann does try to be faithful to the facts, as shown by the many sources he includes in his book. Nevertheless, the letters of Rabbi Shneur Zalman are his main source. He ignores the writs of excommunication issued by the Mitnagdim under the pretext that they contain insults and abuse. Indeed, Heilmann systematically embraces Rabbi Shneur Zalman's version, according to which the Gaon played a critical role in leading the struggle against the Hasidim but did so in good faith. Heilmann also follows Rabbi Shneur Zalman in the effort to justify the Gaon and the other leaders of the Mitnagdim, but his arguments are different.

During the last decades of the nineteenth century the processes of secularization among the Jews of Russia intensified. Correspondingly, the value of cooperation between Hasidim and Mitnagdim increased, for both groups remained faithful to the values of the tradition and came to its defense. Alongside the traditional division between Hasidim and Mitnagdim, the Haredi identity took shape as a shared framework bridging the gaps between them, at least to some extent. From this point of view, it was important to overcome the harsh residue of the struggle between the Mitnagdim and the Hasidim remaining in the collective memory. Consequently, Heilmann tends to emphasize the legitimacy of the phenomenon of controversy by use of an apologetic interpretation. He presents the effort to expel the Hasidim from the Jewish people and the manifestations of hatred, persecution, and excommunication in a soft light as a "controversy for the sake of heaven" based on significant metaphysical grounds.

THE REBBE, RABBI JOSEPH ISAAC: THE VICTORY OF THE HASIDIM IN THE MINSK DEBATE

Another important chapter in Habad historiography is found in the writings of the rebbe Joseph Isaac Schneersohn (1880–1950), the leader of Habad Hasidim between the two world wars and during the Holocaust. Scholars who have discussed this historical writing have commented that portraying the past was an extremely important factor in the spiritual struggles in which Rabbi Joseph Isaac was involved, and that this gave rise to their decidedly anachronistic character. Furthermore, they are characterized by a strange mixture of historical fact and imaginary descriptions that have nothing at all to do with historical sources and are inconsistent with what is known to us about the period under discussion. In sum, Rabbi Joseph Isaac's historical writing is largely arbitrary and partisan.[53]

How did this man describe the phenomenon of opposition to Hasidism? How did he explain to his readers the vexing events that took place in the last decades of the eighteenth century? The reader of Rabbi Joseph Isaac's writings will be surprised to discover that the story of the struggle waged by the Mitnagdim against the Hasidim is barely present in his "history" of Hasidism. In his article "The Fathers of Hasidism," he describes the first three decades of the Hasidic movement but does not discuss the persecution of the Hasidim in itself. This matter is mentioned incidentally when he describes the response of the Hasidim to the persecutions:

> The situation at that time demanded that at the head of the leadership should stand a man with the spirit in him to speak clearly with the Mitnagdim and not to fear the excommunications and the proclamations against the Hasidim, which were then issued by the Mitnagdim, and for that reason it was decided then to choose a leadership committee with a general organizer . . . with the power and authority to act on his own and to give orders to all the centers as he should find necessary for the good of the cause. And that holy band chose—at a general assembly—his honor and holiness our venerable rabbi to be the general and authorized organizer.[54]

Rabbi Joseph Isaac goes on to say that in his capacity of "general organizer," Rabbi Shneur Zalman spent about three years in travels. Among other places, he visited Shklov, Minsk, and Vilna, cities known to be centers of opposition to Hasidim. In those cities he endeavored to gain the sympathy of young scholars. He debated Torah matters with them until they appreciated his greatness and became his followers. This sophisticated propaganda activity was sometimes clandestine. Thus, for example, while he was in Vilna Rabbi Shneur Zalman concealed his identity for some time. He wandered from one house of study to another and debated with all the great Torah scholars. But he did not meet with the Gaon, for he feared lest his identity be revealed.

Rabbi Joseph Isaac does not wish to mention the very phenomenon of opposition to Hasidism. The motives of the Mitnagdim, their means of struggle, the suffering they caused the Hasidim—all these matters are ignored. Even Rabbi Shneur Zalman's terms of imprisonment are not worthy of mention. Instead, he wishes to inculcate the following message in the reader: Rabbi Shneur Zalman stood head and shoulders above the other disciples of the *maggid* of Mezhirech, both as a Torah scholar and as a leader and organizer. For that reason the disciples of the *maggid* chose him as a leader in that emergency period of excommunications and persecutions. Indeed, he succeeded marvelously in drawing masses of young Torah scholars into the ranks of Hasidism.

As noted, Rabbi Joseph Isaac's story abounds with imaginary descriptions. There is no doubt that Rabbi Shneur Zalman was an impressive Torah scholar, and that he was a charismatic leader and talented organizer. However, there is no basis for the statement that the disciples of the *maggid* chose him as a "general organizer," that is to say, an overall leader of the Hasidic movement. Also, the story that he wandered for years among the houses of study of Vilna, Shklov, and Minsk and won souls for Hasidism by demonstrating his great Torah scholarship appears to be imaginary. Naturally it is not impossible that young Torah scholars were drawn to him because of his great erudition. However, the words of Rabbi Shneur Zalman himself show that the message that Hasidism sought to impart to the community was that of a new way of worshiping God, to which prayer in particular was central.[55]

From the account presented above, it appears that Rabbi Shneur Zalman fought the Mitnagdim with their own weapon—Torah scholarship. This message arises even more strongly from the episode known as the Minsk Debate. An account of this episode is included in a typewritten manuscript by Rabbi Joseph Isaac, published with a comprehensive commentary by Rachel Elior.[56]

Here is the essence of the episode: in the winter of 5542 (1782) Rabbi Shneur Zalman decided to initiate a debate with the Mitnagdim. To that end he adopted a strategy: eight young Torah scholars from among the Hasidim were charged with the task of waging a propaganda campaign among the Mitnagdim. They pretended to be Mitnagdim and circulated among communities of Mitnagdim, giving sermons on fear of heaven. At the same time they attacked the dissident sect and explained to their listeners that it was necessary to hold a debate with it. Their plan was successful, and from various communities calls for a debate against the Hasidim reached the leaders of the Mitnagdim in Shklov and Vilna. Disagreement emerged among the leaders of the Mitnagdim in those two centers. The men of Vilna supported holding the debate, but those of Shklov opposed it. The Gaon decided between them, declaring that no debate against the Hasidim should be initiated, "but if the sect should demand it, then we are obliged according to Torah law to respond to them."

In the month of Iyyar, Rabbi Shneur Zalman announced that he invited everyone who disagreed with the ways of the Hasidim to come to Minsk, "and he was prepared to answer everything with proofs from the Talmud and Halakhic authorities." The Gaon took up the challenge and ordered that Torah scholars be sent to Minsk to take part in the debate. Meanwhile hundreds of Rabbi Shneur Zalman's followers also arrived in Minsk, and on the sabbath he taught them Torah as was his wont. Mitnagdim were also among the listeners, trying to find fault with the words of the Hasidic leader. However, Rabbi Shneur Zalman's Torah teachings amazed all those present, including the Mitnagdim. The impression left by the Hasidic leader on the residents of Minsk was so deep that, at the time of the third sabbath meal, the synagogue where he was teaching was not large enough to hold the masses of people who thronged its doors.

Rabbi Shneur Zalman addressed the rabbinical court of Minsk, the body in charge of running the debate, making the following request: since he was unable to respond to all the masses of Mitnagdim who had gathered in the city, let those who debated with him be only those capable of responding properly to questions he would ask them about passages in the Talmud. The rabbinical court acceded to this demand, with one caveat: the senior Mitnagdim would examine Rabbi Shneur Zalman about passages from the Talmud before he examined them. Before the debate the leaders of the Mitnagdim removed the ban under which they had placed the Hasidim in 5532. Moreover, they decreed that the day of the debate should be a day of fasting. Finally they determined which of them should be examined by Rabbi Shneur Zalman and what questions they would pose to him.

It is easy to guess that Rabbi Shneur Zalman astounded his examiners, and they were filled with wonder "at the depth of his intelligence, the power of his memory, and his erudition." However, when their turn came to answer his questions, they were struck dumb and asked to postpone the continuation of the debate until the following day. News of this development spread rapidly throughout the city, and the Mitnagdim were flustered. The next day the leaders of the Mitnagdim held a long consultation. Nevertheless, they were unable to answer the questions that Rabbi Shneur Zalman had posed to them. Hence they changed their strategy and demanded that he should respond to their objections and complaints regarding the ways of the Hasidim. Rabbi Shneur Zalman demanded that they fulfill their part of the bargain and answer his questions. An uproar broke out, and the debate came to an end. Many of the scholars among the Mitnagdim who witnessed the debate were deeply impressed by the great Torah knowledge of the Hasidic leader and became his followers. Rabbi Shneur Zalman's victory was complete.[57]

This is the story of the Minsk Debate as recounted by Rabbi Joseph Isaac. Rachel Elior, who published this document, devotes a detailed discussion to the question of its historical reliability. In addition to general reservations regarding Rabbi Joseph Isaac's historical writings, Elior raises three weighty considerations that cast doubt on the story.[58] First, no support for it is found in other sources, either of the Hasidim or the Mitnagdim. Second, there is a contradiction between the account of the Minsk Debate and the well-known fact that the Gaon condemned all contact with the Hasidim. Finally, in Rabbi Shneur Zalman's epistle of 5557 (1797) to his followers in Vilna, in which he describes the course of confrontations with Mitnagdim since 5532, there is no mention of the Minsk Debate.[59]

Strangely, despite these arguments against it, Elior tends not to deny the historical authenticity of the Minsk Debate. She bases her estimation on the fact that Rabbi Joseph Isaac attributes the story to a family tradition that came down to him from his ancestors. She also claims that "most of the people mentioned in the account of the Minsk Debate can be identified historically, and most of the facts can be reconciled." Therefore she concludes her discussion with the statement "There is no reason to doubt either the veracity of this account, including its historical details, or the likelihood that such a debate could have taken place. Perhaps the publication of this document will lead to confirmation of this episode by another source."[60]

As far as I know, no confirmation of this episode has been found in any other source whatsoever, and I greatly doubt that it will ever be found. As noted, Elior herself points out three considerations that cast doubt on the reliability of this story, and they seem sufficient. Furthermore, it is difficult to believe the story because some of its elements seem imaginary and inconsistent with the concepts of the period: for example, mention of the Hasidic Torah students who disguised themselves as Mitnagdim and attracted audiences with their sermons; the agreement of the Mitnagdim that the debate would open with a battle of brains based on passages of the Talmud; the failure of all the great scholars among the Mitnagdim, including the students of the Gaon, to answer the questions of Rabbi Shneur Zalman; and the astonishing fact that Rabbi Shneur Zalman waived a golden opportunity to respond to arguments of the Mitnagdim against the ways of Hasidism.[61]

On the basis of its contents, structure, and character, the story of the Minsk Debate appears to be hagiography intended to answer an ideological and psychological need of those who told and heard it. Not only did the persecuted Hasidim emerge from darkness into great light, and not only did Rabbi Shneur Zalman win the hearts of his listeners and beholders, but he also vanquished the Mitnagdim with their own weapon —great Torah learning. There could be no more miraculous ending to the Hasidic leader's victory march than his sweeping masses of students from the houses of study of the Mitnagdim into his court.

In a certain sense this story compensates the Hasidic collective memory for two other debates, one that took place and one that did not. The first is the Shklov Debate, which was held in the winter of 5532. As noted, from the Hasidic point of view this was a traumatic event. The Hasidim were unpersuasive in their responses to the accusations leveled against them by the leaders of the Shklov community. For that reason the rabbis of Shklov wrote to the Gaon that the Hasidim were heretics, and the

Gaon adopted their position. Moreover, after their failure to justify the ways of the Hasidim, the Hasidim who took part in that debate were exposed to injurious behavior on the part of the leaders of Shklov. Rabbi Shneur Zalman's letters show that the harsh memory of the failure in Shklov remained with him for decades.[62]

The debate that did not take place is mentioned in Rabbi Shneur Zalman's epistle of 5557 (1797) to his followers in Vilna.[63] As mentioned above, the Hasidim feared the renewal of the persecutions and asked their rabbi to come to Vilna and debate with the Gaon or his representatives and, in that way, bring an end to the controversy. Rabbi Shneur Zalman responded that there was no chance of implementing such a plan, because the Gaon was firm in his refusal to acknowledge that the Hasidim were right or to permit reconciliation with them. In this epistle as well, Rabbi Shneur Zalman mentions the failed debate in Shklov. According to him, it would not be difficult to respond to the challenges of the Mitnagdim, and they had made adequate responses in Shklov, but the Mitnagdim were unwilling to listen.

Thus the debate in Shklov was an utter failure, and the debate that the Hasidim of Vilna wished to hold never took place. Against the background of these disappointments, the miraculous outcome of the Minsk Debate stands out as a glorious victory for the Hasidim, emotional compensation to the collective memory for past suffering. Furthermore, this story also constitutes a statement regarding the status of Habad Hasidim within Haredi society during the first half of the twentieth century. Rabbi Shneur Zalman's proven greatness and wisdom in knowledge of Torah were the spiritual dowry by means of which Rabbi Joseph Isaac sought to strengthen the position of Habad Hasidism over and above other groups of Hasidism and against Lithuanian Torah scholarship.

THE REBBE JOSEPH ISAAC ON HASIDIM, MITNAGDIM, AND MASKILIM

Rabbi Joseph Isaac's historical accounts with the opponents of Hasidism were not settled by proving Rabbi Shneur Zalman's greatness as a Torah scholar. Another argument, whose polemical sting was far greater, was the failure of the Mitnagdim in the struggle against Haskalah.[64] In this matter as well, Rabbi Joseph Isaac offered his readers detailed and colorful accounts containing a mixture of reality and imagination. We shall examine his main points here.

Following the abolition of the Council of the Four Lands in Poland (1764), the senior rabbis decided to place the yoke of community leadership on the shoulders of exceptional individuals. The Gaon was chosen to lead the community of Vilna, though he did not wish to do so: "he was forced to accept the crown of guiding the community." The Gaon not only possessed genius in Torah studies, he also loved the sciences. Furthermore, he believed that science was a vital means for understanding the Torah. Therefore, not only did he himself toil to acquire scientific knowledge, but he also ordered his disciples to translate portions of the Gentiles' books into the holy tongue so that general knowledge would increase among the Jews.

"In the greatness of his righteousness and innocence," the Gaon underestimated the danger entailed in the acquisition of secular knowledge. Consequently he unwittingly caused the penetration of Berlin Haskalah within Vilna. This is how it happened: the Gaon and his associates regretted the lack of a Yiddish translation of the Torah with the addition of "an easily understood explanation . . . accessible to all." When news came to them that in Berlin "there was an erudite scholar of Torah, scrupulous in [keeping] the commandments, who had translated the Pentateuch into the German tongue in clear language," they sent five choice students to this scholar, named Mendelssohn, so they could get to know him. The students remained in Berlin for a long time. They copied pages of Mendelssohn's translation of the Torah and brought them back to the associates of the Gaon in Vilna. These recommended the work to the Gaon, "and with his permission Torah scholars were assigned to make several dozen copies of it and distribute them among people familiar with books, so they would set times to teach it in public before the multitude."

This innocent initiative had disastrous results: "dozens of Torah scholars with excellent talents in the houses of study of Vilna, Shklov, Slutzk, Brisk, and Minsk [began] to drag their legs to Berlin and to study the German language and the science of medicine and the science of engineering." Thus the Haskalah of Berlin penetrated the bastions of Torah in Lithuania. While the Gaon and his associates, in their great innocence, were introducing choice young scholars of Lithuania to Haskalah, the Hasidic leaders knew what lay before them and were properly cautious. This should not be surprising to us, for the Ba'al Shem Tov himself issued a timely warning on this subject. As early as 5503 (1743) the Ba'al Shem Tov gathered his greatest disciples and told them that in one of the cities of Germany there was a scribe named Rabbi Menahem, who was "God-fearing and a great scholar." That man had a talented son, and his father studied Torah with him. But that Rabbi Menahem did not believe in Kabbalah, and he spoke disdainfully to his son about the Holy Zohar. Those words had a bad influence on the lad's faith. When the publication of latter's commentary became widely known, the Hasidic leaders quickly forbade study of that work. To strengthen that prohibition, they also forbade the study of grammar and insisted that the Pentateuch must be studied only with Rashi's commentary.[65]

As noted, Rabbi Joseph Isaac's account is a strange mixture of historical fact with imaginary events. Certain aspects of this topic have been examined above, in the discussion of the Gaon and Haskalah.[66] Here, I shall briefly present the main points. The Gaon believed that knowledge of the sciences should be acquired as an auxiliary for Torah study. This position was adopted by several of his disciples and the idea persisted among a small segment of Torah scholars in Lithuania after his death. However, the claim that the Gaon worked to disseminate Mendelssohn's "commentary" in Lithuania is groundless. Similarly, there is no basis to the claim that the Haskalah movement arose in Lithuania in direct connection with the Gaon. When the first signs of Haskalah arose in eastern Europe, during the first decades of the nineteenth century, there was a clear difference between the response of the Mitnagdim and that of the Hasidim. While the Mitnagdim were ready to support a balanced and controlled mixture of Torah and secular knowledge, the Hasidic leaders objected to this phenomenon absolutely.[67]

These historical facts apparently nourished Rabbi Joseph Isaac's claim that the Gaon and his disciples were to be blamed for the penetration of

Haskalah into Lithuania. However, when he set about proving this severe accusation, he treated the facts with freedom. A prime example of this fanciful presentation of the facts is his dating of the struggle between the maskilim and the Hasidim in eastern Europe several decades too early. He says, "The maskilim waged an aggressive war" against the Hasidim from the mid-1760s! Habad Hasidim were thus stricken doubly: "for they suffered on the one hand from the maskilim and on the other from the Mitnagdim." From here it is not a long step to present both of these enemies of Hasidism as interconnected: "The reader's hair will stand on end when he reads the literature of the maskilim and the literature of the Mitnagdim, which was mainly written by maskilim who hate the Jewish religion and deny the sanctity of the Torah and the Creator."[68]

In sum, the anachronistic projection of the struggle between maskilim and those faithful to the tradition in eastern Europe back to the latter decades of the eighteenth century enabled Rabbi Joseph Isaac to ignore the true struggle that took place in those years: the war of the Mitnagdim against the Hasidim. Thus he is able to exempt the Gaon from the judgment of history for his groundless persecution of the Hasidim, but at the same time he blames him for the penetration of Haskalah into Russia, a sin of which he was not guilty. The advantage that Rabbi Joseph Isaac gains by presenting this picture of the past was double: he clears Hasidism of the accusation of heresy that the Gaon had cast on it, and he fortifies the status of the Hasidim as leaders in the struggle against Haskalah. This picture of the past suits Rabbi Joseph Isaac's position as a fierce opponent of any compromise with modernity.[69]

YEHOSHUA MONDSHINE: A PLOT OF THE *PARNASIM* AND THE WEAKNESS OF THE VILNA GAON

Recently an author identified with Habad Hasidism has addressed the question of opposition to Hasidism once again. The man in question is Yehoshua Mondshine, an important scholar and prolific writer who has contributed greatly to the study of Hasidism both by publishing important documents and by clarifying textual and bibliographical problems.

However, when he examines a historical issue such as the one under discussion here, he identifies clearly with the Hasidic trend to which he is connected. This identification distorts his critical sense to such a degree that one may view Mondshine's historical writing as another example of Habad historiography.

Mondshine presents his view of the motives that underlay opposition to Hasidism in a chapter of his *Kerem Ḥabad*.[70] That chapter is preceded by three chapters that also deal with opposition to Hasidism. In the first of these, Mondshine argues against the claim of the Mitnagdim that the Hasidim introduced changes in ritual. His counterclaim is that the Gaon himself, in his rulings and customs, deviated from accepted practice. Later in this chapter Mondshine responds to the argument that the Hasidim neglected Torah study. In this matter as well, he points an accusatory finger at the Gaon: whereas Rabbi Shneur Zalman of Lyady forbade secular study, even for someone who had studied all of Torah, the Vilna Gaon encouraged his students to acquire secular knowledge.[71] In the second of these chapters Mondshine presents examples showing that the Mitnagdim distorted and mangled Hasidic texts they cited in their works.[72]

The third of these chapters is extremely important to our discussion. It is devoted to the struggle waged between the *kahal* and the rabbi in Vilna.[73] Mondshine presents many documents in order to prove that, in their struggle against the rabbi, the *parnasim* of Vilna acted with malice and did not eschew improper means for advancing their goals. In the author's words, "Judicial and administrative injustice became the norm in the congregation of Vilna."[74] This statement is meant to bolster his proposed account of opposition to Hasidism. His main point is that the struggle against Hasidism was not driven by religious motives and was not led by the Gaon. Those who initiated and led the persecution of the Hasidim were the corrupt *parnasim* of Vilna, who had political motives. The Gaon was nothing but a tool in the hands of those *parnasim*.

Mondshine's point of departure is the assumption that it is inconceivable that Hasidism should have been persecuted for religious reasons, for, to the best of his knowledge, there was no justification for such persecution. To strengthen this assumption he presents quotations from the epistle of Rabbi Shneur Zalman of Lyady, who complains bitterly about the ways of the Mitnagdim.[75] Since opposition to Hasidism cannot be explained on religious grounds, one is constrained to concede that this opposition was politically motivated.

Here is Mondshine's account of the events: Following the decision of the Polish monarchy in 1764 to abolish the Council of the Four Lands, community organization was weakened. In such circumstances the leadership tended "to repress any effort to rebel." Indeed, Mondshine concedes, "I would not define the Hasidim as an 'opposition' in the sense of proposing an alternative to the existing organization. . . . However, the consolidation of a group within the community had in itself always been objectionable to the community administration."[76] For that reason the *parnasim* of Vilna decided to meet the danger and fight the new movement. To that end they hatched a plot "to cast suspicion on the Hasidim of seceding from the community" and to present them as a "sect." To ensure the success of this scheme, the *parnasim* needed a Torah authority who would serve them as a fig leaf. This function was assigned to the Gaon. Since he lived in isolation, cloistered in his house, it was easy to mislead him with false witnesses.

The reader may be surprised to hear that the Gaon was such a naive man and so isolated that he could become a tool in the hands of the *parnasim.* Was he not aware of the terrible injustice being done to the Hasidim? Mondshine anticipates these questions by pointing to the Gaon's silence in the face of the dreadful injustices committed by the *parnasim* in their struggle with the rabbi. He explains that silence by stating that "the Vilna Gaon was isolated and shut up in his room, and he did not know what was happening in the city." If one insists that he must have known something, Mondshine replies: the Gaon benefited from generous financial support from the community, and he was afraid that if he confronted those who supported him, that support would cease.[77]

To bolster the picture he painted, Mondshine relies on the epistles of Rabbi Menahem Mendel of Vitebsk and Rabbi Shneur Zalman of Lyady, who repeatedly state that the Gaon acted under the influence of false witnesses. Mondshine interprets Rabbi Shneur Zalman's statement that the Mitnagdim rely on the Gaon's authority in the following manner: "The

[Hebrew] expression [used by Rabbi Shneur Zalman] 'hanging from a great tree,' which appears again and again in the writings of our venerable rabbi, proves that in his opinion there was no justification and no proof in attributing the harsh persecutions to the Vilna Gaon's opinion. That is merely an excuse."[78]

Mondshine summarizes the motives for the struggle against Hasidism with the following words: "We regard those events as a secular-political struggle, waged by the *parnasim* of the *kahal* in 5532 [1772], in their efforts to strengthen their rule at any cost, feeling that the ground was about to be swept from under their feet." Consequently, the Gaon was not the one who initiated and led the struggle against Hasidism. The *parnasim* were the ones who did so, and "they flaunted the Vilna Gaon and his signature, using him as an effective weapon."[79]

BETWEEN HASIDIC HISTORIOGRAPHY AND CRITICAL RESEARCH

Another characteristic of Mondshine's historical writing is his tendency to challenge scholars connected with the academy. As one who stands on the border of the academic world, contributing to it and drawing from it, he occasionally lashes out against a publication of which he does not approve. He is mainly concerned with studies in the field of Hasidism, in which he is an expert and personally involved.[80] Indeed, the chapter on opposition to Hasidism, surveyed above, was written as a polemical response to an article of my own. In that article I tried to show that the Gaon was the one who initiated and led the struggle against Hasidism, and that his motivations were decidedly religious.[81] Mondshine rejected the reconstruction of events that I proposed, both by proposing an alternative account and by challenging the evidence on which I depended.

Obviously an academic scholar is liable to err, and a historian associated with Hasidism can be correct.[82] Thus Mondshine's connection with Hasidism is not in itself evidence relevant to the truth of his account of events. In other words, only after his claims have been examined on their own merits may the tendentiousness of his writing be taken into account.

The question is whether the picture painted by Mondshine regarding the motives of the opposition to Hasidism can withstand criticism. Did he use valid arguments to refute the account presented in my article? This is not the place for a detailed discussion. Those interested may read my article and Mondshine's criticism and decide for themselves. However, it is impossible to let the matter pass with no further comment.

Let us begin with the *parnasim* of the Vilna community and their motives. The struggle between the community and the rabbi in Vilna is beyond the scope of this discussion. Nevertheless, it is difficult to accept the claim that a gang of corrupt *parnasim* stood at the head of the most important Jewish community in Lithuania. However, even if we assume for the sake of the argument that Mondshine is right about this, it is still surprising that such a vigorous and powerful *kahal* should have seen fit to hatch a plot against Hasidism. The view that Hasidism challenged the community establishment has long since been rejected.[83] Mondshine himself concedes that Hasidism did not constitute opposition to the community administration. Why, then, would the *kahal* perjure itself and deceive the greatest rabbi of the generation?

We cannot determine the exact number of Jews in Vilna who were drawn to Hasidism during the first years of its expansion. Nevertheless, it is difficult to imagine that in 5532, the year when the struggle broke out, their number exceeded a few dozen households.[84] Could it be that a few dozen men who prayed in a separate minyan and recited Psalm 136 before the blessing "Blessed be He who spoke and the world came into being" constituted a threat to the community administration? Furthermore, the first community to declare that the Hasidim were heretics was Shklov. Only after the Sages of Shklov wrote about this matter to the Gaon did he adopt their position, and only then did the community of Vilna begin the campaign against the Hasidim.[85] How does this fact square with the claim that the *parnasim* of Vilna hatched a plot? It must also be asked whether the leaders of the other communities who joined in the war against Hasidism were also evil and corrupt.

There is yet another problem: when relating to the phenomenon of opposition in their letters, why did the Hasidic leaders not state or even hint that the source of the evil was the band of corrupt *parnasim* of Vilna?

Rabbi Shneur Zalman repeatedly argued, as noted, that the Gaon led the struggle by force of his authority, and that the Mitnagdim depended on that authority. Unquestionably, if Rabbi Shneur Zalman had known that the Gaon was not hostile to Hasidism, and that he was merely a stalking horse for the conspiracies of the *parnasim,* he would have said so. Could it be that Rabbi Shneur Zalman did not know what Mondshine knows?

Furthermore, nothing in Rabbi Shneur Zalman's letters supports Mondshine's account. Indeed, they contain evidence that clearly contradicts it. Here is one example: in the epistle in which he debates Rabbi Abraham of Kalisk, Rabbi Shneur Zalman mentions that the *maggid* of Mezhirech was angry at him because he and the members of his band used "to mock Torah scholars and revile them, etc., and to stand with their head down and their feet up, etc., in the streets of Kalisk." Rabbi Shneur Zalman goes on to write that at the time of the Shklov Debate in the winter of 5532, Rabbi Abraham offered no response to these accusations. Following the debate, the sages of Shklov wrote to the Gaon, "so that they made it enter his heart to condemn [us] as rebels, perish the thought, and as Epicureans who revile Torah scholars."[86]

Here we have explicit testimony from Rabbi Shneur Zalman himself regarding the correct sequence of events: the Mitnagdim found severe flaws in the religious behavior of the Hasidim of Kalisk; these accusations had a basis in fact; following the failure of the Hasidic leader to justify these deviant phenomena, the sages of Shklov addressed the Gaon; in the wake of their action and under its influence, and on the basis of decidedly religious considerations, the Gaon determined that the Hasidim were heretics and that they must be persecuted. Here we have neither corrupt *parnasim* nor perjurious witnesses, nor do we have an old man shut up in his room who does not know right from left. We have instead an outstanding example of a radical group of Hasidim whose aberrant behavior was interpreted by the sages of Shklov and by the Gaon as severe religious deviance.[87]

Here is another example: as noted, Rabbi Shneur Zalman sought to explain the Gaon's motives to his Hasidim. Among other things, he told them that a rumor had reached the Gaon regarding a Hasidic interpretation of a passage in the Zohar, and that that interpretation was viewed as deviant. Although Rabbi Shneur Zalman argued that the version of the interpretation sent to the Gaon was incorrect, it is clear from his words that the Gaon acted on his own initiative and from religious considerations. Moreover, his later remarks make it clear that there was a difference of opinion between the Gaon and the Hasidim regarding the understanding of Kabbalistic ideas. As Rabbi Shneur Zalman writes: "In any case it did not occur [to the Gaon] that perhaps the word of God was with them according to Elijah [the Prophet] of blessed memory, to strip away the corporeality that is in the Holy Zohar in a manner that is hidden and beyond his understanding."[88] That is to say, the Gaon found it difficult to believe that the Hasidim had received a revelation from Elijah the Prophet, according to which they had interpreted the Zohar in a manner different from his own. This might refer to the way in which the Hasidim understood the Kabbalistic principle "There is no place vacant of Him."[89] In any event, this was certainly a theological controversy. Furthermore, later in that letter Rabbi Shneur Zalman mentions the controversy between the Gaon and Hasidim regarding the degree of sanctity of the ARI's Kabbalah: the Gaon "does not believe in the Kabbalah of the ARI of blessed memory in general, that it is all from the mouth of Elijah [the Prophet] of blessed memory . . . and that there is any obligation to believe in it"; whereas the Hasidim believe that the entire Kabbalah of the ARI is, in fact, from the mouth of Elijah the Prophet.[90] Here we have explicit testimony that the tension between the Gaon and the Hasidim derived at least in part from a controversy regarding Kabbalah.

All the polemical writings against the Hasidim that were sent from Vilna and Brod in 5532 revolve around matters of religious conduct.[91] Is it conceivable that all the arguments included in these writings are merely a mask for a struggle whose motives were political? For these arguments, or at least the greater part of them, relate to well-known facts. Can it be denied that the Hasidim changed the wording of the prayers and established separate minyanim of their own? Is there any doubt that the Hasidim adopted an enthusiastic style of prayer expressed in abrupt movements and raising of the voice? One could go on listing the innovations introduced by the Hasidim in divine worship that aroused the ire of the Mitnagdim. However, Mondshine finds it difficult to agree that these changes were the cause that justified persecution of the Hasidim.

By contrast, the critical historian must understand the minds of all the parties involved in the conflict. The picture that emerges from that effort is of course more complex: the Hasidim believed that, because they preferred the ARI's version of the prayer book to the traditional Ashkenazic version, their prayers were more effective. By contrast, the Mitnagdim regarded the Hasidim as people who "changed the version established by the Sages" and claimed a high authority of which they were unworthy. What the Hasidim regarded as enthusiastic prayer that broke through the firmament appeared to the Mitnagdim as frenzied prayer, and so on.

As noted, Mondshine sought to refute the conclusions of my article by challenging the reliability of the sources that I used to support them. Here are his words:

> A comparison of my proposed explanation to the method found in I. Etkes shows that our ways are entirely different. . . . This is because of the documents on which each approach relies; I employed historical documents that reflect factually the customs and methods used in the battle by the *kahal* of Vilna in those years, as well as the letters of the Rebbe, Rabbi Shneur Zalman of Lyady, using words that are not tendentious. . . . In contrast, I could not rely on the polemical writings that issued from the circles of Mitnagdim, for the tendency of all those publications—by their very nature—was only to justify their war, "to dress injustice in the cloak of justice."[92]

My lack of objectivity is thus expressed in my use of, among other things, Mitnagdic sources. Thus, for example, Mondshine objects to the trust I placed in article six of the collection, *Zemir 'Aritsim Veḥarvot Tsurim*, for by virtue of its being a Mitnagdic document it cannot be trustworthy.[93] Arguments of this kind reflect an erroneous assumption regarding objectivity. In a controversy like the one under discussion, one does not expect the sources to be "objective." Naturally the documents of both sides reflect their point of view and are intended to serve their ends. The scholar must examine all the sources available in critical and balanced fashion and evaluate the degree of objective truth they contain. This is what I did, to the best of my ability, with respect to both Hasidic and Mitnagdic sources. Moreover, I was pleased to discover that insofar as the facts themselves were discussed, the Hasidic and Mitnagdic sources confirm and complement each other. By contrast, according to Mondshine,

Rabbi Shneur Zalman's letters are worthy of trust, whereas the writings of Mitnagdim are invalid.

Mondshine also accuses other scholars of lacking objectivity. In his opinion they treat the sources with partiality because they cast doubt on Hasidic sources while depending without reservation on Mitnagdic sources.[94] In a "personal confession" with which he concludes the chapter, Mondshine alludes to the conclusion he seeks to reach: "Like many of my predecessors, I, too, am not objective. But unlike them, I admit to this charge. I request of my readers: please try yourselves to be objective."[95] That is to say, there are no objective scholars, and there is no objective research. Just as he himself tends to identify with a certain part in the controversy, so too, in his opinion, do other scholars prefer one side or another. All that remains is for readers to judge which of the tendentious versions is more convincing.

Mondshine draws conclusions about others from his own case. As one for whom the historical controversy between Hasidim and Mitnagdim remains an issue with existential significance, it is difficult for him to imagine the psychological distance with which a critical scholar approaches the subject of his or her research. Hence he suspects me of belonging to the Mitnagdim. In point of fact, the critical scholar is also liable to err. The naive view that it is possible to deal with history with complete objectivity has long since faded away. However, there is a great difference between a scholar committed to discovery of the truth and to striving for it—aware of his or her limitations and of the relative character of historical research—and a scholar bound by religious or ideological commitment who declares that no research can be objective. That difference is conspicuous when one compares Mondshine's discussion of history to that of a critical scholar.

APOLOGETICS, HARMONIZATION, AND INTENTIONAL FORGETFULNESS

The struggle against Hasidism in general, and the role played by the Gaon in that struggle in particular, has continued to preoccupy many and various writers from the end of the nineteenth century until the present. I refer only to writers who are not critical historians and whose concern with the subject is marked by an emotional and ideological affiliation. Some of these writers are connected with Hasidism, and others with Lithuanian Torah scholarship; some are modern orthodox, others are Haredi. What all have in common is the effort to paint a picture of the past with which they can identify.

Three principal tendencies are discernible in the works of these writers: apologetics, harmonization, and purposeful forgetfulness. I will briefly characterize these three tendencies:

1. The apologetic trend argues that the Mitnagdim, led by the Gaon, did indeed struggle against the Hasidim, but that that struggle had a positive influence on Hasidism itself. Had it not been for that struggle, the Hasidim might have strayed from the straight and narrow.
2. The harmonistic trend argues that the struggle between Hasidim and Mitnagdim was a spiritual and doctrinal struggle between two trends within Judaism. The leaders of both groups honored their opposite numbers, even learned from one another, and were positively influenced.
3. The tendency toward intentional forgetfulness seeks to ignore the struggle waged by the Gaon and the Mitnagdim against Hasidism during the last decades of the eighteenth century, either by arguing that it cannot or should not be discussed or by overlooking it completely.

Naturally this list does not exhaust the range of varied positions taken by the writers who have dealt with this topic. Nevertheless, it helps us to map the various directions in which these writers turned. Let us now survey several examples of the three trends. Since I have already noted the approach taken by writers with a Hasidic orientation, I shall devote the following discussion to authors who had an affinity with the Lithuanian school of Torah scholarship and various other types of orthodox Judaism.

A typical expression of the apologetic trend can be found in *Meqor Barukh* by Rabbi Barukh Epstein (1860–1941),[96] who also wrote the commentary on the Pentateuch known as *Torah Temima.* He belonged to a family of prominent Lithuanian Torah scholars. His father, Rabbi Yehiel Mikhal Halevi Epstein, was famous for his Halakhic work, *'Arukh Hashulhan.* The NATSIV (Naphtali Tsvi Yehuda Berlin) of Volozhin was his uncle and later became his brother-in-law. *Meqor Barukh* contains stories and traditions about the author's ancestors; passages of personal memoirs, mainly from the time of his studies in the Volozhin yeshiva; innovative interpretations of Jewish law; and philosophical and historical remarks.[97]

Rabbi Barukh Epstein presents his defense of the Gaon by citing the Hasidic leader Rabbi Menahem Mendel Schneersohn, the third Habad rebbe, known as Hatsemah Tsedek. The author of *Meqor Barukh* describes in detail a monthlong visit that his father had made to the court of the Hasidic leader. During that visit his father heard the following words from Hatsemah Tsedek:

> I shall reveal to you in this matter what has been buried and hidden in my heart forever, . . . and I have never revealed it to anyone . . . except for my father-in-law and my grandfather-in-law, may their souls rest in peace [these are "The Old Rabbi," Rabbi Shneur Zalman of Lyady, and his son the middle rebbe]: and this is that our fellows . . . do not know and are unable to estimate the value and the great benefit and great grace that the Vilna Gaon did for us in disagreeing with us. . . . Because were it not for that controversy, there would have been reason and place to worry and fear that the new system that we paved for ourselves . . . would slowly lead us, step-by-step, forward beyond the border meant for the Torah heritage and the commandments. . . . For by virtue of the power of enthusiasm and fervor of the soul and elevation of spirit in the course of the new system that gripped the hearts of its creators in a storm, . . . in the end the talmudic spirit might have been burned in the flame of the fire of Kabbalah, and that hidden Torah would have diminished most of the figure of the manifest Torah, and the practical commandments might have been cast down in their value before the burning excitement of the secret intentions.[98]

Rabbi Barukh Epstein, or if you will, the rebbe of Habad, knows nothing about the accusations lodged by the Gaon and his followers that Hasidism was heretical. According to him, the error of the Hasidim was limited to violation of the delicate equilibrium between the manifest Torah and the hidden Torah, and between intention and punctilious observance of the commandments. This disequilibrium was indeed liable to end badly, but by virtue of the war that the Gaon waged against them, the Hasidim were saved from a dangerous deviation and returned to the proper balance between the various components of divine worship.

There is a great distance between the view of Rabbi Shneur Zalman—that the brutal aggressiveness of the Mitnagdim led many thousands of Jews to acknowledge the correctness of Hasidism—and the views attributed by Rabbi Barukh Epstein to the third rebbe in the Habad dynasty, namely, that the Gaon and the Mitnagdim had a good influence on Hasidism. Did Rabbi Yehiel Epstein really hear such things from the mouth of Rabbi Menahem Mendel Schneersohn? It is difficult to assume that Rabbi Barukh Epstein or his father invented these things out of whole cloth. Nevertheless, it is doubtful that a Hasidic leader went so far as to express gratitude to the man who led the war against Hasidism. Most likely, Rabbi Menahem Mendel Schneersohn did speak in praise of the Gaon before his "Lithuanian" guest. However, the wording and tone of his remarks as they appear in *Meqor Barukh* reflect the point of view of the Mitnagdim. While the picture painted by Rabbi Barukh Epstein regarding the struggle between Mitnagdim and Hasidim is conciliatory and soft, the price for conciliation is exacted from the Hasidim. They are called on to admit that the Gaon did them a favor by fighting them.

A later example of the apologetic trend is found in an article on the Gaon by Yesh'ayahu Wolfsberg-Avi'ad, published in the mid-1950s.[99] Yesh'ayahu Wolfsberg-Avi'ad (1893–1957) was born in Germany and educated in the neo-orthodox spirit of *Torah 'im derekh eretz.* He made a serious study of not only medicine but also history and philosophy. While still in Germany he was active in the religious Zionist movement, and he remained involved in it after moving to Palestine in 1934. Wolfsberg was prominent as a thinker who wrote about various issues in the fields of Judaism and the philosophy of history.[100]

Wolfsberg's article on the Gaon can be called a biographical essay combining objective and detached observation with unreserved admiration. He portrays the Gaon's asceticism in vivid hues. He then goes on to praise this asceticism, for by means of it the Gaon was capable of fulfilling his historical mission:

> This ascetic feature of Rabbi Eliyahu reflected the need of the hour. Many events, currents, and movements had led to a degree of collapse in the life of the people. . . . Sabbateanism and various other messianic movements, which proclaimed false messiahs, distorted the spirit of the people in the Diaspora. The advent of Hasidism changed the approach to worship and to several fundamental problems. On the other hand, Haskalah was emerging and casting doubt on traditional faith, harming sacred values. In order to prepare the masses of Jews to continue on the traditional path, to restore the Hasidic movement to renewed respect for the study of Torah, and in order to confront Haskalah, . . . there was an immense need for the appearance of such a severe personality, exalted, concentrated without compromise, and fearless, like the Gaon.[101]

Wolfsberg does not speak at length about the danger inherent in Hasidism but contents himself with a hint that it had depreciated the study of Torah. Nevertheless, it is clear that, along with other currents, Hasidism threatened the authority and integrity of the tradition. In those circumstances, a "severe" personality, "without compromise," such as that of the Gaon, was needed to fortify Judaism.

A fine example of the trend toward harmonization can be found in *Zikhron Ya'akov* by Ya'aqov Lifschitz (1838–1921). In truth, a considerable part of Lifschitz's writing about Mitnagdim and Hasidim could be called apologetics for the Gaon and the Mitnagdim. However, in the conclusion of his discussion, he strives for balance and points out the benefits gained by both camps from their involvement in the controversy. This complicated attitude suits both Lifschitz's personal background and the public mission that he took on himself. Having grown up and been educated in the spirit of Lithuanian Torah scholarship, Lifschitz tended to identify with that faction. However, he was also an orthodox functionary who valued cooperation among the various factions of "true believing Jews" in response to the challenges of modernity. Thus his effort to present a harmonious and conciliatory picture of the controversy is understandable.[102]

What impelled the Gaon and other leaders of the Mitnagdim to attack Hasidim? The detailed discussion that Lifschitz devotes to this question is influenced almost entirely by the polemics of Rabbi Ḥayyim of Volozhin against Hasidism.[103] That is to say, we are not dealing here with a sect whose ways of worshiping God were suspect of heresy, but rather with people whose "intentions were for the sake of heaven" and whose religious aspirations were basically holy. However, in their path and in the implementation of these aspirations the Hasidim erred and deviated from the straight and narrow. Following Rabbi Ḥayyim, Lifschitz protests the Hasidim's criticism of the scholarly elite:

> And how grave is this matter, if people who have not been educated fully in Torah . . . learn a lesson from the new Hasidism and say that the study of Torah that is customary among scholars is not at all for its own sake and is worth nothing, [that] fear of punishment without fear of the Exalted One is worth nothing at all, [and that] the performing of a commandment without intention and devotion, they have no value or use at all.[104]

Against the Hasidic criticism of Torah scholars Lifschitz presents the response of the "Rabbis and Geonim," also in the spirit of Rabbi Ḥayyim:

> Indeed love and fear of God, and devotion to Him and study of Torah for its own sake, these are explicit positive commandments in the Torah; . . . but the essence of the commandment to study Torah is first of all the labor, the effort, and the wisdom to know it; . . . but by practicing this severity of "for its own sake" in love and devotion, as a primary obligation above all the scholars of Torah might, perish the thought, bring weakness in the study of Torah, might bring, perish the thought, ignorance and crassness.[105]

In sum, Hasidism's excessive emphasis on the spiritual dimension of the worship of God, so much so as to deny the value of a religious act without proper intention, was erroneous and dangerous. Lifschitz attributes to the leaders of the Mitnagdim—in contrast to Hasidic radicalism, which demanded all or nothing at all—the view that elevation in divine worship is a gradual process.[106]

These are Lifschitz's main points regarding the motivations of the Gaon and the other leaders of the Mitnagdim. It is evident that he completely ignored the true character of the struggle against the Hasidim during the last decades of the eighteenth century, for he describes it as a spiritual and doctrinal controversy, as, during the first decades of the nineteenth century, it in fact appears to be. After defending the Gaon before the tribunal of history, Lifschitz makes way for a festival of reconciliation:

> But in the end the basis and essence of the controversy between the two sides was only for the sake of heaven, . . . for in truth this very controversy brought great benefit to both sides, to Hasidism, which greatly influenced the Mitnagdim, and introduced the flow of the life of the soul for them: . . . [it influenced them] to combine thought and devotion with performing commandments, . . . and to remove some of the sadness that dwells like a heavy cloud on their faces, and to be perfectionists in enhancing the commandments; . . . and on the other hand, the mighty and vigorous opposition of the Geonim who were Mitnagdim, the proclamations and the bans and the threats that were publicized halted the excessive current, . . . and had they not employed such severe means, the enthusiasm of the Hasidim of "5530" would have gone on and burst through all boundaries and borders.[107]

Lifschitz adds to the positive influence exerted by the Hasidim and Mitnagdim on each other until the differences between them are nearly effaced. He concludes his discussion of the topic with an eloquent and self-satisfied statement, one entirely imbued with reconciliation and love: "Behold, everyone who now hears about what happened before and listens to the words of truth and peace that are now uttered like the divine voice from Mount Horeb will readily confess that they embody the principle of 'love truth and peace,' and may peace be upon all of Israel."[108]

Another author who sought to present the relations between Hasidism and its opponents in the light of reconciliation and mutual respect is Rabbi Yehuda Leib Maimon, though his remarks also partake of both apologetics and intentional forgetfulness. In his comprehensive work on the Gaon, Maimon chooses not to treat the topic of the struggle against Hasidism,[109] justifying that decision as follows:

> I do not wish to return to the matter of the controversy between the Mitnagdim and the Hasidim when it first broke out. If only we could com-

> pletely erase this episode from history books; for my part, it is clear that the great rabbis on both sides who led the controversy were not at all guilty of the split that was produced between Hasidim and Mitnagdim. The guilt falls mainly on a single man in that generation, Avigdor of Pinsk, who gave himself the title of rabbi. It was he who inflamed that controversy by means of false and lying accusations. He even brought the Vilna Gaon into this controversy.[110]

Like Lifschitz, Maimon, too, begins by defending the Gaon. True, he is aware of the grievous character of the controversy "when it first broke out." However, the controversy is not worthy of description, for it was based on an error. Maimon again brings forward the well-known argument that the Gaon was deceived by false information transmitted to him. His innovation at this point is the accusation against Rabbi Avigdor of Pinsk, who was active in the struggle against the Hasidim. However, his involvement in the struggle began only in the 1790s, more than two decades after the campaign against Hasidism was begun under the leadership of the Gaon.[111]

As proof that the controversy was unnecessary, Maimon mentions the closeness between the Hasidim and the Gaon. Though he opposed Hasidism, "he himself behaved with great piety *[ḥasidut]*." Not only did the Gaon study Kabbalah extensively, but his disciples and intimates also told marvelous stories about him, like those told by the Hasidim about their rebbes. The Hasidic leaders, too, revered and honored the Gaon. Thus, for example, even Rabbi Shneur Zalman of Lyady admitted that he was the greatest sage of the generation. Maimon concludes his discussion of this topic with his own words of praise for the Gaon: "Indeed this was the great strength of the Vilna Gaon, that he was able to unite the exoteric and the esoteric so that they would complement one another and not vie with each other; the leaders of Hasidism at that time knew and felt this, and they revered him and sanctified him as a Sage of secret doctrine, although he opposed Hasidism and their opinions."[112] Ironically, the Gaon himself bridged the gap between the warring camps, for he embodied and symbolized the spiritual and religious ideal with which both Mitnagdim and Hasidim could identify.

An outstanding representative of the trend toward intentional forgetfulness is Bezalel Landau (1923–96), the author of *Hagaon heḥasid miVilna.*[113] Landau lived and was active within the Haredi community of Jerusalem, and during the decades before his death he was prominent as a journalist, author, and teacher. His journalistic and historical writings are marked by contemporary Haredi ideology, which is to say an uncompromising struggle against secular Jews and secularism. Naturally that struggle necessitated closing ranks and overcoming internecine controversies. Therefore, there is no reason to recall forgotten episodes that could interfere with the unity of the camp. Not surprisingly, Landau devotes an entire chapter to the Gaon's struggle against Haskalah,[114] a struggle that never took place, whereas he did not devote even a single page to the Gaon's campaign against Hasidism.

In a sense Landau is following in the footsteps of Rabbi Joseph Isaac Schneersohn, who, as noted, dated the struggle against Haskalah several decades before it happened. Whereas the Hasidic historian accused the Gaon of inadvertently paving the way for the penetration of Haskalah into Lithuania, Landau portrays him as standing at the barricades and battling fiercely against maskilim. For both writers, Haskalah served as a kind of veil to conceal the war against Hasidism that took place in those years.

Landau does in fact devote one sentence to the struggle against Hasidism: "In his day the Vilna Gaon waged a vigorous ideological struggle against the Hasidic movement." However, even these words are meant only to enhance the praises of the Gaon, as we see from the rest of the sentence: "But even the great leaders of Hasidism did not challenge the Vilna Gaon's status among the Halakhic authorities who are followed by all of the House of Israel."[115] Landau then presents words spoken or written by Hasidic leaders about the Gaon's distinction, quotations that clearly have been taken out of context. Thus, for example, Landau quotes Rabbi Shneur Zalman of Lyady as saying that the Gaon was "unique in his generation." However, he ignores the rabbi's main point, which is that, even though the Gaon was "unique in his generation," he does not have the authority to issue Halakhic rulings against the Hasidim.

Distortion of the historical picture with respect to the relations between the Gaon and the Hasidim reaches its peak in Landau's description of the response of the Hasidim to the Gaon's death. After that event, rumors were rife among the Mitnagdim that the Hasidim were rejoicing at their grief. As a result, persecution of Hasidim was renewed in Vilna, assuming a character of unprecedented cruelty. However, all that Landau mentions in this context is that the Gaon's passing "also made an impression among the Hasidim, with whom he had been involved in a vigorous ideological struggle."[116]

The policy of intentional forgetfulness adopted by Landau is not at all surprising. In the introduction to his book, he reveals that the original manuscript of the book included chapters "on the campaign against the Hasidic movement." Moreover, he states that regarding that topic "there is much dispute," and the chapters he wrote "could shed light on a number of obscure points."[117] Nevertheless, he chose to suppress those chapters, apparently to enable the Gaon to assume his proper place among the great rabbis with whom the Haredi community, in all its varieties and tendencies, can identify. To that end, the Gaon had to lose his image as a zealous warrior against Hasidism. Landau set out to assist him in this task and did his work faithfully.

CONCLUSION

In the first part of this chapter I treated the response of the Hasidim to the struggle waged against them by the Mitnagdim. The character of the available sources constrained me to limit the discussion to the Hasidic leaders' responses, mainly that of Rabbi Shneur Zalman of Lyady. Ordinary Hasidim most probably had responses inconsistent with the position of the leaders, as is indicated by the efforts of Rabbi Shneur Zalman to restrain his followers. The Hasidic leaders, who bore heavy public responsibility, probably responded as they did on the basis of considerations of which ordinary Hasidim were not always aware. In any case, in view of the harsh persecution they underwent, it is impossible not to be impressed by the restraint and self-control exhibited by the Hasidic leaders.

The response of these leaders to opposition was characterized by a position that had been formulated at the start of the controversy, under the inspiration of the *maggid* of Mezhirech: a strategy of restraint, meaning a conscious decision to avoid belligerent responses. Underlying this position was probably apprehension that aggressive responses might exacerbate the conflict and lead to the expulsion of the Hasidim from the Jewish people.

The strategy of restraint entailed taking an ambivalent position toward the leaders of the Mitnagdim, chiefly the Vilna Gaon. This ambivalence was expressed by rejection of all the accusations leveled against them and laying full blame for the continuation of the controversy on the leaders of the Mitnagdim. On the other hand, the Hasidim recognized the moral and religious authority of those leaders. That recognition was predicated on the repeated claim that the Gaon and the other Mitnagdic leaders had been deceived by false witnesses and were acting in good faith.

This complex position was first expressed in the letters that Rabbi Menahem Mendel of Vitebsk sent to the leaders of the communities of Poland and Lithuania from the land of Israel. It persisted in the epistles of Rabbi Shneur Zalman of Lyady, who repeatedly singled out the Gaon as the leader in the struggle against Hasidism by virtue of his authority, and as the one who obstructed any possibility of reconciliation. The sharpest expression of the view that the Gaon bore responsibility for the suffering of the Hasidim is found in his letter to Rabbi Phinehas Horowitz. There, Rabbi Shneur Zalman described the Gaon as the man who "permitted the shedding of our blood like water." However, along with these grave reproaches, Rabbi Shneur Zalman made a conspicuous and tireless effort to defend the Gaon and to present him as acting on the basis of legitimate considerations. The arguments justifying the Gaon became more varied as the years went by and circumstances changed. At first Rabbi Shneur Zalman repeated the claim that the Gaon had been deceived by false witnesses. In addition he made an effort to explain the Gaon's thinking on the basis of that false information. After his release from prison, Rabbi Shneur Zalman was able to praise the Gaon for not supporting the denunciation of rivals to the authorities. A few years after the Gaon's death, Rabbi Shneur Zalman attributed the cessation of persecution to the virtue of the Gaon's Torah.

The ambivalent character of Rabbi Shneur Zalman's response to opposition was not limited to his attitude toward the Gaon. In the late 1790s Hasidism had succeeded in taking root and had even gained strength despite the persistence of the controversy, and Rabbi Shneur Zalman interpreted the struggle against Hasidism in general as a manifestation of divine grace. The vociferous attacks of the Mitnagdim on the Hasidim impelled many people to inquire into the nature of Hasidism, to realize that its way was correct, and to join its ranks. As far as I know, this was the first expression of the dialectical view to find positive aspects in the phenomenon of opposition.

Hasidic leaders' recognition of the Gaon's authority, their willingness to speak in his defense, and their respect for his honor all derived, as noted, from practical considerations. Moreover, this attitude filled a deep psychological need in the Hasidim themselves. By declaring that the Gaon acted in honest error and innocence, they removed a great stain from Hasidism: the fact that the leading scholar of his generation had regarded them as heretics.

The question of the relationship of the Gaon to Hasidism continued to trouble Hasidim even in the first decades of the nineteenth century. Seeking to influence the attitude of Mitnagdim to Hasidism, the author of *Maẓref Ha'avodah* took up the issue again. He now legitimized the Gaon's unintentional error, which had been noted by the Hasidic leaders in the previous generation, by mentioning the important precedents of similar errors in earlier controversies. He also invoked the authority of Rabbi Ḥayyim of Volozhin in order to counterbalance the negative attitude of the Gaon toward Hasidism. An important argument already included in the words of Rabbi Shneur Zalman was now developed considerably: opposition to Hasidism was portrayed as a result of divine providence. It became a kind of veil meant to cover and hide the divine light that shone forth and sparkled in Hasidism.

I devoted a considerable part of this discussion to the manner in which Habad historiography has dealt with the topic of opposition to Hasidism, specifically noting the way Habad historians have depicted the past struggle between Hasidim and Mitnagdim. I focused on three prominent examples: *Beit Rabi* by Ḥayyim Meir Heilmann; the historical writings of Rabbi Joseph Isaac Schneersohn; and a chapter from a work by Yehoshua Mondshine.

Heilmann remained faithful to the facts as they appeared in the many documents that he presented in his work, although those documents specifically express the Hasidic point of view. He blunted the barb of opposition by interpreting the controversy as being "for the sake of heaven" and claiming that secret reasons underlay it. He deepened the legitimation that his predecessors had accorded to the Gaon's error, and he added a new element, arguing that opposition was the fruit of divine providence and served a positive purpose. The Rabbi Joseph Isaac ignored the persecution of the Hasidim and transposed the struggle to the arena of talmudic scholarship. In that arena, Rabbi Shneur Zalman trounced the leaders of the Mitnagdim. Another arena in which Rabbi Joseph Isaac chose to view the rivalry between Hasidim and Mitnagdim was the struggle against Haskalah. To that end, he had to predate the penetration of Haskalah into eastern Europe by several decades. He argued that the leaders of the Mitnagdim, headed by the Vilna Gaon, paved the way for the penetration of Haskalah into Lithuania. By contrast, the Hasidim struggled against Haskalah with determination, and therefore they were victorious. Mondshine discovered, as it were, that the background of the struggle against Hasidism was a plot hatched by the corrupt *parnasim* of Vilna. The role assigned to the Gaon in this wondrous tale was to provide a fig leaf of religious authority to cover the nakedness of the *parnasim.*

Each in his own way, all three of these writers sought to avoid grappling with the harsh truths of the struggle against Hasidism. They found it especially difficult to accept the role that the Gaon played in this episode. Most authors who have dealt with this topic from an orthodox Jewish point of view have shared this difficulty in accepting the picture of the past in which the Gaon appeared as a zealous and uncompromising warrior against Hasidism. Some have overcome the difficulty by writing apologetics on his behalf, others portrayed the confrontation between the Mitnagdim and Hasidim in harmonious tones, and yet others chose to ignore the struggle against Hasidism.

So we see that, in places where the myth of the Vilna Gaon continues to play a vital role and to serve as a focus of identification, critical history is not exactly a welcome guest.

5 Rabbi Ḥayyim of Volozhin's Response to Hasidism

In early 5563 (autumn 1802) Rabbi Ḥayyim of Volozhin published an open letter to all "lovers of Torah" in Lithuania.[1] In that letter, he described the low condition to which study of Torah had sunk and called to the public to voluntarily promote the renewed flourishing of Torah study. The direct purpose of this call was to mobilize support for the new yeshiva that Rabbi Ḥayyim had just established in Volozhin, but it was also a call for the renewal of Torah study throughout Lithuania.

Rabbi Ḥayyim's letter and the establishment of the yeshiva in Volozhin were the first salient manifestations of his new status as leader of the Mitnagdim in Lithuania. This was not an official post but rather leadership status that drew its authority and significance from his personal greatness. Rabbi Ḥayyim achieved this status because he was regarded as the leading disciple of the Vilna Gaon. Nevertheless, in this letter Rabbi

Ḥayyim protested against the practice of presenting him as a disciple of the Gaon: "And I have heard that the name of our great master, Eliyahu, may he rest in peace, has been invoked regarding myself, . . . and that I have been privileged to have his good name called upon for me, saying that I am his disciple, and I view it as an obligation for myself to proclaim in good faith that far be it from me to infringe on the great honor of our great and holy rabbi, may he rest in peace, to have his name invoked for me."[2] Rabbi Ḥayyim's humility and above all his enormous veneration for the Gaon lay behind this claim that invoking the Gaon's name with respect to him was an infringement on the great rabbi's honor. But his protest merely confirms what also emerges from other sources: among those who were close to the Gaon, Rabbi Ḥayyim was regarded as his greatest disciple. During the three decades while the struggle against Hasidism was waged, the figure of the Gaon was a source of authority and inspiration in the Mitnagdic camp. It is no wonder that after his death the Mitnagdim sought a leader to fill the gap that had opened. Rabbi Ḥayyim was a natural candidate for this position.

However, under Rabbi Ḥayyim's leadership, the struggle against Hasidism took on an entirely different form. Ideological confrontation and educational efforts replaced persecution and excommunication. Henceforth, Hasidism—and the Hasidim—was viewed as a legitimate phenomenon, worthy of respect, even though its way must be rejected and its errors protested. The change in the character of the struggle of the Mitnagdim against Hasidism can be explained both by changing circumstances and by the way in which Rabbi Ḥayyim grasped the new circumstances and their significance.

The death of the Gaon and recognition by the Russian government of the Hasidim's right to maintain minyanim of their own put an end to the organized struggle against the Hasidim that had begun at the Gaon's instigation in the spring of 5532 (1772). At the end of that struggle, it was clear that Hasidism had not vanished from the world but, on the contrary, had succeeded in spreading and sinking roots in various regions of eastern Europe. Furthermore, from a persecuted sect it had become a threat to the Mitnagdim who persecuted it. This threat was expressed in the success of Hasidism in drawing into its ranks many young men who frequented houses of study. That development was of particularly grave significance for the Mitnagdim, for Hasidism diminished the status of Torah study and the scholarly elite.

THE DIMINUTION IN THE STATUS OF TORAH STUDY CAUSED BY HASIDISM

From the first, Hasidism combined mystical fervor with a sense of religious mission for all of Jewry, upsetting the religious hierarchy of values accepted within traditional society. From the Mitnagdim's point of view, the diminution in the value of Torah study associated with the rise of Hasidism was particularly grave.[3] The more Hasidism strove to place cleaving to God at the center of religious life, the more it tended to diminish the value of Torah study in the traditional manner.[4] Torah study, as viewed by the traditional society, and Hasidic cleaving to God exemplified two distinct approaches to the goals of religious life.

Traditional society regarded Torah study as a supreme religious value. Over the generations, the relative significance of theoretical study rose, that is to say, study that was not intended to solve concrete Halakhic problems. This development appears to reflect the ritual value attributed to Torah study. The very process of study, even when it did not contribute directly to Halakhic rulings, was regarded as divine service on the highest level. Similarly, those who possessed "greatness" in Torah, measured by the criteria of "sharpness" and "erudition," also enjoyed superior religious status.

Fundamentally speaking, this view appears to be rooted in a transcendental conception of the divinity. Assuming the transcendental distance of God, study of Torah, which derives from divine revelation, is viewed as the highest link with the godhead. It may be said that, because of the divinity's transcendental distance, emphasis was transferred from God Himself to study of a law that was divine in source and character though, in many cases, "secular" in content.

Hasidic religious consciousness, by contrast, made closeness to God Himself its chief aspiration. The Hasid, who sought to cleave to God, strove to "break through firmaments" in order to obtain a mystical experience, a direct and immediate feeling of the divine presence. Hasidism made cleaving to God the principal purpose of religious life by applying a radical interpretation of the Kabbalistic idea that "there is no place vacant of Him." The new movement also strove to clarify the ways that lead to cleaving to God and to remove the obstacles that hinder it. Thus Hasidism sought to bridge the transcendental gap between man and God. From this Hasidic point of view, greatness in Torah, which consisted mainly in intellectual achievements measured by the criteria of "sharpness" and "erudition," was of lesser religious value.

Diminution of the value of Torah study was expressed by, among other things, emphasis on the superiority of prayer as the principal channel for cleaving to God. In Hasidic literature the value of prayer was sometimes emphasized in opposition to the importance of Torah study. This is the spirit in which one must understand the sayings attributed to Rabbi Jacob Joseph of Polna: "A gem in the mouth of the righteous Jacob Joseph of blessed memory, it is easier for him to present ten *ḥiluqim* than to pray the eighteen [benedictions]."[5] A more explicit expression of this idea is found in the words revealed to the Ba'al Shem Tov: "For he had the merit of having exalted things revealed to him, not because he studied many tractates and many rulings [but] only because of the prayer that he always used to pray with great intention; from there he attained a superior elevation."[6] It is to be emphasized that neither the Ba'al Shem Tov nor Rabbi Jacob Joseph speak of Torah study as such. They both refer to the traditional method of study. In using the expression *ḥiluqim,* Rabbi Jacob Joseph alludes to the method of study that emphasized the value of sharpness of wit, whereas the Ba'al Shem Tov alludes to emphasis of quantitative achievement in study. Thus we find that both men present Hasidic prayer as preferable to the traditional mode of study, which attributed great importance to erudition and intellectual acuity.

The argument that one should not study Torah too much is found explicitly in the words of Rabbi Menahem Mendel of Premishlan.[7] That Hasid, who belonged to the circle of the Ba'al Shem Tov, began with the assumption that the psychic activity needed for the effort of cleaving to God and the activity required for Torah study were not consistent with one another. For that reason, and because cleaving to God was undoubtedly more exalted than study, he reached the conclusion that "one should study little and always think about the greatness of the blessed Creator." Rabbi Menahem Mendel distinguishes between "the first generations—whose intellect was strong and who studied with the highest sanctity," and who therefore were capable of studying Torah a great deal without diminishing their attachment to God—and his contemporaries, who were incapable of studying Torah and cleaving to God at the same time. However, this distinction, which was intended to make the proposed, innovative program consistent with the tradition of generations, was of course insufficient to blunt the intensity of the innovation. On the contrary, we find that Rabbi Menahem Mendel himself was aware of the radical character of his words.

The position taken by the Ba'al Shem Tov with regard to Torah study appears more moderate. He does not claim that there is an inherent contradiction between the effort for devotion and the study of Torah. Rather he suggests combining them: "The matter of Torah is not simply study [but] only to cleave by the Torah to His great Name, which is the essence of the purpose."[8] The Ba'al Shem Tov in fact emptied the traditional function of Torah study of its customary content and filled it with new significance. By making cleaving to God the main purpose of religious life, and by viewing all religious activity as means for cleaving to God, he deprived Torah study of its traditional status as the highest religious value and made it, too, into an instrument and a means for seeking to cleave to God. Furthermore, it was only one of several means for seeking to cleave to God and not necessarily the most important of them.

Study as a means of cleaving to God is described in words cited by Rabbi Jacob Joseph in the name of the Ba'al Shem Tov: "According to what I received from my master, the essence of occupation with Torah and prayer is so that one might cling to one's innerness and the spirituality of the infinite light that is in the letters of the Torah and the prayer, and this is called Torah for its own sake."[9] The technique proposed here is based on the assumption that the letters of the Torah and the prayers have a mystical quality. In the Ba'al Shem Tov's opinion, these letters are a kind of container for the divine essence. If a person who studies or prays does so with the right intention, he is capable of drawing down the infinite light and placing it within the letters. At this stage the person studying may make his soul cling to the divine essence that dwells in the letters.

This psychic activity is inconsistent with the traditional way of studying, for the student is not concerned with penetrating the content of the passage being studied. His main efforts are concentrated on the encounter of his innerness with the divine essence, and the text serves solely as a kind of garment or outer skin of that essence. Consequently, intellectual achievement in Torah study, as measured by mental acuity and erudition, loses some of its religious value. This conclusion is reinforced by the Ba'al Shem Tov's interpretation of the concept "Torah for its own sake." Since the times of the Sages, this concept has been viewed as exemplifying the highest level of Torah study. Naturally, thinkers have interpreted it in different ways. According to the Ba'al Shem Tov's interpretation, the term "Torah for its own sake" refers to the method of study that serves as a means of cleaving to God. Hence one must conclude that any Torah study not dedicated to that aim is not study for its own sake.

The assumption that the value of Torah study is conditioned on its being a platform for the effort to cleave to God was common and accepted at the beginning of Hasidism. This assumption also served as the basis for Hasidic criticism of the traditional method of study and of its subjects. A striking example of criticism of this kind is found in the words of Rabbi Meshulam Feibush Heller.[10] The point of departure for Rabbi Meshulam's critique is that the virtues of modesty and humility were essential for cleaving to God, and that pride and the quest for honor cut people off from the creator. In the light of this assumption, Rabbi Meshulam examines the "scholars" and their way of studying:

> A man is teaching Torah to a student who is not worthy. The [teacher's] intention is to make him cleave to God and to remove haughtiness of heart and to uproot it from the heart . . . and if the student is unworthy, then, perish the thought, he will receive more haughtiness of heart from study because he wants to be erudite and his intention is not at all for the sake of heaven, only for his own name, so that he will be eminent in Torah and sharp-minded and expert.[11]

Rabbi Meshulam does not locate the weakness in the system of study itself, but in the quality of the scholar's motivation. However, in the case of "a student who is not worthy," intellectual achievement itself becomes a pitfall, for this achievement itself arouses the instinct for pride and honor.

Use of the term "a student who is not worthy" could be deceptive, for it might seem to refer to isolated and exceptional cases. However, farther on Rabbi Meshulam launches a frontal attack on what was apparently an extensive and considerable phenomenon: "Truly many of our people, who regard themselves as, and are publicly regarded as, learned in the revealed and hidden Torah, and who seem to [live] in awe in all matters, and who are certain they have attained some Torah and *yira,* in truth have not even attained the slightest knowledge of the Torah of our God, which is called Torah because it shows the hidden One [within it] which is the blessed Name."[12] To whom does this passage refer? Who are the people who think of themselves as, and who are seen by the community as, great in Torah, both the revealed and hidden, and on a high ethical level? One is constrained to admit that these words are aimed at the scholars who belong to the spiritual leadership of the Jewish community. One might identify them more precisely: since these men also deal with esoteric doctrine and are regarded as living in "awe," they could be *ḥasidim* of the old kind. In any event, Rabbi Meshulam challenges the spiritual authority of those scholars because their study does not bring them closer to God, which is the only quality that endows Torah study with significance.

Later Rabbi Meshulam comments on the assumption that intellectual achievement itself, which traditional scholars obtain through Torah study, endows them with the virtues of love, awe, and cleaving to God. To refute this mistaken assumption, Rabbi Meshulam offers proof drawn from experience: "Is it not well known that, for our sins, there are several Torah scholars who are adulterers, perish the thought, and known to be sinners, and Gentiles even study our Torah, so how can that be cleaving to God?"[13] The existence of great Torah scholars whose religious awe was doubtful was decisive testimony that intellectual achievement in itself was no guarantee of the scholar's spiritual elevation. It would be difficult to exaggerate the radical nature of this statement in relation to what was common and accepted in traditional Jewish society in that generation.

A striking expression of the change in values ushered in by Hasidism is found in the new distinction proposed by Rabbi Meshulam between what is "revealed" and "hidden" in the Torah. His thoughts on this subject are presented in interpretation of the talmudic expression "A great matter and a small matter—a great matter is *ma'ase merkavah,* and a small matter is the disputes between Abaye and Rava."[14] Throughout the generations this saying has been understood in the spirit of the prevailing distinction between what is hidden and revealed in the Torah. "The disputes between Abaye and Rava" are Halakhic issues concerning various aspects of human life and society, and these are taken to be less valuable than "*ma'ase merkavah*"—divine secrets. Rabbi Meshulam challenges the common interpretation of that saying. On the one hand, he argues, how is it possible to call Halakhic disputes "a small matter"? For "this is the essence of our Torah revealed to Moses on Mount Sinai!" And on the other hand, why is dealing with "the making of the *merkavah*" seen as "a great matter"? "For in our time most people, if not all, are expert in the writings of the ARI of blessed memory, who revealed the matters of *ma'ase merkavah!*" In answer to these questions, Rabbi Meshulam offers a new interpretation of this talmudic dictum:

> But in truth, both the revealed Torah and the hidden Torah, everything is of the same kind. For everything follows a person's intention therein. If the person's intention in it is to know its matter, he does not achieve anything. . . . But if his intention is to desire to cleave to the Blessed Name, to be a chariot [that is, *merkavah*] for him, and there is no way to do that except by Torah and the commandments, then both by the revealed Torah and by the hidden Torah he will make himself cleave; . . . and this, in my opinion, is their meaning [in saying that] a small matter is the disputes of Abaye and Rava. It means to say that the intellect in the *pilpul* of the Gemara, which is the sharp disputes of Abaye and Rava, is a small matter. It means to say: whoever studies for that intellect, who takes pleasure in it, is small and as nothing and he does not touch the Blessed Name. . . . But whoever desires to be a chariot for the Blessed Name by the Torah, that is a great matter. And that is [the meaning of] a great matter is *ma'ase merkavah,* which wishes to say: to make oneself a chariot for the Blessed Name by the Torah.[15]

We have before us a new criterion for distinguishing between a "great matter" and a "small matter" in the study of Torah. The content of the Torah being studied does not determine its category but rather the intention and mind-set of the student. Through emphasis of religious consciousness—the yearning for mystical closeness to God—the classical distinction between "revealed" and "secret" loses its importance. Seeking to cleave to God is what gives Torah study its significance and value. Thus study whose purpose is cleaving to God becomes *"ma'ase merkavah,"* which is "a great matter." In contrast, study motivated by intellectual curiosity, the purpose of which is intellectual satisfaction, becomes "a small matter."[16]

Rabbi Meshulam's words are typical of the criticism lodged by Hasidism against the scholarly elite in the name of the mystical ideal of cleaving to God. By its nature, criticism of the manner in which that elite studied was also a challenge to its authority to lead the community.

SIGNS OF CRISIS IN THE CAMP OF THE MITNAGDIM

From the start of the controversy, the Mitnagdim made repeated accusations that the Hasidim threw off the yoke of Torah, meaning the study of the Talmud and *posqim,* and concentrated instead on the study of Kabbalah, of which they were unworthy. The writings of the Mitnagdim also frequently protested the Hasidim's contempt and disdain for Torah scholars. In fact, from the Mitnagdim's point of view a more severe matter was that the Hasidim were recruiting followers among the young Torah scholars. A letter published in Vilna in 5532, at the beginning of the organized campaign against Hasidism, states:

> For they have seven abominations in their heart to entrap innocent souls, and they prevent many people from studying Torah and remove the yoke of Torah from their necks and from the necks of precious sons who are as precious as gold; . . . and they constantly go off and meet, two by two, and one heretic finds another, and they call [one another] and go forth into impurity, and they say to them every day that they must not spend their days with Torah, but rather in worship, which is prayer.[17]

This is a rather realistic picture of Hasidic propaganda among young Torah students. The author of the epistle accuses the Hasidim of preventing young students from studying Torah, which was regarded as a grave sin. However, it is also possible to view the phenomenon described here in a different light. Young students, who were influenced by Hasidic criticism of the traditional manner of Torah study and who were attracted by Hasidism, were abandoning houses of study and taking up the worship of God in the Hasidic manner. Accusing the Hasidim of snatching souls indicates not only the success of Hasidic propaganda but also reveals the particular sensitivity of the Mitnagdim regarding the penetration of Hasidic influence among Torah scholars.

The damage Hasidism caused to the status of Torah study, its criticism of scholars, and the penetration of its influence among scholars persisted and grew as the Hasidic movement continued to spread at an accelerating pace. The writings of the Mitnagdim during the 1780s repeated the claims familiar to us from the 1770s. The writ of excommunication proclaimed by the community of Slutzk in late 5541 (1781) indicates the severity of these developments and the feeling of crisis that gripped the Mitnagdim: "Like a fertile garden once had been the Land of Judea and Israel, and afterward as bitter as wormwood, and for that reason people burst out in the land and caused us a great sacrilege, and negated the honor of the Torah and those who study it, for our many sins; the Torah wears sackcloth for its students who have ceased and for its scholars who have turned their backs to follow their arbitrary, evil hearts."[18]

In the mid-1780s Rabbi Avraham Katzenelboigen, the rabbi of Brisk, made similar accusations. In his polemical epistle to Rabbi Levi Yitshak of Berditchev, he writes that the Torah "wears sackcloth around its waist for those fools who have repudiated the oral Torah and who think of the commentators of the Talmud as nothing and chaos." Later in the same epistle, the rabbi of Brisk does admit that some Hasidim are among "the men of the Lord and students of Torah," and most likely he was referring to Rabbi Levi Yitshak himself. However, that did not absolve them of responsibility for "the growths that they grew."[19]

During the 1790s Hasidism increased in power, which probably explains the great daring that the Hasidim displayed in the struggle with their persecutors. This daring is expressed in rumors circulated by the Hasidim in 5556 (1796) that the Vilna Gaon had retracted his opposition to Hasidism. At that time the penetration of Hasidic influence among Torah scholars also increased. An indication of that can be found in the words of the *maggid* Rabbi David of Makov, an opponent of Hasidism. In a letter to a relative, Rabbi David says that in response to these rumors the Vilna Gaon roused the communities to renew the persecution of Hasidim. Nevertheless, the Hasidim "still insist on their evil, and Satan has triumphed in attracting women and frivolous people to them; also many students of the Torah have suddenly gone to the opposite side and have been entrapped and snared, and hurried backward [away] from the holy Torah."[20] The claim that Hasidic propaganda was winning souls among "women and frivolous people" is typical of the writings of the Mitnagdim, from the beginning of the controversy, and its polemical character is transparent. However, the argument of the *maggid* of Makov, that "students of the Torah" had also been trapped in the net of Hasidism, is in effect the admission by one involved in the conflict that Hasidic influence had increased in the camp of Torah scholars.

The sources in our possession show that not even the sons of families of aristocratic rabbinic lineage, and not even some from families associated with the Vilna Gaon, were immune to Hasidic influence. Among the students of Rabbi Ḥayyim of Volozhin was preserved a tradition stating that one of their rabbi's relatives tended toward Hasidism. According to the story, Rabbi Ḥayyim demanded of this relative: "In any event accomplish these three things: (1) study Gemara . . . and let this activity of yours be service before the Holy One, blessed be He; (2) preserve 'the law of the Gemara'; (3) do not talk about our master the Vilna Gaon."[21] This response is in keeping with the conciliatory attitude of Rabbi Ḥayyim toward Hasidism, which I shall describe below. Rabbi Ḥayyim did not boycott the relative who was drawn to Hasidism, but he made several demands of him. In these demands one may see what Rabbi Ḥayyim found to be the conspicuous flaws in Hasidic practice at that time.

A fascinating document that also shows the penetration of Hasidism into families that belonged to the scholarly elite is the oath sworn by Rabbi Yitshak the son of Rabbi Phinehas. His father, Rabbi Phinehas the son of Rabbi Judah, served as a preacher in Polozk, and his writings include *Keter Torah,* which will be discussed below. Rabbi Phinehas was an associate of the Vilna Gaon and even taught Torah to his grandchildren. Toward the end of his life he moved to Vilna and served as a preacher and *moreh ẓedeq* in one of its suburbs.[22]

In the oath that Rabbi Yitshak swore before a rabbinical court of three, which included the Vilna Gaon and his father, he states:

> I hereby swear by the Holy Torah and by [my] part in the world to come that I will not be numbered among the sect of Hasidim, . . . and that I will not accept advice from them in worship of the Creator; that is, that I will [not] pray in their special minyan, . . . that I will not sit at their special gathering, . . . and that I will not go to dance with them; that I will never attend a rabbi of theirs; . . . and that if, perish the thought, I ever violate the aforesaid oath intentionally, then may all the curses written in the *Sefer Torah* apply to me, and no permission from any rabbi or rabbinical court will be effective.[23]

The precise background of this oath is unknown. Had Rabbi Yitshak shown some inclination for Hasidism and its ways? If so, the oath was meant to bring the lost sheep back to the flock. Or had some suspicion arisen lest the son might be caught in the snares of Hasidism, and this was sufficient for his father to require him to take this oath? Either way, the stringent oath taken by Rabbi Yitshak the son of Rabbi Phinehas shows the force of Hasidic influence, for it even threatened the sons of scholarly families close to the Gaon.

A similar conclusion may be drawn from the letter of Rabbi Shlomo Zalman of Nashelsk to his son. This man was one of the greatest scholars of his generation and famous for his book of Halakhic *responsa, Ḥemdat Shlomo.* In his letter to his son, "the learned and sharp-witted rabbi," Rabbi Shlomo emphasizes that the bans against Hasidism imposed by the Gaon remained in force. After associating himself with that high authority, the father implores his son, "Thus my beloved son, far be it from you to walk in their path. Keep your feet from their ways, only keep them at a distance of a bowshot." A clause that Rabbi Shlomo added to this letter shows how strong Hasidism had become: "And may these words be hidden with you so as not to defy them. For no good result will come of that. For they will not repent for any [reason], . . . except only [you may] show them to those who are not so much drawn to that notorious sect."[24]

Thus Rabbi Shlomo despairs of the chance of reforming the Hasidim and their followers. His sole hope was limited to saving those who had not yet been swept away by the torrent of Hasidism.

The three incidents described here are representative details that indicate a larger picture. These incidents, together with the evidence presented above, show that at the end of the eighteenth century, with the growth of Hasidism, the crisis in Torah study became more severe. Not only did the Hasidim neglect the study of Halakhah and hold its students in contempt, but they also managed to bring many Torah scholars into their camp.

What impelled those young Torah scholars to cease their studies and join the Hasidic sect? The writings of the Mitnagdim naturally prefer to ignore the willful decision of those who inclined toward Hasidism, and they do not consider its causes. Instead, they describe the influence of Hasidism on Torah scholars as an act of Satan, a pitfall, a trap. However, a more neutral source sheds a different light on the matter.

Shlomo Maimon describes his first encounter with Hasidism in his autobiography. He happened to meet a young man who had just returned from a visit to the court of the *maggid* of Mezhirech. When asked how one might be received by the fellowship of Hasidim, the young man answered, "Anyone who feels in his heart an inclination toward perfection and does not know on what path he will find satisfaction for that inclination . . . has only to turn to the rebbes, and just by doing that he becomes a member of that fellowship." The Hasid went on to tell Maimon some of the Torah teachings he had heard from his new rabbis. Maimon describes the impression made by this conversation: "The man's words inflamed my imagination to an unsurpassed degree. I was struck with a vehement desire to obtain the happiness of becoming a member of that honorable fellowship. I made up my mind to go to the city of M., where Rabbi B. dwelled."[25] Later Maimon recounts that, after his term of service as a teacher, he did not return home but rather went to the *maggid's* court, a journey that lasted several weeks. Thus it was the Hasidic innovation in divine worship that fascinated the young teacher. While Maimon himself did not maintain his affiliation with Hasidism, his case shows why many young Torah scholars were drawn to the Hasidic camp.

THE CRISIS IN TORAH STUDY AS VIEWED BY RABBI ḤAYYIM OF VOLOZHIN

Rabbi Ḥayyim's *Nefesh ha-ḥayyim* provides important insight into the crisis of Torah study in general and into the motivations of Torah scholars attracted to Hasidism in particular. This insight is of special significance for our discussion, since it shows how Rabbi Ḥayyim himself understood the nature of the crisis. At the beginning of the fourth section of *Nefesh ha-ḥayyim,* which is entirely devoted to elucidating the virtue of Torah study, Rabbi Ḥayyim reveals what impelled him to write:

> I also intended to write about the greatness of the obligation to deal with Torah, . . . because it has been many days for Israel that occupation with the holy Torah has been laid low in every generation. And now, in these generations, it has fallen very very far, and it is placed in the obscurity of the lowest step, may the Merciful One save us. As our eyes see now that most of the sons of our nation suffer greatly from bearing the burden of a livelihood, may God have mercy. And some of those who desire closeness to God have chosen for themselves to place the main emphasis of their study in books of *yira* and ethics all the time, without placing the main burden of their occupation with the holy Torah in Scripture and in many Halakhot; . . . may God forgive them, for their intention is for heaven, but this is not the way in which the light of the Torah dwells.[26]

Rabbi Ḥayyim describes the crisis in Torah study as a two-stage process, in which the latter is more severe than the former. In writing about the early stage, Rabbi Ḥayyim appears to allude to slackening support for yeshivot, a point to which we shall return. This phenomenon is connected with the dwindling of economic resources, which he mentions. However, in speaking of "these generations" he refers to the exacerbation of the crisis following Hasidism's rise and the increase in its power. Rabbi Ḥayyim views neglect of the study of Halakhah and concentration on books of *yira* and ethics as a severe symptom of the crisis. But in describing the Hasidim as people "who desire closeness to God," and in saying "may God forgive them, for their intention is for heaven," Rabbi Ḥayyim admits the purity of the intentions of those who depart from Torah study.

Later Rabbi Ḥayyim expands his description of the gravity of the crisis, and the nature of those drawn to Hasidism becomes clearer:

> And now, in these generations, for our many sins, the opposite is the case, and the high one is lowered. For quite a few have placed all the essence of their study most of the day only in books of *yira* and ethics, saying that this is the essence of man in his world, to be occupied always with these, for they inflame hearts, and then his heart will surrender and will subdue and smash the [evil] impulse from its appetites and to straighten itself in good virtues. And the crown of Torah is left in a corner. And with my own eyes I have seen one region where this has spread so much that in most of the houses of study there are mainly many books of ethics, and not even one complete set of Talmud; . . . and soon, with the passage of time, they could be, perish the thought, without a rabbi or guide. And what will become of the Torah?[27]

The turn to occupation with books of *yira* and ethics is described here as a revolution. This probably refers to Torah scholars who once "place[d] the main emphasis of their study" on the Talmud and *posqim,* but who, after they were affected by Hasidic propaganda, turned their backs on that occupation and devoted themselves to the study of ethical works. It is typical of Rabbi Ḥayyim that he did not conceal the positive motivations of those former Torah scholars. They pore over books of *yira* and ethics because that is the path that, in their opinion, promises the smashing of the evil impulse and moral regeneration. These achievements are so important because they are prerequisite to the effort to cleave to God.

Two works by Mitnagdim who argue against the claims that Hasidic propaganda used in order to draw certain scholars away from the traditional mode of Torah study can also teach us about those claims. The works in question are the already mentioned *Nefesh ha-ḥayyim* and an earlier work, *Keter Torah,* by Rabbi Phinehas ben Judah.[28] Following in the footsteps of Rabbi Bahya ibn Paquda, author of the medieval Spanish ethical work *Hovot Halevavot,* the author of *Keter Torah* presents his argument in the form of a debate with the evil impulse. The evil impulse disguises itself and dissembles, piling up arguments whose only purpose is to keep scholars away from their studies. While the author does not identify the responsible party, which is camouflaged behind the "evil impulse," the character and content of the arguments he places in the mouth of the "evil impulse" leave no room to doubt their Hasidic source.

For example, the argument that it is preferable to decrease one's Torah study and devote oneself to prayer because it is of higher value than study has a decidedly Hasidic tone. Another stratagem of the evil impulse is contained in the argument that Torah study is without value if the student has not yet attained the level of religious awe, and that it is, therefore, better to work on moral improvement than to spend a great deal of time studying. Another argument advanced by the evil impulse is that the study of Kabbalah is preferable to the study of Gemara, for by studying Kabbalah one attains the virtue of cleaving to God, which is not true of the study of Halakhah.[29] Regarding the connection between Torah study and cleaving to God, the evil impulse advances another argument: The purpose of Torah study is cleaving to God; "if so, perhaps you can do that, and you vex your mind with *pilpul* of the Gemara and *posqim* day and night; . . . and if so where is your cleaving to God and your devoted contemplation of the Creator? . . . But it would be better for you to decrease your study and to contemplate the ways of God."[30] This argument, describing the traditional mode of study as an obstacle to cleaving to God, appears to echo the words of the Hasid Rabbi Menahem Mendel of Premishlan presented above.

The author of *Keter Torah* also places in the mouth of the evil impulse the Hasidic criticism against those who do not study Torah for its own sake:

> Did not our Sages of blessed memory say that anyone who is occupied with Torah not for its own sake would be better off not having been born? Now, it cannot be possible for you to study for its own sake unless you study in your home in a modest and individual place, . . . which is not the case if you study in a house of study and especially in a group; then your Torah will be full of extraneous considerations and cunning, for you will have no glory except to show your pride and wisdom, . . . and you will make of your Torah a forgery and deceit.[31]

Reproaching scholars because their study of Torah was not for its own sake and because their entire goal is to attain honor apparently played a central role in Hasidic propaganda. This matter occupies an important place in Rabbi Ḥayyim of Volozhin's polemics against Hasidism:

> This is the sinful fruit for several men who prevent themselves from studying the holy Torah, thinking that the meaning of "for its own sake" is with great cleaving to God with no interference. And there is also a sickness greater than that [among those] who believe in their minds that dealing with Torah without cleaving to God means nothing and is of no utility, perish the thought. For this, when they see in themselves that their heart does not go to that high degree, which is study with constant clinging to God, they do not begin to study at all, and therefore their Torah vanishes, perish the thought.[32]

Here we have a fascinating indication that ways of thinking derived from Hasidism had penetrated the circles of Torah scholars. The Hasidic attitude, as presented by Rabbi Ḥayyim, demands that all Torah study must take place "with great cleaving to God with no interference," meaning maximal concentration of consciousness on God. Moreover, Hasidic propaganda states that Torah study that does not involve cleaving to God is worthless. Rabbi Ḥayyim believes that among Torah scholars there are some who are reluctant to study because they fear they cannot meet these demands. In other words, Hasidic propaganda confronted scholars with a dilemma: all or nothing! Thus Hasidism deterred those scholars who could not meet the radical demand of studying "with great cleaving to God with no interference."

Rabbi Ḥayyim goes on to accuse the Hasidim, on the basis of their view regarding the essence of Torah study for its own sake, of fostering a sense of religious superiority and of mocking scholars.[33] He also ascribes grave consequences to that phenomenon: "Because he derides and disdains a man who deals with Torah not for its own sake, he deters him from dealing with Torah, so that he will never reach the level of 'for its own sake.'"[34] These words indicate Rabbi Ḥayyim's position regarding the legitimacy of Torah study that is not for its own sake as a necessary intermediate step toward study that *is* for its own sake.[35]

It seems that neither Rabbi Phinehas the son of Rabbi Judah nor Rabbi Ḥayyim had many illusions regarding the possibility of "reforming" the Hasidim and those inclined to Hasidism. Their main intention was to rescue those who had not yet been swept up by the current, including, it appears, many fence-sitters. One may presume that even those who did not, for example, accept the doctrine of the Zaddik in Hasidism were still able to admit the Hasidic critique of Torah study that was not for its own sake. The Hasidic injunction to study Torah for its own sake, and its rejection of any other approach to study, was based on a value that had been accepted and sanctified for many generations. The innovation of Hasidism lay in the fact that, along with criticism of the traditional mode of study and those who practiced it, it also proposed an extremely attractive alternate path: study as a means for cleaving to God. The words of Rabbi Ḥayyim himself show how far Hasidic influence had gone in this matter: "The clear truth is that 'for its own sake' does not mean cleaving to God, as most people now think."[36] It is difficult to imagine that Rabbi Ḥayyim would be interested in exaggerating the power of Hasidism; thus one should not regard the expression "most people" as a mere superlative.

The blow dealt by Hasidism to the status of Torah study and rabbinical scholars naturally influenced the situation of Torah institutions as well. According to the author of *Keter Torah,* the status of the house of study was also diminished. Rabbi Phinehas describes it as it was in better times: full of "groups and groups" of students who dealt with Torah "until midday." Among the students were prominent "the elders and sages and sons of wealthy men." But now, he writes:

> Our Temple has been destroyed and our house of study is barren, for no one sits there except idlers and poor men who sigh and moan, and anyone who passes them will be appalled and hiss [1 Kings 9:8]. . . . Woe unto us that this has happened in our days. Where is the splendor of the eminence of our Torah and for what will our sons be zealous? . . . And what honor or what prestige does a young Jewish lad see in the house of study that will make him desire it and be zealous for it, since he sees in the house of study only poor men; . . . and what honor does an ignorant person see in a scholar that he would wish to raise his sons to study Torah? Woe to our eyes that see this, that all the Sages refrain from coming to the house of study.[37]

Thus it appears that the important students had abandoned the house of study, and it had ceased to serve as a dwelling for Torah. Rabbi Phinehas's words imply that abandonment of the house of study reflects a decline in prestige attributed by the society to the Torah study and to rabbinical scholars. Rabbi Phinehas even expresses apprehension that, in contrast to a tradition of many generations, the figure of the Torah scholar no longer served as an educational ideal accepted by all levels of the community.

The following remarks indicate the severity of the crisis, in the view of Rabbi Phinehas, and identify the force that he holds responsible for it: "Where is the Jewish religion in general, and has it not fallen prostrate to the earth, a fall from which it cannot rise? . . . Everything comes from the cunning of the power of the seductive Satan . . . with a deceitful ruse and seduction of his words; for he flees from Torah that is not for its own sake or from the pride of the house of study."[38] Thus the increased influence of Hasidic propaganda brought about the seclusion of scholars. The account in *Keter Torah* does not permit us to estimate the extent of the phenomenon described, but judging from the way the author writes, he appears not to refer specifically to communities where Hasidism had complete control. The increase in Hasidism's power also degraded the status of scholars in mixed communities: they were removed from the center of public life and tended to seclude themselves.

Rabbi Ḥayyim speaks of a similar phenomenon: "But there are those who wish to study . . . but they have no rabbi to teach them the true way of learning. For it has been many days for Israel that men who are great in the Torah in our country, each of them builds a room for himself and says: For myself I rescue and withdraw in a generation that does not love Torah."[39] Thus even within Lithuania, the major scholars tended to seclude themselves because of the decline in the status of Torah study. In the view of Rabbi Ḥayyim, this seclusion created a vacuum in the area of Torah instruction.

THE CRISIS IN COMMUNITY YESHIVOT

On the institutional level the crisis of Torah study, as noted earlier, was expressed in the diminished status of community yeshivot.[40] In the late

Middle Ages, the Ashkenazic yeshiva was an institution supported by the local community. The community rabbi usually stood at the head of the yeshiva. The rabbinical contract stipulated the number of *baḥurim* (students) that the community was obligated to support. The supracommunal councils made certain that the communities persisted in fulfilling their duties in supporting yeshivot. The first signs of the weakening of this institution appeared during the mid–seventeenth century. The regulations of the council of the state of Lithuania show that the matter of maintaining yeshivot became more difficult after the pogroms of 1648–49. Quite a few of the councils that convened after those pogroms complained bitterly that the communities were not doing their duty in maintaining yeshivot.[41] Apparently the severe economic distress and the social and institutional crisis that came in its wake resulted in this neglect. The constantly repeated discussion of this phenomenon shows that the crisis of the yeshivot affected many communities and that no essential improvement took place until the 1760s. The Polish government canceled the supracommunal councils in 1764. For years the council of the state of Lithuania had urged communities to do their duty, and when it ceased operations the situation probably worsened.

Sources from the late eighteenth and early nineteenth centuries speak of the vanishing of community yeshivot almost as a fait accompli. This is the picture that emerges from the letter that Rabbi Ḥayyim wrote in early 5563, after the establishment of the yeshiva in Volozhin: "From the time when people ceased supporting yeshivot in this country, since then all those who seek the Lord and His blessed Torah have been scattered like a flock with no shepherd."[42] Rabbi Joseph of Krinik, a student of Rabbi Ḥayyim's, provides a more detailed description of the situation of the yeshivot in Lithuania before the Volozhin yeshiva was established:

> Before the House of God was established by the angel of God, our holy rabbi, the world was barren, truly in chaos, for not even the name of "yeshiva" was known in the world, and what is the purpose of a yeshiva, and what one does there. Nor was the name of public Torah study known, for the world was barren of Torah, and also of sacred books, the books of the Talmud, which were not to be found in the world at all except among exceptional individuals, famous magnates; and even in the

> houses of study from big cities a complete set of the Talmud was not to be found, for it was not required in the world, because there was no one who was occupied with it; and when our holy rabbi founded the yeshiva, many sets of Talmud were demanded, and it was necessary to send to big cities and collect sets of the Talmud for the needs of the yeshiva students.[43]

These words could be somewhat exaggerated. They were written many years after the establishment of the Volozhin yeshiva, and it is not surprising that they endeavor to exaggerate the importance of Rabbi Ḥayyim's project. Nevertheless, Rabbi Joseph's words corroborate the picture that emerges from Rabbi Ḥayyim's letters: namely, that in the early nineteenth century there were no longer yeshivot supported by local communities in Lithuania.

The disappearance of community yeshivot in Poland and Lithuania has not yet been studied systematically. Economic and social factors doubtless underlay the phenomenon. Perhaps it is a manifestation of the crisis that—in the opinion of certain historians—struck the Jewish society of Poland and Lithuania in the first half of the eighteenth century.[44] At the same time it appears quite likely that Hasidism exacerbated that crisis during the second half of the eighteenth century. The Hasidim's depreciation of Torah study, and especially their criticism of Torah scholars and their method of study, could have provided justification to those individuals and groups who found it difficult, or who simply refused to do their part, to maintain the communal yeshivot. In any event, the crisis of the yeshivot added an institutional dimension to the crisis of values regarding Torah study.

Up to now we have examined what could be called the crisis in Torah study in the late eighteenth and early nineteenth centuries. We have seen that, in the wake of the change of values introduced by Hasidism in the manner of worshiping God, Torah study was displaced from the prime position it had hitherto occupied. As a result, the status of Torah scholars was diminished, and Hasidism managed to draw young scholars into its ranks. Moreover, the forgoing developments occurred against the background of the initial crisis in maintaining community yeshivot. In sum, from a persecuted sect Hasidism had become a threat to its opponents.

How severe was the crisis? To what extent did the study of Torah actually decrease? Did the number of Torah scholars decrease? We cannot answer these questions. However, from the point of view of our discussion it is decisive that, as far as Rabbi Ḥayyim of Volozhin was concerned, an extremely grave blow had been dealt to the status of Torah study. He states this explicitly: "And in a little while, as time went on, they could have been, perish the thought, left without priest or teacher, and what will become of the Torah?!"[45] Thus he fears that if Torah study continued to decrease, as described above, the chain of learning and instruction would be broken and the next generation would lack Torah scholars.

This evaluation of the situation lay in the background of Rabbi Ḥayyim's campaign to bring Lithuanian Jewry to grapple with the challenges that Hasidism offered it. That effort had two principal expressions: educational activity that was expressed in his establishing the yeshiva in Volozhin and serving as its head for about twenty years; and literary creativity including both polemics against Hasidism and systematic theology that was a response to the Hasidic challenge. We shall begin by examining first the doctrinal aspect of Rabbi Ḥayyim's response to Hasidism and then the yeshiva he founded.

ON THE STATUS OF TORAH STUDY

Rabbi Ḥayyim's theological response to Hasidism is found mainly in *Nefesh ha-ḥayyim.*[46] A first perusal of this work indicates a new and special stage in the response of the Mitnagdim to Hasidism.[47] First, Rabbi Ḥayyim's polemics stand out because of their tolerant and restrained style. The change that took place in the tone of his writing in comparison to, for example, the way in which his teacher and master, the Gaon, expressed himself is extremely conspicuous. This tolerant attitude derived most probably from the assumption that, even if the Hasidim erred regarding their manner of worshiping God, their intention was pure. The effort to do away with the sect of Hasidism had failed, and Hasidism had become an established fact. On the other hand, some of the intense suspicions raised by those who had banned Hasidism had proved to be groundless. These developments helped consolidate Rabbi Ḥayyim's tolerant position.[48] In any event, this tolerant attitude cleared the way for a relevant and principled discussion, one entirely free of the imprecations and insults that had been so common in the writings of Mitnagdim of the last decades of the eighteenth century.

However, what is special about Rabbi Ḥayyim's response to Hasidism is not only the restrained style and careful language that he uses concerning it but also—and most important—the new direction of his response. Unlike most of his predecessors, Rabbi Ḥayyim was not content with merely pointing out Hasidic deviations from the traditional normative framework and condemning that breach of the rules. With his deeper understanding of the doctrine of Hasidism, Rabbi Ḥayyim was the first in the camp of the Mitnagdim to succeed in getting to the roots of the controversy and even to point out the principal weak points in Hasidic doctrine. Moreover, with a sober estimation of the great attractive power of Hasidism, Rabbi Ḥayyim sought to present a religious doctrine that would provide an answer to the Hasidic challenge. In his reflections, Rabbi Ḥayyim sought to bolster and fortify the traditional manner of worshiping God, which, in his opinion, had been damaged by Hasidism. His main thrust was to present a renewed theological grounding for the status of Torah study as a supreme religious value and as the main way of serving God. Naturally this entailed the strengthening of the status and authority of Torah scholars.

A prominent characteristic of Rabbi Ḥayyim's thought was the effort to base the value of Torah study on ideas and concepts taken from Kabbalah.[49] Rabbi Ḥayyim apparently referred to Kabbalah not only because he himself was involved in it and connected to it, but also because he wished to endow his words with value and authority that would counteract the doctrine of Hasidism, which was also based on Kabbalah. Moreover, Rabbi Ḥayyim proposed a synthesis of the values of cleaving to God and of *yira,* which were preached by Hasidism, with the study of Torah in the traditional manner. Therefore one may say that Rabbi Ḥayyim's thought imparts mystical significance to the traditional manner of Torah study.

Let us now turn to a description of the ideas from which Rabbi Ḥayyim determined that the study of Torah, specifically in the traditional manner, was the major way of serving God. First of all, we shall note several Kabbalistic ideas that served as foundation stones in his edifice.

At the outset of his discussion, Rabbi Ḥayyim first clarifies the principle of dynamic rule of the divinity in the so-called worlds. According to this principle, the creation of the universe was not a unique event that began and ended some time in the past. Indeed, creation is a constant process, infinitely renewed. From the creation of the worlds onward, "all their power and reality and order and existence depends solely on what He, may His Name be blessed, infuses within them with His blessed will every moment with the abundance of power and the abundance of new light. And if He, may He be blessed, removed the power of His influence from them even for a single moment, in an instant everything would be nullity and chaos."[50] After noting that the existence of the worlds depends on the constant flow of divine abundance, Rabbi Ḥayyim goes on to clarify the influence of the Jew in the upper realms.

God gave man power over the upper realms, "and He delivered them into his hand, so that he would be the speaker and their leader according to all the details of the movement of his actions and speech and thoughts and also the orders of his practice either for good or for the opposite, perish the thought."[51] The enormous influence of human action and failing in the upper realms is explained by the high status of the "root" of Jewish souls in the hierarchy of the upper powers. Rabbi Ḥayyim bases this determination on the assumption that the system of supreme powers and worlds is ordered hierarchically, and that every world is like a "soul" in relation to the one beneath it. Hence every world also acts on and influences the worlds beneath it, the way the soul acts on the body. Kabbalah divides the worlds into four: *atsilut* (nobility), *bria* (creation), *yetsira* (formation), and *'asiya* (action). Rabbi Ḥayyim uses parallel concepts—*atsilut, kise hakavod* (the throne of honor), *ḥayot* (divine beings), and *ofanim* (angels)—and claims that the root of Jewish souls is found above the "throne." Therefore a Jew's actions influence all the worlds in that realm and below.[52]

Rabbi Ḥayyim adds a complementary explanation: since man was created last in the order of Creation, all the upper powers and worlds, which preceded him in Creation, are reflected in him. Thus we find that man is "contained" in all the worlds and powers, and thus he embodies in the details of his bodily organs a system parallel to the system of upper worlds. A similar law also applies to the relationship between the commandments and the system of higher powers. Hence Rabbi Ḥayyim derives his conclusion: "When a person does the will of his Creator, may His Name be blessed, and observes one of God's commandments with a bodily organ and the power therein, the reparation touches on that upper world and power that is parallel to it, to repair it or raise it, or to add light to its sanctity."[53]

Influence on the upper worlds was one of the principles of the Kabbalists' divine worship. For that reason they also sought to reveal the secret Kabbalistic meanings of prayer and the commandments.[54] However, Rabbi Ḥayyim does not state in detail what influence on the upper realms was exercised by any given commandment. Nor does he maintain that a Jew ought to be knowledgeable of such things. In contrast, he wants every individual Jew to be aware of the influence of his actions and failures on the upper realms. This awareness did not have to be based on detailed esoteric knowledge but could be on a general understanding of the principle. When a person became aware of the influence of his actions and failures on the upper realms, he discovered the full weight of his responsibility and the significance of the mission imposed on him. Rabbi Ḥayyim views that awareness of mission as a lever to impel the individual to fulfill his obligations:

> And this is the doctrine of man, of every Jewish person: let him not say in his heart, perish the thought, for what am I and what is my power to act? . . . But let him understand and know and determine in the thoughts of his heart that all the details of his actions and speech and thoughts at every time and moment should not be lost, perish the thought, . . . that everyone should rise according to his root and perform its action in the exalted heights; . . . and in truth, for every wise man should understand this in truth so his heart will fear within him with dread and awe and trembling when he sets upon his heart, that if his actions are not, perish the thought, good, how far they will reach.[55]

It should be emphasized that even though Rabbi Ḥayyim was influenced by the Kabbalah of the ARI, and he sometimes relied on it as a source, its messianic element does not play a role in his doctrine. Regarding the purpose of divine worship and its earthly consequences, Rabbi Ḥayyim remains within the boundaries of the conceptions prevalent in Sephardic Kabbalah. Thus he maintains that the principal purpose of the human influence on the upper realms was to bring down the divine "abundance" that gives life to all the worlds and maintains them. In that very matter—the influence of the Jew on the existence of the worlds—Rabbi Ḥayyim states that Torah study is preferable to the other ways of serving God.

Kabbalah attributes influence on the upper realms to keeping the commandments, as well as to prayer and Torah study. Rabbi Ḥayyim's innovation is the transfer of emphasis to Torah study, that is to say, study of Halakhah. He views the very process of studying Halakhah, not accompanied by Kabbalistic intentions, as a decisive and most vital means of bringing down the divine abundance and, of course, of maintaining the existence of the worlds. This determination is founded on a Kabbalistic worldview, according to which the Torah is fundamentally a supreme metaphysical entity.[56] Rabbi Ḥayyim added the notion that the supreme Torah "also preceded, as it were, the world of *atsilut,* may it be blessed." Consequently, since according to the Kabbalistic structural principle every world is a "soul" for the one beneath it, Rabbi Ḥayyim concludes that the upper Torah is the source of divine abundance, by the power of which all the worlds exist.[57]

From here there remained but one step for clarifying the extremely powerful significance of Torah study. By studying the earthly Torah in this world, the Jew, the upper root of whose soul is bound up and connected with the supreme Torah, causes the supreme Torah to infuse all the worlds with its "light." Hence the existence of the entire cosmic system depends on the Jews' study of Torah. This dependence is a permanent law from time immemorial. Therefore, Rabbi Ḥayyim claims, before the Torah was given to the Jews,

> the worlds were weak and shaky and were not on their true foundation; . . . and since it [the Torah] has devolved and descended as it were

> from the source of its hidden root into this world, . . . all the vitality and existence of all the worlds is only by the breath of our mouth and our reflection on it. And in truth without any doubt at all, if the entire world from one end to another of it were, perish the thought, truly vacant for a moment of our dealing with and contemplation of the Torah, at that moment all the upper and lower worlds would be destroyed and become nothing and chaos, perish the thought.[58]

Regarding the influence of Torah study and the descent of abundance and the maintenance of the worlds, Rabbi Ḥayyim goes far beyond the Kabbalistic teachings he depended on. He bases his conclusions on citations from the Zohar, such as "the world was created with the Torah," "everyone who contemplates the Torah and labors in it, as it were, maintains the entire world," and other, similar sayings. However, in Rabbi Ḥayyim's thought these ideas were emphasized and given an unequivocal character as a result of the theosophical basis on which he placed them. I refer to his statement that the highest root of the Torah is "also far, far above the *atsilut* of His sanctity, may He be blessed."[59] On the basis of this declaration, Rabbi Ḥayyim concludes that, just as in the process of Creation, all the worlds "were emanated and created" in the Torah, and "thus since then it has been their soul and existence; . . . and without the abundance of its light in them, truly at every moment to illuminate them and vivify them and maintain them, they would all return truly to chaos."[60] Whereas the Zohar connects the descent of abundance to a certain state of harmony in the relations of the *sefirot*, Rabbi Ḥayyim describes the supreme Torah as the decisive factor in the flow of abundance and the existence of the worlds.[61]

Rabbi Ḥayyim's innovation is even more conspicuous in the matter of Torah study's influence on the flow of abundance: he states that, with respect to influence on upper realms and assurance of the existence of the worlds, Torah study has decisive preference over prayer and performance of the commandments. This is proven by the argument that an absolute cessation of Torah study would bring about the destruction of the worlds, but that the same would not occur with cessation of prayer or the performance of the commandments:

> For even if, perish the thought, all the Jews lay aside and left off prayer to Him, may He be blessed, the worlds would not return to chaos be-

> cause of that. Therefore, prayer is termed "the life of the hour," in the words of the Sages of blessed memory, whereas the Torah is called "eternal life." . . . For the purpose of prayer is to add reparation in the worlds with the addition of sanctity at the time determined for them. Hence if the time has passed it will no longer be effective at all to continue giving an addition of sanctity and blessing in the worlds. However, the study of the holy Torah touches on the very vitality and existence of the worlds, lest they be entirely destroyed. Therefore a person must deal in it all the time always so as to erect and maintain the world at every moment.[62]

The barb in this statement is clearly directed at the Hasidic tendency to be less than scrupulous about the times of prayer. As for the determination that Torah study is preferable to prayer because of the advantage of its influence on the upper worlds, this provides an answer to the Hasidic propensity to attribute great emphasis to prayer as opposed to Torah study.

Thus the doctrine of Rabbi Ḥayyim, as we have seen so far, comprises an effort to block the influence of Hasidism. The fascination and power of Hasidism derived from, among other things, the mystical character it attributed to divine worship. Like Hasidism, Rabbi Ḥayyim draws on Kabbalah. However, whereas Hasidism concentrates on the individual's mystical yearnings, Rabbi Ḥayyim once again emphasizes the classic Kabbalistic goal of influencing the upper realms and bringing down divine abundance. He proposes a supreme religious mission to Torah scholars drawn to Hasidism: responsibility for the existence of the worlds and participation in the act of creation. As he writes, "Everyone who is occupied with Torah for its own sake is called a companion. For as it were, he becomes a partner with the Author of Creation, may His name be blessed. Because now he maintains all the worlds by his dealings with Torah."[63]

TORAH FOR ITS OWN SAKE AND CLEAVING TO GOD

So far we have taken note of one aspect of the mystical meaning underlying Torah study: its influence on the higher worlds. However, Rabbi Ḥayyim also attributes mystical meaning to the study of Torah with respect to the student's personal elevation. He developed these ideas in the course of a direct dispute over the meaning that Hasidism gave to the concept of Torah for its own sake. He writes, "As to the matter of occupation with Torah for its own sake, the clear truth is that 'for its own sake' does not mean cleaving to God, as most of the public now believes."[64] As we shall see below, this declaration was not meant to deny the possibility that, in the process of studying, a student might attain the level of cleaving to God. The declaration sought to challenge the interpretation given by the Hasidim to the concept of Torah for its own sake.

Rabbi Ḥayyim based his argument on quotations from rabbinical literature. First he presents the Midrash recounting that King David asked God to regard everyone who reads the Book of Psalms as if he had been occupied with the talmudic tractates *Nega'im* and *Ohalot,* which deal with aspects of ritual purity. This Midrash implies that occupation with talmudic arguments is more important than reciting psalms. Rabbi Ḥayyim uses the conclusion that he drew from the Midrash as a point of departure for attacking the Hasidic conception of Torah for its own sake: "If we say that 'for its own sake' means specifically cleaving to God, and that the entire essence of occupation with Torah depends solely on that, there is no cleaving to God greater than reciting psalms properly all day long."[65]

The barb here is directed at the ecstatic character of Hasidic prayer and at what Rabbi Ḥayyim thought of as the Hasidic conception of Torah for its own sake. Hasidism attributed primary importance to ecstatic experience, which served as a means of cleaving to God.[66] If Hasidism was right, then reciting psalms was preferable to occupation with talmudic arguments, for there is nothing like reciting psalms, a tried and true method, for arousing religious emotion and the experience of closeness to God. Nevertheless, the Midrash preferred occupation with talmudic arguments to the recital of psalms.

The second proof that Rabbi Ḥayyim presents from rabbinical literature relates to the scope of study. This proof is also one of negation. If Hasidism were correct in its conception of Torah for its own sake, then

> it would be sufficient, for the matter of cleaving to God, to study a single tractate, or chapter, or a single Mishnah, and to be occupied with it all

> one's life while cleaving to God. But this is not what we found in our Sages of blessed memory (*Succah* 28a), where it is said of Rabbi Yohanan ben Zakay that he did not lay aside scripture, Mishnah, Halakhot, and Aggadot, etc.; that is to say, that he always bore in mind that he had not yet fulfilled his obligation of being occupied with Torah by what he had studied until then; hence he was diligent all his life, always adding knowledge, from day to day and from hour to hour.[67]

Here Rabbi Yohanan ben Zakay represents the value of erudition: broad and comprehensive mastery of the Torah. That value stands in opposition to the Hasidic doctrine that mystical experience is the essential meaning of Torah study for its own sake, for that doctrine is inconsistent with the meaning that the Sages attributed to Torah study. Making study a means for an experience deprives it of its primary significance as a process whose essence was deepening and broadening knowledge of Torah, and whose results could be evaluated by the criteria of "sharpness of wit" and "erudition."

Rabbi Ḥayyim based his conception of the term "Torah for its own sake" on the interpretation by the ROSH (Rabbi Asher ben Yehiel, c. 1250–1327) of a passage in the Talmud on that subject. The tractate *Nedarim* (62a) quotes Rabbi El'azar ben Tsadok: "Do things for the sake of their Doer and speak of them for their own sake and do not make of them a crown to be glorified by them and do not make them a hoe to dig with." The ROSH interpreted this saying as follows: "'Do things for the sake of their Doer' means for the sake of the Holy One, blessed be He, who did everything for Himself. 'And speak of them for their own sake' means that all your speaking and discussion of words of Torah will be for the sake of the Torah, such as to know and to understand and to add a lesson and wit and not to grumble or to be proud."[68]

Rabbi Ḥayyim presents his view of the meaning of Torah for its own sake as an interpretation of these words by the ROSH. In his opinion, the ROSH intended to distinguish between keeping the commandments and Torah study. Regarding the commandments, to which the verb "to do" applies, the text states, "Do things for the sake of their Doer," meaning, "for the sake of the Holy One, blessed be He." But regarding Torah study the text states, "Speak of them for their own sake," meaning "to know and to understand and to add a lesson and wit." Consequently, Rabbi

Ḥayyim continues, when a person obeys the commandments, it is proper to accompany performance of the commandments with intention. Obviously, the object of intention is God. However, when a person is occupied with Torah, he has no need at all to accompany his study with intention directed on high. "Study for its own sake" is study whose accompanying religious intention is directed to the Torah itself, and the content of that intention is the aspiration to increase knowledge of Torah.[69] We find that the Torah serves simultaneously as the subject of study and the object of religious intention. This determination is of course connected to the assumption that the Torah with which the scholar is occupied is none other than the earthly reflection of the higher Torah, which is a divine entity.

As noted, Rabbi Ḥayyim's rejection of study combined with cleaving to God in the Hasidic manner is not meant to deny the possibility of cleaving to God through Torah study. On the contrary, Rabbi Ḥayyim maintains that specifically the study of Halakhah in the traditional manner could bring the student to cleave to God if he has reached the high level of studying for its own sake. This outlook is also based on the assumption that the Torah in our possession is the earthly exemplar of the higher Torah. On the basis of this assumption, the Kabbalists tended in particular to reveal the secrets of the Torah, and they sometimes condemned those who were satisfied with the mere study of Halakhah. However, Rabbi Ḥayyim emphasizes the divine character of the Halakhah. Because of our limited intelligence, the higher Torah was garbed in an awkward garment—meaning the Halakhot concerning life in this world—when it came down to our world. However, in contrast to the other higher forces, whose sanctity decreases the more they devolve from level to level, the same level of sanctity that characterizes the higher Torah also characterizes the Torah that is in our possession.[70]

How, then, is it possible to cleave to God by Torah study in the traditional manner? Rabbi Ḥayyim addresses that question in this passage:

> And he shall intend to cleave in his study of the Torah to the Holy One, blessed be He. That is to say, to cling with all his might to the word of God, which is the Halakhah, and thus he cleaves truly to Him, may He be blessed as it were. For He, may He be blessed, and His will are one, as it is written in the Zohar. And every judgment and law from the holy Torah is His will, may He be blessed, for it is decreed that His will shall

> be the law: fit [to eat] or unfit, impure or pure, forbidden or permitted, guilty or innocent.[71]

Thus the possibility of cleaving to God by virtue of occupation with Halakhah is based on the assumption that the Halakhah is identical to God. Halakhah is the embodiment of God with respect to His will. Hence, the deeper the student penetrates the depths of the issue being studied, and the more Halakhic subjects his knowledge encompasses, the more strongly he is connected to the divine will. Thus intellectual achievement in the study of Halakhah, which is measured by the criteria of sharpness of mind and erudition, may serve as an important means for a Jew's religious elevation—although this was the very sort of achievement whose religious significance Hasidism challenged.

The determination that Torah study in the traditional manner can lead to cleaving to God entails a certain difficulty. The tractates of the Talmud contain Aggadah, stories and discussions of ethical and theological matters that are not "relevant to the law" and, therefore, are not revelations of the divine will. Rabbi Ḥayyim responded to this difficulty by citing the well-known words of the Sages: "For the whole Torah in its entirety and in its details and minutiae, and even what a young student asks his teacher, everything issued from His mouth, may He be blessed, to Moses on Mount Sinai."[72] However, Rabbi Ḥayyim was not content with this answer and tried to extend its meaning: "Just as at the time of that sanctified event they cleaved as it were to His word, may He be blessed, so, too, now, truly whenever a person is occupied with it and meditates on it in every word, that very word is then hewn out with a flame from His mouth, may he be blessed, and it is thought of as though now it were received from His mouth, may His Name be blessed, at Sinai."[73] These words convey an actualization of the revelation at Mount Sinai. For the person who studies Torah for its own sake and who manages to cleave to God, the revelation at Mount Sinai is no longer an event that took place some time in the past. It is a constant process in which human consciousness encounters the divinity by means of Torah study. Thus Torah study becomes an occurrence possessing mystical character.[74]

As noted, Rabbi Ḥayyim also sought to endow the intellectual component of Torah study with mystical character. He did so by basing his interpretation on the Kabbalistic conception of the structure of the soul. According to this conception, the soul is divided into three aspects: *nefesh* (psyche), *ruah* (spirit), and *neshama* (soul). These three aspects are graded hierarchically: the *neshama* comes first, then the *ruah,* and finally the *nefesh.* Rabbi Ḥayyim constructs a parallel system of three types of human activity corresponding to these three aspects of the soul: thought, speech, and action. He also makes the three types of service to God parallel to the other two systems: Torah study, prayer, and obeying the commandments. Thus Torah study, which is in the realm of thought, is connected to the *neshama.* Prayer, which belongs to the realm of speech, is connected to the *ruah.* The commandments, which belong to the realm of action, are connected to the *nefesh.*

This structural parallel attributes a hierarchy of values to the three types of divine service. However, the superiority of Torah study to prayer and observance of the commandments is not limited to its connection with the highest aspect of the soul. That superiority emerges in Rabbi Ḥayyim's proposed interpretation of the aspect of the *neshama* within the soul. He argues that the root of the word *neshama* is *neshima* (breath). However, this does not refer to the breath of human beings, "but rather, as it were, to the breath of His mouth, may His Name be blessed, as it is written, 'and He blew the spirit of life into his nostrils' (Genesis 2:7)." On the basis of this interpretation, and on the basis of a rabbinical Midrash that compares blowing the breath of life into Adam to the act of a craftsman blowing a glass vessel, Rabbi Ḥayyim argues that the essence of the soul is not at all invested in the human body. The soul is a divine entity concealed in the upper realms, and "only sparks of light sparkle from it onto a person's head, and God favors each individual according to his level."[75]

What is the nature of this divine inspiration embodied in the "sparks of light" with respect to the soul? Rabbi Ḥayyim responds, "It is what gives a person greater understanding to comprehend the hidden and buried insights of the holy Torah." Ostensibly this refers to penetration to the hidden level of Torah. However, from Rabbi Ḥayyim's remarks elsewhere, we find that this divine inspiration may occur also during the study of Halakhic literature. In this case, the divine inspiration is expressed in the fertilization and enrichment of the student's mind, and thereby it helps him to overcome the complications of the Halakhic issue.[76]

It seems that we have here the transfer of an idea derived from the world of Kabbalah into the realm of occupation with Halakhah. An idea frequently encountered in Kabbalah and Hasidism is that superior individuals may discover the "secrets of the Torah." In the Kabbalistic context, these "secrets" belong to the realm of the esoteric Torah. The discovery is viewed in this context as surpassing the limitations of human intellect, which, by its own nature, is incapable of revealing the hidden secrets of the Torah. However, Rabbi Ḥayyim, who seeks to endow the study of Halakhah with mystical character, describes divine intervention as fertilization and enrichment of the intellect, and the object of study is Halakhic literature. Recall the Vilna Gaon's view on the matter of intellectual labor in Torah study, which is that the achievements of his intellect appear to him as words that God places in his mouth. It would not be unreasonable to suggest that Rabbi Ḥayyim was inspired by the Gaon's personal example in developing his ideas about divine intervention in the process of Torah study.

BETWEEN TORAH AND *YIRA*

As noted earlier, the Hasidic critique of traditional Torah study pointed out the gap between the intellectual attainments of the scholars and the degree of their *yira.* The scholars were accused of neglecting the value of *yira* and making their Torah studies an instrument for obtaining honor. Rabbi Ḥayyim's thought on this topic may be viewed as an effort to rehabilitate the traditional idea of combining Torah with *yira.* Hence, he was essentially responding favorably to the Hasidic critique. However, in contrast to the Hasidim, who interpreted *yira* as cleaving to God or as preparation for it and so rejected traditional Torah study, Rabbi Ḥayyim suggested what he regarded as the correct combination of Torah and *yira.* He condemned the Hasidic tendency to neglect the study of Halakhah and to concentrate on ethical works. In his opinion, the Halakhah was "the body of the Torah."[77] Therefore, neglect of Halakhic study was neglect of Torah study. Nevertheless, he admits that "certainly it is impossible to say that for the purpose of occupation with the Torah there is no need of any purification of thought and *yira* of God, perish the thought. For we have studied an entire Mishnah that states that if there is no *yira*, there is no wisdom."[78] What emphasis, then, should be placed on developing *yira* alongside Torah study?

Rabbi Ḥayyim clarifies the correct relationship between the two by interpreting the Talmud in the tractate *Shabat* (31a): "Resh Lakish said: What is the meaning of the verse 'Faithfulness to Your charge was [her] wealth, wisdom and devotion [her] triumph,' etc. [Isaiah 33:6]. 'Faithfulness' is the Order *Zera'im*, 'Your charge' is the Order *Mo'ed*, and 'wealth' is the Order *Nashim* . . . and even so '*yira* for the Lord—that was his treasure.'" Rabbi Ḥayyim interprets the word "treasure" as a granary and compares Torah to produce and *yira* to a granary, whose purpose is to preserve the produce. Thus, "if a person has not first prepared a granary of *yira*, most of the produce of the Torah will be as if left in the field to be trampled by the hooves of oxen, perish the thought, and it is not maintained by him at all."[79]

Following the comparison of Torah to produce and of *yira* to the granary in which it is stored, a clear conclusion emerges: Torah study is the main objective, and *yira* is a means to it. However, *yira* is an essential means, without which one cannot study Torah. Indeed, the meaning of this example is double: It contains a polemical barb aimed at Hasidism: "Could it possibly occur to a person, since all of the existence and preservation of the produce is the granary, that he might be occupied all or most of his time only in building the granary, and that he would never put produce in it! Similarly, how could it occur to anyone to say that this is the purpose of a Jewish person, that he should place all of his determined study in building the granary of *yira* . . . , and that the granary would be empty."[80] At the same time, the example of the granary also states that *yira* is an essential accompaniment to Torah study.

Now that we have seen what Rabbi Ḥayyim regarded as the correct balance between the values of Torah and *yira*, a question arises: is there any interdependence between them? Rabbi Ḥayyim did maintain that success in Torah study depended on the level of the student's *yira.* As noted, we found that success in Torah study depends on divine inspiration, which enriches and fertilizes the scholar's mind. However, the achievement of intellectual inspiration and its scope depend on "the granary of *yira*" that one has prepared for it: "For if a person has prepared a large granary of pure *yira* for God, God will give him wisdom and understanding and great abundance, as much as the granary will hold. Everything is according to the size of his granary."[81] Hence a man's greatness in Torah also testifies to the degree of his *yira,* for he gained that greatness because of it.

What is the character of *yira* that Rabbi Ḥayyim invokes, and how is it to be integrated in the process of study? The following provides an indication:

> Hence it is proper for a person to prepare himself all the time, before he begins to study, to reflect somewhat upon his Creator, may His name be blessed, in purity of heart and *yira* for God, and to purify himself of his transgressions with thoughts of repentance, so that during his occupation with the holy Torah he can connect and cleave to His word and His will, may His name be blessed. And he should also take it upon himself to do and fulfill everything written in the written and oral Torah, and then he will see and understand His way and His guidance in the holy Torah. And so when he wishes to look into a Halakhic matter, it is proper for him to pray that He, may He be blessed, will permit him to reach conclusions according to the Halakhah, to direct himself to the truth of the Torah.[82]

The *yira* that Rabbi Ḥayyim requires as an accompaniment to Torah study is therefore a certain state of consciousness, and it must serve as a framework for the process of study. The consciousness of *yira* is acquired by a conscious mental effort to purify one's thinking of sinful ideas. Therefore it is accompanied by a spiritual accounting and atonement for sins, based on thoughts of repentance. Consciousness of *yira* is a necessary prerequisite for cleaving to God during one's study. Rabbi Ḥayyim's proposal to prepare a reverent consciousness before beginning to study is strikingly similar to the preparations that the Hasidim instituted prior to prayer. This structural similarity brings out the difference in values between the two approaches. Hasidic literature regards cleaving to God as the main thing, and Torah study is sometimes presented as one of the ways of preparation for prayer. In contrast, for Rabbi Ḥayyim, Torah study is the main thing, and he regards *yira* as a necessary preparation for study.

Rabbi Ḥayyim makes two additional demands, and these too may be regarded as prerequisites that enable Torah study to serve as a path to cleaving to God. First, the scholar is asked to obligate himself to apply in his practical life all conclusions that might emerge in the course of his study. This demand is not limited to the actions commonly agreed on and found in works of Halakhic authorities and compilations of Halakhah but also refers to practical conclusions that emerge from give and take regarding passages in the Talmud, including the Aggadic portions. This demand was intended to supplement abstract study of the Halakhah with the dimension of study that leads to action, by means of sensitivity and awareness of all the consequences that can be deduced from the words of the Sages.[83]

Second, the scholar is asked "to direct himself to the truth of the Torah." This demand opposes the method of study in which sharpness of mind becomes an end in itself. Only the commitment to reveal the truth inherent in the text must guide the scholar. In this matter, Rabbi Ḥayyim follows in the footsteps of the Vilna Gaon. However, in addition to the methodological aspect this demand has spiritual significance: whoever seeks to cleave to God by virtue of Torah study, based on the assumption that the Halakhah embodies the divine will, must of course strive with all his ability to discover the truth in the Torah.

Thus we have found that Rabbi Ḥayyim rejected the Hasidic method of Torah study as a way of cleaving to God, and in place of it he proposed a method of his own for that purpose. It is appropriate now to raise the question: What is the nature of cleaving to God that can be consistent with the traditional manner of Torah study? Evidently, when the student of Torah "for its own sake" cleaves to God, as described by Rabbi Ḥayyim, it is quite different from the cleaving to God of which Hasidism speaks. The essence of the experience according to Hasidism is the immediate feeling of the divine presence. This experience, though it may be attained on various levels and have different qualities on each level, is bound up with a certain separation from consciousness of the material world. In contrast, the student of Torah "for its own sake," according to Rabbi Ḥayyim's approach, still focuses most of his attention on Halakhic issues, all of which belong to the material world. In his prayer or by other means the Hasid seeks to achieve ecstasy and rapture, whereas the Torah scholar must strive for lucidity of thought and clarity of sensation. Thus, even though Rabbi Ḥayyim uses the term "cleaving to God," the meaning of the experience of Torah study is not the same as the mystical experience of Hasidism.

Are we to conclude that Rabbi Ḥayyim's remarks on the combination of cleaving to God with Torah study are merely an abstract construct with no application to the psychological reality of the student? I believe such a conclusion would be erroneous. It appears that a person who identifies with the ideas set out by Rabbi Ḥayyim regarding the meaning of Torah study, and who applies his directives regarding study for its own sake, could, while studying Torah, experience a profound religious experience unique in its power. A scholar who studies Torah for its own sake who is aware of the divine character of the Halakhic issues with which he is dealing and of the power of the influence of Torah study on the higher realms; who attributes the success of his study to divine inspiration, which fertilizes his intelligence; who acknowledges that this inspiration depends on the degree of his *yira;* and who purifies his soul and his thoughts before studying—such a scholar is likely to feel, in the course of his study, a solemn sense of sanctity, elevation, and enthusiasm bound up with awareness of his religious mission. All these feelings may join together to produce an intense religious experience, which might border on mystical experience, though it is doubtful that it would cross that border.

BETWEEN INTENTION AND DEED

In responding to the Hasidic challenge Rabbi Ḥayyim also sought to show the proper way to pray and perform the commandments, because

Hasidism impaired the traditional patterns of serving God in that area too. Central to Rabbi Ḥayyim's polemics was the claim that the Hasidic manner of serving God raised the danger of antinomianism. This danger had two causes. The first was the distortion inherent in the Hasidic view of God's presence in the "worlds" and the practical conclusions derived from it. The second cause was the radical spiritualization of prayer and observation of the commandments.

Divine Immanence

The idea of divine immanence occupied a central place in Hasidic doctrine. Hasidic thought also has a pronounced tendency to give this concept a far-reaching interpretation. Kabbalistic literature usually emphasizes the graduated character of divine immanence in the worlds, whereas Hasidic thought sometimes speaks of the immanence of the divine substance itself.[84] This radical conception of divine immanence served as the doctrinal basis for some of the ways Hasidism renewed divine worship. Prominent among these were the raising up of "alien thoughts" and worship in corporeality.[85] The latter term means that even mundane actions, such as eating and drinking, may be regarded as worship of God if the proper intention accompanies them.[86] Thus divine immanence supplied justification for Hasidism to enlarge the scope of service of God to include Halakhically neutral actions, neither specifically enjoined nor expressly prohibited.

Rabbi Ḥayyim begins his polemics against Hasidism on the issue of divine immanence with a protest that this arcane matter, which should have been passed over in silence, had become a matter of public discussion in the Hasidic camp. In this way Hasidism had broken down the barriers of the tradition in the area of belief and opinion as well. Moreover, in the absence of a restraining authority, things had gone so far "that a man [may find] any path suitable in his eyes to walk after the tendency of his mind . . . and above all, that it is the doctrine of everyone, and it has also become a maxim in the mouths of fools, namely, that in every place and every thing is absolute divinity."[87]

The belief that the divine presence is found in everything, and the identification of that presence with the very substance of the divinity, was regarded by Rabbi Ḥayyim as a simplistic distortion of the idea of divine immanence. He based his view on the literature of Kabbalah, which distinguishes between divine immanence in the realm of the world of *atsilut* and that which is in the realm of the worlds—*bria, yetsira,* and *'asiya.*

Rabbi Ḥayyim connects the distorted understanding of the idea of divine immanence with the fact that Hasidism opened the gates of Kabbalah before people who were unworthy of it. However, he regards the Hasidic tendency to "worship in corporeality" as even more dangerous. This path was perilous because it could lead a person to permit himself to meditate on the words of the Torah even in polluted places. Such conduct, which is contrary to the Halakhah, is presented by Rabbi Ḥayyim as a pronounced example of the blurring of boundaries between sacred and profane.[88] That blurring of boundaries implied a grave possibility of "destroying several foundations of the holy Torah,"[89] for the entire Halakhah is based on the distinction between sacred and profane, between impure and pure, between what is prohibited and what is permitted, and so on.

In a response to one of his students, we find a similar argument against worship in corporeality. His student had asked, "What is service for its own sake?" Rabbi Ḥayyim responds, "[Adherents of] the well-known sect say that with them everything is service for its own sake; [but] if so, why do we have 613 commandments, so that everything that is for the sake of heaven one should do and what is not for the sake of heaven one should not do, even if it is a commandment?!"[90] With these words Rabbi Ḥayyim expresses the depth of the chasm between the idea of "worship in corporeality" and the traditional conception of the Halakhah. If religious intention has the power to sanctify even a profane act, what is the purpose and place of the Halakhah? For the entire essence of the Halakhah is that it draws the boundary between sacred and profane, on the basis of the objective definition of actions that are desired by God and those He prohibits.

Rabbi Ḥayyim is not content with merely rejecting the Hasidic interpretation of the idea of divine immanence. He wishes to place it on its true foundation. His interpretation is based on the dual wording of the Zohar, which states that God "surrounds all the worlds," and that He "fills all the worlds." He regards this dual wording as the basis for the distinction between two different perspectives in conceiving the connection between the divine substance and the worlds. From the divine perspective, to which man is not privy because of his limitations, God "fills all the worlds." That is to say, "He fills all the worlds and the places and the creatures with absolute equality and simple unity." Not even the act of creation caused a change in the simple unity of the divinity. However, from the human point of view, God "surrounds all the worlds." In the process of creation the divine substance contracted so as to allow "the existence of the worlds and the powers and creatures renewed in different aspects and matters and divided in divisions of different holy and pure places and, on the contrary, polluted and filthy."[91]

Rabbi Ḥayyim conceives of the idea of *tsimtsum* (contraction), which derives from the Kabbalah of the ARI, not as a withdrawal of the divine substance from the space in which the work of creation took place, but as the garbing of the divine substance in material garments, which conceal it from human senses. Consequently, humans conceive the cosmic being as a system of various and contradictory elements. This human perspective creates the framework for the necessity and possibility of the existence of the Halakhah, for against the background of that system of contrary elements the Halakhah defines the boundaries between sacred and profane. Thus man's service to God must take place in the framework of the conception of the divinity as "surrounding all the worlds."

To sum up, the distinction proposed by Rabbi Ḥayyim between "surrounding all the worlds" and "filling all the worlds" is meant to bridge the gap between the transcendental view of the divinity and the Kabbalistic idea of divine immanence in the worlds. By virtue of this distinction, Rabbi Ḥayyim sought to sustain the idea of immanence in its full power, meaning that the divine substance itself fills all the worlds with simple unity. At the same time he sought to avert the danger that this idea might serve as the basis for divine service in practical life and thus threaten the authority of the Halakhah.[92]

Intention in Prayer and the Commandments

Another element of Hasidism with which Rabbi Ḥayyim argues is the demand, exaggerated in his opinion, for the spiritualization of divine service. Hasidism demands that the performance of every commandment and the utterance of every prayer be done with a pure mind and cleaving to God. This demand appears to be positive, for it seeks to raise people to a high level in service to God. But in fact, Rabbi Ḥayyim argues, it is no more than the counsel of the evil impulse, "which disguises itself so as to appear to a person as the good impulse . . . and deceive him."[93] The evil impulse seeks to convince a person that "the main essence of the Torah and commandments is [fulfilled] specifically when they are [observed] with immense intention and true cleaving to God; and any time when a person's heart is not full [of desire] to do them with holy intention and cleaving to God and pure thought, it is not regarded as a commandment or as service at all." Hence, making the value of prayer or the commandments depend on one's attaining purity of thought ultimately impairs the Halakhic framework of that commandment or prayer. Thus, for example, a person who believes that "all Torah and commandments without cleaving to God are nothing" will ultimately prefer prayer with intention, but at an improper time, to prayer at the proper time uttered without the necessary intention. By using this example, Rabbi Ḥayyim alludes to the Hasidic custom of praying late as a result of the preparations prior to prayer. In his opinion that phenomenon is only the first break in *yira* for the law, and it could expand and become "destruction of the entire Torah."[94]

To illustrate this danger, Rabbi Ḥayyim describes a hypothetical case: suppose a person spends the entire Seder night purifying his soul in order to perform the commandment to eat an "olive-size" portion of matza. In the end he would eat the matza only after dawn, and he would not have performed his Halakhic duty to eat it on the Seder night. In this spirit Rabbi Ḥayyim goes on to describe other ridiculous possibilities: "And what is the difference between him and someone who sounds the shofar with enormous intention on the first night of Pesah, instead of the commandment to eat an olive-size portion of matza, and he eats an olive-size portion of matza on Rosh Hashana, and he fasts on the day before Yom Kippur, and on Yom Kippur he waves a *lulav,* instead of the commandment to fast, and where is the place of the Torah?"[95] These examples, which are of course greatly exaggerated, were intended to reveal the antinomian potential contained in the Hasidic manner of serving God. Rabbi Ḥayyim did not belittle the intention that must accompany the service of God, but he was apprehensive lest overemphasizing intention might detract from precise observance of the details of actions as defined by the Halakhah.

Rabbi Ḥayyim's fears that the Hasidim might diminish the Halakhah's status had no basis in their behavior. The path of "service in corporeality" was not widely practiced. As for undermining Halakhah by overemphasizing intention, except for lateness in the time of prayers this potential danger was never actualized. In the end, conservative tendencies prevailed among the Hasidim, and these blocked or restrained the danger of antinomianism. Thus we find that, rather than condemning the actual behavior of the Hasidim, Rabbi Ḥayyim sought to warn about the potential dangers inherent in the Hasidic approach.

Rabbi Ḥayyim's response to the Hasidic view of the connection between intention and action was ambivalent. On the one hand, he fears it might impair the authority of the Halakhah. On the other hand, he admits the positive element inherent in it. Hence the course that Rabbi Ḥayyim charts regarding prayer and the commandments was a middle way between radical spiritualization, with the danger it entailed, and service of God devoid of any awareness or inner religious experience. This path is predicated on three basic assumptions: (1) all religious action ought to be performed within the bounds of the Halakhah; (2) performing a commandment or reciting a prayer has religious value, even if not accompanied by intention; and (3) the path toward perfection in service of God traverses a gradual course, and progress in it depends on the personal qualifications of every individual.

The first assumption underlay the alternative that Rabbi Ḥayyim proposed for "service in corporeality." In a response to his students on this matter, he states that such service had been legitimate before the giving of the Torah. Similarly, even today a "son of Noah," meaning a non-Jew, may worship God in any way that he wishes. "But to us, the children of Israel, the Torah has given a fence and a boundary, and every action is comprised in a command and a warning. . . . And it the way of Hasidism [is] to be precise in the [commandments] to the very limit, and to withdraw . . . from the gate of prohibition, and to be careful in all the precise instructions of the rabbis and the warnings."[96] Identifying scrupulousness and precision in observing the commandments as the essence of piety is not in itself an innovation. That view had been common in the tradition for generations. However, by emphasizing that this was the legitimate path to pious action, and by directing his students to act in that fashion, Rabbi Ḥayyim is in fact expressing reservations about "service in corporeality," as conceived by Hasidism. The determining principle is that, since the giving of the Torah, no service of God is possible, for Jews, that goes beyond the bounds of the Halakhah, no matter how exalted the intention underlying the act might be.

In response to the danger entailed in Hasidism's excessive emphasis on intention, Rabbi Ḥayyim declares, "For in truth, the entire matter of purity of heart in serving Him, may He be blessed, is [to enhance] the commandment but not vital to it; . . . and anyone who observes the commandments of God, as commanded to us in the holy written and oral Torah, even without cleaving to God, he, too, is called a servant of God and beloved before Him, may He be blessed."[97] With these words Rabbi Ḥayyim establishes a principled and sharp distinction between obligation and voluntary action in keeping the commandments. There is a Halakhic obligation to observe the commandments. This is a fundamental demand from which one may not deviate. The intention accompanying the performance of a commandment is a very desirable addition to it, but not a necessary one. Consequently, the absence of intention does not nullify the value of performing a commandment.

Rabbi Ḥayyim finds a doctrinal basis for this statement in the Kabbalistic view regarding the effect of human actions in the upper worlds. He observes that, when a Jew performs a commandment properly, according to the detailed definition of the Halakhah, this action has an effect in the higher realms, even if not accompanied by intention or knowledge of the Kabbalistic intentions: "For thus the Creator, may His Name be blessed, determined the nature of the worlds, that they would be affected by human actions. And that every commandment rises up by itself to do the action particular to it."[98]

The determination that performance of a commandment in itself acts on the upper realms casts doubt on the necessity for Kabbalistic intention. Indeed, Rabbi Ḥayyim's words imply that there is no need to use these intentions. According to him, in recent generations Rabbi Shimon Bar Yoḥai and his students and the ARI discovered only a few of the secrets of the commandments' influence on the higher realms. Even that discovery was meant only to endow Jews with some concrete knowledge about the power and influence of their actions on the higher realms, so as to arouse them to keep the commandments "with utter precision and veneration and mighty love and sanctity and purity of heart; . . . by so doing [the Jew] will cause great reparations in the worlds, . . . but the essence of all the commandments . . . are the details of action in them."[99] We find that the desired intention in performing the commandments is not a mystical intention like that of the Kabbalists. The Jew who performs the commandment does not know the exact influence of his action on the higher realms, and there is certainly no need to intend to exert that specific influence. The intention that Rabbi Ḥayyim recommends is more general in character: "And it is worthy of every man from the holy nation . . . to combine this thought and the desired purity of intention with the study of Torah and performing all the commandments, to continue to add sanctity and light in the worlds with that nourishment."[100] However, this intention, too, is "very desirable but not vital."

Rabbi Ḥayyim even takes this principle and applies it to prayer. Here, too, he depends on a Kabbalistic view regarding the influence of prayer on the higher realms. By means of the holy spirit and the power of prophecy with which they were imbued, those who composed the prayers, the members of the Great Assembly, knew the order of the higher realms and the divine powers. Therefore, "they established and ordained the wording of the benedictions and prayers in those specific letters, since they saw and understood in what way would dwell the light of every individual letter of them, which is needed greatly for the greatest reparation of the worlds and the higher powers and the arrangement of the *merkavah*."[101] Rabbi Ḥayyim concludes from this that by pronouncing the words of the prayers themselves in their standard formulation, a Jew has influence on the higher realms even if no intention accompanies them. Regarding the Kabbalistic notion of intention, not only is it not a prerequisite in order for prayer to influence the higher realms, its use is impossible. Everything that the masters of Kabbalah discovered in this regard "does not even have the value of a drop in the whole sea in contrast to the deep innerness of the intention of the men of the Great Assembly who instituted the prayers; . . . and any person of understanding will understand that no person on earth can make a reparation as marvelous and awesome as that."[102]

The statement that the acts of prayer and observing the commandments influence the higher realms, even when they are not accompanied by an intention, is made only to avert the danger bound up with the exaggerated emphasis Hasidism gave to the value of intention. However, at the same time, Rabbi Ḥayyim seeks to arouse Jews and impel them to serve God on the highest level possible. His intention is expressed in his principle of degrees in the service of God. This principle is based on psychological observation that takes into account the following givens: the continuous and graduated process of education, ascents and descents in the individual's spiritual life, and the differences in individuals' condition and spiritual power. Rabbi Ḥayyim concludes from these that the path to perfection in the service of God is a ladder with many rungs. Ascending the ladder is a slow and prolonged process that differs from one person to another. Describing the service of God as a course that is by nature one of many stages legitimizes even the lowest levels of that course. This, then, is Rabbi Ḥayyim's answer to Hasidic radicalism calling for all or nothing.

Regarding the intentions of prayer, Rabbi Ḥayyim proposes a detailed model of the principle of graduation. The first level, a relatively low one, is that in which the person praying fulfills the obligation prescribed in the Torah as praying "with your whole heart." Two components are included in this level: The first is the demand that the worshiper must concentrate on the meaning of the words of the prayer without attaching any other thought to them. Purifying the mind of alien thoughts assures that the prayer will be offered "with a whole heart and from the depth of the heart." A second demand is added to this: "[One should endeavor], while praying, to uproot from his heart the pleasures of the world and its enjoyments entirely," so that the person's full intention "is drawn only upward to take pleasure in God alone."[103] The second demand is more difficult than the first, for it requires one to ignore all matters of this world, even when they are mentioned in the body of the prayer itself.

A higher level in the intention of prayer, meant for "those who know and understand a little," is that by which the worshiper fulfills the Torah's demand to pray "with your entire soul." This intention has a decidedly mystical character, and its purpose is to cause the worshiper to cleave to God. The prayer service takes the place of the service of sacrifice: "And, as the matter of sacrifice is to raise the soul of the beast upward, . . . so the essence of prayer is to raise and deliver and have the soul cleave upward." Prayer may accomplish this because "speech is the essence of the human soul, which is the superiority of man over animals." However, in order for a man truly to pour his soul into the words of his prayer, he must attain a certain condition:

> He shall strip away his body from his soul, . . . and before standing in prayer he must nullify and remove from himself in his thought all the pleasures of the body and its enjoyments and all its concerns, so that it will be determined in his thought to abhor the body as if he had no body at all, and only his soul alone is speaking in his prayer. And in uttering each letter, which is a power and part of his soul, he shall greatly make his will cling to give and truly pour his soul into it completely, and make it cling to the upper root of the letters of the prayer, which stand at the pinnacle of the world; . . . and then he will be thought of as if he were removed from this world.[104]

Here, then, we have a description of cleaving to God in prayer that is attained by virtue of stripping away corporeality and on the basis of an assumption regarding the mystical characters of the letters of the prayer. Detachment of the soul from the body, which takes places in the consciousness of the worshiper, permits him to pour his soul into the letters of the prayers, and they raise him to their upper root in the realm of the divinity. Within this level of intention in prayer Rabbi Ḥayyim also notes several secondary degrees, for every person is likely to cleave to God "according to the power of the purity of his heart," and even the very same person may experience ascents and descents in purity of thought.[105]

Later Rabbi Ḥayyim describes a higher level of intention in prayer:

"And it is to direct yourself to the details included within the soul, but education is necessary to make oneself accustomed [to rise] from level to level. For after one is used in one's prayer for some time to the matter of pouring out and cleaving with the entire soul, after that one will transfer oneself to aiming at the aspect of the details of which one's soul is composed."[106] This intention is based on the division of the soul into aspects: *nefesh, ruah,* and *neshama.* These are parallel to the aspects of action, speech, and thought. Now, these aspects are also present in the letters of the prayers, and they are embodied in the letters, the vocalization, and the accentuation. Thus the worshiper on this level must pour each part of his soul into the aspect parallel to it in the letters of the prayer. In so doing each of the aspects of the soul will be connected to its upper root.

Thus the higher degrees of intention in prayer, which Rabbi Ḥayyim describes, have a decidedly mystical character. As one involved with the literature of Kabbalah, Rabbi Ḥayyim did not need the intermediary of Hasidism in order to reach this conception of the intentions of prayer. Moreover, the character of prayer in cleaving to God described by Rabbi Ḥayyim is different from prayer in cleaving to God as known to us in Hasidism. The ecstatic element that characterizes Hasidic cleaving to God is blocked and restrained by the need to attach the details of the aspects of the soul to the aspects parallel to them in the letters of prayer. Nevertheless, it appears that when he decided to include instructions regarding prayer with cleaving to God in his book, Rabbi Ḥayyim was responding to the Hasidic challenge. For at that historical moment in Judaism, Hasidism had placed cleaving to God at the center of religious life.

Torah Not for Its Own Sake

The dialectical approach that characterized Rabbi Ḥayyim's position regarding the relationship between intention and action in prayer and observance of the commandments is also be found in relation to Torah study. As noted, the Hasidim severely criticized traditional Torah scholars because their study was not for its own sake. Rabbi Ḥayyim maintained that this criticism was liable to deter scholars and lead to the cessation of Torah study. His response to this threat was to emphasize the high value of Torah study for its own sake, as well as demand recognition of the value of Torah study that was not for its own sake.

Rabbi Ḥayyim bases permission for studying Torah not for its own sake on a quotation from the Sages in the tractate *Pesahim* (50b): "A person must always engage in Torah [study] and the commandments, even if not for their own sake, since from not being for its own sake, it will come to be for its own sake." And he casts a new light on this famous quotation, which was usually interpreted as limited and temporary permission to study Torah not for its own sake:

> For in truth it is almost impossible to arrive right away in the beginning at placing one's study on the level of for its own sake as should be done. For occupation with Torah not for its own sake is a level, from which one can come to the level of for its own sake. Therefore, it, too, is beloved and cherished before Him, may He be blessed. Just as it is impossible to ascend from the ground to an attic except on the rungs of a ladder. And on this the [Sages] said: "A person must always engage in Torah and the commandments, even if not for their own sake." They said always, meaning constantly, that is to say, at the start of his study he is required only to study constantly always day and night. And even if some thought of his own benefit may come to his mind, and he thinks about pride and honor or the like, nevertheless he should not pay attention and withdraw or slacken in it because of that, perish the thought; but on the contrary he should fortify himself greatly in occupation with the Torah and let his heart be ready and secure that certainly he shall come into the level of for its own sake; . . . and anyone who swells his heart to deride and belittle, perish the thought, someone occupied with Torah and the commandments even not for their own sake, his evil will not be cleansed, and in the future he will face judgment, perish the thought.[107]

Thus, study not for its own sake was no longer deficient, so that it could only be permitted retroactively. Rather it was a necessary step on the path leading to the level of study for its own sake. Therefore, not only was it legitimate, but it also had value of its own. Furthermore, in the talmudic statement that he cites, Rabbi Ḥayyim also finds the promise that whoever is diligent in his study not for its own sake will ultimately have the merit of studying Torah for its own sake.

Up to now we have seen Rabbi Ḥayyim defending Torah study not for its own sake as a necessary stage on the way to Torah study for its own sake. In continuing to discuss this topic he expands permission for the former even further:

> And even if it appears that all the days of his life, from his youth until venerable old age, his occupation with it was not for its own sake, even so you must treat him with respect, and even more so not despise him, perish the thought. For since he was constantly occupied with Torah, without doubt many times his intention was also for its own sake, as our Sages of blessed memory have promised, since from not being for its own sake, it will come to be for its own sake. For that does not mean that he shall come to it for its own sake so that finally he always will be occupied with it all his days only for its own sake. Rather, [it means] that every time he studies . . . several hours in succession, even though in general his intention was not for its own sake, nevertheless it is completely impossible that a worthy intention for its own sake should not enter his heart in the midst of the study, at least for a short time. Henceforth, everything he had hitherto learned not for its own sake is sanctified and purified by that short time that he intended it for its own sake.[108]

It should again be emphasized that Rabbi Ḥayyim's repeated efforts to justify Torah study that was not for its own sake were intended only to counteract the grave danger that he saw in Hasidic criticism and its influence on scholars. However, at the same time, Rabbi Ḥayyim spoke at length emphasizing the high spiritual level attached to Torah study when it was for its own sake. Among other things, he wrote, "A person who accepts upon himself the yoke of the holy Torah for its own sake and its truth . . . is raised above all the matters of this world, and he is watched over by Him, may He be praised, with personal providence, above all the laws of nature. Since he truly cleaves to the Torah and to the Holy One, blessed be He, . . . indeed the forces of nature are obedient to him, to whatever he decrees regarding them."[109]

We have found two tendencies in the thought of Rabbi Ḥayyim of Volozhin. One seeks to preserve and reinforce traditional patterns and values that Hasidism impaired or threatened to impair. The other tendency combines and integrates the values of *yira* and cleaving to God within traditional patterns and values. Thus it may be said that the theological system developed by Rabbi H.ayyim was a synthesis of the patterns and values accepted by the Mitnagdim and those in whose name Hasidism campaigned and whose neglect it protested.

The special quality and strength of Rabbi Ḥayyim's thinking derives from its being interwoven with Kabbalah. Indeed, he wished to make Kabbalah a conscious theological framework for Jewish service to God. At the same time he was far from intending to turn the Jewish people into a nation of Kabbalists. This explains the popularizing tendency of his use of Kabbalah. He mainly emphasized general principles without expounding on the details. On the one hand, Rabbi Ḥayyim wanted every Jew to be aware of the strong influence of his actions on the higher worlds. On the other hand, he did not make that influence depend on detailed knowledge of the secrets of the divinity or on the use of Kabbalistic intentions. Similarly, he did not demand deep study of esoteric doctrine.[110]

Particularly striking was Rabbi Ḥayyim's use of ideas and concepts from Kabbalah in order to place Torah study once again at the top of the hierarchy of Jewish values. As noted, Rabbi Ḥayyim presents Torah study as a decisive factor in influencing the upper worlds and bringing down abundance. This view identifies scholars as bearing the main responsibility for the very existence of the worlds. At the same time, Rabbi Ḥayyim represents Torah study as the most promising channel for elevating the individual. Torah study for its own sake was the ideal path of cleaving to God. In a general way, Rabbi Ḥayyim responds to the spiritual challenge presented by Hasidism by endowing Torah study with mystical significance. He does not, however, advocate study of Kabbalah, but rather study of Halakhic literature, as practiced in houses of study and yeshivot.

Rabbi Ḥayyim's theology was extremely influential among the Mitnagdim in Lithuania during the nineteenth century. One prominent expression of that influence is the popularity of his book *Nefesh ha-ḥayyim.* Nahum Lamm found that seven editions of it appeared during the fifty years after its first publication in 1824.[111] Since then, many other editions have been published, and it continues to be published even today. The popularity of his book shows that the theological system he proposed responded to a true need. Another expression of its importance is the frequency with which *Nefesh ha-ḥayyim* is cited as an authoritative work. In light of all this, it may safely be said that Rabbi Ḥayyim's ideas made a significant contribution to the process of the renewal of Torah study in Lithuania. In other words, his teachings gave ideological support to the community of scholars and those who supported them.[112]

It is no exaggeration to say that the ideas that Rabbi Ḥayyim developed in *Nefesh ha-ḥayyim* also guided him in establishing and administrating the yeshiva he founded in Volozhin; that is, his ideas served as its educational program. In the beginning of this chapter, I argued that the yeshiva was established in response to the crisis in Torah study caused by the rise of Hasidism.[113] We shall now examine the character of that yeshiva and consider the role it played in the struggle with Hasidism.

THE ESTABLISHMENT OF THE YESHIVA IN VOLOZHIN

In 5562 (1802) Rabbi Ḥayyim gathered a number of students in Volozhin and began to teach them Torah. He supplied the needs of those students with his own money.[114] By so doing he renewed the existence of the institution of the yeshiva and suggested a new direction to look for its support. Soon afterward, in early 5563, he addressed the Jews of Lithuania with his famous epistle. Some scholars have interpreted this epistle as nothing more than a request for financial support for the new yeshiva. However, it was in fact a call to the Jews of Lithuania to restore the Torah institutions that had been weakened and to place them on a new foundation. Rabbi Ḥayyim regarded the yeshiva he established in Volozhin as the cornerstone of this extensive process of renewal.

In founding the yeshiva in Volozhin, Rabbi Ḥayyim was not acting on personal initiative alone. In his epistle he states that he was acting as an emissary for many "whose hearts worry within them and who moan for the Torah that is forgotten by the Jews and that has become depleted and thin."[115] These words should not be viewed merely as a show of modesty, for later on in the epistle we find a more detailed description of the many appeals and entreaties that spurred him into action. The appeals to Rabbi Ḥayyim express public recognition of his prominence among the spiritual leaders of the Mitnagdim in Lithuania.[116]

In his epistle Rabbi Ḥayyim mentions the crisis in Torah study, and he also mentions an apprehension that if the current situation continued, the present generation would be left "without priest or teacher." The danger that the chain of great Torah scholars might be broken is what impelled him to overcome his doubts and assume the yoke of the mission imposed on him. After some words about the great virtue of Torah study and the grave sin of preventing it, Rabbi Ḥayyim presents his public appeal: "Brethren, Children of Israel, perhaps the time has come to mend that break in the fence and let us once again cling to the Torah of God with all our power; and who will be the volunteers to teach the pupils, and who will be the volunteers to be among the pupils? And who will be the volunteers to support the Torah with all their might?"[117] Rabbi Ḥayyim does not demand that the communities renew the previous custom of maintaining yeshivot. His appeal has no institutional character at all. It is addressed to individuals and is based on the commandment to study Torah and support those who study it. Rabbi Ḥayyim asks individuals to take action that can be defined as personal volunteerism. He presents his project in Volozhin as an example of what he expects of others: "And I will be the first among the volunteers, without an oath, to be among the teachers, and by the grace of God who has always shepherded me in affluence, in Whom I trust and in Whom I take refuge, that He will prosper me to supply the needs of the students; . . . and after my heart has filled me to leap to the forefront and volunteer to be among the teachers, let other men of my kind do like me."[118]

The method that Rabbi Ḥayyim chose in attempting to establish yeshivot was fitting to the circumstances of his times. He probably believed that it was impossible to restore the old model of community maintenance of yeshivot. Therefore he chose to address "lovers of Torah" as individuals, wherever they might be, outside the local community framework. Thus the yeshiva became the joint enterprise of many individuals from various communities: those who studied in the yeshiva, those who taught there, and those who supported it. Unlike its predecessors, the new yeshiva was free of any institutional tie to the local community where it was situated. The new system on which support of the Volozhin yeshiva depended also contributed to the prestige of the yeshiva students. Under the previous system, yeshiva students had eaten at the tables of householders on certain days of the week, but now they were freed of the humiliation which that entailed, and their needs were met by the yeshiva treasury.[119]

In the wake of Rabbi Ḥayyim's epistle came a letter of support from the famous *naggid,* Rabbi Yehoshu'a Zeitlin, a prominent figure among the Mitnagdim at that time.[120] Zeitlin's words show the hopes that Rabbi Ḥayyim's supporters pinned on the recently established yeshiva: "Everyone whose heart has been touched by *yira* for God will understand and realize by himself the quantity and quality of this great thing; and may heaven have mercy on him, with the help of heaven may the thing be concluded, and multiply and flourish, and may it be a great merit to the generation and a tree of life to those who support it."[121] These words support my assumption that Rabbi Ḥayyim, his supporters, and those he represented all viewed establishment of the yeshiva in Volozhin as the first step toward broader and more comprehensive change.

A letter written by several Jewish notables from Vilna about a year and a half later contain the first echoes of the success of the Volozhin yeshiva. The notables recount that "many excellent men have gathered for the sacred task," and that they are diligent in their study of Torah. Similarly the notables relate that until then they had supported the yeshiva with their money. But now,

> since we have seen that the will of God has succeeded by his hand, and that we find that people go in to him every day and seek him, therefore we proclaim to those afar that this is the path of Torah; from a distance shall it bring its bread, and we must acknowledge that this great thing is being done in our days, in an orphaned generation like ours; and we here and you there, let us come and strengthen their hand and let us not be negligent, perish the thought, . . . for we shall do that which is good and honorable in the eyes of the Lord, to strengthen the column of the Torah that had been weakened.[122]

Ten Jewish notables from Vilna signed the letter, which was written in the month of Iyyar 5564. It was intended to expand the circle of the yeshiva's supporters. The call to join the contributors was justified by the large numbers of students who came to Volozhin. This was thus an additional step in the process of basing the finances of the yeshiva on the voluntary support of individuals who identified with the yeshiva and with the values it represented. In the ensuing years this system was improved with the help of a special organization of delegates and emissaries who collected contributions for the yeshiva.[123]

Rabbi Joseph of Krinik, Rabbi Ḥayyim's student, describes repercussions of the Volozhin yeshiva's establishment:

> In the first year after the house of the Lord was founded in Volozhin, I saw that many merchants went out of their way to be in Volozhin and to see what the yeshiva was, and what was done there. And seeing that several quorums of devoted Torah scholars were sitting and studying all day and all night long with marvelous diligence, they were astonished and amazed by that, for they had never seen or imagined anything like it. And many merchants remained for several days and did not want to depart from there.[124]

The Volozhin yeshiva was thus an innovation that aroused wonder and astonishment among the Jews of that generation. The fact that wandering merchants passed through the yeshiva and even stayed there certainly helped spread the word about it over an extensive area.

The successful experiment of the Volozhin yeshiva appears to have prepared people's hearts and paved the way for the establishment of other yeshivot on the same model in Lithuania. Indeed, several of the new yeshivot were established by direct disciples of Rabbi Ḥayyim himself. The founders of these yeshivot followed in their master's footsteps, not only in the organization and financial basis of the yeshiva but also with respect to the method of study and the prevailing educational atmosphere.[125] Rabbi Joseph recounts what he heard from Rabbi Ḥayyim himself regarding his connection with the "daughters" of the Volozhin yeshiva: "From the yeshivot in Minsk I have more delight and pleasure than from my own yeshiva, because from my yeshiva I have great vexation from the details of yeshiva's needs, but from the yeshiva in Minsk I have no vexation at all, and it is all mine." The general view of the role played by the Volozhin yeshiva as the mother of the yeshivot of Lithuania is presented by Rabbi Joseph of Krinik: "For in truth it is the mother and source of all the yeshivot, . . . for they are like pipes that flow from the source."[126]

The Volozhin yeshiva differed from the communal yeshivot that preceded it in ways other than its organization. From testimony about the ways of the Volozhin yeshiva, and mainly from the pamphlets describing Rabbi Ḥayyim's religious practice as well as the advice he gave to his students, we find that this yeshiva was not an institution for the teaching of Torah in the narrow sense of the word.[127] Rather it was an educational institution that sought to develop a man who combined the virtues of an erudite Torah scholar and those of a pious Jew. The educational ideal resulting from the synthesis contained in Rabbi Ḥayyim's teachings was that of a scholar whose sharpness of mind and erudition in Torah was combined and interwoven with *yira.*

A prominent characteristic of the yeshiva under Rabbi Ḥayyim's direction was the great importance attributed to the value of perseverance. Rabbi Ḥayyim encouraged his students to devote themselves almost absolutely to Torah study.[128] The traditional value of perseverance in Torah study was given extra force and authority in his teachings because of their Kabbalistic foundation. For the continued existence of the worlds depended on Torah study and required uninterrupted perseverance in that study. In practical life the ideal of maximal devotion to Torah studies that prevailed in the Volozhin yeshiva was translated into an incessant struggle to exploit every hour and every minute of the student's day. Rabbi Ḥayyim gave his students practical instructions whose purpose was to assist them in their struggle against the impulse to stop studying. These instructions show the rabbi's sensitivity and psychological insight, for they vary from case to case, depending on the personal traits of the student.[129] The phenomenon of the "watches" was an impressive expression of the value of perseverance at the Volozhin yeshiva: some continued to study until the wee hours of the morning, and others arose then to commence studying. Thus Torah study continued at the yeshiva day and night.

At the same time that he urged his students in maximal devotion to

Torah study, Rabbi Ḥayyim also instructed them in *yira.* Some of the students expressed their doubts and difficulties in this area and asked his advice. Among other things they asked him how to overcome alien thoughts, the sin of nocturnal emission, and similar things. Sometimes these questions included a personal confession, showing an intimate fabric of relations between the rabbi and his students. One of the subjects about which Rabbi Ḥayyim often warned his students was the matter of pride. Among other things, he warned against the pride involved in accepting a rabbinical post.[130]

Rabbi Ḥayyim's personal example served as a significant factor in guiding the students. This is true regarding both his behavior in Halakhic areas in which there was an element of doubt and his scrupulous observance of the commandments. The head of the yeshiva was also a personal model in his acts of piety. These acts of piety were not viewed as going beyond the letter of the law but rather were characterized by total application of the Halakhah in every area of life. Indeed, this was a form of piety based on erudition and expertise. The pious scholar knew how to lay bare implications of the law that were also implicit in acts and situations to which most people did not even know that the Halakhah applied. The tendency to base pious action specifically on the Halakhah appears to be a response to the Hasidic tendency to sanctify even secular actions through intention. In any event, Rabbi Ḥayyim's students observed his manner of serving God and recorded it in detail in pamphlets. Most likely they also sought to imitate it.[131]

Thus Rabbi Ḥayyim's role was not limited to teaching Torah and to concern with supplying the financial needs of his yeshiva. As the head of the yeshiva, he was a living model and guide in the service of God. In this respect the role of a Lithuanian head of a yeshiva is somewhat similar to that of a Hasidic Zaddik. Moreover, the students attributed a degree of supernatural power to their rabbi, which added a magical tinge to his figure. This, too, may be seen as a counterpoise to the power of the Hasidic Zaddik.[132]

In the Volozhin yeshiva and in the yeshivot that arose in Lithuania after it, there was yet another parallel with Hasidism. The Hasidic movement provided a framework for organization on a voluntary, supracommunal basis. Similarly, the Volozhin yeshiva and those that arose in its pattern also served as a focus for supracommunal spiritual activity. Around the new yeshiva, which severed its dependence on the local community, was a concentrated public of scholars, graduates, supporters, and sympathizers from many localities. This public regarded the yeshiva not only as an educational institution preparing students for life but principally as a spiritual center where religious ideals were exemplified in the highest fashion.

6 Talmudic Scholarship and the Rabbinate in Lithuanian Jewry during the Nineteenth Century

During the nineteenth century, the Jewish community of Lithuania was famous primarily as a center of Torah study.[1] Although the renown of Lithuanian Jewry has sometimes been related in idealized terms, it is grounded in reality. From many and various sources we find that there was indeed impressive growth in Torah study in Lithuania during the nineteenth century.[2] This phenomenon was reflected in the large number of young men who occupied the benches of houses of study and yeshivot, in the famous *gedolei torah* (masters of Torah), in the different types of Torah institutions, and in the veneration for studiousness and erudition among broad segments of the community. In this chapter I shall clarify the relationship between scholarship and the institution of the rabbinate. One might expect that the two would form harmonious relations of mutual support, for erudite Jewish men were natural candidates to serve as rabbis, and a rabbinical post rewarded the learned Jew and provided him with a livelihood, prestige, and influence. But was this expectation fulfilled in reality? What was the attitude of learned Jews to the post of the rabbinate? To what degree could such a post offer a learned man an adequate reward for his achievements?

The following remarks are based on three kinds of sources: (1) biographies of rabbis written by their descendants or their admiring students; (2) memoirs written by men who were raised in the house of study but who were influenced by modernization later in their lives; and (3) the personal letters of traditional scholars, which reveal their inner world. In our discussion the autobiographical work of Rabbi Eliahu David Rabinowitz-Teumim, known as the ADERET, receives special consideration.[3] This work is exceptional because its author belonged to the group known in nineteenth-century Russia as the "Old Generation." Rabbis of his type usually did not write memoirs. Moreover, the ADERET's book is uncommon in the degree to which it openly describes trying and painful events without disguise.

Academic scholars have not yet examined the questions that we will deal with here, so the following remarks will leave more questions than definite answers. Some of the statements and suppositions presented here require grounding and proof in sources other than the ones available to us now. Thus I do not claim to offer a definitive account of the subject but only open the discussion.

THE ATTITUDE TOWARD THE POST OF THE RABBINATE

In the biographies of Torah scholars in nineteenth-century Lithuania, reluctance to undertake a rabbinical career appears consistently. Even in the cases of men who served in rabbinical posts for many years, their biographers take pains to emphasize that these men did not initially intend to accept such a post, and that they did so merely because of economic need or some other constraint. A typical example of this phenomenon is Rabbi Hillel Milikovsky, also known as Rabbi Hillel Salanter. As his biographer recounts, "Nor did it occur to him to make his Torah a hoe with which to dig food, and therefore he was not ordained with the ordination of Sages and Geonim who lived in that generation, to pass judgment and issue Halakhic instruction. However, when his name became renowned in glory and splendor for his great knowledge of the Talmud and its medieval commentators, he had the merit of serving first in glory in the post of rabbi in the community of Creva."[4] Rabbi Hillel's reluctance to serve as a rabbi thus derived from the conviction that it was improper to make one's Torah knowledge "a hoe with which to dig" (*Avot* 4:5). A practical expression of that reluctance can be seen in his refusal to accept ordination. Later, his biographer says that the rabbi initially rejected the invitation to fill the post that had opened in the community of Creva, and that he agreed to retract his refusal only after Rabbi Ḥayyim of Volozhin intervened.

That which is said of Rabbi Hillel is repeated, with unimportant variations, in the biographies of other rabbis as well.[5] This relieves us of the necessity of evaluating the accuracy of the testimony in each instance. For the purposes of our discussion, it is enough to state that, among the Torah scholars of Lithuania during the nineteenth century, there was general agreement that it was not fitting for a young scholar to study Torah in order to become a rabbi. This attitude is also the background of the controversy between Rabbi Israel Salanter and some of his students during the 1850s. We learn of this controversy from Rabbi Yitshak Blaser, Rabbi Israel Salanter's disciple and first biographer. Blaser reports that even though Rabbi Israel did not himself serve as a rabbi, he tried to convince his students to prepare themselves for that post. Several of Rabbi Israel's greatest students, who were determined to devote their lives to the study of Torah without making it "a hoe with which to dig," argued that the study of Halakhic rulings as preparation for the rabbinate was contrary to the principle of Torah for its own sake. Rabbi Israel responded:

> There is no "for its own sake" greater than that. For you have erred in your imaginations to assume that you can withstand the trial. For when, perish the thought, you are in an hour of need to support your household, all of your wisdom will be swallowed up. Then not only will need

> bring you to take upon yourselves the burden of [rabbinical] instruction, but you will also not yet be complete and ready to fulfill all the needs of instruction. . . . Hence the goal of study is not for the sake of the rabbinate . . . [but rather] so that in a time of need, when necessity forces you, you will not, perish the thought, mislead the multitude.[6]

The pragmatic character of Rabbi Israel's response to his students is evident: since they will ultimately be required to serve as rabbis because of financial need, they had better prepare themselves for that position. It seems likely that this consideration was neither the sole nor the chief consideration that guided Rabbi Israel. He probably wanted his students to assume leadership positions and to influence society. Nevertheless, his remarks contain no hint that the rabbinate is a public mission that should be taken up as a primary aim. He apparently expressed himself in this manner because he did not want to detract from the value of Torah study for its own sake, as it was then understood among his students.

A personal incident that indicates the general situation is that of Rabbi Shmuel of Kelme and his son Arieh Leib Frumkin.[7] Rabbi Shmuel sent many letters to his family containing instructions to his son regarding Torah study. Even before the period of his support *(mezonot)* was over, his father began to urge him to study *posqim*. In a letter from the month of Av 5527 (1867), Rabbi Shmuel reproaches his son because his regimen of study was inefficient and he still was not prepared to receive ordination. In that letter Rabbi Shmuel adds, "And if it occurs to you that the blessed Lord will save you, and you will succeed in becoming a guide in Halakhah and a judge, that is not a bad thing in these times, but rather it is a great benefit and a commandment."[8] These words might seem surprising: why did Rabbi Shmuel have to persuade his son that there was nothing wrong with a rabbinical post? The answer lies in another letter that Rabbi Shmuel wrote to his son at that time: "And even to study in this age, so that you can become a rabbi and guide in Halakhah in some city, even that is for the sake of Torah, so that you will not, perish the thought, have to neglect your studies in business and to make a living."[9]

We find that the young Arieh Leib's reluctance to become a rabbi was also connected to the widespread idea noted above: that studying for the rabbinate was contrary to studying Torah for its own sake. However, like

Rabbi Israel Salanter, Rabbi Shmuel of Kelme does not try to present the post as a mission or a goal but instead presents it as the lesser evil: since Arieh Leib ultimately will be forced to find a source of livelihood for his family, work in the rabbinate is preferable because, more than any other occupation, it permits the young scholar to continue his Torah studies. Two questions about this aversion to the rabbinate arise: First, can one point out factors that connect this phenomenon particularly to nineteenth-century Lithuania? Second, is it true aversion to the rabbinate, or could it be a symbolic gesture, a kind of lip service?

The sayings of the Sages and later authors on the superior value of Torah study for its own sake and on the fault of making it a "a hoe with which to dig" made a deep impression on Torah scholars in various places during various periods. Nevertheless, it appears that the social convention stating that studying for the rabbinate lacks the value of study for its own sake is particular to nineteenth-century Lithuania. To be more precise, evidence shows that this convention was prevalent among Lithuanian Torah scholars during the second half of that century.

It is possible to point to several phenomena that could have nourished the development of this attitude. One of them is the personal model of the Gaon. As noted, one of the prominent features of his image, as viewed by his students and admirers and as transmitted by them to succeeding generations, was withdrawal from the world for the sake of Torah study.[10] Among other things, this withdrawal entailed almost absolute detachment from public affairs. Thus the message embodied in his personal example emphasized Torah study as a value in its own right, unconnected with direct intervention in public affairs. Only a few of the Gaon's students tried to adopt that way of life in its full severity. The most pronounced effort in this direction was made by those known as *perushim* (the withdrawn), who immigrated to the land of Israel in the early nineteenth century. Nevertheless, the personal example of the Gaon undoubtedly influenced all Torah scholars of nineteenth-century Lithuania.

Rabbi Ḥayyim of Volozhin's teachings are another factor that probably encouraged aversion to studying for the rabbinate.[11] Although Rabbi Ḥayyim promoted the concept of Torah study for its own sake, significantly he expressed no aversion to the rabbinate. On the contrary, he believed in training even young scholars for the rabbinate at the yeshiva he established and ran. At the same time, his statements regarding the meaning of Torah study as a value in its own right likely fostered the conception of Torah study for the rabbinate as study that was not for its own sake.

Another factor that could have influenced the formation of this attitude was the position of Haskalah regarding Torah study and the training of rabbis. The new attitude is manifest as early as *Divrei Shalom Veemet* by Naftali Hertz Wessely, one of the first expressions of the Haskalah program. Wessely argues that specialization in Halakhic literature is not suitable for every Jew, but only for the few who are preparing themselves for a Torah occupation.[12] This attitude is distinctly expressed in the conception underlying a new type of institution for the training of rabbis: *beit hamidrash lerabbanim,* the rabbinical seminary. Institutions of this type were established in various places in Europe during the nineteenth century, and they differed from one another in the political, social, and cultural circumstances that attended their establishment, as well as in their character and nature. Nevertheless, they had a common denominator: the close connection between Torah study and the rabbinate. This connection was expressed both in the declared aim of these institutions and in their curricula. The fundamental assumptions on which the rabbinical seminaries stood clearly contrasted strongly with the traditional value of Torah study for its own sake as interpreted by Lithuanian Jews at that time.

Traditional Lithuanian Torah scholars were exposed to the Haskalah attitude regarding Torah study and rabbinical training in several stages. In the late 1840s the Russian government established two rabbinical seminaries, one in Zhitomir and the other in Vilna.[13] In those institutions, which were under direct government supervision, instruction in Jewish subjects was placed in the hands of maskilim. The hopes that the maskilim pinned on these seminaries were disappointed, because their graduates, who were outstanding neither as Torah scholars nor as pious men, were not accepted by the public. Hence the communities continued to choose rabbis of the old type.[14] However, those rabbis became the objects of blunt and incessant criticism from maskilim during the 1860s and 1870s.[15] In this spirit, the Society for the Promotion of Enlightenment among the Jews encouraged young men to attend the rabbinical seminary in Breslau. In the 1870s the government-established rabbinical seminaries were closed in Russia, and another effort was made to establish such an institution there in the early 1880s. This time the initiative came from the Jewish aristocracy of wealth in St. Petersburg and Moscow. This initiative also failed, because it did not receive the support of the important rabbis in Russia.

The challenge and threat that the Haskalah movement posed to Torah study and the training of rabbis naturally influenced the general Jewish community in Russia. However, it had particular bearing on Torah scholars in Lithuania, who in their opinions and way of life embodied the traditional conception of Torah study.[16] Hence, it is understandable that the view that studying for the rabbinate was a betrayal of the value of Torah "for its own sake" developed in reaction to, among other things, the position of Haskalah, which sought to limit specialization in Torah study to those who aspired to a rabbinical career.

Now let us address the question of whether the various expressions of aversion to the rabbinate are evidence of a real phenomenon or whether they should be interpreted as lip service. At first glance it does appear that these expressions were in fact lip service. Most of the men described as shunning rabbinical posts ultimately accepted them. However, a second examination of the matter shows that this conclusion is superficial. Aversion to the rabbinate in the name of the ideal of Torah for its own sake appears to have been especially typical of young men who were not yet financially independent. The idealism of youth and the fact that these young men were still exempt from the need to support families combined to encourage that attitude. Indeed, when their period of support *(mezonot)* came to an end, many of these young men overcame their aversion to the rabbinate. Nevertheless, the fact that they held the opinion that Torah study for its own sake was superior to the rabbinate did influence the way they performed as rabbis. This applies especially to those who viewed the rabbinate as a livelihood that would enable them to avoid abandoning their Torah studies. These scholars found that their aspirations to persevere in Torah study were incompatible with their duties as rabbis.

The frustration and sorrow of a rabbi whom the vexations of the rabbinate did not permit to engage in Torah study as he wished emerges in the letters of Rabbi Eliyahu Rogoler. In a letter to his brother, Rabbi Shmuel of Kelme, written in 5607, when he was the rabbi of Kalisz, Rabbi Eliyahu says:

> Since the day when I became a man I have not had such hard work as in the rabbinate of our congregation, with my whole body, with my whole soul, at all times. And there is no free time to study at all in an orderly fashion, only at intervals. . . . Perhaps the Lord will favor me to be relieved of the iron yoke of the rabbinate, without swearing an oath, and I will be able to amuse myself with you in words of Torah. . . . My request—to go on the eve of the New Moon of Adar or on the eve of the New Moon of Nissan to the graves of our righteous fathers in the city of Rosein, and to remember them for myself and for my sons and daughters, so that we will not depend on flesh and blood and so that I can be released with goodness and joy from my hard yoke so that I can always study our holy Torah.[17]

Recognition of the conflict between the obligations of a rabbinical post and the aspiration to persevere in Torah study was shared by other rabbis.[18] Some sought to overcome the difficulty by choosing to live in small communities, though they were offered posts in larger and more affluent ones.[19] Rabbi Hillel Milikovsky found a slightly different solution when he served as rabbi of Khoslovitz, as his biographer tells us: "Our rabbi, when he was the head of the rabbinical court, chose to dwell in the second room that belongs to the house of study, and he dwelled in seclusion and in great abstention, studying night and day with enormous diligence. He conducted himself in that manner for a long time, so that the vexations of the entire city would not disturb him. Only matters of instruction in law were resolved by him, and he did not thrust his head into other matters of the city."[20] Here we have a Torah scholar who combined a rabbinical post with seclusion for the purpose of Torah study according to the example of the Gaon.

THE RABBINATE AS A LIVELIHOOD

Until now we have dealt with the attitude of traditional scholars to the rabbinate from the point of view of ethics and values. However, in the eyes of prospective rabbis, the status of the rabbinate was doubtless influenced by economic and social considerations as well. Here a basic question arises: Did the rabbinate offer an honorable livelihood to rabbis?

Much evidence indicates that communities paid their rabbis a meager salary, and the rabbis of nineteenth-century Lithuania suffered from poverty and want. One indication of the low salary offered to rabbis was the important role played by their wives in supporting the family.[21] During the nineteenth century, many rabbis' wives ran stores. Occasionally the wife's economic activity was included in the contract between the rabbi and the community. In some instances the rabbi's family remained dependent on the wife's parents for several years. For example, this was the fate of Rabbi Yitshak Elhanan Spektor during his first years in the rabbinate at Zublin.[22] An anecdote that illustrates the precarious financial position of the rabbis is told by Rabbi David, who served as the rabbi of Novhardok until 1838. Once he was asked how much money he earned, and he answered, "Three rubles this week." The questioner was surprised and asked, "Why did you say 'three rubles this week' and not 'three rubles a week'?" Rabbi David answered, "During a week when I am paid, I receive three rubles, and during a week when I'm not paid, I don't receive anything."[23]

A gloomy and dreary picture of the economic distress that was the lot of the rabbi of a large town was painted by Rabbi Eliahu David Rabinowitz-Teumim (the ADERET) in his autobiography. He began to serve as rabbi of Ponivezh in 1875. Hundreds of the Jews of the town signed his rabbinical appointment. A formal reception was held in his honor, and at it he was showered with signs of affection and honor.[24] Nevertheless, his salary as rabbi was only nine rubles per week, so the shop managed by his wife played a decisive role in supporting the family. In 1883 the ADERET was offered the rabbinical post in Vilkomierz. When this became known to the leaders of community of Ponivezh, they promptly sent a delegation of three notables to him. These emissaries implored him to remain in their town and offered to increase his salary by six rubles per week. Later the ADERET learned that the notables had been authorized to offer him a larger salary increase, almost double, but that he had not received it because he had not bargained hard enough. In any event, the leaders of the Ponivezh community did not pay the

ADERET the fifteen rubles he had been promised, and this is how he describes the course of events:

> Then I began [to suffer] from want and need, may we be spared this, in horrific fashion. In my innocence I trusted their words without written assurance, as was common. Therefore, after I refused the offer from Vilkomierz, and they hired another rabbi, the people of Ponivezh no longer saw to my salary for weeks and months. Therefore, we stopped issuing decisions about what was forbidden and what was permitted, and there was no response. It even happened that for forty straight weeks they did not pay my salary. And the business in my store became weaker and weaker, and the expenses for bread increased with the number of children. The people of the city said: How is it possible that my father-in-law, the rich man of Warsaw, who had successful businesses, did not provide for me? My father-in-law thought to himself: How is it possible that a wealthy town like Ponivezh should leave its rabbi in oppression and need and not keep their promise to give him fifteen silver rubles a week?[25]

In 5646 the ADERET married his daughter to the man who was later to become famous as Rabbi Avraham Yitshak Hacohen Kook. The expenses incurred because of the wedding, and the fact that the leaders of the community of Ponivezh continued to withhold his salary, caused further deterioration of his financial position. At that time he did not have enough money to pay the doctor. However, the ADERET goes on to relate,

> the heart of the townsmen is as hard as granite, their ear is heavy to hear, and their eyes avoided me until we agreed not to issue Halakhic instruction even on holidays, not a single question, even though this was as difficult for me as "the burden of sand" [Proverbs 27:3]. But necessity forced me to heed this advice . . . and men greater and better than I in Torah and good deeds, and wealthy rabbis, do such actions every day. Nevertheless I was not bold enough to do it by myself then, until I had asked the eldest of the great authorities of the generation, the Gaon of Kovna, and he answered me that there was no hint of a prohibition in this and also he had done so, and so was it done in all the Jewish Diaspora.[26]

Because of their poverty, the ADERET and his family were forced to vacate the apartment where they had lived until then and move into a smaller dwelling.[27] Another result of his poverty was the ADERET's inability to continue to support his daughter and son-in-law at his table, as was the practice at that time. "And I," the ADERET writes, describing his emotions, "wept bitterly in my heart that my sins forced him to accept the rabbinate in the spring of his days because of financial pressure and want, because it was impossible to support him in my home."[28]

Perhaps the ADERET's case was exceptionally severe. Nevertheless, his words suggest that it was a well-known and even common phenomenon at that time for rabbis to strike and refuse to rule on the Halakhah because the community did not pay their salaries. It is even possible that the ADERET's case was indicative of the situation of many other rabbis, and that he was only exceptional in that he describes it without hiding the ugly truth. Naturally, in biographies of rabbis written by their descendants or disciples, one cannot expect realistic descriptions of that kind. One way or another, the plentiful evidence regarding the low salaries of rabbis during the nineteenth century leaves no room for doubting the existence of the phenomenon. Moreover, this state of affairs contrasts strongly with the situation in earlier times, when the rabbinate in Poland and Lithuania was regarded as a substantial source of income. This is clearly evident from the many cases during the seventeenth and eighteenth centuries in which posts were purchased. Willingness to spend considerable sums in order to acquire a rabbinical post shows that the position was regarded as a worthwhile investment by the men of that age.[29]

Why did the salary of rabbis fall? The first factor we can point to is the change that took place in the legal status of the rabbinate. The Russian constitution of 1835 included regulations concerning the functions and obligations of rabbis. The purpose of these regulations was to make the rabbinate an instrument of the government. Among other things, rabbis were obligated to keep a registry of births, deaths, marriages, and divorces. In order to do so, they had to master the Russian language. The communities awarded this function to Jews with general education, who were regarded as "official rabbis," whereas the traditional functions of the rabbinate were still carried out by old-style rabbis. However, because the legal basis for the functions of these rabbis had been removed, their financial status was also seriously damaged. According to an order of the

Russian government of 1839, which was repeated in 1844, communities were forbidden to pay the salaries of men known as "clergymen" from the revenues of the tax on meat, which hitherto had been the principal source of the community budgets for the payment of rabbinical salaries. Henceforth the communities were permitted to pay the salaries of rabbis unrecognized by the government only from individual contributions. Communities sought to get around the government regulations in various ways. Some of them granted their rabbis the monopoly on sales of salt or yeast. Others made certain that the rabbis could purchase the right to farm the meat tax for a fee lower than its value and then resell it to private entrepreneurs for a much higher fee. The difference between these two sums financed various needs of the community, including the rabbi's salary. However, the necessity of paying the rabbis' salaries from contributions or from illegal income caused a decline in those salaries and, as a result, in the rabbis' public status.[30]

Another factor that negatively influenced the salary and status of rabbis was the change in the social class of scholars and in their numbers. During the seventeenth and eighteenth centuries, to a large degree the class of scholars and the oligarchy of Jewish society in Poland and Lithuania overlapped. Consequently, the livelihood of rabbis did not depend to a decisive degree on the salary they received from the community. Rabbis were occasionally involved personally in various economic initiatives, including some available to them because of their post, and these were even included in the contract between them and their communities.[31] During the nineteenth century, by contrast, many scholars came from families of limited means, so their salaries as rabbis were a significant factor in supporting their families. Moreover, the sources give the impression that a great increase in the number of Torah scholars took place in nineteenth-century Lithuania. Since many of them were not, as noted, affluent, the main source of livelihood open to them was the rabbinate. Thus a gap was created between the demand for rabbinical positions and their supply. Naturally this gap had an adverse affect on the rabbis' bargaining ability and permitted the community leaders to impose harsh conditions of employment on them. Furthermore, intense, occasionally fierce, competition emerged for rabbinical posts in general, and especially for those regarded as prominent and lucrative.

Clearly, that competition itself detracted from the rabbis' honor and prestige.

Rabbis who wished to obtain a position with a community commonly traveled to that community to solicit its leaders and notables. Sometimes the candidates used intermediaries who accompanied them and strove to gather supporters for them. In some cases those competing for the rabbinate offered the community payment or a loan in return for the desired post.[32] The negative aspects of the effort to obtain a rabbinical post became more severe when two candidates were competing with one another for the same position. Occasionally such competition was connected to struggles for power and prestige between wealthy and aristocratic families in the community, with each family supporting its own candidate. In such cases the candidates became pawns in the game between rival magnates.[33]

The ADERET's memoirs contain a concrete description of a struggle for a rabbinical post. He recounts that for several years he used to spend the summer months in Riga. Because of this, the Jews of the city came to know and respect him. When the rabbi of that city died, before Passover of 5642, many members of the community leaned toward choosing the ADERET to replace him. The ADERET describes the course of events following that initiative:

> After Passover I received letters and a telegram from the official rabbi, the late Pombiansky, . . . and he asked me whether I would favor receiving the rabbinical post in Riga. But before I could consult on the question of how and what to respond, Rabbi Moshe Shapira, who was from Vilkomierz, came by himself and in person. Although he received much dishonor and contempt from many who did not want him at all, he paid no attention to all that and came with his assistants to act and endeavor to conclude the matter. After great labor, which he and they performed, and for my part I did nothing, thereafter they were able to ask the rabbi of Kovna, the senior rabbi in the state, the Gaon Rabbi Yitshak Elhanan Spektor. . . . I, too, trusted his integrity because he had already promised me in a letter . . . that he would respond to the congregation of Riga when they asked him for the better advice.[34]

However, Rabbi Yitshak Elhanan Spektor's decision caused the ADERET bitter disappointment, for he ruled that the community of

Riga should prefer the competing candidate. The ADERET emphasizes that most of the men of Riga supported him, and even the minority who supported the competitor did so only because of their hatred for the "official rabbi." The ADERET justifies his anger against Rabbi Yitshak Elhanan with the claim that instead of relating to the essence of the question, which of the two candidates was the greater Torah scholar, he passed judgment according to considerations of "mercy," meaning that the rival candidate was needier economically. Regarding his feelings after this affair, the ADERET writes:

> The humiliation that I had from this cannot be described in words, and only His blessed Name alone knows. Everyone who knew me and Rabbi Moshe Shapira [the rival candidate] knows whom it was proper to select. Many rabbis reproved Rabbi Yitshak Elhanan for his injustice in this matter. . . . In my great grief I immediately wrote a letter to Kovna overflowing with reproaches for his deeds, for placing a warden over the community not in accordance with the Torah, and for responding to a question improperly. . . . I stated in detail everything he had committed and done against the Halakhah, deeds that should not be done, only from the malice of his heart and some favoritism that he had.[35]

The ADERET's sorrow for the injustice that, in his opinion, had been done to him illustrates one point that is almost self-evident: the struggle for rabbinical posts involved more than economic considerations. Since the acknowledged criterion for choosing rabbis was great Torah knowledge, preference for one candidate over his rival affected the status and prestige of Torah scholars.

The status of the rabbinate was severely damaged because of the negative side effects accompanying the process of selecting rabbis. Recognition of this led to efforts to mend fences by establishing improved and obligatory norms of conduct. The ADERET describes two efforts in which he personally was involved. At a meeting of several rabbis in 5646 he proposed that every region should establish an arbitration board composed of three rabbis, who would be authorized to intervene, decide, and determine in case of a difference of opinion. Another effort in this direction was made in 5653, when more than twenty rabbis gathered in Kovna to choose their representative for the convocation of rabbis initiated by the government in St. Petersburg. Along with Rabbi Alexander Moshe Lapidot from the city of Rosein, the ADERET addressed Rabbi Yitshak Elhanan and proposed passing legislation that would regulate the matter of ordaining young rabbis, the competition for rabbinical posts, and so on. However, this initiative, like the former one, produced no results.[36]

These failed efforts to regulate the ordination and selection of rabbis demonstrate the lack of central, supracommunal authority within Russian Jewry. Before the dismantling of the Council of the Four Lands and the Council of the State of Lithuania in the 1760s, issues such as these were subject to their supervision. The special authority enjoyed by Rabbi Yitshak Elhanan as the senior rabbi of the generation was apparently insufficient to fill that gap.

A far-reaching effort to institute reforms in the ordination and choice of rabbis was made in 1899. At a meeting in which nearly twenty rabbis participated, most of whom were from Lithuania, these subjects were discussed and, at the end of the discussion, regulations were instituted. Four of the seven regulations regarding the choice of rabbis were:

1. A rabbi or a man ordained as a rabbi who wishes to be chosen as the rabbi of a city with a vacant post that seeks a rabbi may not travel by himself to that city unless he is called from his place of residence and returned to that place.
2. If the congregation that seeks a rabbi wishes to see the rabbi before appointing him, that congregation has permission to invite that rabbi by means of a letter, but on condition that the letter be signed by ten householders; and aside from that, the wardens of the Great House of Study in that city must attest that the letter was written according to the instructions of an assembly. Then he has permission to come there and to stay for a week. And after a week the rabbi is required to return to his home, and he has no right to receive a rabbinical appointment while he is there, but the letter must be sent to his home.
3. If [the rabbinical post of] a community remains vacant for a year and a half, and no rabbi is appointed there for the aforementioned time, then, after that time, it is permitted for rabbis and those ordained as rabbis to travel there to seek the rabbinate.

4. Regarding the eventuality that in one of the cities a rabbi might give of his own money for the needs of the community as a gift or a loan at the time he is appointed as rabbi, we have agreed here to forbid that strenuously both to the rabbi and also to the community.[37]

Thus we find that the main apprehension of the authors of these regulations concerned initiatives that candidates were liable to take in order to mobilize support among the members of the community. Clearly, this apprehension derived from deleterious phenomena that had taken root and needed to be combated.

Eli'ezer Gordon, the rabbi of Telz and the head of its yeshiva, played a central role in formulating these regulations and in the effort to make them obligatory. In a letter to prominent rabbis who had not taken part in the meeting, Rabbi Eli'ezer emphasizes that without their support the regulations would have no force. Therefore he asks them to add their signatures.[38] In his letter Rabbi Eli'ezer mentions another problem that concerned those who drafted the regulations: "This is that there is great neglect in the granting of rabbinical ordination, and many who are unworthy of ordination are ordained, and this is a stumbling block and an obstacle for the Jews. And the majority of the rabbis at the convocation agreed to draft regulations for that, too, and a regulation was also drafted by them at that time."[39] Regrettably, that regulation has not come down to us. Nevertheless, it may be deduced from Rabbi Eli'ezer's words that the regulations were meant to prevent the ordination of young men who were unworthy of it. The need for regulations of this sort proves that many young scholars sought rabbinical posts as a way of earning a living. In the end, these regulations remained merely good ideas that were never implemented. Rabbi Eli'ezer Gordon and his friends could not mobilize enough support for them among the prominent rabbis.

THE STATUS OF THE HEADS OF YESHIVOT

Admiration for "masters of Torah" among broad segments of the Jewish community in Lithuania might have counterbalanced the decline in the status of rabbis. Nevertheless, the position of rabbi in nineteenth-century Lithuania did not generally provide sufficient avenues of expression for the rabbis' erudition. The framework within which a learned rabbi could give maximal expression to his knowledge of Torah was that of teacher in a yeshiva. From the late Middle Ages until the eighteenth century, there was a large overlap in Poland and Lithuania between the post of rabbi and that of head of a yeshiva. In that period, yeshivot were supported by local communities, and the rabbi of the community usually served as head of the yeshiva as well.[40] Despite the yeshiva's economic dependence on the local community, the rabbi exerted almost sole authority within the yeshiva. Needless to say, the rabbi's prestige as a scholar, which was nourished by his teaching in the yeshiva, also reinforced his status and authority within the community.[41]

This type of yeshiva head gradually disappeared during the eighteenth century, a process that has not yet been exhaustively researched—so that I cannot offer a full and certain explanation of it. In any event, it is clear that at the beginning of the nineteenth century we no longer find that kind of yeshiva in Lithuania. In other words, if someone wished to establish a yeshiva, he could no longer count on the commitment of the local community to support it, and he was forced to find alternative sources. A famous example illustrative of this new situation is the yeshiva of Volozhin. As noted, when Rabbi Ḥayyim founded the yeshiva in Volozhin, the town where he served as rabbi, he did not pin his hopes on the local residents. Rather, he issued a call to all lovers of Torah in Lithuania to make contributions. The yeshiva as a private institution based on contributions from individuals—a phenomenon that appears self-evident to us—was actually an innovation.[42]

With the establishment of that yeshiva, Rabbi Ḥayyim created not only a new kind of yeshiva but also a new kind of yeshiva head. The position of the yeshiva head no longer depended on the rabbinate and it even outshone it. Not only was the Volozhin yeshiva independent of the place where it was located, but its status also enhanced that of the community, and in time it came to provide a livelihood for its inhabitants.[43] This was also true of the relationship between the rabbinate and the position of yeshiva head. Rabbi Ḥayyim did not derive his status and authority from the rabbinate, but on the contrary, his position as head of the yeshiva enhanced his status as a rabbi. The independence of the Volozhin yeshiva in relation to the community, and the fact that the rabbinate in Volozhin became a kind of adjunct to the position of yeshiva head, is shown by adoption of the principle that the head of the yeshiva was authorized to bequeath his position to his son or son-in-law.[44] For those concerned, it was self-evident that the rabbinate of Volozhin would pass as a legacy along with the position of yeshiva head. A controversy arose between Rabbi Naphtali Zvi Yehuda Berlin (the NATSIV) and Rabbi Yosef Dov Soloveitchik as to which of the two would be regarded as the first head of the yeshiva and who would be the second. The rabbis who were invited to arbitrate this controversy ordained that the NATSIV would serve as the first head of the yeshiva, and that it was therefore fitting that the rabbinate should also be placed in his hands and not in those of Rabbi Yosef Dov, who was appointed as the second head of the yeshiva.[45] The rabbinate of Volozhin, which had been held by Rabbi Ḥayyim and afterward by his son and heir, Rabbi Yitshak, thus became identified with the position of yeshiva head. It was evident to both parties in the controversy that the main concern was heading the yeshiva, whereas they viewed the rabbinate of Volozhin as a kind of ornament accompanying the position of yeshiva head and embellishing it.

In nineteenth-century Lithuania there arose a model of a Torah scholar—following the example of Rabbi Ḥayyim of Volozhin and, to a certain degree, his inspiration—who derived his prestige and public authority, and usually his salary, from being the head of a yeshiva. The position, including its organizational and economic character, took various forms, depending on the talents and initiative of the scholar and according to conditions that changed from place to place and from time to time. Some yeshiva heads, like Rabbi Ḥayyim, occupied that post while serving as community rabbis as well. A famous scholarly figure who combined the position of yeshiva head with that of rabbi was Rabbi Eli'ezer Gordon. As a young man, he studied in the Kloiz (house of study) of Neviyozer in Kovna, under the tutelage of Rabbi Israel Salanter. Even then he acquired a reputation as a teacher with a talent for fascinating students. In a letter written many years afterward, Rabbi Eli'ezer recounts:

> The pious master Rabbi Israel Salanter of blessed memory implored me to begin giving lessons to the young men, for he thought that, in *pilpul* close to the truth and in my labor to understand everything with common sense and depth and direct assumptions, . . . I would have great influence on the young men who studied Torah, and that the worth of Torah would increase among the young men.[46]

Rabbi Eli'ezer's letter goes on to say that he acceded to Salanter's request, and indeed the lessons that he gave were favorably received. In 1864, after the death of his father-in-law, who had served as a preacher in Kovna, Rabbi Eli'ezer was offered a combined position: that of preacher, which had been held by his father-in-law, and a teaching position in the Kloiz of Neviyozer. He was paid separately for each of these two positions.[47] After a short while, he was invited to serve as the rabbi of Kelme. Such was his renown as head of the yeshiva, however, that soon a group of young scholars formed around him to hear his lessons. Thus a yeshiva was founded in Kelme.[48] In 1883, when Rabbi Eli'ezer was invited to serve as the rabbi of Telz, the *parnasim* of that community were primarily considering their need for a gifted yeshiva head who would enhance the reputation of the local yeshiva. Indeed, under Rabbi Eli'ezer's leadership, the yeshiva of Telz became famous for its organization and for the system of study practiced there, and it was acclaimed in the Torah world of Lithuania.[49]

Public recognition of the special quality of a rabbi who was also a yeshiva head is expressed in a letter that Rabbi Eli'ezer wrote in 5667, in response to the offer of the post of rabbi of Jerusalem. When he explains his financial demands, which were apparently higher than was common, he claims, among other things, that "there are many great scholars in Jerusalem and also those greater than I in Torah and in piety, but nevertheless they are not gifted at giving lessons; . . . for I only . . . am gifted at that, and I have also done this work for twenty-five years; [therefore] the students of the great yeshiva want me to give them lessons."[50] As with Rabbi Ḥayyim at the start of the century, so too with Rabbi Eli'ezer Gordon at its end, the position of yeshiva head appears to have outshone that of the rabbinate in prestige and glory.

The highest dream of any scholar of stature in nineteenth-century

Lithuania was probably to serve as the head of one of the established and renowned yeshivot such as Volozhin or Telz. However, positions of that sort were naturally few, and obtaining them usually depended on appropriate family connections as well as greatness in Torah learning. Alongside the large and famous yeshivot in Lithuania were many other Torah institutions, which differed in level, in organizational character, and in the extent of their influence.[51] The variety of these institutions offered diverse opportunities to scholars who did not choose to pursue the rabbinate. However, since the positions that these institutions could offer were few in relation to the number of men interested in them, scholars established yeshivot of their own. The salary of these yeshiva heads was paid from the students' tuition fees or from the contribution of a local philanthropist.[52] Another way of making a living by teaching Torah was to tutor boys in the Talmud. This does not refer to a teacher in a *heder,* the traditional Jewish primary school, but to a scholar who served as a private tutor to talented boys of thirteen or more. The task of such a tutor was to provide the boys with tools for studying so that they would be able to continue on their own. Rabbi Shmuel of Kelme, mentioned above, was a tutor of that kind. His letters show that there was a mutual and productive relationship between his personal studies and his activity as a tutor: while he was teaching he achieved several of the original insights that he considered important.[53]

As noted, the position of yeshiva head varied from place to place with respect to its character, status, extent, and influence. But in every instance it offered the scholars who held it a suitable channel for expressing their achievements in Torah study, as well as relatively high rewards for those achievements.

CONCLUSION

In this chapter we have noted that spiritual, political, social, and economic factors caused a decline in the status of the rabbinate in nineteenth-century Lithuania. The increasingly common view that studying for the rabbinate was contrary to the value of Torah for its own sake was related to a number of elements: the model of the Vilna Gaon, who withdrew from the world for the sake of Torah study; the mystical meaning that Rabbi Ḥayyim of Volozhin attributed to Torah study, which emphasized the virtue of study as a value in its own right; and the attitude of the Haskalah movement, which advocated limiting specialization in Halakhic literature to those who were preparing themselves for the rabbinate. According to the prevalent view, to become a rabbi did not mean taking on an important public mission, but rather it was a response to economic constraint.

However, those scholars who expected to find in the rabbinate an honorable way of making a decent living for their families generally met with disappointment. The legal status of the rabbinate was undermined by policies of the Russian government, which dealt a severe blow to the salaries of rabbis and to their public position. Another factor in this development was the fierce, sometimes unbridled competition for rabbinical posts. Efforts to reform the procedures for choosing and ordaining rabbis were not fruitful, apparently because of the absence of a central leadership institution that could impose its authority on all communities.

This state of affairs most probably had considerable influence on the decisions of young scholars, who had to choose between a rabbinical and a commercial career. Quite possibly—though this must be verified—many of those who chose the rabbinate were young men without independent financial resources who had no other way of supporting their families. In contrast, young scholars from affluent families probably preferred to engage in commerce. Perhaps this can explain a phenomenon that became rather widespread in nineteenth-century Lithuania: the learned householder. This term refers to excellent Torah scholars who divided their time between business and diligent study of Torah.

Unlike the rabbinate, which steadily decreased in status and prestige, the post of yeshiva head developed in nineteenth-century Lithuania as a position not necessarily connected with the rabbinate and even in competition with it. Heading a yeshiva had a conspicuous advantage over serving as a rabbi, since the yeshiva position offered an ideal channel of expression for outstanding erudition in Torah. Unlike the rabbi, whose communal responsibilities limited his ability to study Torah diligently, the yeshiva head could expand and deepen his knowledge and even be well rewarded for doing so. While the rabbi was dependent to varying degrees on the householders in his community, and he was frequently embroiled in conflicts with aggressive magnates, the yeshiva head was virtually sole master of the yeshiva that he ran. This development might account for the change that took place during the nineteenth century in the curriculum and methods of study in Lithuanian yeshivot. In Volozhin at the beginning of the century, the students also studied books of *posqim*. The testimony of students of Rabbi Ḥayyim shows that he considered it important to prepare his students to serve as rabbis.[54] Later on, students stopped studying *posqim* at the Volozhin yeshiva. Moreover, new methods of study were introduced, connected with the names of Rabbi Ḥayyim of Brisk and Rabbi Shimon Shkop and others.[55] These approaches entailed deep theoretical analysis of the talmudic text, with a certain distance from its practical application, perhaps reflecting the spiritual world of yeshiva heads who, at that time, were not involved in offering practical Halakhic guidance.

In view of the foregoing, it is not surprising that, in the social hierarchy of scholars, yeshiva heads stood above community rabbis. Of course this statement demands a certain modification: the rabbi of a large and aristocratic community had a status higher than that of the head of a small and obscure yeshiva. However, heading a large and famous yeshiva was regarded as preferable to serving as the rabbi of a large community. At the two extremes of this social hierarchy stood the heads of large yeshivot versus the rabbis of medium-sized and small towns. An anecdote reflecting this social polarization in its full severity is found in Ben-Ẓion Dinur's memoirs. Before going to study in the Telz yeshiva, Dinur obtained letters of recommendation from several rabbis in the towns in the area where he lived. These rabbis were very impressed by his knowledge, and their letters contained extravagant praise for him. When he arrived in Telz, he was called forward to be tested by the heads of the yeshiva. At the end of the test, Rabbi Eli'ezer Gordon said to him, "True, . . . you know where the sayings appear and are referred to, but you do not understand their content at all! The rabbis who wrote letters of recommendation for you are great ignoramuses, whom we would not even accept in the lowest class, but we might accept you in that class!"[56]

In conclusion one may point out a similarity between the status of the rabbinate in areas influenced by Hasidism and its status in the Lithuania of the Mitnagdim. It is well-known that Hasidism detracted from the status of the rabbinate by making cleaving to God central to the service of God and by elevating the Zaddik as the spiritual leader of the congregation. Jacob Katz characterized this development aptly when he wrote that, in areas under Hasidic influence, the rabbi became a "technician" of the Halakhah.[57] In the Lithuania of the Mitnagdim, by contrast, there was a decline in the status of the rabbinate, even though Torah studies flourished, and to some degree that decline took place *because* Torah studies flourished. The Hasidic Zaddik and the Lithuanian yeshiva head, each in his own way, displaced the rabbi from the preeminent status he had hitherto enjoyed.

7 Torah and *Yira* in the Thought and Practice of the Vilna Gaon

The unique authority enjoyed by the Vilna Gaon was not based solely on his achievements as a scholar, but, as we have seen, it was based on the combination of those achievements with a pious and ascetic way of life.[1] In this chapter I shall discuss extensively the character and purpose of the Gaon's ascetic withdrawal. I shall also attempt to clarify his conception of the reciprocal relations and correct equilibrium between the value of *yira* and that of Torah study. In the background of this discussion is the assumption that the issue of how the value of Torah study relates to that of *yira* has been immanent within Jewish culture for generations. While the Sages highly prized Torah study and Torah scholars, at the same time they modulated that esteem by requiring that the Torah scholar be morally impeccable and scrupulous in the observance of the commandments. Hence, over the generations, questions constantly arose: How much emphasis should one place on Torah study versus the fostering of *yira?* Moreover, is there any mutual dependency between the two, and if so, to what degree?

In his writings, the Gaon did not leave a systematic presentation of his doctrine concerning *yira,* its acquisition, and the proper balance between it and Torah study. Fragmentary reference to these topics can be found in his commentaries on the Bible and Kabbalistic works. His attitudes in these matters are also reflected in the ethical will that he left to his family and in oral remarks recorded in his name by his disciples. In addition to his explicit statements on these matters, the Gaon's legacy in this area was conveyed by the example he set by his way of life, as it was understood and described by his disciples. In this chapter, I shall attempt to reconstruct the Gaon's views on these subjects as well as possible from the available sources.

THE NATURE OF *YIRA* AND THE WAYS IT IS ACQUIRED

The Vilna Gaon's greatness in Torah resulted from more than his intellectual genius and prodigious memory. No less important were his constant effort and infinite persistence. His way of life, as described by his sons and students, was outstanding in its maximal subjection of his physical and mental powers to a sole purpose: Torah study. Actually, the Gaon regarded the value of absolute devotion to Torah study as one side of a coin, the other side of which was ascetic withdrawal as a guiding principle and a way of life. Needless to say, in emphasizing the virtue of ascetic withdrawal in worshiping God, the Gaon was following in the footsteps of earlier moralists. Nevertheless, his uniqueness derives from his conception of the purpose of this withdrawal.

For example, the author of *The Duties of the Heart* regarded withdrawal as paving the way to love of God on an exalted level. An ascetic way of life permits a person to detach his soul from any connection with the values of this world and its pleasures. Thus the soul is entirely open to fully devoting itself to the love of God.[2] In Kabbalistic ethical literature, withdrawal is conceived as being intended to enable one to cleave to God. Withdrawal from society and from the occupations of this world allows the formation in the soul of a consciousness known as "the stripping away of corporeality." This consciousness is a precondition and a suitable leaping-off point for the attainment of cleaving to God.[3] The causal connection between withdrawal and cleaving to God is epitomized by the author of *Sefer Haredim,* who writes, "And know this in truth that the greater your withdrawal from the world, the greater will be your cleaving to Him, may He be praised."[4]

Unlike his predecessors, the Gaon regarded the essence of the meaning of ascetic withdrawal as the concentration of most of a man's physical and spiritual resources on Torah study. Consequently he especially emphasized the value of withdrawal from human society, since social contact naturally leads to neglect of Torah, and reclusion promotes perseverance in study.[5] Thus the Gaon adopted the ideal of ascetic withdrawal as formulated in ethical literature, especially by Kabbalistic moralists, but he diverted its goal: Torah study now took the place of contemplation intended to attain cleaving to God!

The ideal of withdrawal from the world for the sake of Torah study expresses a view that denies any intrinsic value to worldly possessions and mundane activity. This is combined with the virtue of *bitaḥon* (assurance), which depends on a fatalistic assumption that "all of a person's nourishment is allotted to him on Rosh Hashana."[6] Therefore, human endeavor in the area of economics is neither beneficial nor detrimental.[7] However, application of the virtue of *bitaḥon* in practical life sometimes gives rise to a difficult ordeal, for this virtue entails denial of the distress of one's family members. Thus it is not surprising that, when he describes an elevated degree of divine service, the Gaon combines ascetic withdrawal for the sake of Torah study with the virtue of *bitaḥon:*

> Men of valor are the noblemen of the heart [who], entirely in the fullness of *bitaḥon,* constantly perform commandments and meditate on the Torah day and night, though in his house there is no bread nor any garment, and his sons and the members of his household shout to him, Bring us a livelihood to sustain us and support us; and he does not pay any attention to them at all and does not fear their voice, . . . for all his

loves are nullified before the love of God and His Torah and His commandments.[8]

We find that, although the Gaon viewed the essence of the virtue of ascetic withdrawal as the devotion of one's time and forces to Torah study, he also attributed great importance to it as a defense against the evil impulse. He was convinced that contact with the world, especially social contact, was replete with obstacles and impediments. Therefore ascetic withdrawal serves as a safe haven for anyone who tends to be drawn after his appetites.[9] Further, ascetic withdrawal can serve as preventive medicine for anyone who wishes to avoid entanglement in difficult trials. In the spirit of this view, the Gaon recommended to his family that they have as little social contact as possible, even for the sake of performing a commandment.[10]

The Gaon expressed his position regarding the ideal of ascetic withdrawal for the sake of Torah study in his way of life more than in any other manner. His reclusion, as described by his sons and his disciples, stands out in its severity and its uncompromising character. As a youth he studied Torah in seclusion. After his marriage he went into "exile," during which he wandered extensively among the communities of Prussia.[11] At that time he also practiced self-mortification. Later on, however, he rejected extreme asceticism, because a person who fasts is unable to properly fulfill his obligations of divine service. Moreover, one must take care because ascetic practices might violate the precept of the Torah that states, "And you shall preserve your souls" (Deuteronomy 4:15). Nevertheless, the Gaon justified his youthful asceticism, claiming that then he was strong enough not to succumb to those risks.[12]

After returning to Vilna from "exile," the Gaon continued to maintain his reclusion. This was expressed by maximal restriction, almost to the point of total detachment, from contact with anything beyond the four ells of Halakhah. Even if we concede that there was a degree of exaggeration in the well-known descriptions of the Gaon's withdrawal from the entire world beyond the closed shutters of his study, there is no reason to doubt that, in their main thrust, those descriptions are truthful.[13] The severity with which the Gaon limited his contacts with people is also reflected in the small number of his students. Just a few men had the privilege of being in his company and being numbered among "those who saw his face."[14] The culmination of the Gaon's seclusion is found in his relations with members of his family. He repressed his natural affection for his children, refrained from taking an interest in their livelihood, and spent little time in their company.[15] As noted, the most characteristic feature of the Gaon's withdrawal lay in its close connection with Torah study. Here is a description of that connection in the words of one of his admirers:

> Anyone who observed and scrutinized in our rabbi of blessed memory his labor in Torah and his marvelous perseverance day and night without negligence or slackening even for the wink of an eye and who looks to see [could see] how he was cleared in his mind of any matters of the transitory world and its desires and preoccupations and vexations as though he were not in the world but only standing and serving above like one of the heavenly host.[16]

In the life of the Gaon, absolute detachment from the world, as demanded in ethical and Kabbalistic works as a condition for cleaving to God, served as a psychic matrix for maximal devotion to the study of Torah.

The Gaon apparently approved of the tendency of some of his disciples to live in reclusion, and he even encouraged that. When his student Rabbi Yoel of Amcislaw asked him for instructions in achieving reclusion, the Gaon answered, "If you are tenacious, you shall succeed."[17] Similarly the Gaon instructed his disciples that a person who wishes to live in seclusion must not fear being accused of "haughtiness": "For in this age, the accusation of haughtiness is irrelevant, and on the contrary it is correct to publicize." Moreover, "whoever wishes to withdraw from the world should cry out in the streets that he wishes to withdraw and justify himself, otherwise he will not free himself."[18] Thus a public announcement can assist someone who wishes to live in reclusion in overcoming his attraction to mundane pleasures, apparently because social pressure will serve as a powerful psychological motivation for the individual. After these instructions, which express a positive attitude toward reclusion, come two reservations: "that he should not be excessive in his withdrawal and appear to be separate from the world, and especially that it should be for the sake of heaven."[19] The Gaon certainly did not suggest ascetic withdrawal as a path for the multitude; however, seeing the instructions cited in his name in the writings of his disciples, it does appear that he regarded positively the adoption of a reclusive way of life on the part of individuals whose profession was Torah study.[20]

The Gaon's *ḥasidut* was also expressed in his scrupulous observation of the commandments. In this area, his path was characterized by uncompromising obedience to the Halakhah, which meant he tried to observe commandments even in the most difficult of circumstances and he took care to observe precepts that it had become customary to regard with lenience. However, the singularity of the Gaon in this area lies in the renewal of certain laws and the correction of "debased" customs, even those that had long since become prevalent among Jewish communities. According to testimony by his disciple, the Gaon had reservations regarding the term *ḥasid,* which clung to him, arguing, "The word *ḥasid* only applies to one who is *ḥasid* with his Creator and goes beyond the letter of the law imposed by our Sages of blessed memory, but as for someone who does not move beyond all that was explained in the Talmud and the four parts of the *Shulḥan 'Arukh* should not rightly be called *ḥasid,* but rather a proper Jew."[21]

Thus the Gaon's *ḥasidut* was not expressed in conduct beyond the letter of the law, but rather in an effort for maximal application of the Halakhah in life on the basis of exhaustive recourse to its primary sources. Consequently, his *ḥasidut* in the observance of the commandments was connected and conditional on his unique ascendancy and authority as a scholar.

The Gaon attributed great importance to *tiqun hamidot* (the improvement of character traits). This importance is expressed in his acceptance of a scheme according to which service of God depends on three things: Torah, the commandments, and moral virtue.[22] The Gaon regarded the special excellence of *tiqun hamidot,* and its advantage with respect to Torah and the commandments, as the principal defense against sin. Although Torah study and the performance of commandments also defend against the evil impulse, the influence of *tiqun hamidot* is more comprehensive and profound because the virtues "teach a person the path that he should tread."[23] In other words, since the virtues are deeply rooted in the soul, they dictate patterns of behavior and distance a person from sin. The Gaon also pointed out the excellence of moral virtue by a negative example: if someone neglects the *tiqun hamidot,* the "fences" and "barriers" that he has erected for himself will not succeed in overcoming his appetites. Moreover, even the "fence" that he has built around himself by dint of Torah study will be powerless to save him from sin.[24] Another expression of the excellence of moral virtue in the Gaon's view is his statement that only a person whose *midot* (moral qualities) have been perfected is likely to merit discovery of the secrets of the Torah in the course of his study.[25]

The great importance attributed by the Gaon to *tiqun hamidot* derives from his view regarding the place and function of *midot* within the soul: "*Midot* belong to the soul that clings to the body, and they are garments of the upper soul, which is the rational soul, and by means of the rational soul they become *midot.*"[26] According to this view, the body is the "garment" of the animal soul, which in turn is the "garment" of the rational soul. Consequently, the power of *midot* to shape a person's patterns of behavior derives from the close connection between the body and the animal soul, in which *midot* are located.[27]

The Gaon conceived of the process of *tiqun hamidot* as a fierce struggle to subdue and control oneself: "For the wicked man knows by himself that his path is evil and bitter, but it is hard for him to leave it. This is the essence of man: not to leave him to his desire but with a bit to restrain and halt him, and until the day of his death a person must afflict himself, not in fasts and mortification but only to restrain his mouth and his appetite."[28] The Gaon points to the tension between the power of consciousness, which distinguishes between good and evil, and the appetites rooted in vices. The ascendancy of moral judgment over the appetites is a task that entails psychological torments, and a person must expect to persist in it all his life. The Gaon regarded the virtues as part of a dualistic system: every virtue is matched by a vice that is its opposite.[29] Thus *tiqun hamidot* has two sides: the acquisition of virtues, on the one hand, and the "breaking" of vices, on the other.

Following the views prevalent in Jewish ethical literature, the Gaon recommended habit formation as an important means for *tiqun hamidot* "because speech and virtue require great habit, and habit controls everything, and the beginning is always difficult."[30] We find that the principal difficulty lies in the first stages of the process of *tiqun hamidot.* The more a person persists in acting morally, the more that conduct will become rooted in his soul and it will be easier for him. The Gaon believed that the way to acquire virtue through the force of habit was the scrupulous observance of the commandments. Repetition and persistence in the performance of the commandments cause virtues to take root in the soul. He also discusses the opposite situation: contempt for the commandments causes vice to take root in the soul.[31] Thus the commandments and virtue are mutually dependent: virtue guarantees that a person will be able to observe the commandments even when he is oppressed by the seductions of his appetites; and the acquisition of virtue depends on scrupulous and constant performance of the commandments.

The Gaon describes the breaking of vices—uprooting them from the soul—as a gradual and prolonged process "because for the person who wishes to break his appetite it is impossible to leap immediately and instantly grasp the final end and the opposite of what he is used to. Rather he must distance himself little by little until he comes to the final end, and then he will break his appetite until he stands on the straight path."[32]

It would be erroneous to interpret the Gaon's words as though he were following in the footsteps of Maimonides and holding up the moral ideal of the "golden mean." His affiliation with Maimonides is limited solely to the methodological sphere. In fact the act of breaking the vices has the character of a personal struggle in which every single individual imposes on himself "fences" and "restrictions" that gradually distance him from the transgressions he tends to succumb to: "Because every person must walk in the path necessary for him, for people's *midot* are not identical to one another, and because of that one is habituated to the transgression that comes with a certain virtue, and one must greatly fence himself off against that from which one's fellow does not need to preserve himself, and one's fellow requires something else."[33]

In this context it is fascinating to see how the Gaon distinguished between the positive and negative aspects of *tiqun hamidot:* "How to walk in the way of the Lord: a person must seek advice from Sages and saints who walk in the way of the Lord and have not tripped on the stumbling block, which is the evil impulse; and to battle against the evil impulse he himself must use stratagems, and for that purpose advice alone is not effective without a stratagem."[34] Insofar as one speaks of the adoption of positive patterns of behavior, it is good to seek advice from "Sages and saints," whose lives comprise an example worthy of imitation. However, the advice of "Sages and saints" cannot save someone who is struggling against his evil impulse. In that struggle the individual remains in isolation, and he must find "stratagems" appropriate to his own personal circumstances.

The Gaon found that the study of moral instruction and reproach was an important aid in the struggle to subdue and restrain the appetites.[35] The booklet of the Gaon's practices contains the following instruction: "Books of moral instruction several times every day."[36] He also recommends the study of ethical works in his ethical will to his family. Similarly, he instructs them to read Proverbs and Ecclesiastes, the Ethics of the Fathers, and *Avot de Rabbi Nathan.* He writes that the virtue of Ecclesiastes is that it "makes vanity of the matters of this world."[37] The vanity of this world was apparently one of the most important lessons that one was supposed to learn from ethical works. However, this was not sufficient. The Gaon also warns against occupation with ethical works, the purpose of which was "reading alone, for therein a person is not moved, for how many people read ethical works and are not moved, and it is for the aforementioned."[38] The emotional effect that the Gaon regarded as the main fruit of consulting ethical works is apparently emotional upheaval that results from feelings of remorse and from purification, and it has the power to motivate a person to reform his behavior.

However, the Gaon expresses reservations about the value of studying ethical works and made such study conditional on withdrawal from society. A person who is aroused by the study of moral works but who does not limit his contacts with other people is similar to someone "who sows without plowing so that the wind takes it and nourishes the birds, etc., and it is because he cannot block himself and fence himself off."[39] Thus we find that, while ethical writings may arouse a certain motivation in the soul and help restrain the appetites, reclusion continues to be a vital defensive barrier, without which ethical works have no beneficial effect.

THE RELATIONSHIP BETWEEN TORAH AND *YIRA*

Until now we have seen how the values of Torah and *yira* are combined in the Gaon's teachings and way of life. Reclusion, which expresses rejection of the values of this world and serves at the same time as a shield and shelter from the assaults of the evil impulse, is principally intended to free most of a person's time and energy for Torah study. We have found, too, that the Gaon's *yira* was also expressed in scrupulous observation of the commandments and *tiqun hamidot.* Now it is appropriate to ask: What was the Gaon's opinion regarding the proper balance between Torah and *yira* and their relative significance in human life? Can Torah study in itself also serve as a means of moral elevation? Are Torah study and *yira* conditional on one another, and if so, to what extent?

In the Gaon's commentaries on the Bible, and in teachings attributed to him by his disciples, one may discern a tendency to attribute decisive preference to Torah study with regard to both the commandments and *tiqun hamidot.* The Gaon expresses his preference for Torah study over the commandments with an analogy: "For the Torah is like the bread on which a man's heart feeds, . . . and it is always needed like bread, and therefore you shalt meditate on it day and night; but the commandments are like preserves. They are good intermittently and in their own time, like preserves, which come from time to time."[40] This analogy reflects not only the special significance of Torah study versus that of the practical commandments but also the proper division of time between them. Preference for Torah study over the commandments received exaggerated expression in the statement that every word a person learns is equal in weight to all the commandments.[41] A typical expression of the way this conception is translated into practical instruction can be found in the words spoken by Rabbi Ḥayyim of Volozhin in the name of the Gaon: "Our rabbi [Rabbi Ḥayyim] said that it is not good to seek out commandments, and he said in the name of the Gaon that it was better to go to the house of seclusion and cross one's arms than to go to the market and seek out a commandment."[42]

The Gaon also expresses his view about the relationship between Torah study and *yira* with an analogy: "And if there is no wisdom, even if he has *yira,* this is nothing, for *yira* cannot bring about anything, . . . because *yira* is only a treasury for wisdom, as it is written [Isaiah 33]: *yira* is His treasury."[43] In comparing *yira* to a treasury, the purpose of which is to preserve wisdom within it, it emerges that *yira* in itself is of no value when not combined with Torah study. This view also yields instruction in a practice attributed to the Gaon: "for *yira* and severe observance of the commandments and scrupulousness do not endure and are not worthwhile to undo the yoke of Torah even for a moment; and the most excellent form of repentance is also the yoke of Torah."[44]

The preference for Torah study, as opposed to the pursuit of commandments and fostering of *yira,* can be understood in light of the unique significance that the Gaon attributed to it. However, in addition, the Gaon was certain that study in itself was an important measure of defense against the evil impulse. In this spirit he interprets words of the Mishnah in the Ethics of the Fathers: "Turn it over and turn it over, for everything is in it": "This means to say that with the Torah he will merit all deeds; . . . it is known that when a man studies Torah in his childhood, then the evil impulse does not rule over him later."[45] Moreover, not only does the Torah protect those who are occupied with it from the evil impulse, but "the *yira* comes from the Torah, and if he does not study, he will not have *yira.*"[46] In light of this, the Gaon distinguishes between those for whom Torah is not their profession, to whom the recommendation to make use of stratagems for *tiqun hamidot* is directed, and those who are occupied with Torah for its own sake, who achieve *tiqun hamidot* by virtue of their study.[47]

Along with expressions of preference for Torah study and statements that study in itself is an important means for attaining *yira,* one may also find in the writings of the Gaon remarks that restrict the virtue of study and make it conditional on connection with *yira.* Such a conditional status can be found in his statement that, when the student is motivated by *yira,* he has a qualitative advantage regarding the essence of his study:

"For if a person has *yira* he will study to know what to preserve himself from; and it is human nature that if someone wants something and finds it precious to him, he will preserve it. But if he does not have *yira* and does not fear sin, even if he studies several times he will not find it, because he does not study so that he will know what to be careful of."[48] A more far-reaching expression of the value of study as dependent on that of *yira* is the statement that the influence of Torah study on the soul is even liable to be negative, because study "irrigates" the soul and strengthens the forces contained in it, including the negative forces. Therefore, the Gaon believed, both before and after study the student must "purify the dross from himself with fear of sin and with good actions."[49] Finally, one must again recall here the Gaon's words regarding the ascendancy of *tiqun hamidot:* if one does not toil to improve his *midot,* even the "fence" that he built around himself by virtue of Torah study will be destroyed: it cannot save him from sin.

The value of Torah study was made conditional on its connection with *yira* in yet another way: the demand that Torah study must be for its own sake. In other words, the ascendancy of Torah study is conditional on the nature of the student's spiritual motivation. Needless to say, by emphasizing the virtue of Torah study for its own sake, the Gaon was adopting a position accepted universally from the time of the Sages. However, his uniqueness is apparent in his severe attitude regarding the degree to which one may forgive study that is not for its own sake. Halakhic scholars were called on to address that matter as part of their effort to explain the presence of contradictory statements in the sources. For example, the Sages harshly condemned study that was not for its own sake, as in the saying "For anyone who is occupied with Torah not for its own sake, it becomes a death potion" (*Ta'anit* 7a). And another well-known saying stated, "A person should always be occupied with Torah and the commandments, even if not for its own sake, for from being not for its own sake, it comes to be for its own sake" (*Pesahim* 50b). Both Rashi and the Tosafists explain this contradiction by distinguishing between two aspects of "not for its own sake." The Tosafot states, "What is said, that one should always be occupied with Torah even if not for its sake, that is so that one will be called 'rabbi' or be honored. And what is said here, that for anyone who deals with Torah not for its sake it becomes a death potion, this refers to someone who learns in order to quibble."[50]

Against the background of the position taken by Rashi and the Tosafists, with which other Halakhic authorities concurred, the Gaon's position stands out in its severity: "There are those who study for the sake of enjoyment, so that they will have pleasure because they study or are called 'rabbi,' and this is a very bad lot."[51] The Gaon's words are directed against the student who does not study Torah "for its sake," whom other Halakhic authorities viewed with tolerance. The Gaon proposes two reasons for rejecting study for the sake of honor: first, such study is defective because of the defective motive that underlies it; second, it is an instance of love that depends on its object, as opposed to unconditional love: if the motivation is removed, the study will also cease. For these and other reasons, the Gaon spares no condemnation of the student who seeks to achieve honor and social prestige by means of his study. For example, he describes those who study Torah in order to glorify themselves as "children of Gehenna from the side of the mixed multitude."[52] From this position the Gaon interprets the permission to study Torah not for its own sake ("for from being not for its own sake, it comes to be for its own sake") as referring to a student "who does not aim at anything, and merely pursues his ancestral custom, but not for someone whose study is mainly for the sake of honor."[53] The degree to which the Gaon rejected study that was not for its own sake emerges from his statement that it is better to study a little bit but without any extraneous goal than to study a great deal but not for its own sake.[54]

In conclusion, while considering both their particular significance and the resources that should be applied to them, the Vilna Gaon decisively preferred Torah study over the pursuit of commandments and development of *yira.* Nevertheless, he made the value of study conditional on a strong connection with *yira.* Just as *yira* without study is valueless, study detached from *yira* is worthless. These two are bound up with one another in mutual dependence and fruitfulness. Thus the ideal is the combination of Torah with *yira:* one concentrates on Torah study, and *yira* both fosters study and results from it.

Notes

1. HA-GAON HE-HASID: IN HIS OWN TIME AND FOR SUCCEEDING GENERATIONS

1. Vilensky, *Ḥasidim umitnagdim,* 1:200.
2. See chaps. 3 and 4.
3. Sons of the Vilna Gaon, introduction to *Shulḥan 'arukh, oraḥ ḥayyim.*
4. This refers to *Aliyot Eliyahu,* written by Rabbi Yehoshu'a Heschel Levine, published in Vilna in 5616 (1856). On reliance upon the introductions to the Vilna Gaon's writings, see the publisher's introduction to *Aliyot Eliyahu.*
5. Ḥayyim of Volozhin, introduction to *Sifra deẓeni'uta.*
6. Sons of the Vilna Gaon, introduction to his commentary on the Aggadot.
7. See chap. 2.
8. Israel of Shklov, introduction to *Peat hashulhan.*
9. Ibid.

10. Sons of the Vilna Gaon, introduction to *Shulḥan 'arukh, oraḥ ḥayyim.*
11. Ḥayyim of Volozhin, "Sheiltot," sig. 56.
12. Ḥayyim of Volozhin, Iggeret 'al yesud hayeshivah.
13. Sons of the Vilna Gaon, introduction to *Shulḥan 'arukh, oraḥ ḥayyim.*
14. Abraham Simḥah of Amcislaw, introduction to *Zohar Ḥadash.*
15. Kaplan, "Ledarkho shel rabbi Ḥayyim miVolozhin bahalakhah."
16. I am grateful to Professor Israel Ta-Shma for clarifying this matter.
17. For an example of this, see Y. L. Maimon, *Toledot HaGRA*, 47. On the Vilna Gaon's revisions of the Jerusalem Talmud, see Goronchik, "HaGRA vehayerushalmi."
18. Israel of Shklov, introduction to *Taqlin hadetin.*
19. Ibid.
20. Sons of the Vilna Gaon, introduction to *Shulḥan 'arukh, oraḥ ḥayyim.* On the Gaon's commentary on the *Shulḥan 'arukh,* see Czernowitz, *Toldot haposqim*, 3: 10–33.
21. Ḥayyim of Volozhin, introduction to *Sifra deẓeni'uta.*
22. Ibid.
23. On the relationship between the Halakhah and the Zohar, see J. Katz, "Hakhra'ot hazohar bidvar halakhah."
24. Ḥayyim of Volozhin, introduction to *Sifra deẓeni'uta.*
25. Menahem Mendel of Shklov, introduction to *Sefer mishlei, 'im beur hagaon.*
26. Israel of Shklov, introduction to *Taqlin hadetin.*
27. Abraham Ben Eliyahu miVilna, *Se'arat Eliyahu.*
28. Abraham Simḥah of Amcislaw, introduction to *Zohar Ḥadash.*
29. Israel of Shklov, introduction to *Peat hashulhan.*
30. Ḥayyim of Volozhin, introduction to *Seder zera'im.*
31. Ḥayyim of Volozhin, introduction to *Sifra deẓeni'uta.*
32. Israel of Shklov, introduction to *Peat hashulhan.*
33. On this see Dinstag, "Haim hitnaged HaGRA lemishnato hafilosofit shel HaRAMBAN?," 253–68.
34. A prominent example of this is the Hasidism of Ashkenaz during the Middle Ages. See Marcus, ed., *Dat veḥevra bemishnatam shel ḥasidei Ashkenaz.*
35. Schechter, "Safed in the 16th Century."
36. For a comprehensive discussion of this subject, see Rosman, *Founder of Hasidism*, 27–41; Etkes, *Ba'al Hashem, HaBESHT*, 164–78. On groups of Hasidim who were active in the framework of the *kloiz* (a certain type of house of study), see Reiner, "Hon, ma'amad ḥevrati, vetalmud torah," 287–328.
37. Ḥayyim of Volozhin, introduction to *Sifra deẓeni'uta.*
38. Tishby, "Qudsha brikh hu oraita veYisrael kula ḥad"; Y. Avivi, *Qabalat HaGRA*, 30.
39. Vilensky, *Ḥasidim umitnagdim*, 1:201–2.

40. Ḥayyim of Volozhin, introduction to *Sifra deẓeni'uta*.
41. Avivi, *Qabalat HaGRA*, 28 ff.
42. H. H. Ben-Sasson, *Ishiyuto shel HaGRA vehashp'aato hahistorit*, 45–50.
43. Ḥayyim of Volozhin, introduction to *Sifra deẓeni'uta*.
44. On the angelic herald of Rabbi Joseph Karo, see Werblowsky, *Joseph Karo, Lawyer and Mystic*, 9–23; Elior, "R. Yosef Karo veR. Yisrael ba'al shem tov," 675–84. On the *maggid* of Rabbi Moses Ḥayyim Luzzatto, see Benayahu, "Hamaggid shel RAMḤAL," 299–336.
45. Karo's book *Maggid meisharim* was first published in Lublin in 5405 (1645) and then in 5409 (1649) in Venice. Since then, many editions of it have been printed. On the controversy, see S. Ginzburg, *R. Moshe Ḥayim Luzzatto uvnei doro.*
46. Rabbi Joseph Karo was referred to by the name of his Halakhic work, *Beit Yosef.*
47. Ḥayyim of Volozhin, introduction to *Sifra deẓeni'uta*.
48. Rabbi Yeḥezqel Feivel of Dretshin wrote a biography of Rabbi Shlomo Zalman, *Toldot Adam*. See also Bloch, *Ruaḥ Eliyahu*, 109–35.
49. The information in the Vilna Gaon's possession was not exact. Rabbi Joseph Karo had received the revelation of the *maggid* even before he immigrated to the land of Israel.
50. Braver, *Galicia veyehudeiha*, 197–275.
51. Vilensky, *Ḥasidim umitnagdim*, 1:66–67.
52. Abraham Simḥah of Amcislaw, introduction to *Zohar Ḥadash*.
53. See "Iggeret HaBESHT," in *Shivḥei HaBESHT*, ed. Y. Mondshine (Jerusalem, 1982), 233–37; see also *Shivḥei HaBESHT*, 133–34, 154–55, and passim.
54. See Idel, *Kabbalah*, 88–96.
55. Benayahu, *Sefer toldot HaARI*, 164–66.
56. "Iggeret HaBESHT."
57. Ḥayyim of Volozhin, introduction to *Sifra deẓeni'uta*.
58. Ibid.
59. Ibid.
60. Ibid.
61. Ḥayyim of Volozhin, introduction to *Seder zera'im*.
62. Abraham Ben Eliyahu miVilna, introduction to *Shenot Eliyahu*.
63. Ḥayyim of Volozhin, introduction to *Sifra deẓeni'uta*.
64. Menashe of Ilia, *Alfei Menashe*, fol. 73 a–b.
65. Ḥayyim of Volozhin, introduction to the Vilna Gaon's commentary on the Zohar.
66. H. H. Ben-Sasson, *Ishiyuto shel HaGRA vehashp'aato hahistorit*, 40–41 and passim.

2. THE VILNA GAON AND HASKALAH

1. Barukh of Shklov, trans., introduction to *Uqlidos.*

2. For an extensive biographical discussion of Rabbi Barukh of Shklov, see Fishman, *Russia's First Modern Jews,* 22–45. See also Mahler, *Divrei yemei Yisrael,* 4:53–57; Twersky, "R. Barukh of Shklov," 77–81.

3. Levinsohn, *Te'udah beYisrael,* 151–52.

4. Etkes, *Te'udah beYisrael,* 13.

5. Fin, *Safah laneemanim,* 132–34, 138–43. On Fin and his writings, see Feiner, *Mehaskalah loḥemet lehaskalah meshameret,* 1–47.

6. On Rabbi Eliyahu Rogoler, see Frumkin, *Toldot Eliyahu.* For the correspondence between Rabbi Eliyahu and his brother, Rabbi Shmuel of Kelme, see Etkes, *Lita biYerushalayim.*

7. Rogoler, *Yad Eliyahu,* 34.

8. Levine, *Aliyot Eliyahu,* 57–63; see also 31, n. 5; 34–35.

9. Ibid., 60–61, n. 31.

10. Ibid., 61–64, n. 34.

11. Ibid., 59.

12. Ibid., 30–31.

13. On Levine, see Citron, "Milḥemet hadinastiot beyeshivat Volozhin," 123–35.

14. A short biographical note on Rabbi David Luria appears as an appendix to Luria's book, *Qadmut sefer hazohar,* 14–15. See also Steinschneider, *'Ir Vilna,* 157–59; Ginzburg, *Ketavim historiim,* 28–29.

15. Levine, *Aliyot Eliyahu,* 10.

16. Druk, "Hagaon R. Ya'aqov Ẓvi Meklenburg," 171–79.

17. This refers to "Divrei hayamim hahem," which was distributed in a typed edition and in a limited number of copies (Jerusalem, 1962). The following quotations come from fols. 4–11. On Joseph Isaac's ways and motivations as a historian, see chap 4, n. 53, in the present volume.

18. Raisin, *The Haskalah Movement in Russia.*

19. Ibid., 72–75.

20. Naftali Hertz Wessely (1725–1805), one of the most prominent literary figures of the early Haskalah, published *Divrei shalom veemet* in 1782, the first literary expression of the Haskalah movement's educational program. See Eliav, *Haḥinukh hayehudi beGermania biymei hahaskalah vehaemantsipaẓia,* 25–51.

21. Hirschberg, "Toldot R. Z. Yavetz," 14:123–63. On the Vilna Gaon, see Yavetz, *Toldot Yisrael,* 13:230–31, 234–35.

22. See B.-Ẓ. Katz, *Rabanut, ḥasidut, haskalah,* 2:38–43; B.-Ẓ. Katz, *Hazman,* 1–7; J. Klausner, *Hahistoria shel hasifrut ha'ivrit heḥadasha,* 3:17–18; Zinberg, *Toldot sifrut Yisrael,* 3:292–99 (for an English version, see I. Zinberg, *A History of Jewish Litera-*

ture, 6:220–32); Greenberg, *The Jews in Russia*, 22–23; Mahler, *Divrei yemei Yisrael*, 4:14–16.

23. B.-Ẓ. Katz, *Rabanut, ḥasidut, haskalah*, 2:10–15. A critical attitude toward these legends is also found in the article by Twersky, "R. Eliyahu miVilna," 113–14.

24. B.-Ẓ. Katz, *Hazman*, 2.

25. Zinberg, *Toldot sifrut Yisrael*, 3:299.

26. J. Klausner, *Hahistoria shel hasifrut ha'ivrit heḥadasha*, 3:18.

27. Mahler, *Divrei yemei Yisrael*, 4:14.

28. Klausner and Zinberg employ the word *harbinger* (in Hebrew, *mevasser*) explicitly, while Mahler, who is more cautious, distinguishes between "first signs of the renascence of traditional Jewry" and the actual "harbingers of the Haskalah," and includes the Gaon in the former category.

29. I have treated this issue more extensively in Etkes, "Leshealat mevasrei hahaskalah bemizraḥ Eiropa."

30. At this point one should distinguish between a pioneer and a harbinger. Unlike a harbinger, a pioneer strives to change the society in light of a predetermined picture of the future.

31. As early as 1877, in Berlin, Rabbi Barukh published *Yesod 'olam* by Rabbi Isaac, the son of Rabbi Joseph Hayisraeli, on the science of astronomy, and his own work, *'Amudei hashamayim vetiferet adam*, dedicated partly to astronomy and partly to anatomy. See Fishman, *Russia's First Modern Jews*, 22–45.

32. Rabbi Abraham Simḥah's letter is published in the beginning of Josephus, *Milḥamot haYehudim*.

33. Fin, *Qiryah neemenah*, 161. See also B.-Ẓ. Katz, *Rabanut, ḥasidut, haskalah*, 2:43. The Vilna Gaon's views about astronomy were discussed in a lecture by Zvi Mazeh at a conference on the Vilna Gaon at Bar-Ilan University in January 1998. Basing his talk on the Gaon's commentary on *Sefer Yeẓira*, Mazeh showed that the Gaon's views were innovative and original in comparison to those prevalent in the Middle Ages. However, he was entirely unaware of the revolutionary developments that took place in that field during the seventeenth century.

34. The Gaon's book on grammar is partly a précis of an earlier text by Eliyahu Bakhur. See Y. L. Maimon, *Toledot HaGRA*, 21.

35. Sons of the Vilna Gaon, introduction to *Shulḥan 'arukh, oraḥ ḥayyim;* Abraham Ben Eliyahu miVilna, *Se'arat Eliyahu;* the eulogy of the Vilna Gaon by Danzig, *Ẓavaat yehezkel*, esp. fol. 13; see also the introductions written by the Gaon's disciples to the works cited in chap. 1 in this volume.

36. Israel of Shklov, introduction to *Peat hashulhan*.

37. See, for example, Sons of the Vilna Gaon, introduction to *Aderet Eliyahu*.

38. Kupfer, "Lidmuta hatarbutit shel yahadut Ashkenaz veḥakhameihah bameot hayod-dalet-hatet-vav," 113.

39. Isserles, *Shu"t HaREMA,* sig. 7, p. 29 ff.; Kleinberger, *Hamaḥshavah hapedagogit shel HaMAHARAL miPrague,* 148 ff.; Bachrach, *Ḥavot Yair,* question 29; Shoḥet, *'Im ḥilufei tequfot,* 199–200; Ḥelma, introduction to *Merkevet hamishneh.*
40. For further information about occupation with secular studies in Ashkenazic society at the end of the Middle Ages, see S. Assaf, *Meqorot letoldot haḥinukh beYisrael,* 1:63, 113, 211, 288–89; 4:38. See also Breuer, "Qavim lidmuto shel R. David Ganz ba'al 'Ẓemah David,'" 97–118.
41. G. Scholem, "Hatnu'ah haShabtait bePolin," 2:36 ff.; H. H. Ben-Sasson, *Hagut vehanhagah,* 13–16.
42. On the Gaon's reservations about philosophy, see Dinstag, "Haim hitnaged HaGRA lemishnato hafilosofit shel HaRAMBAN?," 253–68.
43. Isserles, *Shu"t HaREMA,* sig. 6; S. Assaf, *Meqorot letoldot haḥinukh beYisrael,* 1:288; Ḥelma, introduction to *Merkevet hamishneh.*
44. Rabinowitz, "'Aqevot shel ḥofesh-de'ot barabanut shel Polin bameah hatetzayin."
45. On the Gaon's alleged struggle against Mendelssohn's *Habeur,* see Zinberg, *Toldot sifrut Yisrael,* 5:327–328, which completely refutes that assertion.
46. In addition to Raisin, whose assessment is mentioned above, see B.-Ẓ. Katz, *Hazman,* 7.
47. Sons of the Vilna Gaon, introduction to *Shulḥan 'arukh, oraḥ ḥayyim.*
48. On traditional education in the late Middle Ages, see J. Katz, *Tradition and Crisis,* chap. 18. For a survey that emphasizes the weak points in traditional education, see Kleinberger, *Hamaḥshavah hapedagogit shel HaMAHARAL miPrague,* chap. 2.
49. Etkes, *Te'udah beYisrael,* 7 ff.
50. S. Assaf, *Meqorot letoldot haḥinukh beYisrael,* 1:45–51, 61–63, 65–66.
51. Wessely, *Divrei shalom veemet,* chap. 1, first letter.
52. On that, see chap. 1 in this volume.
53. See S. Assaf, *Meqorot letoldot haḥinukh beYisrael,* 1:45–51, 61–63, 65–66; for a typical expression of criticism of *pilpul* among the Gaon's admirers, see Yeḥezqel Feivel of Dretshin, *Toldot Adam,* 20 ff.; for an up-to-date survey of this topic, see Dimitrovski, "'Al derekh hapilpul," 111–81.
54. For a typical example of a claim for such awareness, see Phinehas ben Judah of Polozk, *Rosh hagiv'a,* fol. 11a.
55. Levinsohn, *Te'udah beYisrael,* 6–7, note on 7–8.
56. For a list of rabbis who condemned *pilpul,* see Reines, *Hapilpul.*
57. For a detailed discussion of the Gaon's textual emendations of the Jerusalem Talmud, see Goronchik, "HaGRA vehayerushalmi," 45–107.
58. L. Ginzberg, *Students, Scholars, and Saints,* 133–38; A. H. Weiss, "Reshit ẓemiḥat hahaskalah beRusia," 9 ff.
59. Goronchik, "HaGRA vehayerushalmi," 56.

60. Y. L. Maimon, *Toledot HaGRA,* 44; L. Ginzberg, *Perushim veḥidushim baYerushalmi,* 127.
61. Czernowitz, *Toldot haposqim,* 3:210 ff., and esp. 219, 225–26.
62. The Gaon's religious practices were described by Rabbi Yissacher Ber ben Tanḥum in *Ma'aseh rav,* first published in Zulkowa in 1808 and reprinted in later editions.
63. As noted earlier, I have treated this issue more extensively in Etkes, "Leshealat mevasrei hahaskalah bemizraḥ Eiropa."
64. As mentioned above, an extensive biographical discussion of Rabbi Barukh of Shklov is found in Fishman, *Russia's First Modern Jews,* 22–45. See also Mahler, *Divrei yemei Yisrael,* 4:53–57.
65. These matters are presented in Shoḥet, *'Im ḥilufei tequfot,* 199–200.
66. See Sons of the Vilna Gaon, introduction to *Shulḥan 'arukh, oraḥ ḥayyim;* Fin, *Qiryah neemenah,* 163–70; Landau, *Hagaon heḥasid miVilna,* 266 ff. On Rabbi Menasseh of Ilya, see M. Plongian, *Ben Porat;* Rosenfeld, "R. Menasseh Ilyer," 250; B.-Ẓ. Katz, *Rabanut, ḥasidut, haskalah,* 2:187–203; Zinberg, *Toldot sifrut Yisrael,* 6:153–61; Mahler, *Divrei yemei Yisrael,* 4:63–68.
67. We have no information about contacts between Rabbi Barukh of Shklov and the Vilna Gaon other than the visit mentioned in Rabbi Barukh's introduction to *Uqlidos.* Ben-Ẓion Katz's conjecture that Rabbi Barukh was the Gaon's algebra tutor (B.-Ẓ. Katz, *Rabanut, ḥasidut, haskalah,* 2:41) seems baseless.
68. Among the autobiographical writings of the early maskilim in Lithuania are Gottlober, *Zikhronot umas'aot;* M. A. Ginzburg, *Avi'ezer;* and S. Y. Fin, "Dor dor vedorshav," 259 ff. Fin relates that he was first drawn to Haskalah ideas by I. B. Levinsohn's book *Te'udah beYisrael.* Although he had studied as a youth in a study house named for the Vilna Gaon, which followed some of the Gaon's personal traditions, he learned of the "Gaon-as-maskil" motif only as an adult, when he himself had become a maskil. At that stage he resorted to the motif in his critique of traditional society. On the Gaon and his literary output in relation to the spiritual development of the early maskilim, this conclusion is reinforced by the new research of Dr. Mordecai Zalkin presented at the conference on the Vilna Gaon held at the Zalman Shazar Center in Jerusalem in January 1998. Zalkin studied a number of men from eastern Europe who wrote or translated works of science during the first decades of the nineteenth century. It emerges that these authors did not refer to the Gaon to justify that initiative.
69. See chap. 3.
70. For example, see Lebensohn, introduction to *Beurim ḥadashim,* 6. The high value placed on the image of the Vilna Gaon as a maskil by the maskilim of Lithuania is shown by the effort to "clear" him of opposition to the philosophy of Maimonides. See Dinstag, "Haim hitnaged HaGRA lemishnato hafilosofit shel HaRAMBAN?," 255.

71. See Lillienblum, "'Al HaGRA vehaBESHT," 228; Ish Horowitz, "haḤasidut vehaHaskalah," 31–33; Verses, "Hagaon R. Eliyahu miVilna be'olamah shel sifrut hahaskalah," 25–66.
72. See Reines, "Hapilpul besifrut Yisrael."
73. One of the most important avenues for the propagation of the Gaon's influence in this respect was the yeshiva of Volozhin, headed by Rabbi Ḥayyim, the Gaon's leading disciple. On his method of study, see Kaplan, "Ledarkho shel rabbi Ḥayyim miVolozhin bahalakhah."
74. See Steinschneider, *'Ir Vilna,* 250–52. On Rabbi David Luria, see the biographical note in the appendix to his *Qadmut sefer hazohar.* See also Steinschneider, *'Ir Vilna,* 157–59; and S. Ginzburg, *Ketavim historiim,* 28–29. Ẓevi Kaplan ("Ledarkho shel rabbi Ḥayyim miVolozhin bahalakhah," 16) points out Rabbi Ḥayyim of Volozhin's attention to the question of wording. However, from his discussion it does not appear that Rabbi Ḥayyim actually engaged in textual editing.
75. In 1802 Rabbi Abraham published a collection of Midrashim, including the Midrash to Genesis known as *Aggadat bereshit.* To the latter work he added a critical introduction, which was held in high regard by some later scholars and reprinted by Solomon Buber in his edition of *Aggadat bereshit* (Cracow, 1903). Rabbi Abraham also published another work, *Rav pe'alim,* on the sources of various Midrashim. It is worth mentioning that two of the other Vilna figures just mentioned, Strashun and Luria, also devoted some efforts to researching midrash, possibly under the influence of the Gaon, who had emphasized the need to study all branches of Tannaitic and Amoraic literature.
76. The customs of the Vilna Gaon, with a commentary intended to reveal their sources, were described, as noted, in Yissacher Ber ben Tanḥum, *Ma'aseh rav;* see also Ḥayyim of Volozhin, "Sheiltot."
77. Fishman, *Russia's First Modern Jews,* 108–12.
78. Abraham Ben Eliyahu miVilna, *Gevulot haarets.*
79. On Rabbi Ya'aqov Barit, see Barit, *Toldot Ya'aqov;* Dinur, "Reshima otobiografit shel Ḥ. Z. Margoliot," 254 ff.
80. Ya'aqov Moshe Ben Abraham, *Ayil meshulash,* was published in Vilna and Horodna in 1834; the citations below come from the introduction to that edition by Rabbi Ya'aqov Moshe.
81. See Phinehas ben Judah of Polozk, *Keter torah,* at the beginning of the book. On Rabbi Phinehas, see Fin, *Qiryah neemenah,* 236–37. On Rabbi Phinehas's polemics against Haskalah, see Nadler, *The Faith of the Mitnagdim,* 135–38.
82. The *haskamah* given by Rabbi Abraham Abeli to the first edition of *Te'udah beYisrael* was omitted from later editions. In the introduction to the second edition of his book (1857), Levinsohn wrote as a comment, "The true Gaon Rabbi Abeli, rabbi and head of the rabbinical court, of blessed memory, after giving his

approval of it, was asked by the notables of the community of Vilna at a great assembly, saying, What is this book? What is its nature? What is its flaw? And the Rabbi answered publicly: 'There is no flaw in it except that it was not composed by our great rabbi Eliyahu the Hasid of Vilna.'" On Rabbi Abraham Abeli, see Steinschneider, *'Ir Vilna,* 19–31.

3. THE VILNA GAON AND THE BEGINNING OF THE STRUGGLE AGAINST HASIDISM

1. Dubnow, *Toldot haḤasidut,* 108. Citations of Dubnow are paraphrased from the Hebrew edition.
2. Ibid., 111.
3. Ibid., 108.
4. Ibid., 111.
5. J. Katz, *Tradition and Crisis,* 202–13.
6. Ibid., 210.
7. Ibid., 241.
8. H. H. Ben-Sasson, *Ishiyuto shel HaGRA vehashp'aato hahistorit,* 204.
9. Ibid., 206.
10. B.-Z. Katz, *Rabanut, ḥasidut, haskalah,* 2:111–21.
11. Scholem, "Shtei ha'eduyuot harishonot 'al ḥavurot haḤasidim veha-BESHT," 228–40.
12. Liberman, "Keiẓad ḥoqrim Ḥasidut beYisrael," 1:38–49; Piekarz, *Biyemei ẓemiḥat haḤasidut,* 320.
13. *Shivḥei HaBESHT,* 81.
14. Ibid., 61.
15. Vilensky, *Ḥasidim umitnagdim,* 1:64–67. On the anthology *Zemir 'aritsim veḥarvot tsurim,* see Vilensky's introduction (1:27–35).
16. The author of article six says of himself, following his description of the course of events, "All the foregoing my eyes saw and not those of a stranger" (Vilensky, *Ḥasidim umitnagdim,* 1:66). His close relationship with the leadership may be surmised from the information he possessed about contacts between the Vilna Gaon and the *parnasim* of the community.
17. Shneur Zalman of Lyady, *Igrot qodesh,* letter no. 34, pp. 85–90; and letter no. 51, pp. 120–29. The consistency between these letters of Rabbi Shneur Zalman and the account in *Zemir 'aritsim veḥarvot tsurim* has been noted by Vilensky, *Ḥasidim umitnagdim,* 1:29–30.
18. The name Mendel of Minsk refers to Rabbi Menahem Mendel of Vitebsk.

19. Vilensky, *Ḥasidim umitnagdim,* 1:64, and cf. the Babylonian Talmud, *'Avoda zara* 26b.
20. See Shneur Zalman of Lyady, *Igrot qodesh,* 86.
21. Vilensky, *Ḥasidim umitnagdim,* 1:64, n. 4, suggests that the passage in the Zohar mentioned here is to be identified with the one mentioned in the letter of the opponent of Hasidism, Rabbi David of Makov.
22. Shneur Zalman of Lyady, *Igrot qodesh,* 86–87. *Gilui eliyahu* literally means "the revelation of Elijah." The prophet Elijah may appear to a person and teach him the secrets of the Torah. Among Jewish mystics, *gilui eliyahu* is regarded as a high level of revelation.
23. The contents of these rumors may be inferred from the letters sent from Vilna calling for other communities to join in the struggle against Hasidism. These letters are published in Vilensky, *Ḥasidim umitnagdim,* 1:36–69. For a detailed list of the accusations contained in these letters, see Vilensky's introduction, 1:28–29.
24. Gris, "Mimitos leetos," 2:117–46; Haran, "R. Avraham miKalisk veR. Shneur Zalman miLadi," 2:399–428.
25. The Babylonian Talmud, *Sanhedrin* 99b, states, "An *apikoros:* Rav and Rav Hanina both said that it is someone who scorns Torah scholars." The remark about turning the feet upward refers to the sins of the Israelites at Ba'al Pe'or (Numbers 25). The Babylonian Talmud, *Sanhedrin* 60b, states, "Whoever bares [*po'er*] to Ba'al Pe'or, that is its worship," which is to say, even though the person who bares himself intended to show scorn for Ba'al Pe'or, he is subject to the death penalty, since baring oneself is the ordinary way of worshiping that god. Apparently the Vilna Gaon regarded the Hasidic custom of standing on one's head as verging upon idolatry, similar to the worship of Ba'al Pe'or.
26. Shneur Zalman of Lyady, *Igrot qodesh,* 125–26.
27. On this matter see the explanations in Vilensky, *Ḥasidim umitnagdim,* 1:29, n. 24.
28. Ibid., 64.
29. Vilensky has pointed out the important role played by the community of Shklov in the beginning of the struggle against Hasidism. He states that "the community of Shklov began the battle against the sect[,] and it provoked the community of Vilna to wage war aggressively against the sect" (ibid., 29). The function filled by Shklov in the early struggle against Hasidism has been discussed in detail in the recent book by Fishman, *Russia's First Modern Jews.* Fishman also emphasizes the contribution of Shklov as the first community to take a stand regarding Hasidism and as the one that impelled the Vilna Gaon to take action. Fishman also points out that Shklov was a center of opposition in the areas annexed to Russia in 1772. Fishman believes that, following the debate held in Shklov in the winter of 5532, in the spring a special assembly was convened there,

at which it was declared that Hasidim were heretics. Furthermore, the community of Shklov sent letters to other communities, including Vilna, reporting the decision of the assembly. It seems doubtful that such an assembly was actually convened. Fishman offers no explicit evidence to that effect, and he apparently bases his claim on two passages in *Zemir 'aritsim veḥarvot tsurim,* where it is stated that the Hasidim were declared heretics in the community of Shklov (see Vilensky, *Ḥasidim umitnagdim,* 1:63–64). However, this does not oblige us to conclude that a special assembly was convened, and it is highly possible that at the end of the debate the rabbis of Shklov announced their position regarding the Hasidim. Nor is there any clear evidence to support Fishman's conjecture that the community of Shklov sent letters to other communities, aside from the "writings" that were sent to Vilna.

Vilensky and Fishman appear to exaggerate the importance of Shklov's influence on the Gaon. As noted above, the Gaon had assumed a hostile position regarding Hasidism before the Shklov debate took place. Nevertheless, the outcome of the debate undoubtedly influenced him, as we shall see below. From the point of view of this discussion, decisive weight must be attributed to the fact that, while Shklov preceded Vilna in actually proclaiming that the Hasidim were heretics, action to suppress Hasidism was not begun before the Gaon approved the position of the rabbis of Shklov.

30. Fishman, in *Russia's First Modern Jews,* suggests that Rabbi Jacob, the son of Rabbi Judah, the rabbi of Shklov, played a central role in that community's struggle against Hasidism. He supports this supposition with evidence that Rabbi Jacob was persecuted by the Hasidim.

31. This is how Vilensky interprets the course of events, in *Ḥasidim umitnagdim,* 1:29.

32. Ibid., 64–65.

33. Ibid., 65.

34. Ibid.

35. Ibid.

36. Ibid., 66.

37. From the Vilna Gaon.

38. Shneur Zalman of Lyady, *Igrot qodesh,* letter no. 34, p. 87.

39. Ibid., 87–88.

40. Ibid., letter no. 61, p. 144.

41. Although the community of Shklov preceded that of Vilna in declaring that the Hasidim were heretics, from all that is known to us, that declaration does not appear to have been accompanied by suppressive measures, and it is doubtful that the Shklov community could have conscripted other communities in the struggle, as did the Gaon.

42. See the beginning of this chapter on opposition to Hasidism, which pre-

ceded the Gaon's intervention. On opposition to Hasidism after the Gaon's death, see chap. 5.

43. See, for example, article one in *Zemir 'aritsim veḥarvot tsurim,* in Vilensky, *Ḥasidim umitnagdim,* 1:37–44.

44. See the letters against the Hasidim of the Brod community, ibid., 44–49.

45. A rabbi sympathetic to Hasidism, although he did not actually join the movement, was Rabbi Eliezer Halevi of Pinsk. See M. Nadav, "Qehilat Pinsk-Karlin bein Ḥasidut lehitnagdut," 98–108.

46. My opinion—that the Vilna Gaon's response to Hasidism was not necessitated by reality, and that in response to the dilemma posed by Hasidism for the spiritual leadership of the generation it would have been possible to respond differently—is consistent with the conclusion reached by Mordecai Nadav in his study of the struggle between Hasidim and Mitnagdim in the Pinsk community. Nadav states—contrary to the common view that the Jews of eastern Europe were divided between Hasidim and Mitnagdim—that the picture was more varied: there were Hasidim, non-Hasidim who were not opponents, moderate Mitnagdim, and militant Mitnagdim. See ibid.

47. Vilensky, *Ḥasidim umitnagdim,* 1:66. Cf. the quotations Vilensky presents from *Shever posh'im* (ibid., n. 29). Vilensky maintains that the various accusations leveled against the Hasidim in polemical writings "cannot explain the unrestrained outburst against the Hasidim. The opponents did not refrain from personal persecution and economic and social harassment" (ibid., 17). Thus Vilensky concludes that the motive for the outbreak of the struggle against Hasidism was its offense against the status of Torah study and scholars: "The heads of the opponents believed with complete faith that the new sect wanted to introduce changes in the hierarchy of values that had been traditional in Judaism, especially among the Jews of Lithuania, a hierarchy in which the highest position was Torah study and the elite member of the Jewish community was the scholar, who constantly studied Torah. Hence, when a sect organized that, in the opinion of the Mitnagdim, held that hierarchy of values in contempt, and that chose leaders whose expertise in Torah was in many cases dubious in the eyes of the Mitnagdim, it was necessary to combat that sect by all possible means" (ibid., 18). Vilensky is certainly correct in attributing great significance to the issue of the status of Torah study in the controversy between Hasidim and Mitnagdim. However, this subject became a central issue in the controversy at a later stage, after the Gaon's death. Furthermore, it is difficult to accept the argument that this was the matter that influenced the decision to begin all-out warfare against the Hasidim; for transfer of emphasis from Torah study to other forms of divine worship—as grave as this may have been from the viewpoint of the Mitnagdim—would still not have justified the verdict that the Hasidim were heretics.

48. See J. Katz, *Tradition and Crisis,* 202–13.

49. Shlomo Maimon also understood the struggle against Hasidism in this manner. See S. Maimon, *Ḥayei Shlomo Maimon*, 134.
50. See H. H. Ben-Sasson, *Ishiyuto shel HaGRA vehashp'aato hahistorit*, 204.
51. A prominent example of this was the struggle regarding Hasidic ritual slaughter. See Shmeruk, "Mashma'uta haḥevratit shel hashḥita haḥasidit," 47–72.
52. Vilensky, *Ḥasidim umitnagdim*, 1:94.

4. THE VILNA GAON AND THE MITNAGDIM AS SEEN BY THE HASIDIM

1. Dubnow's survey of the struggle against Hasidism, *Toldot haḤasidut*, 107–69, 242–89, remains the most comprehensive. A valuable collection of documents and bibliographical and historical information can be found in Vilensky, *Ḥasidim umitnagdim.*
2. Vilensky, *Ḥasidim umitnagdim*, 1:90–93. On the various editions of this letter and the one to be cited presently, see Vilensky's introduction, 90. The letter was also printed in the collection Barnai, ed., *Igrot Ḥasidim meerets-Yisrael*, 62–65. A different interpretation of these letters is found in D. Assaf, "Sheyaẓa shmu'a sheba mashiaḥ ben David," 337.
3. "Behold, in order to clear ourselves in truth of all the suspicions falsely raised against us, we swear by heaven and earth[:] . . . if in rebellion or in dishonesty, perish the thought, we have violated even any extension of enlargement of a commandment . . . may none of us be redeemed" (Vilensky, *Ḥasidim umitnagdim*, 1:92).
4. "Behold we forgive all of them entirely, validly and permanently, anyone who has vexed us, whether bodily or monetarily[,] . . . and from now on our princes, our lords, our brothers, our flesh, what has happened is no more, and is as though it never was, but we pray for the future" (ibid.).
5. "Whom will the kings of Israel pursue, after a single flea, as if they were hunting a partridge in the hills [1 Samuel 26:20]. And now I call to you men, and yours is this commandment, to be in a covenant with us for life and peace" (ibid.).
6. Ibid., 91–92. Perhaps the "orator" mentioned here is the "procurer" mentioned in the letter of Rabbi Shneur Zalman cited below. This identification was suggested by D. Assaf, "Sheyaẓa shmu'a sheba mashiaḥ ben David," 337, n. 93.
7. See chap. 3 in this volume for a discussion of this event.
8. Vilensky, *Ḥasidim umitnagdim*, 1:93–97.
9. Ibid., 1:94–95. This apparently refers to the followers of Rabbi Abraham of Kalisk, who were accused of deriding Torah scholars and of standing on their heads. See chap. 3 in the present volume.

10. Vilensky, *Ḥasidim umitnagdim,* 1:94.
11. Etkes, "'Aliyato shel R. Shneur Zalman miLiadi le'emdat manhigut," 429–39.
12. On the struggle between Hasidim and Mitnagdim in White Russia, see Fishman, *Russia's First Modern Jews,* 7–21. On Rabbi Shneur Zalman's Hasidim in Lithuania, see Zalkin, "Meqomot shelo maẓa 'adayin haḤasidut ken la."
13. On the imprisonment of Rabbi Shneur Zalman, see Ḥayyim Meir Heilman, *Beit rabi,* 51–77; Vilensky, *Ḥasidim umitnagdim,* 1:230–95; Mondshine, *Kerem ḥabad,* 27–108.
14. Vilensky, *Ḥasidim umitnagdim,* 1:161–67.
15. Ibid., 162–64.
16. Ibid., 164; see also the Babylonian Talmud, *Baba metsi'a* 59b.
17. Vilensky, *Ḥasidim umitnagdim,* 1:187–90.
18. Ibid., 198–203.
19. Ibid., 200.
20. For a discussion of this episode, see the section "The Course of Events before the Spring of 5532" in chap. 3 in this volume.
21. This letter was first published in Mondshine, *Kerem ḥabad,* 1:111–13.
22. Ibid., 111.
23. Sections of the letter were published in Heilman, *Beit rabi,* 48–58; Vilensky, *Ḥasidim umitnagdim,* 1:40. For the full text of the letter, see Shneur Zalman of Lyady, *Igrot qodesh,* 120–29.
24. Mondshine, *Kerem ḥabad,* 1:111–12.
25. For a Hasidic tradition on this matter, see Rodkinson, *'Amudei beit ḥabad,* 21–23. See also Glitzenstein, *Harav rabi Shneur Zalman zatsal,* 23–25, 36–38.
26. Mondshine, *Kerem ḥabad,* 1:112.
27. Ibid.
28. See Vilensky, *Ḥasidim umitnagdim,* 1:204, 210–22.
29. As noted earlier, on the imprisonment of Rabbi Shneur Zalman, see Heilman, *Beit rabi,* 51–77; Vilensky, *Ḥasidim umitnagdim,* 1:230–295; and Mondshine, *Kerem ḥabad,* 27–108.
30. Vilensky, *Ḥasidim umitnagdim,* 1:305–6.
31. Ibid., 305–6, 308, and cf. the footnotes there.
32. Ibid., 311.
33. Ibid., 312.
34. On the author's identity and on various versions of the work, see Mondshine, "Hasefarim 'maẓref ha'avodah' 've'vikuḥa raba,'" 165–75. For biographical details about Ya'aqov Qidner, see Nigal, *Melaqtei hasipur haḤasidi,* 59–77.
35. Qidner, *Maẓref ha'avodah,* fol. 5–13.
36. This issue is discussed in chap. 5 in this volume. Also see N. Lamm, "Excursus 1: The *Maẓref ha'avodah:* A Pro-Hasidic Response to the *Nefesh ha-ḥayyim,*"

in *Torah Lishma, Torah for Torah's Sake in the Works of Rabbi Hayyim of Volozhin and His Contemporaries*, 308–24. Perhaps Lamm exaggerates in that he regards the response to *Nefesh ha-ḥayyim* as the principal concern of *Maẓref ha'avodah*. This subject does indeed occupy an important place in the work, but it has broader contents and goals.

37. Qidner, *Maẓref ha'avodah*, fol. 17a.

38. Ibid., fols. 17b–18a. Cf. the letter of Rabbi Shneur Zalman, cited above.

39. Qidner, *Maẓref ha'avodah*, fol. 18.

40. Ibid., fols. 18b–19a.

41. Qidner cites Rabbi Ḥayyim on behalf of Hasidism, an approach also found in his collection of Hasidic tales, *Sipurim noraim*. Qidner recounts that Rabbi Ḥayyim greatly admired the erudition and wisdom of Rabbi Shneur Zalman (112–16).

42. Qidner, *Maẓref ha'avodah*, fol. 19.

43. Vilensky, *Ḥasidim umitnagdim*, 1:218. Recognition by the Russian government of the right of the Hasidim to maintain separate minyanim was included in the constitution of 1804. See Ettinger, "Taqanat 1804," 234–56.

44. Heilman, *Beit rabi*, 6.

45. For a detailed discussion of Heilman as a Hasidic historian, see Karlinkski, *Historia shekenegged*, 109–65. See also Karlinkski, "Bein biografia lehegiograpia," 161–68.

46. Heilman, *Beit rabi*, 6.

47. Ibid., 7. Rabbi Yeḥezqel Landau (1713–1793) was one of the greatest rabbis of the eighteenth century. Among other things, he served as the rabbi of the Jewish community of Prague. He was famous because of his book of Halakhic responsa, *Hanod'a beYehudah* (Renowned in Judea).

48. Ibid.

49. See Mishnah, *Avot* 5:17.

50. Heilman, *Beit rabi*, 7.

51. Scholem, *Major Trends in Jewish Mysticism*, 244–86; Tishby, *Torat har'a vehaqelipah beqabalat HaARI*, 134–43.

52. Heilman, *Beit rabi*, 7.

53. For a detailed account of Rabbi Joseph Isaac's historical writing, see Rapoport-Albert, "Hagiography with Footnotes," 119–59. In "Hasidism after 1772," Ada Rapoport-Albert offers an apt description of Rabbi Joseph Isaac's historical writing when she says, "The admor Joseph Isaac, who was not a professional historian but a leader of a large community in extremely difficult circumstances, subordinated the writing and documentation of history to the needs of making of history, in which indeed he took an active part" (125). For a discussion of Rabbi Joseph Isaac's historical writings in the broader context of orthodox Jewish historiography, see Bartal, "Shimon Hakofer," 243–68.

54. Schneersohn, "Avot haḤasidut," 3.
55. See, for example, the words of Rabbi Shneur Zalman as cited by Mondshine, *Kerem ḥabad,* 1:46–47.
56. Elior, "Vikuaḥ Minsk."
57. Ibid., 218–31.
58. On general reservations regarding these writings, see ibid., 182.
59. Ibid., 200.
60. Ibid., 206–7.
61. Cf. Gris, "Mimitos leetos," 2:130, n. 41.
62. For a discussion of this event, see the section "The Course of Events before the Spring of 5532" in chap. 3 in this volume.
63. Vilensky, *Ḥasidim umitnagdim,* 1:198–203.
64. This subject occupies an important place in Rabbi Joseph Isaac Schneersohn's "Divrei hayamim hahem." This matter, discussed briefly in chap. 2, is discussed at much greater length in this chapter.
65. Ibid., 4–10.
66. See chap. 2.
67. See Etkes, *Te'udah beYisrael;* Etkes, "Parshat ha'haskalah mit'am' vehatemura bema'amad tenu'at hahaskalah beRusia," 264–313; Stanislawski, *Tsar Nicolas I and the Jews,* 49–96; Fishman, *Russia's First Modern Jews,* 101–21. For a different approach to this issue that emphasizes the opposition of the Mitnagdim to Haskalah, see Nadler, *The Faith of the Mitnagdim,* 127–50. For new and significant findings on the expansion of the Haskalah movement in Russia in the first half of the nineteenth century, see Zalkin, *Be'alot hashaḥar.*
68. Schneersohn, "Divrei hayamim hahem," 11–12.
69. See Piekarz, *Ḥasidut Polin,* 25–26, 30–31; Bacon, *The Politics of Tradition,* 194.
70. Mondshine, "Parnasei Vilna vehaGRA umilḥamtam bahasidut," 182–221.
71. Ibid., 151–57. Here Mondshine shows a clear affinity with the views of Rabbi Joseph Isaac regarding the Gaon's responsibility for the penetration of Haskalah into Lithuania.
72. Ibid., 158–61.
73. Ibid., 162–81. On the struggle between the *kahal* and the rabbi in Vilna, see Y. Klausner, *Vilna bitekufat hagaon.*
74. Mondshine, *Kerem ḥabad,* 184.
75. Ibid., 183–84.
76. Ibid., 186–87.
77. Ibid., 185.
78. Ibid., 191.
79. Ibid., 192–93. See also the concluding remarks, 219.
80. See for example Mondshine, ed., *Shivḥei HaBESHT.* Mondshine's introduction is full of critical comments about earlier scholars, some of which are important and useful.

81. The article in question is an earlier version of chap. 3 of the present volume.

82. Thus, for example, it seems that Hayim Liberman was correct in his criticism of Gershom Scholem. See Liberman, "Keiẓad ḥoqrim Ḥasidut beYisrael," 38–49. Similarly, I believe that Mondshine is correct in his dispute with Ra'aya Haran. See Haran, "Shivḥei harav," 22–58; Mondshine, "Aminutan shel igrot hahasidim meereẓ Yisrael," 63:65–97, 64:79–97; Haran, "'Atara leyoshna," 98–102.

83. See Etkes, "The Study of Hasidism," 447–64; Rosman, *Founder of Hasidism*, 63–82.

84. The relatively small number of Hasidim in Vilna in the early 1770s can be deduced from the remark of Bulgakov, the civil governor of Lithuania, in 1798: "The number of the members of the sect is still small, and it could have been done away with by exiling thirty Jews." Bulgakov's letter is presented by Mondshine, *Kerem ḥabad*, 33–35.

85. See Vilensky, *Ḥasidim umitnagdim*, 1:29.

86. Shneur Zalman of Lyady, *Igrot qodesh*, 125–26.

87. As noted, Rabbi Menahem Mendel of Vitebsk also admitted, in the letter cited above, that there were some instances of faulty conduct among some of the Hasidim.

88. Vilensky, *Ḥasidim umitnagdim*, 1:199.

89. See Elior, "Ha ziqa shebein qabbalah leḤasidut," 199.

90. Vilensky, *Ḥasidim umitnagdim*, 1:201–2. See Avivi, *Qabalat HaGRA*, 30.

91. Vilensky, *Ḥasidim umitnagdim*, 1:37–49, 58–64.

92. Mondshine, *Kerem ḥabad*, 193.

93. Ibid., 194.

94. Ibid., 220.

95. Ibid., 221.

96. Epstein, *Meqor Barukh*.

97. On Barukh Epstein, see Tarshish, *Rabbi Barukh Halevi Epstein ba'al "torah temimah."* On *Meqor Barukh*, see Barlev, "'Olamam haruḥani vehatarbuti shel halomdim bayeshivot haLitaiyot bamaḥaẓit hashniyah shel hameah hayod-tet ubameah hakaf, kefi shemishtaqef misifrut hazikhronot."

98. Epstein, *Meqor Barukh*, 3:519.

99. Wolfsberg, "Hagaon miVilna keishiyut ukheparshan," 163–69.

100. For a biography of Wolfsberg, see Raphael, ed., *Sefer Avi'ad*, 1–10.

101. Wolfsberg, "Hagaon miVilna keishiyut ukheparshan," 164.

102. On Ya'aqov Lifschitz and his book *Zikhron Ya'akov*, as an alternative, orthodox version of history, see Bartal, "'Zikhron Ya'aqov' leR. Ya'aqov Lifschitz," 409–14.

103. This topic is discussed at length in chap. 5.

104. Y. Lifschitz, *Zikhron Ya'akov*, 1:10.

105. Ibid., 11–12.

106. This argument is also in the spirit of Rabbi Ḥayyim's views. Lifschitz states too that the Gaon and his disciples rejected Hasidism because of their interpretation of the idea of God's immanence and because the Hasidim changed the wording of the prayers. See ibid., 12–14.
107. Ibid., 14. The expression "the Hasidim of '5530'" alludes to the group of Hasidim associated with Rabbi Abraham of Kalisk who were accused of insulting rabbis in the year 5530.
108. Ibid., 15.
109. Y. L. Maimon, *Toledot HaGRA.*
110. Ibid., 72–73.
111. Vilensky, *Ḥasidim umitnagdim,* 1:230 ff.
112. Y. L. Maimon, *Toledot HaGRA,* 73.
113. Landau, *Hagaon heḥasid miVilna.*
114. Ibid., 227–36.
115. Ibid., 339.
116. Ibid., 344.
117. Ibid., introduction to the 2d ed. (Jerusalem, 1978).

5. RABBI ḤAYYIM OF VOLOZHIN'S RESPONSE TO HASIDISM

1. We do not yet have a comprehensive and exhaustive biography of Rabbi Ḥayyim of Volozhin. A first step in that direction was taken by Rabbi M. S. Schmuckler, in *Toldot Rabenu Ḥayyim miVolozhin.* In several respects this is an incomplete study, and its main importance lies in presenting the outline of the biography and the relevant sources. Other studies dealing with Rabbi Ḥayyim and his life work are Kamelhar, *Dor de'ah,* 2:130–34; Tsharna, "R. Ḥayyim miVolozhin betor pedagog"; Mirsky, *Mosdot hatorah beEiropa,* 1–30; Bialovloẓki, "Merkazei hatorah beLita," 1:185–90; Virzburg, "Rabbi Ḥayyim miVolozhin," 26–38; Weinberg, "Ba'alei hamusar, R Israel Salanter," 292–94. On Rabbi Ḥayyim's relationship with the Vilna Gaon, see H. H. Ben-Sasson, *Ishiyuto shel HaGRA vehashp'aato hahistorit;* on Rabbi Ḥayyim's educational doctrine, see Y. Ben-Sasson, "'Olamam haruḥani umishnatam haḥinukhit shel meyasdei hayeshiva haLitait," 155–216. For other aspects of Rabbi Ḥayyim's biography, see Lamm, *Torah Lishma,* 3–58; for a discussion of Rabbi Ḥayyim's thought, see Lamm, *Torah Lishma,* 101–307; Gross, "'Al tfisat 'olamo shel R. Ḥayyim miVolozhin," 121–60. On Rabbi Ḥayyim as the founder of the yeshiva in Volozhin, see Stampfer, *Hayeshiva halitait behithavutah,* 25–54. For an uncritical, hagiographical treatment of his life, see Eliakh, *Avi hayeshivot.*
2. Ḥayyim of Volozhin, Iggeret 'al yesud hayeshivah.

3. My intention here is not to present an exhaustive and balanced discussion of the attitude of Hasidism toward the study of Torah. The following discussion focuses on the more radical expressions of the relationship of Hasidism to Torah study—for they were most insulting to the Mitnagdim—and explains the background of Rabbi Ḥayyim's response. On the relationship of Hasidism to Torah study, see J. Weiss, "Torah Study in Early Hasidism," 56–68; Schatz-Uffenheimer, *Hasidism as Mysticism,* 310–25.

4. The innovation of Hasidism with respect to *devekut* (cleaving to God) is explained in Scholem, "Devekut, or Communion with God," in *The Messianic Idea in Judaism,* 203–27; see also Tishby and Dan, "Torat haḤasidut," 17:800–804; Idel, *Kabbalah,* 35–58; Piekarz, *Bein ideologia lemiẓiut,* 150–78. On *devekut* in the manner of the Ba'al Shem Tov, see Etkes, *Ba'al Hashem, HaBESHT,* 122–62.

5. *Shivḥei HaBESHT,* 182.

6. *Liqutim yeqarim* (Jerusalem, 1974), 5.

7. The summary of his position and the citations below come from *Darkhei yesharim, vehu hanhagot yesharot meharav haẓadik rabi Mendel miPermishlan,* 3.

8. Ya'aqov Yosef of Polna, *Toldot Ya'akov Yosef,* fol. 4a.

9. Ibid., fol. 25a.

10. On Rabbi Meshulam Feibush Heller and his teaching, see Krassen, "Devequt and Faith in Zaddiquim." See also a recent doctoral dissertation concentrating on the writings of Rabbi Meshulam Feibush: Altschuller, "Mishnato shel R. Meshulam Feibush Heller umeqomah bereshit hatnu'ah haḤasidit." Unfortunately, this dissertation contains many statements that are unsupported by the sources on which it is ostensibly based. The work of Rabbi Meshulam Feibush Heller, *Yosher divrei emet,* is composed of two epistles. The first was written in Sivan 5537, and the second was apparently written a few months later. The work was published in *liqutei yeqarim* (Lemberg, 5552). A more accurate edition of the letters of Rabbi Meshulam Feibush was printed by one of his descendants: *Yosher divrei emet;* the citations below are taken from that edition. On the various editions of *Yosher divrei emet,* see Altschuller (8–19).

11. Heller, *Yosher divrei emet,* fol. 12a.

12. Ibid.

13. Ibid., fol. 12b.

14. The Babylonian Talmud, *Succah* 28a.

15. Heller, *Yosher divrei emet,* fol. 12b.

16. See also the words that Rabbi Meshulam Feibush attributes to Rabbi Menahem Mendel of Premishlan, ibid., fol. 18b.

17. Vilensky, *Ḥasidim umitnagdim,* 1:38.

18. Ibid., 118–19.

19. Ibid., 128.

20. Ibid., 2:229 ff.
21. Z. Lifschitz, ed., *Hanhagot ve'etsot*, pt. 1, para. 44.
22. On Rabbi Phinehas the son of Rabbi Judah, see Fin, *Qiryah neemenah*, 236–37. On his writings, see Nadler, *The Faith of the Mitnagdim*, 177–84. Nadler discusses the views of Rabbi Phinehas in various parts of his book.
23. Vilensky, *Ḥasidim umitnagdim*, 1:323. The date of this oath is unclear, though it was certainly administered before the Vilna Gaon's death in 5558.
24. Dubnow published this epistle for the first time in *Toldot haḤasidut*, 461–65. It was published again in Vilensky, *Ḥasidim umitnagdim*, 2:234–38. There are some differences between the manuscript copied by Dubnow and that copied by Vilensky. One is the difference in the date of the epistle (see Vilensky's introduction to the letter). The quotations here are taken from Dubnow.
25. S. Maimon, *Ḥayei Shlomo Maimon*, 143.
26. Ḥayyim of Volozhin, *Nefesh ha-ḥayyim*, fol. 38a.
27. Ibid.
28. On Rabbi Phinehas see Fin, *Qiryah neemenah*, 236–37. *Keter torah* was first printed in Shklov in 5545 (1785) and most probably reflects the state of affairs in White Russia during the 1770s and early 1780s. Since he visited Vilna, Rabbi Phinehas might have known about the situation in Lithuania, so his remarks could also be applicable there.
29. Phinehas ben Judah of Polozk, *Keter torah*, fols. 7b, 8b, 11a.
30. Ibid., fols. 9b, 10a.
31. Ibid., fol. 13a.
32. Ḥayyim of Volozhin, *Nefesh ha-ḥayyim*, fol. 38a.
33. Rabbi Shneur Zalman's reproach against young Hasidim who derided Torah scholars can be viewed as a kind of admission of guilt on the part of a litigant: "The rumor that my ear has heard is not good, . . . of young members of the flock who made their voices heard . . . to pour derision and calumny upon all scholars of the Torah . . . who are not allied with us, saying that only our congregation is holy" (Vilensky, *Ḥasidim umitnagdim*, 1:390).
34. Ḥayyim of Volozhin, *Nefesh ha-ḥayyim*, fol. 35a-b.
35. Rabbi Ḥayyim attributed great importance to proving the value of Torah study even when it was not "for its own sake." This topic is treated below.
36. Ḥayyim of Volozhin, *Nefesh ha-ḥayyim*, fol. 38a.
37. Phinehas ben Judah of Polozk, *Keter torah*, fols. 14b, 15a.
38. Ibid.
39. Ḥayyim of Volozhin, Iggeret 'al yesud hayeshivah.
40. On communal yeshivot during the sixteenth and seventeenth centuries, see J. Katz, *Tradition and Crisis*, 156–69; Breuer, "Hayeshivah haashkenazit beshilhei yemei habeinayim," 9–39; J. Katz, "Jewish Civilization as Reflected in the Yeshivot," 698–700.

41. Dubnow, ed., *Pinqas medinat Lita, va'ad taf-yod, takana* [regulation] no. 459; *Va'ad taf-yod-bet, takana* no. 484; *Va'ad taf-kaf-bet, takana* no. 528; *Va'ad taf-kaf-zayin, takana* no. 587.
42. Ḥayyim of Volozhin, Iggeret 'al yesud hayeshivah.
43. For the testimony of Rabbi Joseph of Krinik, see Schmuckler, *Toldot Rabenu Ḥayyim miVolozhin,* 33.
44. Dubnow, *Toldot haḤasidut,* 8–18; Dinur, *Reshita shel haḤasidut veyesodoteiha hasoẓyaliim vehameshiḥiim,* 92–139; J. Katz, *Tradition and Crisis,* 195–201.
45. Ḥayyim of Volozhin, *Nefesh ha-ḥayyim,* fol. 38a.
46. For a detailed discussion of *Nefesh ha-ḥayyim,* see Lamm, *Torah Lishma,* 59–101. Lamm supposes that the book was written during the last years of Rabbi Ḥayyim's life and, in any event, after the fire of 1815, which destroyed many of his writings. According to this conjecture, the book was written between 1815 and 1822, when Rabbi Ḥayyim died. Even if we concur that the book was written after 1815, most probably many of the ideas included in it had taken shape many years before then. Evidence of this can be found in Rabbi Ḥayyim's introduction to the Vilna Gaon's commentary on the Zohar, which was printed in 1810. This introduction includes several of the ideas found in *Nefesh ha-ḥayyim* regarding the relationship between intention and action. The great importance that Rabbi Ḥayyim attached to this book can be inferred from the fact that he ordered his son to print it even before his Halakhic *responsa* (see the introduction by Rabbi Yitshak to *Nefesh ha-ḥayyim*). The following discussion is based on both *Nefesh ha-ḥayyim* and *Ruaḥ ḥayyim,* Rabbi Ḥayyim's commentary on the Ethics of the Fathers, and on some of the sermons published in *Derashat MAHARAḤ,* as well as on pamphlets that contain his *responsa* to his students and a description of his practice, which is elucidated below.
47. In *Torah Lishma,* Lamm presents a detailed and profound discussion of several of the principal ideas in *Nefesh ha-ḥayyim.* In his opinion, one should not view Rabbi Ḥayyim's thought regarding Torah study as a response to Hasidism. On Lamm's work and my response to his position on the subject, see Etkes, "Lamm, Naḥum," 638–48.
48. Recall that in chap. 4 I presented the testimony of the author of *Maẓref ha'avodah* regarding personal contacts between Rabbi Ḥayyim and Hasidim.
49. In *Nefesh ha-ḥayyim* Rabbi Ḥayyim presents a doctrinal system that is an original combination of elements taken from various levels of Kabbalistic literature. In general he formulates his ideas in his own way, and following every idea he produces confirmation from rabbinical literature and various works of Kabbalah. The main sources he depends on are the Zohar and its various parts, and *'Ets hayyim* and *Sha'arei qedusha* by Rabbi Ḥayyim Vital. His approach to Kabbalistic sources is marked by a harmonizing tendency. Rabbi Ḥayyim was probably also influenced by works of Kabbalah that he does not mention explicitly. On

ways that Rabbi Ḥayyim might have been influenced by *'Avodat haqodesh* by Rabbi Meir Ibn Gabai, see Gottlieb, "Hayesod hateologi vehamisti shel tefisat ye'ud haadam baqabbalah," 145.

50. Ḥayyim of Volozhin, *Nefesh ha-ḥayyim,* fol. 6a.

51. Ibid., fol. 6b.

52. Ibid., fol. 8b.

53. Ibid., fols. 9b ff.

54. On the concept of intention in Kabbalah, see Tishby, *Mishnat hazoahar,* 2:247 ff.

55. Ḥayyim of Volozhin, *Nefesh ha-ḥayyim,* fol. 7a.

56. On the Kabbalistic conception of Torah, see Scholem, *On the Kabbalah and Its Symbolism,* 32–86.

57. Ḥayyim of Volozhin, *Nefesh ha-ḥayyim,* fol. 41b.

58. Ibid., fols. 40b, 41a.

59. Ibid., fol. 41b.

60. Ibid.

61. On the connection of abundance to harmony in the relations of the *sefirot,* see Tishby, *Mishnat hazoahar,* 1:219–20, 268–70; 2:261–68.

62. Ḥayyim of Volozhin, *Nefesh ha-ḥayyim,* fol. 47a. On the preference of Torah study as opposed to the commandments, see ibid., fol. 48a. It should be emphasized that certain Kabbalists specifically emphasized the performance of commandments in relation to the study of Torah. Rabbi Meir Ibn Gabai, for example, argues that the commandments are preferable to Torah study in influence on the unification of upper realms and the bringing down of abundance (Ibn Gabai, *'Avodat haqodesh,* chap. 66). Similarly, in the introduction to De Vida, *Reshit ḥokhmah,* there is a conspicuous tendency to emphasize the value of the commandments, making the value of Torah study depend on its relationship to the performance of commandments.

63. Ḥayyim of Volozhin, *Nefesh ha-ḥayyim,* fol. 41a.

64. Ibid., fol. 38b.

65. Ibid.

66. Etkes, *Ba'al Hashem, HaBESHT,* chap. 4.

67. Ḥayyim of Volozhin, *Nefesh ha-ḥayyim,* fol. 38b.

68. Ibid.

69. Ibid.; see also Ḥayyim of Volozhin, *Ruaḥ ḥayyim,* chap. 6, Mishnah 1.

70. Ḥayyim of Volozhin, *Nefesh ha-ḥayyim,* fol. 47a.

71. Ibid., fol. 39b.

72. Ibid.

73. Ibid., fol. 42a; see also ibid., fol. 39b.

74. A similar idea that also endows the Halakhah with mystical significance was expressed by Rabbi Meir Ibn Gabai: "For that great voice in which [the

Torah] was given has not ceased, . . . for it calls out eternally forever, and everything that the prophets and Sages instructed and innovated in all the generations, they received it from that voice[;] . . . and for that voice in every generation they are like the image of a trumpet at the mouth of the man who sounds it[,] . . . and there is no innovation in it from their knowledge or intellect" (Ibn Gabai, *'Avodat haqodesh,* chap. 23). Rabbi Ḥayyim might also have been influenced on this subject by Rabbi Meir. However, the image of the trumpet used by Rabbi Meir blurs the active intellectual element in the study of Halakhah, whereas, as we shall see below, Rabbi Ḥayyim specifically sought to sanctify that very element.
75. Ḥayyim of Volozhin, *Nefesh ha-ḥayyim,* fol. 16a.
76. Ibid., fols. 16b, 18b.
77. Ibid., fol. 38a.
78. Ibid., fol. 39a.
79. Ibid.
80. Ibid., fol. 40a.
81. Ibid., fol. 39a.
82. Ibid., fol. 39b.
83. This demand is connected with the tendency to seek to base the Halakhic decisions once again on the Talmud itself. See the introduction by Rabbi Ḥayyim to the Vilna Gaon's commentary on *Shulḥan 'arukh, oraḥ ḥayyim.*
84. On the concept of immanence in Hasidism, see Tishby and Dan, "Torat ha-Ḥasidut," 17:775; Schatz-Uffenheimer, *Hasidism as Mysticism,* 189–203; Elior, "Ha ziqa shebein qabbalah leḤasidut—reẓifut utemura," 107–14; Etkes, *Ba'al Hashem, HaBESHT,* 144–47.
85. This issue of "alien thoughts" is examined in an article by J. Weiss, "Reshit ẓemiḥata shel haderekh haḤasidit," 46–105.
86. See Etkes, *Ba'al Hashem, HaBESHT,* 151–54.
87. Ḥayyim of Volozhin, *Nefesh ha-ḥayyim,* fol. 29b.
88. On the Halakhah's stricture against meditating on the Torah in polluted places, see the Babylonian Talmud, *Brakhot* 24b.
89. Ḥayyim of Volozhin, *Nefesh ha-ḥayyim,* fol. 29b.
90. Z. Lifschitz, ed., *Hanhagot ve'etsot,* pt. 1, para. 41.
91. Ḥayyim of Volozhin, *Nefesh ha-ḥayyim,* fols. 29b, 30a.
92. Rabbi Ḥayyim's distinction is similar to the approach of Rabbi Shneur Zalman of Lyady to the same topic, as noted by Teitelbaum, *Harav miLadi umifleget ḥabad,* 2:43–61. Teitelbaum also tried to prove that Rabbi Ḥayyim was directly influenced by the *Tanya,* a claim that was hotly denied by Virzburg, "Rabbi Ḥayyim miVolozhin," 36–37. A comparative and detailed discussion of the positions of these two thinkers is found in Ross, "Shnei perushim letorat haẓimẓum," 153–69.
93. Ḥayyim of Volozhin, *Nefesh ha-ḥayyim,* fol. 36a.

94. Ibid.
95. Ibid., fol. 36b.
96. Ḥayyim of Volozhin, "Sheiltot," para. 71. This is a collection of *responsa* and instructions that Rabbi Ḥayyim gave his students and a description of his practices. They were copied by Rabbi Eli'ezer Landau, the Vilna Gaon's grandson, from a manuscript left by his father-in-law, Rabbi Asher Hacohen of Tiktin, who was a student of Rabbi Ḥayyim. With slight changes in wording and in a different order, they were also published under the title "Keter ROSH—orhot hayyim" as an appendix to the prayer book *Ishei yisrael 'al pi derekh HaGRA* (Jerusalem, 1935). Much of what is included in these compilations is parallel in content to the manuscript "Hanhagot ve'etsot" (Z. Lifschitz, ed., *Hanhagot ve'etsot*). For other practices of Rabbi Ḥayyim recorded by his student Rabbi Zundel of Salant, see Rivlin, *Hazadik R. Yosef Zundel miSalant verabotav*.
97. Ḥayyim of Volozhin, *Nefesh ha-ḥayyim*, fol. 35a.
98. Ibid., fol. 19b.
99. Ibid.
100. Ibid., fol. 23b.
101. Ibid., fol. 24a.
102. Ibid., fol. 25a.
103. Ibid., fol. 20a.
104. Ibid., fol. 26a.
105. Ibid., fol. 26b.
106. Ibid.
107. Ibid., fol. 35b.
108. Ibid., fol. 36a.
109. Ibid., fols. 43b, 44a.
110. This applies to the community at large, for Rabbi Ḥayyim did guide individual students in the study of Kabbalah. See Z. Lifschitz, ed., *Hanhagot ve'etsot*, pt. 1, para. 25, 26; Y. Lifschitz, *Zikhron Ya'akov*, 1:87.
111. Lamm, *Torah Lishma*, 60.
112. An example of the role played by *Nefesh ha-ḥayyim* in the education of young scholars in Lithuania during the nineteenth century can be found in Etkes, *Lita biYerushalayim*, 52–58.
113. Shaul Stampfer disagrees with this statement. He argues that "the lack of public action against Hasidism and Hasidim on the part of Rabbi Ḥayyim raises doubts as to the importance of the struggle against Hasidism in his considerations when founding the yeshiva." Stampfer also notes that in sources of that period, including the writings of Rabbi Ḥayyim himself, the establishment of the yeshiva is not connected with the struggle against Hasidism. Stampfer argues, too, that use of the term *crisis* in reference to the state of Torah study in Lithuania is not justified. In his opinion, Rabbi Ḥayyim's remarks on the decline in Torah study refer to Poland and White Russia, but not to Lithuania. Stampfer con-

cludes, "The most important factor in establishing the yeshiva was the sincere wish to help young men fulfill the ideal of Torah study, and not the desire to change Jewish society or struggle against trends in Jewish society" (Stampfer, *Hayeshiva halitait behithavutah*, 38).

It is difficult for me to agree with Stampfer's conclusions. True, the state of Torah study in Lithuania might not have been so grave. But that cannot overshadow the fact that Rabbi Ḥayyim acted out of a profound sense of crisis that threatened the status of Torah study and the authority of its scholars. Therefore, one cannot separate his desire "to help young men fulfill the ideal of Torah study" from the general context. Ultimately, the Rabbi Ḥayyim who established the yeshiva in Volozhin was the same Rabbi Ḥayyim who wrote *Nefesh ha-ḥayyim.* Hence his preoccupation with the status of Torah study on the theological level was interconnected with and complementary to the efforts to provide a solution on the organizational and educational level.

114. Rabbi Ḥayyim's main income derived from a textile factory that he owned. He appears to have been a wealthy man in the terms of his period. See Berlin, *MiVolozhin 'ad Yerushalayim*, 1:98.

115. Ḥayyim of Volozhin, Iggeret 'al yesud hayeshivah.

116. Berdyczewski ("Toldot yeshivat 'eẓ heḥayyim," 132) and Ya'veẓ (*Toldot Yisrael*, 14:10) claim that by establishing this yeshiva, Rabbi Ḥayyim was fulfilling the last will and testament of the Vilna Gaon. For a recent, colorful biographical version of this view, see Eliakh, *Avi hayeshivot*, 95–96. Nevertheless, in the writings of those who lived at the time the yeshiva was founded, there is no reference to such a will and testament, and it is mentioned neither in the letter of the notables of Vilna, which is presented below, nor in the testimonials to *Nefesh ha-ḥayyim.* Moreover, Rabbi Ḥayyim never mentions such a testament. Most probably, had he acted under the inspiration and guidance of the Gaon, his supporters would have mentioned that fact prominently. Hence this story is probably merely a late legend connecting the work of the disciple to the figure of his master (cf. Stampfer, *Hayeshiva halitait behithavutah*, 31).

117. Ḥayyim of Volozhin, Iggeret 'al yesud hayeshivah.

118. Ibid.

119. Berlin, *MiVolozhin 'ad Yerushalayim*, 1:81.

120. On Rabbi Yehoshu'a Zeitlin, see Fin, *Qiryah neemenah*, 271; Ya'veẓ, *Toldot Yisrael*, 14:6; Fishman, *Russia's First Modern Jews*, 57–59.

121. Rabbi Yehoshu'a's letter is published in Schmuckler, *Toldot Rabenu Ḥayyim miVolozhin*, 43. The quotation here is from Ḥayyim of Volozhin, *Derashat MAHARAḤ.*

122. Ḥayyim of Volozhin, *Derashat MAHARAḤ.* Among the signatories to the epistle of the Vilna notables were Rabbi Abraham, the son of the Gaon, and Rabbi Abraham Abeli.

123. See Stampfer, *Hayeshiva halitait behithavutah*, 39–41.

124. The words of Rabbi Joseph of Krinik are cited in Schmuckler, *Toldot Rabenu Ḥayyim miVolozhin,* 33 ff.
125. Ibid., 34. See the remarks of Yehiel Mikhel of Neshviz, *Lezekher leYisrael,* in the preface and introduction to the book.
126. Schmuckler, *Toldot Rabenu Ḥayyim miVolozhin,* 33 ff. For further estimates of Rabbi Ḥayyim's contemporaries regarding his contribution to the renewal of the yeshiva in Lithuania, see the testimonials in *Nefesh ha-ḥayyim.*
127. On the advice he gave to his students, see n. 96 above.
128. See his interpretation of the difference of opinion between Rabbi Shimon Bar Yoḥai and Rabbi Yishma'el in *Nefesh ha-ḥayyim,* fols. 12b, 13a. See also Z. Lifschitz, ed., *Hanhagot ve'etsot,* pt. 1, para. 34; pt. 2, para. 15.
129. Z. Lifschitz, ed., *Hanhagot ve'etsot,* pt. 1, paras. 6, 61, 115, 127; pt. 2, para. 15: Ḥayyim of Volozhin, "Sheiltot," para. 68.
130. Z. Lifschitz, ed., *Hanhagot ve'etsot,* pt. 1, paras. 5, 7, 31, 104, 110; pt. 2, paras. 3, 8: Ḥayyim of Volozhin, "Sheiltot," paras. 32, 35, 36, 57, 78, 122. See also the comments presented by Ya'veẓ, *Toldot Yisrael,* 14:11.
131. Descriptions of Rabbi Ḥayyim's practice in matters of Halakhah, of his manner of enhancing the commandments, and of his acts of piety are plentiful in the pamphlets written by his students.
132. The miracles that the Hasidim attributed to their Zaddikim raised doubts among the Mitnagdim. Some of them denied everything and accused the Zaddikim of deceit. It is said of the Vilna Gaon that he admitted the supernatural abilities of the Zaddikim but attributed them to the forces of pollution (Z. Lifschitz, ed., *Hanhagot ve'etsot,* pt. 1, para. 119). In the imaginary debate between a Hasid and a Mitnaged presented in *Maẓref ha'avodah,* which reflects states of mind in the early nineteenth century, the Mitnaged points to the Gaon's holy spirit as a counterpoise to the holy spirit that the Hasidim attributed to their rebbes. Rabbi Ḥayyim himself wrote that a person who studies the Torah for its own sake is not subject to the laws of nature and merits special providence; "indeed, the forces of nature are obedient to him, to whatever he decrees regarding them" (*Nefesh ha-ḥayyim,* fol. 44a), because, by the power of his studies, he acts upon and influences the higher realms. Similarly, Rabbi Ḥayyim presents a story about David ben Shmuel HaLevi—the author of *Turei zahav,* a Halakhic work—who brought a sick man back to life by the power of his Torah. Rabbi Ḥayyim sums up the moral of the story: "For in all occupation with Torah, by the force of his cleaving to God, he has the merit of bringing the dead to life" (*Ruaḥ ḥayyim,* fol. 4b). Stories circulated among Rabbi Ḥayyim's students about the Vilna Gaon's power to exorcise demons, his esoteric knowledge, his ascent of the soul, and the like (Ḥayyim of Volozhin, "Sheiltot," paras. 103–9; Z. Lifschitz, ed., *Hanhagot ve'etsot,* pt. 1, paras. 120–26). Rabbi Ḥayyim's students said of him that he was able to talk to the dead and to discover hidden sins, and even that things happened to him that bordered

on the miraculous (Ḥayyim of Volozhin, "Sheiltot," para. 33; Z. Lifschitz, ed., *Hanhagot ve'etsot*, pt. 1, paras. 80, 81, 101, 76).

6. TALMUDIC SCHOLARSHIP AND THE RABBINATE IN LITHUANIAN JEWRY DURING THE NINETEENTH CENTURY

1. S. Bialovloẓki, "Merkazei hatorah beLita," 1:185–205; Stampfer, *Hayeshiva halitait.*
2. See, for example, the epistle of Rabbi Avraham Sackheim in M. A. Ginzburg, *Devir,* 102 ff.; Dick, *Haoreaḥ,* 5–6; Y. Lifschitz, *Zikhron Ya'aqov;* Epstein, *Meqor Barukh;* Buqi Ben Yogli, *Ma sherau 'einai vesham'u oznai;* Dinur, *Be'olam sheshaq'a;* Nisnboim, *'Alei ḥeldi;* and many others.
3. Rabinowitz-Teumim, *Seder Eliyahu.*
4. Zalmanovitz, *Zikhron Hillel,* 18.
5. See, for example, Eliasberg, *Shvil hazahav,* 8; Barit, *Toldot Ya'aqov,* 12; Rabiner, *Rabbi Eli'ezer Gordon zatoal,* 34. And cf. J. Katz, "Kavim lebiografiah shel haḥatam sofer," 128–29.
6. Blazer, *Or Yisrael,* 112.
7. Etkes, *Lita biYerushalayim,* 17–62.
8. Ibid., 167.
9. Ibid., 171.
10. See chaps. 1 and 7 in this volume.
11. See chap. 5.
12. Wessely, *Divrei shalom veemet,* chap. 8, first letter.
13. Slutzky, "Beit hamidrash lerabbanim beVilna," 29–49; Shoḥet, *Mosad 'harabbanut mita'am' beRusia,* 9–60 (Slutzky's article and part of Shoḥet's book also are included in I. Etkes, ed., *Hadat vehaḥayyim: tenu'at hahaskalah haYehudit bemizraḥ Eiropa,* 217–68 [Jerusalem, 1993].)
14. Shoḥet, *Mosad 'harabbanut mita'am' beRusia,* 33 ff.
15. Ibid., 61–144.
16. For a fine example of the orthodox response to the rabbinical seminary, which is based on the value of Torah for its own sake, see Etkes, *Rabbi Israel Salanter and the Musar Movement,* 275–88.
17. Etkes, *Lita biYerushalayim,* 197–98.
18. See, for example, the will of Rabbi Mordecai Gimpel Yafe in Yafe, *Mivḥar ketavim,* 63.
19. Rabbi Mordecai Eliasberg, when he served as the rabbi of Boisk, and Rabbi Yehiel Mikhal Halevi Epstein, when he served as the rabbi of Novhardok, both

acted in this manner. See Eliasberg, *Shvil hazahav*, xix; Epstein, *Meqor Barukh*, 3:1644–45, para. 1.

20. Zalmanovitz, *Zikhron Hillel*, 23.

21. See Etkes, "Mishpaḥa velimud torah beḥugei ha'lomdim' beLita bameah hayod-tet," 87–106. Reprinted in Etkes, *Lita biYerushalayim*, 63–84.

22. Y. Lifschitz, *Toldot Yiẓḥak*, 6.

23. Epstein, *Meqor Barukh*, 3:1186, para. 1. Further information about the low salaries of rabbis can be found in ibid., 1206–7, para. 3; Rabinowitz-Teumim, *Seder Eliyahu*, 19. In this context the testimony of Rabbi Nahman Reuven Meirovitz is fascinating. He was a student of Rabbi Yitshak of Volozhin, and in his book he lists the communities where he served as a rabbi and "they supported me with honor" (Meirovitz, *Ḥelqat Reuven*, 18). On this book and its author, see Yudlov, "Sefer 'Helkat Reuven,'" 139–41. Meirovitz's writing indicates that some rabbis had a better fate than ADERET, and that their living conditions were not identical everywhere in Lithuania. Nevertheless, perhaps the fact that this rabbi took the trouble to indicate the communities that supported him with honor indicates that this was exceptionally good treatment.

24. Rabinowitz-Teumim, *Seder Eliyahu*, 50.

25. Ibid., 62.

26. Ibid., 64–65. The "Gaon of Kovna" was Rabbi Yitshak Elhanan Spektor.

27. Ibid.

28. Ibid., 67.

29. For ordinances against the purchase of rabbinical posts, see Heilperin, ed., *Pinqas va'ad arb'a arẓot*, 62–66, 400 ff. On criticism of this phenomenon in homiletic literature, see Dinur, *Reshita shel haḤasidut veyesodoteiha hasoẓyaliim vehameshiḥiim*, 106–7.

30. On the change in the legal status of the rabbis and on its consequences for their salary and status, see Shoḥet, *Mosad 'harabbanut mita'am' beRusia*, 9–10, 13–15.

31. Dinur, *Reshita shel haḤasidut veyesodoteiha hasoẓyaliim vehameshiḥiim*, 103–4; Nadav, "Toldot qehilat Pinsk," 1:147, 193–94. An outstanding example of a young man who was appointed to the rabbinate of Vilna in return for a huge payment to the community by his wealthy father-in-law is that of Rabbi Samuel, the son of Rabbi Avigdor. His contract stipulated in detail the money-lending and commercial businesses that he was entitled to engage in. See J. Klausner, *Vilna bitekufat hagaon*, 50–53.

32. Rabinowitz-Teumim, *Seder Eliyahu*, 48–49; see also below, the regulations regarding payment by rabbis to communities for rabbinical posts.

33. Eliasberg, *Shvil hazahav*, xix.

34. Rabinowitz-Teumim, *Seder Eliyahu*, 60.

35. Ibid., 60–61.

36. Ibid., 89, 90. ADERET placed the blame on Rabbi Yitshak Elhanan Spektor, because, as a senior rabbi, he had the power to institute reforms but did not respond to those who addressed him on that matter.
37. Cited by Rabiner, *Rabbi Eli'ezer Gordon zatsal,* 149–50.
38. Ibid., 147–48.
39. Ibid., 147.
40. J. Katz, *Tradition and Crisis,* 156–69; Dubnow, ed., *Pinqas medinat Lita,* paras. 49, 141, 280, and passim.
41. A description of the prestige of yeshivot heads in Poland before the events of 1648–49 appears in Hanover, *Yeven meẓulah,* 87.
42. See the section "The Establishment of the Yeshiva in Volozhin" in chap. 5 in this volume; Stampfer, *Hayeshiva halitait,* 39–43.
43. Berlin, *MiVolozhin 'ad Yerushalayim,* 1:107–11.
44. Stampfer, *Hayeshiva halitait,* 55–88.
45. On the verdict of the arbitrators, see Karlinsky, *Harishon leshushelet Brisk,* 107–9).
46. Ostrovsky, ed., *Ish Yerushalayim,* 67–69.
47. Rabiner, *Rabbi Eli'ezer Gordon zatsal,* appendix B, pp. 176–77.
48. Friedman, *Sefer hazikhronot,* 98–100.
49. Stampfer, *Hayeshiva halitait behithavutah,* 252–92; Dinur, *Be'olam sheshaq'a,* 62–81; S. Assaf, "Shnot limudai beyeshivat Telz," 34–45.
50. See Ostrovsky, ed., *Ish Yerushalayim,* 67–69.
51. Here are several examples of yeshivot of local character: on the yeshiva of Rabbi Meile in Vilna and on the controversy surrounding the position of head of that yeshiva, see Etkes, *Rabbi Israel Salanter and the Musar Movement,* 80–83; on the yeshiva of Rabbi Ya'akov Harif in Vilan, see Friedman, *Sefer hazikhronot,* 87–90; on the two yeshivot in Slutzk, see Lisitzki, *Eleh toldot Adam,* 19–25.
52. A scholar named Rabbi David Halle ran a yeshiva with two classes in Kovna during the mid–nineteenth century. The students in the lower class paid tuition, while those in the higher class, more advanced students, were exempt from payment (see Etkes, *Lita biYerushalayim,* 213–19). Another example of a young scholar who established a small yeshiva and made a living from it is that of Moshe Lillienblum (see Lillienblum, *Ketavim otobiografiim,* 128). Rabbi Ya'akov Barit was a scholar who made a living by giving lessons in a house of study maintained by the contributions of a philanthropist, Rabbi Nahman Parnas of Vilna. Young men who were studying for ordination attended it (see Barit, *Toldot Ya'aqov,* 11 ff.).
53. Etkes, *Lita biYerushalayim,* 21–24. For other examples of Torah scholars who made a living as Talmud tutors, see Barit, *Toldot Ya'aqov,* 4; Y. Lifschitz, *Toldot Yiẓḥak,* 5; Eliasberg, *Shvil hazahav,* 5; Bialovloẓki, "R. Itseleh miPonivez," 1:394.

54. The testimony of Rabbi David Tevil of Minsk, a student of Rabbi Ḥayyim of Volozhin, is important here. See Tevil, introduction to *Beit David.*
55. Zevin, *Ishim veshitot,* 39–85.
56. Dinur, *Be'olam sheshaq'a,* 129.
57. J. Katz, *Tradition and Crisis,* 211.

7. THE TORAH AND *YIRA* IN THE THOUGHT AND PRACTICE OF THE VILNA GAON

1. See chap. 1.
2. Baḥye ibn Paqudah, *Ḥovot halevavot,* esp. the section "Sha'ar haprishut" (522) and the beginning of "Sha'ar ahavat HaShem" (555–56).
3. Pechter, "Sifrut hadrush vehamusar shel ḥakhmei Ẓefat bameah hatet-zayin uma'arekhet ra'ayonoteiha ha'iqariim," 430–35.
4. Cited in ibid., 430.
5. Eliyahu Ben Shlomo Zalman, *Aderet Eliyahu,* Devarim I, 1.
6. Eliyahu Ben Shlomo Zalman, *Iggeret haGRA.* Cf. the Babylonian Talmud, *Beitsa* 16a, *Baba batra* 10a.
7. Remarks in this spirit are common in *Iggeret haGRA.* See also Ḥayyim of Volozhin, "Sheiltot," para. 97.
8. Eliyahu Ben Shlomo Zalman, *Beur haGRA lemishlei* (the Gaon's commentary on Proverbs), 23:30.
9. Ibid., 21:19.
10. Eliyahu Ben Shlomo Zalman, *Iggeret haGRA.*
11. Levine, *Aliyot Eliyahu,* 65–67.
12. Ibid., 65, n. 36.
13. Ibid., 66 and passim. In two famous cases, the Vilna Gaon emerged from his withdrawal and took part in public controversies: that of the rabbi of Vilna and the struggle against Hasidism. These two cases are so exceptional that they establish the validity of the rule.
14. Ibid., 70 ff. Typically, those who were not among his intimates but who managed to be received by him singled out the event as very special. Thus, for example, Rabbi Yeḥezqel Feivel of Dretshin writes in the introduction to his *Toldot Adam:* "In the first half of the month of Adar in the year 5557, I was called to come to the house of our rabbi the Gaon[,] . . . and God gave me grace and mercy in his eyes so that I had the privilege of speaking with him five times."
15. Levine, *Aliyot Eliyahu,* 67–68; see also Ḥayyim of Volozhin, introduction to *Sifra deẓeni'uta.*
16. Yissacher Ber ben Tanḥum, introduction to *Ma'aseh rav.*
17. Ḥayyim of Volozhin, "Sheiltot," para. 47; see also paras. 48 and 49.

18. Ibid., para. 14.
19. Ibid.
20. See also ibid., para. 68.
21. Yissacher Ber ben Tanḥum, introduction to *Ma'aseh rav.*
22. Eliyahu Ben Shlomo Zalman, *Beur haGRA lemishlei,* 22:5.
23. Ibid.
24. Ibid., 24:31.
25. Ibid., 11:16.
26. Ibid.
27. In his conception of the structure of the soul and of the place of *midot* in it, the Gaon follows Kabbalistic ethical literature. See Vital, *Sha'arei qedusha,* pt. 1, sec. 2.
28. Eliyahu Ben Shlomo Zalman, *Iggeret haGRA.*
29. Eliyahu Ben Shlomo Zalman, *Beur haGRA lehabakuk* (the Vilna Gaon's commentary on Habakuk), 2:4. Cf. Vital, *Sha'arei qedusha,* pt. 1, sec. 2.
30. Eliyahu Ben Shlomo Zalman, *Iggeret haGRA.*
31. Eliyahu Ben Shlomo Zalman, *Beur haGRA lemishlei,* 11:22.
32. Ibid., 4:15.
33 Ibid., 14:2.
34. Ibid., 20:18.
35. Ibid., 1:23.
36. Yissacher Ber ben Tanḥum, *Ma'aseh rav,* para. 60.
37. Eliyahu Ben Shlomo Zalman, *Iggeret haGRA.*
38. Ibid.
39. Ibid.
40. Eliyahu Ben Shlomo Zalman, *Beur haGRA lemishlei,* 4:4.
41. Melzen, *Even shlema,* 70.
42. Z. Lifschitz, ed., *Hanhagot ve'etsot,* para. 115.
43. Eliyahu Ben Shlomo Zalman, *Beur haGRA lemishlei,* 2:5. Cf. the position of Rabbi Hayyim of Volozhin on this topic, described in the section "Between Torah and *Yira*" in chap. 5 in this volume.
44. "Hanhagot pratiyot mehaGRA zatsal," in Rivlin, *Hazadik R. Yosef Zundel miSalant verabotav,* 111.
45. Eliyahu Ben Shlomo Zalman, *Beurei Aggadot,* 108.
46. Eliyahu Ben Shlomo Zalman, *Beur haGRA lemishlei,* 11:2.
47. Ibid., 31:11.
48. Ibid., 1:7.
49. Ibid., 24:31.
50. See the Tosafot, Babylonian Talmud, *Ta'anit* 7a. Similar statements are to be found in *Nazir* 23b, *Pesahim* 50b, and *Brakhot* 17a, and in Rashi's commentary to *Brakhot* 17a.
51. On the position taken by other Halakhic authorities, see *Shulḥan 'arukh,*

yoreh de'ah, 246:20; see also the commentary of Shakh there. The Gaon's position is stated in *Beur haGRA lemishlei,* 23:1.

52. Melzen, *Even shlema,* 80. For further remarks condemning study for the sake of honor, see *Beur haGRA lemishlei,* 12:8, 31:30.

53. Melzen, *Even shlema,* 77.

54. Eliyahu Ben Shlomo Zalman, *Beur haGRA lemishlei,* 15:16–17, 17:1. The severe position taken by the Vilna Gaon regarding study not for its own sake is similar to that found in Vistinetsky and Freimann, eds., *Sefer hasidim,* sig. 753.

Glossary

dybbuk The soul of a dead person that has possessed the body of a living person and taken control of it because the dead person's sins were not expiated in the next world. Sometimes a dybbuk takes the form of a demon or demons that penetrate the person's body and take control of it. The exorcism of a dybbuk involves a complex ceremony, and it is performed by *ba'alei shem* (magicians), Hasidic leaders, or rabbis.

Gaon (pl. Geonim) An honorary title held by the heads of the yeshivot in Babylonia during the Middle Ages. Starting in the eleventh century, this title was also given to the heads of yeshivot in North Africa and Germany. During the sixteenth and seventeenth centuries, the title was widely applied to the heads of yeshivot in Poland. Gradually, the title also came to be applied to outstanding scholars who were not heads of yeshivot.

ḥasid (pl. *ḥasidim*) In the Bible this term describes a person who performs acts of loving-kindness for other people. In rabbinical literature the term describes a person who goes far beyond the letter of the law to serve God.

From the Middle Ages on, *ḥasid* became a personal title applied to someone whose worship of God was viewed by the members of his generation as exceptional in its quality and intensity. The word *ḥasidut* refers to the *ḥasid's* high spiritual level and his way of life. Over the generations, the term *ḥasidim* was used to describe the members of groups whose spiritual inclinations, manner of worshiping God, and way of life were regarded as worthy of that title. A prominent example of such a group is the *Ḥasidut ashkenaz,* who were active in Germany during the twelfth and thirteenth centuries. Inspired by the center of Kabbalah that was active in Safed during the sixteenth century, the phenomenon of *ḥasidism* was linked to occupation with esoteric studies and with the particular patterns of worship and the ascetic way of life influenced by Kabbalah. *Ḥasidim* of that kind existed in Poland during the eighteenth century. Rabbi Israel Ba'al Shem Tov, his associates, and his disciples were called *ḥasidim* in that spirit. However, when the *ḥasidic* movement expanded and became consolidated in the form of *ḥasidic* "courts" that grew up around the figure of the Zaddik, the term *ḥasid* received new meaning: a person known as a Lubavicher Hasid, a Gerer Hasid, and so on is a person who has accepted the leadership of the Lubavicher rebbe, the Gerer rebbe, and so on.

kahal The leadership of the Jewish community organization, which enjoyed extensive autonomy and administered all community matters.

lulav A palm branch, one of the "four species" used in the rituals of the Sukkot festival in autumn.

ma'ase merkavah This term appears in the Talmud and refers to the secrets of creation and of the divinity. The source of the concept is the *merkavah* (chariot) described in the first chapter of Ezekiel.

maggid (pl. *maggidim*) A metaphysical entity such as an angel or the soul of an eminent person, who appears to a person and tells him secrets of the celestial worlds. Sometimes a *maggid* speaks from the mouth of the person to whom he reveals himself, and sometimes he conveys messages to him by means of automatic writing.

maggid meisharim The title of the community preacher.

maskil Among the Jews of eastern Europe during the nineteenth century, the term *maskil* referred to a person who was familiar to some degree with European culture of the time and who identified with the values and goals of Haskalah, the Jewish Enlightenment movement.

Mitnagdim Literally, the opponents: those who opposed the Hasidim and Hasidism and struggled against them.

moreh ẓedeq Literally, a teacher of righteousness: a religious head with extensive Torah education, authorized to issue Halakhic rulings. His status was ordinarily below that of the rabbi of the community.

morenu A title indicating possession of Torah education. This title was usually given to men who had studied Torah for several years after their marriage.

pilpul and *ḥiluqim* The term *pilpul* appears in the Talmud, where it refers to a Halakhic discussion in which a specific question is discussed from every angle. The word continued to be used in that sense during the Middle Ages. During the fifteenth century it began to be applied to a new method of study that was spreading in Poland. During the sixteenth century, this method took on a new aspect and became known as *ḥiluqim.* This method of study encouraged the development of intellectual brilliance at the expense of fidelity to the literal meaning: the authentic interpretation of a text according to common sense. For that reason, several of the greatest rabbis of the sixteenth and seventeenth centuries vehemently criticized this method of study. However, those rabbis admitted that they did not succeed in eradicating the system of *pilpul* and *ḥiluqim,* because it had won great popularity among Torah scholars.

qelipa Literally, a shell. This term is common in the Lurianic Kabbalah, and it refers to demonic powers.

sugiya (pl. *sugiyot*) A talmudic discussion focused on a specific subject.

Torah 'im derekh eretz Literally, "Torah with the way of the world," this was the motto of the ideology developed by Samson Raphael Hirsch (1808–88), the leader of German orthodoxy. *Torah 'im derekh eretz* describes the effort to establish an ethos founded on a synthesis between commitment to Halakhah and the values of the Jewish tradition, on the one hand, and European culture as it had developed in nineteenth-century Germany, on the other hand.

yira Literally, fear or fear of God. In the homiletical and ethical literature of the traditional Jewish society that this book discusses, the term *yira* has a far more general meaning. *Yira* is the entire complex of spiritual and religious qualities that a person is supposed to develop. Among them are scrupulous and precise performance of the commandments, the emotional dimension expressed in worship of God, moral virtues, and the like. The ideal of this society was that a great Torah scholar should also be distinguished by great *yira.*

Bibliography

Abraham Ben Eliyahu miVilna (Rabbi). Critical introduction to *Aggadat bereshit* [The legend of creation]. 1802. Reprinted in S. Buber, ed., *Aggadat bereshit* (Cracow, 1903).

———. *Gevulot haarets* [The borders of the land]. Berlin, 5661 [1901].

———. Introduction to *Shenot Eliyahu* [The years of Elijah]. In *Mishnayot, seder zera'im.* Vilna, 5670 [1920].

———. *Rav pe'alim* [Multifarious works]. Warsaw, 5654 [1894].

———. *Se'arat Eliyahu* [The storm of Elijah]. Warsaw, 5638 [1878].

Abraham Simḥah of Amcislaw (Rabbi). Introduction to *Zohar Ḥadash.* In *Sefer midrash Ruth heḥadash.* Warsaw, 5625 [1865].

Altschuller, M. "Mishnato shel R. Meshulam Feibush Heller umeqomah bereshit hatnu'ah haḤasidit" [The teaching of Rabbi Meshulam Feibush Heller]. Ph.D. diss., Hebrew University, Jerusalem, 1995.

Assaf, D. "'Sheyaẓa shmu'a sheba mashiaḥ ben David': or ḥadash 'al 'aliyat haḤasidim bishnat 5537" ["That a rumor was afoot that the messiah, the son of David, has come": New light on the immigration of the Hasidim to Palestine in 5537]. *Ẓion* 61 (1997): 319–46.

Assaf, S. *Meqorot letoldot haḥinukh beYisrael* [Sources for the history of Jewish education]. 4 vols. Tel Aviv, 5695–708 [1935–48].

———. "Shnot limudai beyeshivat Telz" [My years of study in the Telz yeshiva]. *He'avar* 2 (1954): 34–45.

Avivi, I. *Qabalat HaGRA* [The Kabbalah of the Vilna Gaon]. Jerusalem, 1993.

Bachrach, Yair (Rabbi). *Ḥavot Yair* [The farms of Yair]. Frankfurt, 5459 [1799].

Bacon, G. *The Politics of Tradition: Agudat Yisrael in Poland, 1916–1939*. Jerusalem, 1966.

Baḥye ibn Paqudah (Rabbi). *Ḥovot halevavot* [The duties of the heart]. Tel Aviv, 1964.

Barit, Ya'aqov (Rabbi). *Toldot Ya'aqov* [The history of Jacob]. Vilna, 5643 [1883].

Barlev, N. "'Olamam haruḥani vehatarbuti shel halomdim bayeshivot haLitaiyot bamaḥaẓit hashniyah shel hameah hayod-tet ubameah hakaf, kefi shemishtaqef misifrut hazikhronot. 'iyun besefer 'Meqor Barukh' leR. Barukh Halevi Epstein" [The spiritual and cultural world of the students in Lithuanian yeshivot in the second half of the nineteenth and the twentieth centuries as reflected in memoir literature: An examination of *Meqor Barukh* by Rabbi Barukh Halevi Epstein]. Master's thesis, Hebrew University, Jerusalem, 1997.

Barnai, Y., ed. *Igrot Ḥasidim meerets-Yisrael.* Jerusalem, 1980.

Bartal, I. "'Shimon Hakofer'—a Chapter in Orthodox Historiography." In *Keminhag Ashkenaz vepolin,* ed. I. Bartal, H. Turnianski, and E. Mendelssohn, 243–68. Festschrift in Honor of Khone Shmeruk. Jerusalem, 1993.

———. "'Zikhron Ya'aqov' leR. Ya'aqov Lifschitz—historiografia ortodoksit?" [*Zikhron Ya'aqov* by Rabbi Ya'aqov Lipschitzs—orthodox historiography?]. *Milet* 2 (1984): 490–14.

Barukh of Shklov. *Uqlidos* [Euclid]. The Hague, 5540 [1780].

Benayahu, M. "Hamaggid shel RAMḤAL" [The Maggid of Rabbi Moshe Ḥayyim Luzzatto]. *Sefunot* 5 (1961): 299–336.

———. *Sefer toldot HaARI* [The history of the ARI]. Jerusalem, 1967.

Ben-Sasson, H. H. *Hagut vehanhagah* [Ideas and leadership]. Jerusalem, 1959.

———. *Ishiyuto shel HaGRA vehashp'aato hahistorit* [The personality of the Vilna Gaon and his historical influence]. *Ẓion* 31 (1966): 39–86, 197–216.

Ben-Sasson, Y. "'Olamam haruḥani umishnatam haḥinukhit shel meyasdei hayeshiva haLitait" [The spiritual world and educational doctrine of the founders of the Lithuanian yeshiva]. In *Ḥinukh haadam veye'udo,* 155–216. Jerusalem, 1967.

Berdyczewski, M. Y. "Toldot yeshivat 'eẓ heḥayyim" [The history of the Eẓ Hahayyim yeshiva]. *Heasif* 3 (1886): 231–42.

Berlin, M. *MiVolozhin 'ad Yerushalayim* [From Volozhin to Jerusalem]. 2 vols. Jerusalem, 1971.

Bialovlozki, S. "Merkazei hatorah beLita" [Torah centers in Lithuania]. In *Yahadut lita,* 1:185–90. Tel Aviv, 1960.

———. "R. Itseleh miPonivez" [Rabbi Itseleh of Ponevitz]. In *Yahadut lita,* 1:394. Tel Aviv, 1960.

Blazer, Y. *Or Yisrael* [The light of Israel]. Vilna, 1900.

Bloch, A. M. *Ruaḥ Eliyahu* [The spirit of Elijah]. New York, 1954.

Braver, A. I. *Galicia veyehudeiha, meḥqarim betoldot Galicia bameah hashnoneh-'esreh* [Galicia and its Jews: Studies in the history of Galicia during the eighteenth century]. Jerusalem, 1965.

Breuer, M. "Hayeshivah haAshkenazit beshilhei yemei habeinayim" [The Ashkenazi yeshiva at the end of the Middle Ages]. Ph.D. diss., Hebrew University, Jerusalem, 1967.

———. "Qavim lidmuto shel R. David Ganz ba'al 'Ẓemah David'" [Outlines of the figure of Rabbi David Ganz, the author of *Ẓemah David*]. *Bar-Ilan* 11 (1973): 97–118.

Buqi Ben Yogli. *Ma sherau 'einai vesham'u oznai* [What my eyes saw and what my ears heard]. Jerusalem, 1947.

Citron, S. L. "Milḥemet hadinastiot beyeshivat Volozhin." *Reshumot* 1 (1925): 123–35.

Czernowitz, H. *Toldot haposqim* [The history of the Halakhic decision makers]. New York, 5508 [1948].

Danzig, Abraham (Rabbi). *Ẓavaat yehezkel* [The testament of Ezekiel]. Vilna, 5631 [1871].

De Vidas, Eliyahu. *Reshit ḥokhmah* [The beginning of wisdom]. Warsaw, 5635 [1875].

Dick, A. M. *Haoreaḥ* [The guest]. Vilna, 1844.

Dimitrovski, Ḥ. Z. "'Al derekh hapilpul" [On the way of pilpul]. In *Sefer yovel likhvod Shalom Baron,* 111–81. Jerusalem, 1975.

Dinstag, I. "Haim hitnaged HaGRA lemishnato hafilosofit shel HaRAMBAN?" [Did the Vilna Gaon object to the philosophical doctrine of Maimonides?]. *Talpiyot* 4 (1949): 253–68.

Dinur, B.-Z. *Be'olam sheshaq'a* [In a world that has declined]. Jerusalem, 1958.

———. "Reshima otobiografit shel Ḥ. Z. Margoliot" [An autobiographical article by Ḥ. Z. Margaliot]. *He'avar* 15 (1968): 254–58.

———. *Reshita shel haḤasidut veyesodoteiha hasoẓyaliim vehameshiḥiim* [The origins of Hasidism and its social and messianic foundations]. In *Bemifne Hadorot.* Jerusalem, 1955.

Druk, D. "Hagaon R. Ya'aqov Ẓvi Meklenburg" [The Gaon Rabbi Jacob Ẓvi Meklenburg]. *Horev* 7–8 (1938): 171–79.

Dubnow, S. *Toldot haḤasidut* [The history of Hasidism]. Tel Aviv, 1960.
Dubnow, S., ed. *Pinqas medinat Lita.* Berlin, 1925.
Eliakh, D. *Avi hayeshivot* [The father of the yeshivot]. 2 vols. Jerusalem, 1991.
Eliasberg, M. *Shvil hazahav* [The golden path]. Warsaw, 5657 [1897].
Eliav, M. *Haḥinukh hayehudi beGermania biymei hahaskalah vehaemantsipaẓia* [Jewish education in Germany during the Haskalah and emancipation periods]. Jerusalem, 1961.
Elior, R. "Haziqa shebein qabbalah leḤasidut—reẓifut utemura" [The connection between Kabbalah and Hasidism]. In *Proceedings of the Ninth World Congress of Jewish Studies,* sec. 3, pp. 107–14. Jerusalem, 1986.
———. "R. Yosef Karo veR. Yisrael ba'al shem tov: metamorfozah mistit, hashraah qabalit, vehafnamah ruḥanit" [Rabbi Joseph Karo and Rabbi Israel the Ba'al Shem Tov: Mystical metamorphosis, Kabbalistic inspiration, and spiritual internalization]. *Tarbiẓ* 65 (1996): 675–84.
———. "Vikuaḥ Minsk" [The Minsk debate]. *Meḥqarei Yerushalayim bemaḥshevet Yisrael* 1 (1982): 179–235.
Eliyahu Ben Shlomo Zalman (Rabbi). *Aderet Eliyahu* [The cloak of Elijah]. Dubrovna, 5584 [1824].
———. *Beurei Aggadot* [Commentaries on Aggadot]. Warsaw, 1886.
———. *Beur vegam hagahot 'al kol hazohar* [Commentary and corrections on the whole Zohar]. Vilna, 5570 [1810].
———. *Iggeret haẓavaah shehotir HaGRA livnei mishpaḥato keshe'amad laẓet leereẓ Yisrael, 'alim litrufah* [The testament that the Vilna Gaon left for his family when he was about to leave for the land of Israel, medicinal leaves]. Minsk, 5596 [1836].
———. *Sefer Ḥabaquq im perush rabenu HaGRA* [The Book of Habakuk, with the commentary of the Vilna Gaon]. In *Sefer Zot-Neḥamati.* Pitekov, 1899.
———. *Sefer mishlei 'im perush rabenu HaGRA* [The Book of Proverbs, with the commentary of the Vilna Gaon]. Vilna, 5643 [1883].
Epstein, Barukh Halevi (Rabbi). *Meqor Barukh* [The source of Barukh]. 4 vols. Vilna, 5688 [1928].
Etkes, I. "'Aliyato shel R. Shneur Zalman miLiadi le'emdat manhigut" [The ascent to leadership of Rabbi Shneur Zalman of Lyady]. *Tarbiẓ* 54 (1985): 429–39.
———. *Ba'al Hashem, HaBESHT— magiah, mistiqah, hanhagah* [The Besht—magic, mysticism, leadership]. Jerusalem, 2000.
———. "Lamm, Naḥum: Torah lishma bemishnat R. Ḥayyim miVolozhin uvemaḥshevet hador" [Lamm, Naḥum: Torah Lishma: Torah for Torah's sake in the works of Rabbi Ḥayyim of Volozhin and his contemporaries]. *Qiryat sefer* 50 (1975): 638–48.
———. "Leshealat mevasrei hahaskalah bemizraḥ Eiropa" [On the question

of harbingers of the Haskalah in eastern Europe]. *Tarbiẓ* 57 (1989): 95–114. Reprinted in I. Etkes, ed., *Hadat vehaḥayyim: tenu'at hahaskalah haYehudit bemizraḥ Eiropa* (Jerusalem, 1993), 24–44.

———. *Lita biYerushalayim, ha'ilit harabanit beLita veqehilat haprushim biYerushalayim leor igrot ukhetavim shel R. Shmuel miKelm* [Lithuania in Jerusalem, the rabbinical elite in Lithuania, and the community of *perushim* in Jerusalem in the light of the letters and writings of Rabbi Shmuel of Kelme]. Jerusalem, 1992.

———. "Mishpaḥa velimud torah beḥugei ha'lomdim' beLita bameah hayodtet" [Family and Torah study in the circles of "Lomdim" in nineteenth-century Lithuania]. *Ẓion* 51 (1986): 87–106. Reprinted in *Lita biYerushalayim, ha'ilit harabanit beLita veqehilat haprushim biYerushalayim leor igrot ukhetavim shel R. Shmuel miKelm* (Jerusalem, 1992), 63–84.

———. "Parshat ha'haskalah mit'am' vehatemura bema'amad tenu'at hahaskalah beRusia" [Government-sponsored Haskalah and the change in the status of the Haskalah movement in Russia]. *Ẓion* 43 (1978): 264–313. Reprinted in I. Etkes, ed., *Hadat vehaḥayyim: tenu'at hahaskalah haYehudit bemizraḥ Eiropa* (Jerusalem, 1993), 167–216.

———. *Rabbi Israel Salanter and the Musar Movement*. Philadelphia, 1993.

———. "The Study of Hasidism: Past Trends and New Directions." In *Hasidism Reappraised*, ed. A. Rapoport-Albert, 447–64. London, 1996.

———. *Te'udah beYisrael, bein temurah lemasoret, mavo lemahadurah meẓulemet* . . . ["Te'udah beYisrael," between change and tradition, introduction to the photographic reprint]. Jerusalem, 1977.

Etkes, I., ed. *Hadat vehaḥayyim: tenu'at hahaskalah haYehudit bemizraḥ Eiropa* [Religion and life: The Jewish enlightenment movement in eastern Europe]. Jerusalem, 1993.

Ettinger, S. "Taqanat 1804" [The regulations of 1804]. In *Bein Polin leRusia*, 234–56. Jerusalem, 1995.

Feiner, S. *Mehaskalah loḥemet lehaskalah meshameret* [From combative Haskalah to conservative Haskalah]. Jerusalem, 1993.

Fin, S. Y. "Dor dor vedorshav" [Every generation and its commentators]. *Hakarmel* 4 (1879).

———. *Qiryah neemenah* [The faithful city]. Vilna, 5675 [1915].

———. *Safah laneemanim* [A tongue for the faithful]. Vilna, 1881.

Fishman, D. E. *Russia's First Modern Jews: The Jews of Shklov*. New York, 1995.

Friedman, A. A. *Sefer hazikhronot* [The book of memories]. Tel Aviv, 1926.

Frumkin, A. L. *Toldot Eliyahu* [The history of Elijah]. Vilna, 1900.

Ginzberg, L. *Perushim veḥidushim baYerushalmi* [Interpretations and new insights on the Jerusalem Talmud]. New York, 1941.

———. *Students, Scholars, and Saints*. Philadelphia, 1928. Reprint, New York, 1958.

Ginzburg, M. A. *Avi'ezer.* Vilna, 5624 [1864].

———. *Devir* [Sanctum]. Vilna, 1844.

Ginzburg, S. *Ketavim historiim* [Historical writings]. Tel Aviv, 1944.

———. *R. Moshe Ḥayim Luzzatto uvnei doro, osef igrot vete'udot* [Rabbi Moshe Ḥayyim Luzzatto and his generation, a collection of letters and documents]. 2 vols. Tel Aviv, 5697 [1937].

Glitzenstein, S. *Harav rabi Shneur Zalman zatsal—admor hazaken (harav miLadi) ḥayav toldato umif'alav* [Rabbi Shneur Zalman of blessed memory—the old rebbe (the rebbe of Lyady) his life, his history, and his deeds]. Jerusalem, 1945.

Goronchik, S. "HaGRA vehayerushalmi" [The Vilna Gaon and the Jerusalem Talmud]. In *Sefer HaGRA,* IV: *kovez̧ maamarim vehe'arot 'al mishnat HaGRA vetalmidav* [The book of the Vilna Gaon: Collection of articles and comments on the teaching of the Vilna Gaon and his students], ed. Y. L. Maimon, 4:45–107. Jerusalem, 1954.

Gottlieb, E. "Hayesod hateologi vehamisti shel tefisat ye'ud haadam baqabbalah" [The theological and mystical basis of the conception of man's purpose in the Kabbalah]. In *Studies in Kabbala Literature,* 29–37. Tel Aviv, 1976.

Gottlober, A. B. *Zikhronot umas'aot* [Memories and travels]. Jerusalem, 1976.

Greenberg, L. *The Jews in Russia.* New York, 1976.

Gris, Z. "Mimitos leetos—qavim lidmuto shel R. Avraham miKalisk" [From myth to ethos—outlines of the figure of Rabbi Abraham of Kalisk]. In *Uma vetoldoteiha,* ed. S. Ettinger, 2:117–46. Jerusalem, 1984.

Gross, B. "'Al tfisat 'olamo shel R. Ḥayyim miVolozhin" [On Rabbi Ḥayyim of Volozhin's worldview]. *Bar-Ilan* 22–23 (1988): 121–60.

Hanover, N. N. *Yeven mez̧ulah* [Quicksand]. Tel Aviv, 1966.

Haran, R. "'Atara leyoshna—haomnam?" [The restoration of past glory—truly?] *Katedra* 64 (Tammuz 1992): 98–102.

———. "R. Avraham miKalisk veR. Shneur Zalman miLadi—yedidut shenifseqah" [Rabbi Abraham of Kalisk and Rabbi Shneur Zalman of Lyady—friendship broken off]. In *Qolot rabim, sefer hazikaron leRivka Schatz-Uffenheime,* ed. R. Elior and Y. Dan, 2:399–428. Jerusalem, 1996.

———. "Shivḥei harav: lesheelat aminutan shel igrot haḤasidim meerets Yisrael" [Praises of the rabbi: Regarding the reliability of the letters of Hasidim from the land of Israel]. *Katedra* 55 (Nissan 1990): 22–58.

Ḥayyim of Volozhin (Rabbi). *Derashat MAHARAḤ* [The sermon of Rabbi Ḥayyim of Volozhin]. Jerusalem, 1961.

———. Iggeret 'al yesud hayeshivah [Letter on the establishment of the yeshiva]. In *"Leḥoqrei qadmoniot," Hapeles* 2, no. 15 (5672 [1912]): 140–43.

———. Introduction to *Seder zera'im.* In *Perush 'al kamah Aggadot,* by Eliyahu Ben Shlomo Zalman. Warsaw, 5622 [1862].

———. Introduction to *Sifra deẓeni'uta 'im beur hagaon . . . Eliyahu miVilna.* Vilna, 5580 [1820].

———. *Nefesh ha-ḥayyim* [The soul of life]. Vilna, 5634 [1874].

———. *Ruaḥ ḥayyim, perush lepirqei avot* [Spirit of life: a commentary on the Ethics of the Fathers]. Vilna, 5619 [1859].

———. "Sheiltot" [Inquiries]. In *Ma'aseh rav,* by Ya'aqov Kahana. Jerusalem, 5656 [1896].

Heilman, H. M. *Beit rabi* [The house of my rabbi]. Berdichev, 5672 [1912].

Heilperin Y., ed. *Pinqas va'ad arb'a arẓot* [The register of the Council of the Four Lands]. Jerusalem, 1945.

Heller, Meshulam Feibush (Rabbi). *Yosher divrei emet* [Righteous words of truth]. Munkacz, 5665 [1905].

Ḥelma, Shlomo (Rabbi). *Merkevet hamishneh* [The chariot of the Mishneh]. Frankfurt am Oder, 5511 [1751].

Hirschberg, A. S. "Toldot R. Z. Yavetz" [The story of Rabbi Zeev Yavetz]. In *Toldot Yisrael,* by Z. Yavetz, 14: 123–63. Tel Aviv, 1963.

Ibn Gabai, Meir (Rabbi). *'Avodat haqodesh* [Holy worship]. Jerusalem, 1973.

Idel, Moshe. *Kabbalah: New Perspectives.* New Haven, 1988.

Ish Horowitz, S. Y. "haḤasidut vehaHaskalah" [Hasidism and Haskalah]. *He'atid* 2 (1923): 31–33.

Israel of Shklov (Rabbi). Introduction to *Peat hashulhan.* Safed, 5596 [1836].

———. Introduction to *Taqlin hadetin.* In *Talmud Yerushalmi, Sheqalim.* Minsk, 5572 [1812].

Isserles, Moses (Rabbi). *Shu"t HaREMA* [The *responsa* of the REMA]. Jerusalem, 5731 [1971].

Josephus. *Milḥamot haYehudim* [The wars of the Jews]. Trans. Kalman Shulman. Vilna, 5621 [1861].

Kamelhar, Y. *Dor de'ah* [A generation of knowledge]. New York, 1953.

Kaplan, Ẓevi. "Ledarkho shel rabbi Ḥayyim miVolozhin bahalakhah" [On the method of Rabbi Ḥayyim of Volozhin in Halakhah]. In *Me'olamah shel Torah,* 9–43. Jerusalem, 5734 [1974].

Karlinkski, N. "Bein biografia lehegiograpia: hasefer 'beit rabi' vereshita shel hahistoriografia haḤasidit-Ortodoqsit" [Between biography and hagiography: *Beit rabi* and the Hasidic-Orthodox historiographical method]. In *Proceedings of the Eleventh World Conference of Jewish Studies,* sec. 3.2, pp. 161–68. Jerusalem, 1994.

———. *Historia shekenegged, "igrot Ḥasidim meereẓ-Yisrael," hateqst vehaqonteqst* [Oppositional history: The letters of Hasidim from the land of Israel, the text and the context]. Jerusalem, 1998.

Karlinsky, H. *Harishon leshushelet Brisk* [The founder of the Brisk dynasty]. Jerusalem, 1984.

Karo, Joseph (Rabbi). *Maggid meisharim* [The direct herald]. Lublin, 5405 [1645]; Venice, 5409 [1649].

Katz, B-Ẓ. *Rabanut, ḥasidut, haskalah* [The rabbinate, Hasidism, Haskalah]. 2 vols. Tel Aviv, 1956.

———. "Toldot Haskalat haYehudim beRusia" [The history of Jewish enlightenment in Russia]. *Hazman* 2 (St. Petersburg, 5673 [1913]), 1–7.

Katz, J. "Hakhra'ot hazohar bidvar halakhah" [Determinations by the Zohar in matters of Halakhah]. In *Halakhah veqabbalah*, 34–51. Jerusalem, 5744 [1984].

———. "Jewish Civilization as Reflected in the Yeshivot—Jewish Centers of Higher Learning." *Journal of World History* 10 (1967): 698–700.

———. "Kavim lebiografiah shel haḥatam sofer" [Outlines for a biography of the Ḥatam Sofer]. In *Meḥqarim baqabbalah uvetoldot hadatot mugashim le G. Shalom* [Studies in Kabbalah and in the history of religions offered to G. Scholem], 128–29. Jerusalem, 1968.

———. *Tradition and Crisis: Jewish Society at the End of the Middle Ages*. New York, 1993.

Klausner, J. *Hahistoria shel hasifrut ha'ivrit haḥadasha* [The history of modern Hebrew literature]. Vol. 3. Jerusalem, 1953.

Klausner, Y. *Vilna bitekufat hagaon, hamilḥamah haruḥanit vehaḥevratit beqehilat Vilna bitequfat HaGRA* [Vilna in the time of the Gaon, the spiritual and social battle in Vilna at the time of the Gaon]. Jerusalem, 1942.

Kleinberger, A. F. *Hamaḥshavah hapedagogit shel HaMAHARAL miPrague* [The pedagogical thought of the Maharal of Prague]. Jerusalem, 1962.

Krassen, M. A. "Devequt and Faith in Zaddiquim." Ph.D. diss., University of Pennsylvania, Philadelphia, 1990.

Kupfer, A. "Lidmuta hatarbutit shel yahadut Ashkenaz veḥakhameihah bameot hayod-dalet-hatet-vav" [Toward the cultural image of Ashkenazic Jewry and its rabbis in the fourteenth and fifteenth centuries]. *Tarbiẓ* 42 (1973): 113–47.

Lamm, N. *Torah Lishma, Torah for Torah's Sake in the Works of Rabbi Hayyim of Volozhin and His Contemporaries*. New York, 1989.

Landau, B. *Hagaon heḥasid miVilna* [The righteous Gaon of Vilna]. Jerusalem, 1965.

Lebensohn, A. D. *Beurim ḥadashim* [New commentaries]. Vilna, 5618 [1858].

Levine, Rabbi Yehoshu'a Heschel. *Aliyot Eliyahu* [The ascents of Elijah]. Vilna, 5616 [1856].

Levinsohn, Isaac Baer. *Te'udah beYisrael* [A testimony in Israel]. Vilna, 5588 [1828].

Liberman, Ḥ. "Keiẓad ḥoqrim Ḥasidut beYisrael" [How research in Hasidism is conducted in Israel]. In *Ohel Raḥel* 1:38–49. New York, 1980.

Lifschitz, Ya'aqov. *Toldot Yiẓḥak* [The history of Isaac]. Warsaw, 5657 [1897].

———. *Zikhron Ya'aqov* [The memory of Jacob]. 3 vols. Frankfurt-Kovna, 5684–90 [1924–30].
Lifschitz, Zelig, ed. *Hanhagot ve'etsot meet R. Ḥayyim miVolozhin* [Customs and advice by Rabbi Ḥayyim of Volozhin]. MS London, Pedro 1.14, sig. 8800. Institute for the Photography of Hebrew Manuscripts, National and University Library, Jerusalem.
Lillienblum, M. L. "'Al HaGRA vehaBESHT" [On the Vilna Gaon and the BESHT]. *Hashiloaḥ* 18 (1908): 228.
———. *Ketavim otobiografiim [ḥatat ne'urim]* [Autobiographical writings (the sins of youth)]. Jerusalem, 1970.
Lisitzki, A. *Eleh toldot Adam* [This is the story of Adam]. Jerusalem, 1944.
Luria, David (Rabbi). *Qadmut sefer hazohar* [The antiquity of the book of the Zohar]. Warsaw, 1887.
Mahler, R. *Divrei yemei Yisrael dorot aḥaronim* [History of the Jews, latter generations]. Vol. 4. Tel Aviv, 1962.
Maimon, S. *Ḥayei Shlomo Maimon* [The life of Shlomo Maimon]. Tel Aviv, 1958.
Maimon, Y. L. *Toledot HaGRA 'im hosafot misifrei HaGRA* [The history of the Vilna Gaon, with additions from the books of the Vilna Gaon]. Jerusalem, 5730 [1970].
Maimon, Y. L., ed. *Sefer HaGRA*, IV: *koveẓ maamarim vehe'arot 'al mishnat HaGRA vetalmidav* [The book of the Vilna Gaon: Collection of articles and comments on the teaching of the Vilna Gaon and his students]. Jerusalem, 1954.
Marcus, I. G., ed. *Dat veḥevra bemishnatam shel ḥasidei Ashkenaz* [Religion and society in the doctrine of Ḥasidei Ashkenaz]. Jerusalem, 1987.
Meirovitz, N. R. *Ḥelqat Reuven* [The portion of Reuben]. Vilna, 5667 [1907].
Melzen, Shmuel (Rabbi). *Even shlema* [A whole stone]. Vilna, 5650 [1890].
Menaḥem Mendel of Shklov (Rabbi). Introduction to *Sefer mishlei, 'im beur hagaon . . . Eliyahu ben Shlomo Zalman* [The Book of Proverbs, with the commentary of the Gaon . . . Eliyahu Ben Shlomo Zalman]. Shklov, 5558 [1798].
Menashe of Ilia (Rabbi). *Alfei Menashe* [The thousands of Menashe]. Vilna, 1822.
Mendel of Premishlan (Rabbi). *Darkhei yesharim, vehu hanhagot yesharot meharav haẓadik rabi Mendel miPermishlan* [The ways of the righteous, correct practices of the saintly Rabbi Mendel of Permishlan]. Jerusalem, 1965. Photo-offset reproduction.
Mirsky, S. K. *Mosdot hatorah beEiropa* [Torah institutions in Europe]. New York, 1956.
Mondshine, Y. "Aminutan shel igrot hahasidim meereẓ Yisrael" [The reliability of letters of Hasidism from the land of Israel]. *Katedra* 63 (Nissan 1992): 65–97 and 64 (Tammuz 1992): 79–97.
———. "Hasefarim 'maẓref ha'avodah' 've'vikuḥa raba'" [The Books "Maẓref ha'avodah" and "Vikuḥa raba"]. *'Alei sefer* 5 (1978): 165–75.

———. *Kerem ḥabad* [The vineyard of Ḥabad]. Vol. 4, pt. 1. Kfar Ḥabad, 1992.
———. "Parnasei Vilna vehaGRA umilḥamtam baḥasidut" [The Parnasim of Vilna and the Gaon in their war against Hasidism]. In *Kerem ḥabad.* Vol. 4, pt. 1, pp. 182–221. Kfar Ḥabad, 1992.
Mondshine, Y., ed. *Shivḥei HaBESHT* [The praises of the BESHT]. Jerusalem, 1982.
Nadav, M. "Qehilat Pinsk-Karlin bein Ḥasidut lehitnagdut" [The community of Pinsk-Karlin between Hasidism and opposition]. *Ẓion* 34 (1969): 98–108.
———. "Toldot qehilat Pinsk" [The history of the community of Pinsk]. In *Pinsk,* 1:147, 193–94. Tel Aviv and Haifa, 1973.
Nadler, A. *The Faith of the Mitnagdim: Rabbinic Responses to Hasidic Rapture.* Baltimore, 1997.
Nigal, G. *Melaqtei hasipur haḤasidi* [Collectors of Hasidic stories]. Jerusalem, 1996.
Nisnboim, Y. *'Alei ḥeldi* [On my youth]. Jerusalem, 1969.
Ostrovsky, M., ed. *Ish Yerushalayim* [A man of Jerusalem]. Jerusalem, 1937.
Pechter, M. "Miẓefunot Ẓefat" [Of the mysteries of Safed]. In *Meḥqarim umeqorot letoldot Ẓefat veḥakhameiha bameah hatet-zayin.* Jerusalem, 1994.
———. "Sifrut hadrush vehamusar shel ḥakhmei Ẓefat bameah hatet-zayin uma'arekhet ra'ayonoteiha ha'iqariim" [The homiletic and ethical literature of the rabbis of Safed in the sixteenth century and its principal ideas]. Ph.D. diss., Hebrew University, Jerusalem, 1976.
Phinehas ben Judah of Polozk (Rabbi). *Keter torah* [The crown of the Torah]. Jerusalem, 5656 [1896].
———. *Rosh hagiv'a* [The top of the hill]. Jerusalem, 1965.
Piekarz, M. *Bein ideologia lemeẓiut* [Between ideology and reality]. Jerusalem, 1994.
———. *Biyemei ẓemiḥat haḤasidut* [In the days of the growth of Hasidism]. Jerusalem, 1978.
———. *Ḥasidut Polin—megamot ra'ayoniot bein shtei milḥamot ubegzerot tav shin-tav shin heh ("hashoah")* [Polish Hasidism—trends of thought between the two wars and during the holocaust]. Jerusalem, 1990.
Plongian, M. *Ben Porat* [Fertile son]. Vilna, 5618 [1858].
Qidner, Ya'aqov. *Maẓref ha'avodah.* [The refinement of worship]. Koenigsberg, 5618 [1858].
———. *Sipurim noraim* [Wonderful tales]. Ed. G. Nigal. Jerusalem 1992.
Rabiner, Z. A. *Rabbi Eli'ezer Gordon zatsal* [Rabbi Eliezer Gordon of blessed memory]. Tel Aviv, 1968.
Rabinowitz, S. P. "'Aqevot shel ḥofesh-de'ot barabanut shel Polin bameah hatet-

zayin" [Traces of freedom of opinion in the rabbinate of Poland in the sixteenth century]. Jerusalem, 1959.

Rabinowitz-Teumim, E. D. (Rabbi). *Seder Eliyahu, toldot hagaon Eliyahu David Rabinovitz-Teumim ketuvim biyedei 'aẓmo.* [The order of Eliyahu, the story of the Gaon Eliyahu David Rabubiwitz-Teumim, written by himself]. Jerusalem, 1984.

Raisin, J. S. *The Haskalah Movement in Russia.* Philadelphia, 1913.

Raphael Y., ed. *Sefer Avi'ad, qoveẓ maamarim umeḥkarim lezekher dr. Yesha'ayahu Wolfsberg-Avi'ad* [The Book of Aviad: Collection of articles and inquiries in memory of Dr. Isaiah Wolfsberg-Aviad]. Jerusalem, 1986.

Rapoport-Albert, A. "Hagiography with Footnotes: Edifying Tales and the Writing of History in Hasidism." *History and Theory: Studies in the Philosophy of History (Essays in Jewish Historiography)* 27 (1988): 119–59.

———. "Hasidism after 1772: Structural Continuity and Change." In *Hasidism Reappraised,* ed. A. Rapoport-Albert, 76–140. London, 1996.

Reiner, E. "Hon, ma'amad ḥevrati, vetalmud torah—hakloiz baḥevrah haYehudit bemizraḥ eiropah bameot hayod-zayin-yod-ḥet" [Wealth, social class, and Torah study—the *kloiz* in Jewish society in eastern Europe in the seventeenth and eighteenth centuries]. *Ẓion* 58 (1993): 287–328.

Reines, M. "Hapilpul besifrut Yisrael" [Pilpul in Jewish literature]. In *Knesset Yisrael* 3. Warsaw, 5648 [1888], 137–72.

Rivlin, A. *Hazadik R. Yosef Zundel miSalant verabotav* [The saintly Rabbi Yosef Zundel of Salant and his rabbis]. Jerusalem, 1927.

Rodkinson, M. Levi. *'Amudei beit ḥabad* [The pillars of the house of Ḥabad]. Koenigsberg, 5636 [1876].

Rogoler, Eliyahu (Rabbi). *Yad Eliyahu* [The hand of Elijah]. Warsaw, 1900.

Rosenfeld, Z. "R. Menasseh Ilyer." *Hatequfa* 2 (Berlin, 1930): 250–88.

Rosman, M. *Founder of Hasidism: A Quest for the Historical Ba'al Shem Tov.* Berkeley, 1996.

Ross, T. "Shnei perushim letorat haẓimẓum: R. Ḥayyim miVolozhin ver. Shneur Zalman miLadi" [Two interpretations of Tsimtsum: Rabbi Ḥayyim of Volozhin and Rabbi Shneur Zalman of Lyady]. *Meḥqarei Yerushalayim bemaḥshevet Yisrael* 2 (1982): 153–69.

Schatz-Uffenheimer, R. *Hasidism as Mysticism.* Princeton, 1993.

Schechter, S. "Safed in the 16th Century." In *Studies in Judaism* II (Philadelphia, 1908), 203–306.

Schmuckler, M. S. (Rabbi). *Toldot Rabenu Ḥayyim miVolozhin* [The history of our Rabbi Ḥayyim of Volozhin]. Vilna, 5669 [1909].

Schneersohn, Joseph Isaac (Rabbi). "Avot haḤasidut" [The fathers of Hasidism]. *Hatamim* 2 (Kislev 5696 [1936]).

———. "Divrei hayamim hahem" [Events of those days]. Typewritten manuscript, 1964.

Scholem, G. "Hatnu'ah haShabtait bePolin" [The Sabbatean movement in Poland]. In *Beit Yisrael bePolin,* ed. Y. Heilprin, 2:36–76. Jerusalem 1954.

———. *Major Trends in Jewish Mysticism.* New York, 1961.

———. *The Messianic Idea in Judaism.* New York, 1971.

———. *On the Kabbalah and Its Symbolism.* New York, 1969.

———. "Shtei ha'eduyuot harishonot 'al ḥavurot haḤasidim vehaBESHT" [The two first testimonies regarding societies of Hasidim and the BESHT]. *Tarbiẓ* 20 (1949): 228–40.

Shivḥei HaBESHT [In Praise of the BESHT], with introduction and annotation by A. Rubinstein. Jerusalem, 1991.

Shmeruk, K. "Mashma'uta haḥevratit shel hashḥita haḤasidit" [The social significance of Hasidic ritual slaughter]. *Ẓion* 20 (1955): 47–72.

Shneur Zalman of Lyady (Rabbi). *Igrot qodesh meet kvod qdushat admor hazaqen, kevod qdushat admor haemẓa'I, kevod qdushat admor haẓemaḥ ẓedeq* [Holy letters from his holy honor the elder rebbe, his holy honor the middle rebbe, his holy honor the Ẓemaḥ Ẓedeq]. New York, 1980.

Shoḥet, A. *'Im ḥilufei tequfot* [Beginning of the Haskalah among German Jewry]. Jerusalem, 1960.

———. *Mosad 'harabbanut mita'am' beRusia* [The institution of the official rabbinate in Russia]. Haifa, 1976.

Slutzky, Y. "Beit hamidrash lerabbanim beVilna" [The rabbinical seminary in Vilna]. *He'avar* 7 (1960): 29–49.

Sons of the Vilna Gaon. Introduction to *Aderet Eliyahu.* Dubrovna, 5584 [1824].

———. Introduction to *Perush 'al kamah Aggadot,* by Eliyahu ben Shlomo Zalman. Koenigsberg, 5622 [1862]; first printed in Vilna in 5560 [1800].

———. Introduction to the Vilna Gaon commentary on *Shulḥan 'arukh, oraḥ ḥayyim,* by Joseph Caro. Shklov, 5563 [1803].

Stampfer, S. *Hayeshiva halitait behithavutah* [The Lithuanian yeshiva]. Jerusalem, 1995.

Stanislawski, M. *Tsar Nicolas I and the Jews.* Philadelphia, 1983.

Steinschneider, H. N. M. *'Ir Vilna* [The city of Vilna]. Vilna, 5660 [1900].

Tarshish, A. Z. *Rabbi Barukh Halevi Epstein ba'al "torah temimah"* [Rabbi Barukh Halevi Epstein, author of *Torah temimah*]. Jerusalem, 1967.

Ta-Shma, I. *Hanigleh shebanistar: Leḥeqer sheqi'ei halakhah besefer hazohar* [The visible in the hidden: Toward the study of residua of the Halakhah in the Zohar]. Tel Aviv, 5755 [1995].

Teitelbaum, M. *Harav miLadi umifleget ḥabad* [The rabbi of Lyady and the Habad faction]. 2 vols. Warsaw, 1913.

Tevil, D. *Beit David* [The house of David]. Warsaw, 5614 [1854].

Tishby, Y. *Mishnat hazoahar* [The wisdom of the Zohar]. Jerusalem, 1957–61.
———. "'Qudsha brikh hu oraita veYisrael kula ḥad'—meqor haimrah be-ferush 'Idra raba' leRAMḤAL" ["The Holy One blessed be he, Torah, and Israel are all one"—the source of the saying in the commentary on *Idra Raba* by Rabbi Moshe Ḥayyim Luzzatto]. *Qiryat Sefer* 3 (1975): 480–92.
———. *Torat har'a vehaqelipah beqabalat ḤaARI* [The doctrine of evil and the qelipa in the Kabbalah of the ARI]. Jerusalem, 1992.
Tishby, Y., and Y. Dan. "Torat haḤasidut" [The doctrine of Hasidism]. In *Haentsiklopedia ha'ivrit*, 17:800–804. Jerusalem, 1965.
Tsharna, S. Y. "R. Ḥayyim miVolozhin betor pedagog" [Rabbi Ḥayyim of Volozḥin as a pedagogue]. *Shvilei haḥinukh* 4, no. 6 (1929).
Twersky, I. "R. Eliyahu miVilna" [Rabbi Elijah of Vilna]. *He'avar* 1 (1953): 109–14.
———. "R. Barukh of Shklov." *He'avar* 4 (1957): 77–81.
Verses, S. "Hagaon R. Eliyahu miVilna be'olamah shel sifrut hahaskalah" [The Gaon Rabbi Eliyahu of Vilna in Haskalah literature]. In *"Haqiẓah 'ami," sifrut hahaskalah be'idan hamodernizaẓia*, 25–66. Jerusalem, 2000.
Vilensky, M. *Ḥasidim umitnagdim—Letoldot hapulmus shebeineihem bashanim taf quf lamed bet taf quf 'ayin heh* [Hasidim and Mitnagdim—toward a history of the controversy between them in the years 5532–5565]. 2 vols. Jerusalem, 5730 [1970].
Virzburg, V. S. "Rabbi Ḥayyim miVolozhin" [Rabbi Ḥayyim of Volozhin]. In *Notrei moreshet*, ed. L. Jung, 26–38. Jerusalem, 1968.
Vistinetsky, Y., and Freimann, Y., eds. *Sefer hasidim* [The book of the righteous]. (Parma version.) Frankfurt, 1924.
Vital, Ḥayyim (Rabbi). *Sha'arei qedusha* [The gates of sanctity]. Jerusalem, 1985.
Weinberg, Yeḥiel Ya'aqov (Rabbi). "Ba'alei hamusar, R. Israel Salanter" [Masters of ethics, Rabbi Israel Salanter]. *Sridei esh* 4 (Jerusalem 1969): 292–94.
Weiss, A. H. "Reshit ẓemiḥat hahaskalah beRusia" [The emergence of Haskalah in Russia]. *Mimizraḥ umima'arav* 1 (1894); 1:9 ff.
Weiss, J. "Reshit ẓemiḥata shel haderekh haḤasidit" [The first flowering of the Hasidic way]. *Ẓion* 16 (1951): 46–105.
———. "Torah Study in Early Hasidism." In *Studies in Eastern European Jewish Mysticism*, 56–68. Oxford, 1985.
Werblowsky, R. J. Z. *Joesph Karo, Lawyer and Mystic.* Philadelphia, 1980.
Wessely, Naftali Hertz. *Divrei shalom veemet* [Words of peace and truth]. Berlin, 5542 [1782].
Wolfsberg, Y. "Hagaon miVilna keishiyut ukheparshan" [The Vilna Gaon as a personality and a commentator]. In *Sefer HaGRA*, ed. Y. L. Maimon, 4:163–69. Jerusalem, 1954.

Ya'aqov Moshe Ben Abraham (Rabbi). *Ayil meshulash.* Vilna and Horodna, 5594 [1834].

Ya'aqov Yosef of Polna (Rabbi). *Toldot Ya'akov Yosef* [The story of Ya'aqov Yosef]. Koretz, 5540.

Yafe, M. G. *Mivḥar ketavim* [Selected writings]. Jerusalem, 1978.

Ya'veẓ, Z. *Toldot Yisrael* [The history of the Jews]. Tel Aviv, 1963.

Yeḥezqel Feivel of Dretshin (Rabbi). *Toldot Adam* [The history of man]. Dyhernfurth, 5561–69 [1801–09].

Yehiel Mikhel of Neshviz. *Lezekher leYisrael* [Of memory to Israel]. Vilna, 1833.

Yissacher Ber ben Tanḥum (Rabbi). *Ma'aseh rav* [A great deed]. Zulkowa, 5568 [1808].

Yudlov, Y. "Sefer 'Helkat Reuven'" [The book *Ḥelqat Reuven*]. *'Alei sefer* 14 (1987): 139–41.

Zalkin, M. *Be'alot hashaḥar, hahaskalah haYehudit baimperia haRusit bameah hatsh'a 'esreh* [A new dawn: Jewish enlightenment in the Russian empire in the nineteenth century]. Jerusalem, 2000.

———. "'Meqomot shelo maẓa 'adayin haḤasidut ken la'—bein hasidim umitnagdim beLita bameah hayod-het" ["Places where Hasidism has not yet found a nest"—between Hasidim and their opponents in eighteenth century Lithuania]. In *Bema'agalei Ḥasidim* [Within Hasidic circles: studies in Hasidism in memory of Mordecai Vilensky], ed. I. Etkes, D. Assaf, I. Bartal, E. Reiner, 21–50. Jerusalem, 1999.

Zalmanovitz, M. M. *Zikhron Hillel* [Memory of Hillel]. Vilna, 1902.

Zevin, S. Y. *Ishim veshitot* [Men and methods]. Jerusalem, 1979.

Zinberg, Y. *Toldot sifrut Yisrael* [The history of Jewish literature]. 7 vols. Tel Aviv, 1959–1971. English version published as I. Zinberg, *A History of Jewish Literature* (New York, 1978).

Index

Compositor: G&S Typesetters, Inc.
Text: 10/14 Palatino
Display: Snell Roundhand Script and Bauer Bodoni
Printer and Binder: Maple-Vail Manufacturing Group